D1491525

# A FLOATING COMMONWEALTH

# A Floating Commonwealth

## Politics, Culture, and Technology on Britain's Atlantic Coast, 1860–1930

CHRISTOPHER HARVIE

OXFORD
UNIVERSITY PRESS

# OXFORD
UNIVERSITY PRESS

Great Clarendon Street, Oxford OX2 6DP

Oxford University Press is a department of the University of Oxford.
It furthers the University's objective of excellence in research, scholarship,
and education by publishing worldwide in

Oxford New York

Auckland Cape Town Dar es Salaam Hong Kong Karachi
Kuala Lumpur Madrid Melbourne Mexico City Nairobi
New Delhi Shanghai Taipei Toronto

With offices in

Argentina Austria Brazil Chile Czech Republic France Greece
Guatemala Hungary Italy Japan Poland Portugal Singapore
South Korea Switzerland Thailand Turkey Ukraine Vietnam

Oxford is a registered trade mark of Oxford University Press
in the UK and in certain other countries

Published in the United States
by Oxford University Press Inc., New York

© Christopher Harvie 2008

British Library Cataloguing in Publication Data

Data available

Library of Congress Cataloging in Publication Data

Data available

Typeset by Laserwords Private Limited, Chennai, India
Printed in Great Britain
on acid-free paper by
Biddles Ltd., King's Lynn, Norfolk

ISBN 978-0-19-822783-0

1 3 5 7 9 10 8 6 4 2

# *Preface*

> World is crazier, and more of it
> than we think, Incorrigibly plural . . .
> Louis MacNeice, 'Snow', 1935[i]

Louis MacNeice must have come to the mind of my editors at Oxford University Press over the last twenty years. His 'The Character of Ireland', took decades *not* to be published during an earlier Oxford regime, owing to the distractions of poetry, Fitzrovia, alcohol, the BBC, and so on. I had my excuses. In Scotland and Wales Marx's line 'Philosophers have sought to understand the world. Our purpose is to change it' diverted a historian who was also involved in politics as an adviser and commentator and since May 2007 as a Member of the Scottish Parliament. The collapse of devolution legislation in 1979 provided the initial motive for research into 'Celtic nationalism', a powerful but also inchoate and sometimes downright misleading presence within the study of elitism and democracy in the British Isles which I began in *The Lights of Liberalism: University Liberals and the Politics of Democracy, 1860–86* (1976). This had, however, to compete with such projects as the BBC's *Scotland 2000* television series in 1986–7, which gave the kiss of life to the cause of autonomy, and the books—on political fiction, North Sea oil, European regionalism, and Scottish history—launched by it. Only with the actuality of home rule after 1999 could a balance be reckoned.[ii]

This audit is important. Hence the time taken 'to arrive where we started, | and know the place for the first time', or to reconstruct the *mentalité* in which the Anglo-American T. S. Eliot lived: the 'latter days' which produced *The Waste Land* in 1922. Ironically, writing this preface coincides with the Scots' decision that no one is interested any more in Thomas Carlyle, who began the tradition that led to Eliot—so they're closing down the two museums that deal with him—just when the carnage

[i] In *Collected Poems* (London: Faber and Faber, 1966), 24.

[ii] See *The Centre of Things: Political Fiction in Britain from Disraeli to the Present* (London: Unwin Hyman, 1991); *The Rise of Regional Europe* (London: Routledge, 1993; Cardiff: University of Wales Press, 2008); *Fool's Gold: The Story of North Sea Oil* (London: Hamilton, 1994); *The Road to Home Rule* (Edinburgh: Polygon, 2000); *Scotland: A Short History* (Oxford: Oxford University Press, 2002). And, for a general background, *Travelling Scot* (Colintraive: Argyll, 1999). It is at this point that I must record a 'running debt' to the following factual sources, used so frequently that detailed references would be burdensome: *The Encyclopaedia Britannica*, 12th edn, 32 vols. (New York: Encyclopaedia Britannica, 1923), which includes the 11th edn, 29 vols. (Cambridge and New York: Cambridge University Press, 1910–11) plus three volumes on World War I; the *Oxford Dictionary of National Biography* (Oxford: Oxford University Press, 2004), both online and bound versions; *Baedeker's Guide to the United Kingdom* (Leipzig: Karl Baedeker, 1930), *The Ordnance Gazetteer of Scotland*, 6 vols. (London: William Mackenzie, 1868 and 1896).

in the London streets seems to endorse his view of history and human action, which was synoptic as well as apocalyptic.

To bring the ship into port is to make out the geography: hills, promontories, settlements, the impact of social capital; and on the quayside, various notables of Eliot's generation: some obvious enough, and recurrent in the narrative: besides Carlyle, Yeats, Buchan, Patrick Geddes, and James Bryce; and others whose presence is episodic or impressionistic: Meredith, Conrad, Lloyd George, Cunninghame-Graham, Hardy, Joyce. These supplement two images so firmly embedded that they are unlikely ever to go away: the Kim's game of knowledge that poured out of Arthur Mee's *Children's Encyclopaedia* (1903), part of that populist enlightenment surrounding the unlikely figure of Lord Northcliffe, and, more abstract, R. G. Collingwood's injunction 'all history is the re-enactment of past thought in the historian's own mind'. Both bring back childhood and a Rilke poem:

> Wo ich, einem dunklen Rufe
> Folgend, nach Gedichten griff,
> Und auf einer Fensterstufe
> Tramway spielte oder Schiff.[iii]

*Then* the environment I am trying to recapture was still alive. It persisted into my postgraduate years: a quite different world from that of a parliamentarian and professor, with chairs in three countries. But modern mobility has provided the means, in the interstices of teaching, writing, and politics, to travel, research, and explore: an accumulation of experience which strengthened an earlier awareness that under the urban and industrial surface of imperial Britain—taken for granted by free marketeers and Marxists alike—were more complex, and questionably British, force fields.[iv] Hence a series of enquiries into the consciousness of the western littoral: conveyed by literature, religion, history, the arts, but with the elitist discourse within these further

---

[iii] My translation:

> Where, following the enigmatic
> I grasped at poems,
> And on the window-seat
> Played at ships or trams.

[iv] My main stalking-horses were respectively David Landes, *The Wealth and Poverty of Nations*, 1998 (London: Abacus, 1999), and Eric Hobsbawm, *Industry and Empire* (London: Weidenfeld, 1968), useful throughout for their narrative elements and intellectual stimulus, while intriguingly ham-fisted with regard to the nuts and bolts of technology and the commercial geography of 'These Islands'. Adam Smith appears frequently in Landes, Scotland (and Ireland and Wales) not at all. His map of English canals must be one of the worst ever drawn (navigable rivers vanish, and the 'Black Country' is shifted to the Black Mountains of Brecon . . .). Its few accurate elements are cribbed from a map of mine in Kenneth O. Morgan, ed., *The Oxford History of Britain* (1983). Hobsbawm's graphics are admirable, but his Anglo-Marxian centralism made him oblivious of technological change happening in front of his nose. He holidayed for three decades in the Croesor valley, but the role of the nearby Festiniog Railway in the development of the 'Cape gauge' along which European imperium advanced after 1870 (see Chapter 3) escaped him completely.

interrogated by technology, commerce, politics, and the ideas and organizations usually stuffed into—but not fitting—the grab-bag of 'nationalism'.

Two books were inspirational: Fernand Braudel's *The Mediterranean* (1949) on the sea as highway and world, was written while in a prisoner-of war camp, and working from *Mitteleuropa* is in some ways similar. Source material is, if not exiguous—certainly not since e-mail and the Web—sometimes unpredictable. But this challenges one to speculate, and use visual material and the social sciences, both to fill in the gaps and to suggest empirical comparisons. Neal Ascherson's *Black Sea* (1995) was a brilliant blend of travel writing, reportage, and occasionally terrifying meditation on man, his natural and political milieu, and cultural and political change: making the point that you can't just read about such a habitat, you have to see, taste, and walk it.

Each part of the book has its own history, and grasping how it has evolved is important, for *mentalités* are constructed by amassing perspectives. University departments and groups of scholars wanted papers on the general area, which suggested the pull of my theme, while I tried to be systematic in the choice and chronology of the talks to be given, and seminars to be organized. The Prelude and the Aftermath, 'Night's Candles are Burnt Out', were undertaken in 2002–5, trying to test the overall rationale, and bring about a thematic reordering.

The first chapter, on the language of nationality, contract, and fear, had perhaps the most complex history. Its roots were in a paper given to Tom Devine's and Douglas Gifford's Scottish–Canadian research conference at Connel Ferry near Oban in 1991. It was then modified through a commission from Jeffrey Richards and the Lancaster-based journal *Cultural Values*, and was given a remarkable going-over by Owen Dudley Edwards. It reached its final development in a 2002 paper for Valentina Bold at Glasgow University's new Crichton Campus, Dumfries. 'Why do I speak about Burns?' 'Because you're in Dumfries!' might be too cynical; it led me to look at Burns's political ideas and their links to the *Edinburgh Review* (the publishers of early Carlyle), whose bicentenary fell in 2002, into which ideas from Liam McIlvanney about Burns, contract, and Whiggery got incorporated.

The ideas about technology and geography of the second and third chapters crystallized when McIlvanney and I climbed Garron Top, above MacNissi's College, where Edna Longley had invited me to talk about engineering and ideology to the John Hewitt Summer School. At sunset we saw Kintyre, the southern Hebrides, and the Firth of Clyde laid out below us. The Protestant engineers acquired a local habitation in this inland sea; and the ideas generated here still seemed to stand up when the sea widened to the broad Atlantic. A further paper given in 1996 to Win Bogaards's 'Nation and Region' conference at St John, New Brunswick—building-ground of the softwood clippers, birthplace of Bonar Law and Beaverbrook—was honed through discussions with Colin Matthew at Oxford, about James Bryce, John Buchan, and much more. Further south, Terence Brown of Trinity College Dublin asked for a paper on the Scots and Celticism, which examined the erosion of a dogmatic Anglo-Saxonism through aesthetic and historiographical developments; a

critique by Luke Gibbons of *Field Day* wired this back to the 'sympathy' that underlay enlightenment social science, while Boris Proskurnin, inviting paper and self to
Perm, stimulated reflection on Scotland, empire, and the sciences. Roderick Murch-
ison had geologized the Urals in the 1830s—hence Permian sandstone—part of the
cataloguing and commodifying which underlay Scottish techno-imperialism and its
diffusion.

Wales, my honorary chair in politics at Aberystwyth, and the friendship of Principal Kenneth O. Morgan brought about a British Academy John Rhys Lecture in
1991: an enquiry into the persistence in both countries, despite headlong industrialization and urbanization, of a rural, religiously derived standard of civility represented by the folk or the *gwerin*; this led to an analysis of Ireland's complex response to the
industrial and imperial challenges, something which went far beyond technology or
ultramontanism. Religious identity was moving by 1900 towards the secular, and
Peter Stead turned me into a sport historian for a conference in Swansea in 1993,
to the amusement of my sister Dr Jane George, who is the real thing, while my colleagues and students of the Tübingen Anglo-Irish Theatre Group, twenty-five years
a-growing, got me deconstructing the synoptic system-building of Bernard Shaw.
A conference organized by Barbara Korte on the culture of World War I led to a
reappraisal of the barons of the industrial basins who in the contest of attrition organized a Phyrric victory.

Such marshalling of argument is only part of the story. As the devolved assemblies were being set up, market forces remoulded British History plc into something near-feral in its metropolitanism: Atlantic print capitalism (which stemmed
from the Copyright Treaty of 1891) imprisoned its identity in ways rejected in the
North and West. In contesting this the use of the media, civil society, and social
overhead capital to project ideas to a civic public, and (maybe) receive back theirs,
gained its old importance. A book of essays, *Travelling Scot*, published by my friend
Derek Rodger at Argyll in 1999, allowed me to advance some experimental notions
about the culture of what Patrick Geddes called 'palaeotechnic', carbon-burning,
technology—besides, in Heisenberg's sense, considering the effect a public life has on
research, writing, and the dissemination of ideas. There was always the worry that an
empirical approach would hatch a pre-Copernican monster like Mr Casaubon's 'Key
to All Mythologies' in George Eliot's *Middlemarch*, but 'history as the new rock 'n
roll | gardening' and its market-driven distortions had already queered its pitch. I am
as politically compromised in this business as Simon Schama and Niall Ferguson on
the other side of the argument, or in their day Samuel Smiles or Rudyard Kipling.

In this, teaching at Tübingen, in Baden-Württemberg, Europe's main manufacturing region, has proved critical. *Lehrfreiheit*—freedom to teach—enabled me to run a
seminar in which students were encouraged to take on their own projects, and many
of these have fed back into my own work: Helmut Zaiser on Carlyle, Ruskin and
economic theory, Carola Ehrlich on the 'synthetic regionalism' of Sir Arthur Quiller-
Couch's Cornwall, Christoph Meister on technology clusters and innovation, Karin
Straub on psychoanalysis and Scots literature, Paddy Bort and Christine Frasch on

politics and drama in Ireland, Simone Holzschuh and Dorothea Flothow on children's literature and, respectively, social reform and war, Ya-Fe Hsu on families and patterns of industrial enterprise in Scotland, Württemberg, and Taiwan. In 1996 Tübingen made me co-chair of the Baden-Württemberg Forum with Prof. Adolf Wagner, a symposium in which many of the links between artisan technology (Swabian has a word for it: *tüfteln*), society, and economic policy became clarified — just at the point where my former colleague Gordon Brown shuffled manufacturing off the British scene. My 'International Economics' students have been a continual stimulus: in 2004 *Der Spiegel* voted Tübingen's economics faculty the best in Germany and I feel privileged to have been part of this.

Tübingen's collaboration with the Welsh universities, in the Welsh Studies Centre, has been an important link since 1993, with the alternation of literary and social history seminar leaders. My debt to Dai Smith and Hywel Francis, Wynn Thomas, Jane Aaron, Merfyn Jones, Neil Evans, Stephen Knight, Peter Lord, Kenneth Morgan, and Tony Brown is immense, and visible in the footnotes. This has been strengthened by the Freudenstadt Symposia on Regionalism, which have run since 1991, involving the likes of Tom Nairn, Neal Ascherson, Joseph Lee, Nuala O'Faolain, John Osmond, David Walker, and Phil Williams. Further, the effect on my students of the collapse of national frontiers after 1989, and the ease with which they have gone Anglophone (not altogether reciprocated from an Anglo-Saxon standpoint) has shown some of the residual magnetism of the littoral environment on writers from Engels to Enzensberger. At Aberystwyth, the friendship of Prof. Ieuan Gwynnedd Jones and his wife Maisie until her death has been a continual stimulus. Ieuan has read through all the book's chapters and acted as my conduit to the Welsh language. I wanted to dedicate the book to them.

I ought to remind Oxford that my delays gave me the immense bonus of harnessing the *Oxford Dictionary of National Biography* in 2004–5. Not just because engineers, *commerçants*, and women get better coverage; its systems of cross-reference have thrown illumination on many otherwise neglected clusters of intellectual and technical activity. The anoraks of the Web ought also to take a bow, being particularly valuable for transport and engineering history.[v]

> Self under self, a pile of selves I stand
> Threaded on time, and with metaphysic hand
> Lift the farm like a lid and see
> Farm within farm, and in the centre, me.
>
> Norman MacCaig, 'Summer Farm'[vi]

---

[v] My attitude to one immense fortune accumulated over this period is more qualified. About half this book was written in WordPerfect, a simple, reliable, and academically civilized text programme. This was despatched to the Gulag by Bill Gates's Word, whose ambitions are not matched by reliability, and which makes simple operations like footnotes into an extended torture, where a change in font or margin produces alphabet soup. By fussily intervening where the author ought to be left alone, the Microserfs may have done more to wreck the English language than Orwell's Newspeakers.

[vi] In *The Sinai Sort* (London: Hogarth, 1957).

'Worlds' as envisaged by MacNeice and Braudel start off subjective: impressions which cohere, and then with study consolidate. The personal can't be left out, particularly when one's own experience runs from that still common to author and reader to one in which only memory and the historical record remain. Images stay put. Teenage days on the steamers of the Clyde and Hebrides or the Irish or Manx packets, also part of my parents' youth. The father of my first girlfriend Julie MacWhirter, Bob, remembering being filmed on one of 'the boats' at the Tail o' the Bank, seeing emigrant uncles off to Canada in 1908. A group of old folk in an Edinburgh gallery, who had been painted by William MacTaggart on Machrihanish beach. The Celtic revivalist Sir Shane Leslie, splendid in saffron kilt, addressing the Royal High Literary and Debating Society: 'Did you know Bernard Shaw?' 'Yes, and more important, Bernard Shaw knew me!' Arthur Geddes at an anti-war demonstration in Edinburgh Old Quad, handing round little maps of the Vietnamese ecosystem. My neighbour Sophia Thomas talking of the last pre-war meet of the Ceredigion hunt in Llanbadarn Square in 1914: the milling horsemen and intrusive motors, the young squires, Pryse of Gogerddan, Williams of Nanteos, who would die in the trenches, their estates with them. A returnee's empty Skye mansion reached on a sailing dinghy: a bath poised in mid-air, held up by its pipes where the floor had rotted to nothing.

Such recollections are not random: writing on the history of Victorian industrial Scotland proved the centrality of imaginative autobiography; and biographical 'constellations' (researched through the *Oxford DNB*) showed how socialization and intellectual innovation extend far beyond the marriage-family alliances of Noel Annan's 'Intellectual Aristocracy'.[vii] Two such interpretative networks emerged while writing: the literary innovators who publicized Blake and Whitman (see Prelude) in the 1850s and 1860s, and a later linked group foregrounding architecture, design, and drama around E. W. Godwin and James Abbot MacNeill Whistler (see Chapter 7). Notionally, a third—inevitably dwarfed by total war—can be seen spanning literature and nationalism in World War I.

James Joyce was right about epiphanies. They remain important in recapturing a period and environment for a post-electronic readership which has no direct experience of it. I hope the cumulative effect of my chapters in imagining this—his or her—past will justify the reader in tackling my narrative as a consecutive effort. Can an ageing modernist sell his literary imagination to an age heavy with defensive theory and 'long words which make us sad'? I hope so, because 1860–1930 laid the mantraps which still lie before us: not Fukuyama's fanciful End of History but Geddes's Necropolis.

At this point museums must figure, both as repositories and reconstructions of history, and as evidence in themselves: something seen more recently 'from the inside' as Adviser to the new Glasgow Museum of Transport. Back in 1976 I came upon the open-air museum at Lillehammer in the Gudbrandsdal: opened in 1884 and the

---

[vii] See Christopher Harvie, 'Industrialisation and the Condition of Scotland', in Douglas Gifford, ed., *The History of Scottish Literature*, iii: *The Nineteenth Century* (Aberdeen: Aberdeen University Press, 1988).

first of its kind in the world. Ibsen had written *Peer Gynt* only seventeen years before, and the old steamer at the quay had been plying Lake Mjöse since 1856; antiquities which 'froze' the peasant society from which 'little Gynt'—archetype of the international wheeler-dealer—set out. There are the great collections: the Science Museum, Museum of London, and Docklands Museum, and Imperial War Museum, all in London, the National Railway Museum in York, the National Museum of Scotland in Edinburgh and Kelvingrove Art Galleries in Glasgow, the Ulster Museum in Belfast, the National Museum of Wales. Ships and trade figure naturally in the National Maritime Museum in Greenwich, the Liverpool Maritime Museum, the maritime museums of Bergen, Rotterdam, and Amsterdam, the Berlin and Mannheim technology museums, and the vast Deutsches Museum in Munich. North America offered the Smithsonian complex in Washington, the Museum of South Carolina in Columbia, the New York Maritime Museum, the McCord and Montreal history museums—where else would I have found out that the Montreal 'duplex' (two-storey block of flats) is derived from Victorian Scotland's 'improved artisans' dwellings'?—and New Brunswick Museum in St John. All of these have managed to combine visual evidence and impressions and give notions of scale and environment that one can't get from books, though some may be at a tipping point where 'access' (translation: 'dumbing-down') begins to evict specialist knowledge.

A compensation is the rise of outfits like the Estorick Collection in Islington with its Futurist shows, the whaling and Arctic/Antartic exploration at Discovery Point in Dundee, Brunel's *Great Britain* at Bristol, the Discovery Centre in Newcastle for the Tyne shipyards and Parsons's *Turbinia*, the Emigration Museum in Antwerp, and the Taxation Museum (really!) in Rotterdam. There are tiny powerhouses like Cromarty's Court House Museum, and there have recently been pretentious disasters: the car-boot sale which was the twentieth-century floor at the National Museum of Scotland, the huge vacuity of Daniel Liebeskind's Imperial War Museum North, set appropriately in the waste of what once was Salford docks.

That said, my debt to librarians, particularly at the British Library, the National Libraries of Scotland and Wales, the London Library, and the excellent reference collection in Ceredigion Library, Aberystwyth, remains immense. I have also depended greatly on the book collections and personal knowledge of a host of friends (besides those mentioned earlier) accumulated in forty years of teaching and research: Arthur Marwick, Bill Purdue, Clive Emsley, Cicely Havely, Bernard Waites, Anne Laurence, Henry Cowper, Joan Bellamy, the late Graham Martin, and the late David Englander at the Open University; Paul Addison, Victor Kiernan, John Brown, Bob Morris, and the late Hamish Henderson at Edinburgh; Ian Wood and Alan Burnett at Napier; John Hume, Hamish Fraser, and Richard Finlay of Strathclyde, Tom Hart, Douglas Gifford, Colin Kidd, Irene Maver, and Ted Cowan at Glasgow; Douglas Dunn, Bill Knox, Chris Smout, and Robert Crawford at St Andrews; the late Raphael Samuel and Bob Purdie at Ruskin College, Oxford; elsewhere in that hospitable city Geoffrey Best, Michael Brock, Karen Hewitt, and the late Colin Matthew; Eugenio Biagini and Tim and Charlotte Benton at Cambridge, Helen Meller at Nottingham, David Daniell at University College London and Bill Fishman at Queen Mary University of London, Donald Munro of the Institute of Historical Research, and among local, transport, and cultural historians Billy Kay of Dundee, Lester Borley, and David Alston of Cromarty, Pat Kane of Glasgow, George Rosie of Edinburgh, Allan Massie of Selkirk, Paul Salveson of Yorkshire, the late Charles Hadfield, the late John McGrath, and the late L. T. C. Rolt. In Germany Hans-Werner Ludwig, Rudolf Hrbek, Roland Sturm, Hans Schwarze, Gerhard Stilz, Gerd and Helga Ebrecht, and Eckhard Auberlen; in France the late François Bedarida and Christian Civardi; in Canada and the USA Gary Geddes, Win Bogaards, Pascal Benoit, Martyn Thompson, Patrick Scott, Jim Smyth, and Newton Key. And thanks to my agents, Tony Peake and Kate Jones: 'The long trick's over.'

Families finally: to be thanked for endless hospitality, but also lodged in the narrative. On my own side the west-coast Scottish bourgeoisie: engineers, managers, clergy, teachers: my two grandfathers at Dalzell Steelworks and Anderson Boyes Coal-cutters, my great-uncle Alex at the Grangemouth dockyard. Their story is a chapter of *Travelling Scot*. On my wife's? Christopher Foulis Roundell, whose father had reported in 1865 on the Governor Eyre case in Jamaica and helped reform Oxford, saw in 1910 the young widow of Harry Vivian on the battlements of the Scots baronial Trelowarren (built in Cornwall out of South Wales tinplate profits) and determined there and then to marry her. Roundell was Virginia's grandfather, from a family of Yorkshire merchants who married into the Cheshire gentry. In 1921 as a civil servant he devised the co-ordination schemes which frustrated the Triple Alliance and the General Strike (see Aftermath).[viii] Lady Maude Vivian, née Clements, was the grand-niece of Lord Leitrim, killed in 1878 by his Donegal tenants. Virginia, who could wolf a Tolstoy novel in a day, was a hawk-eyed editor, saw my books through the press—'Focused has only one s.': 'They won't understand what you mean by anti-syzygy. I don't.': 'Put fewer words in quotes.' I write this preface in the weeks after she died, ending a companionship of twenty-eight years. This book, along with our daughter Alison, is her memorial.

---

[viii] See Keith Jeffrey and Peter Hennessy, *States of Emergency: British Governments and Strikebreaking since 1919* (London: Routledge, 1983), chap. 1.

# Contents

# *Illustrations*

1. Trade emblem of the Amalgamated Society of Engineers, Machinists, Millwrights, Smiths, and Pattern Makers, engraved by James Sharples 1852. © Trades Union Congress, London/Bridgeman Art Library

2. John Patrick Crichton-Stuart, Third Marquess of Bute. National Portrait Gallery, London

3. Mount Stuart, Isle of Bute, the west front, photograph by H. B. Lemare, 1904. Reproduced courtesy of the Royal Commission on the Ancient and Historical Monuments of Scotland

4. Cathays Park Cardiff, postcard of 1930. Author's collection

5. The Glasgow Stock Exchange, May 1908. Reproduced courtesy of the Mitchell Library, Glasgow

6. Pat and Tommy. Author's collection

7. Jack Butler Yeats (1857–1951), *The Greater Official.* © The Estate of Jack B. Yeats/DACS, London 2007. Photo © The National Gallery of Ireland

8. Pushing and Going. National Library of Wales

9. Sean Keating, *Night's Candles are Burnt Out* (1929). Reproduced courtesy of the Gallery, Oldham

10. 'Work as if you lived in the early days of a better nation'. © Trustees of the National Library of Scotland

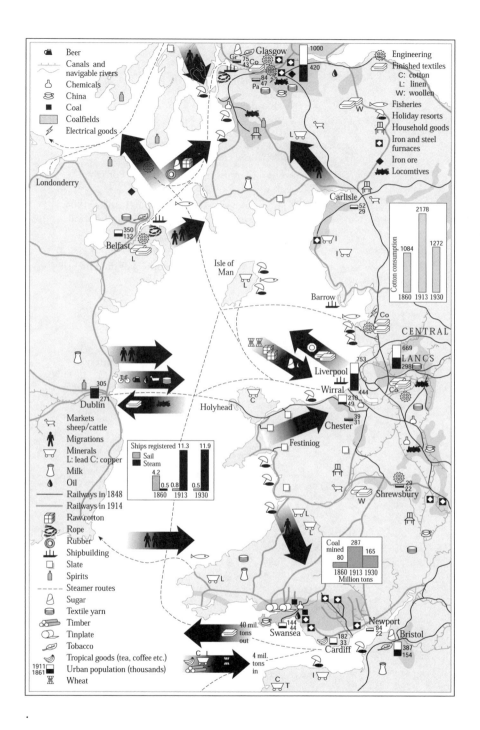

# Prelude

Behold the sea!
And on its myriad, heaving breast, the ships;
See, where their white sails, bellying in the wind, speckle the green and blue,
See the steamers, coming and going, steaming in and out of port,
See, dusky and undulating, the long pennants of smoke.

Walt Whitman, 'Song of the Exposition', 1871[1]


## I BEHOLD THE SEA!

On 12 October 1912, at the Leeds Festival, the massed choirs of Yorshire boomed out the opening strophes of Ralph Vaughan Williams's *Sea Symphony*, a vast oratorio-scale setting of poems—'Song of the Exposition', 'Sea Drift', 'A Passage to India'—by Walt Whitman. A new, radical voice was injected into an English musical scene which, with Elgar, Stanford, Parry, Delius, had been in furious movement for over a decade. 'Write choral music as befits an Englishman and a democrat' had been Sir Hubert Parry's injunction to the composer, and this was what the Leeds audience got: a music-drama which celebrated the sea on which the country's prosperity depended, but did so in a way which wasn't imperial, but liberal and inclusive:

> O we can wait no longer,
> We too take ship O soul,
> Joyous we too launch out on trackless seas,
> Fearless for unknown shores on waves of ecstasy to sail,
> Amid the wafting winds (thou pressing thee to me, I thee to me, O soul,)
> Caroling free, singing our song of God . . .[2]

Vaughan Williams conducted himself. He was forty, from a family partly Welsh in origin, but related to the English commercial and intellectual aristocracy. His uncle, Lord Justice Vaughan Williams, commended the mix: 'The working of the leaven of Celtic genius, Celtic aestheticism, Celtic athleticism, and Celtic love of first principles, and last but not least, Celtic altruism upon the more practical, more industrious, more selfish and more material mass of the Anglo-Saxons'.[3] His Wedgwood and Darwin relatives had already proved themselves revolutionary innovators in industry

---

[1] In *The Portable Whitman*, ed. Mark van Doren, 1944 (Harmondsworth: Penguin, 1979), 269.
[2] Ibid. 281.
[3] In *Wales* (Feb. 1913), 61, quoted in Aled Jones and Bill Jones, 'The Welsh World and the British Empire', *Journal of Imperial and Commonwealth History*, 31/2 (2003).

and science: developing the assembly-line production of pottery, launching the theory of natural selection. His wife, Adelina Fisher, was the sister of the historian H. A. L. Fisher, who became Lloyd George's education minister in 1916. 'Uncle Ralph' would, for a further half-century, bestride English music, a cultural counterpart to the slightly younger Winston Churchill in the country's politics.[4]

'Uncle Ralph' looked like a farmer in his tweeds, or someone—organist, architect, lawyer—from one of the cathedral closes of the Three Choirs Festival. The conservative publicist Simon Heffer has tried to reclaim him for an embattled Englishness. But he was an agnostic, collected folk songs with the communist Bert Lloyd, taught amateur and working-class musicians, voted Labour. He had studied under Max Bruch in Berlin and Maurice Ravel in Paris: a German Jew and a French Basque. He would dedicate the most English of his symphonies, the Fifth, in the middle of World War II, to Jean Sibelius, in troubled, neutral Finland. His literary tastes were catholic: his first song-setting, of R. L. Stevenson's *Songs of Travel*, anticipated the mood of the *Sea Symphony*, and his first major choral work set another Whitman poem, 'Toward the Unknown Region'. His closest musical friend was another European, Gustav von Holst, from a Swedish family, likewise leftish in his politics, and drawn to oriental mysticism. Vaughan Williams's own nationalism was complex. Years later, he would quote the German liberal statesman Gustav Stresemann: 'To be an internationalist, one first has to be a nationalist', yet he believed in a federal Europe, and the key to his own Englishness, his engagement with folk song, stemmed from the internationality of another friend, Cecil Sharp, in recording migrant farmers of English stock in the Appalachians.[5]

And Whitman! The poet of the railroad and steamboat, of the stump-speech and the navvy-gang, American and cosmopolitan, unnervingly democratic and ambiguous in his sexuality: in the latter half of the nineteenth century he became as influential as what he called the 'kosmic intellect' of Thomas Carlyle had been two generations earlier, on writers and thinkers as various as Patrick Geddes, Standish O'Grady, Edward Carpenter, and Robert Louis Stevenson. Vaughan Williams's own commitment to democracy had come through the 'personalism' of Whitman's poetry, first published in Britain in the 1850s and owing much to Carlyle. Among the other grand figures of Edwardian music-making, little orthodox nationalism was visible. Frederick Delius was a German Nietzschean from the Bradford wool-merchant colony. Arnold Bax, London-born, was in politics an Irish nationalist, Edward Elgar came from a Worcester lower-middle-class Catholic family, Sir Charles Stanford was wholly Irish, and Sir Hubert Parry part-Welsh, another Whitman-obsessed seafarer.[6]

---

[4] Michael Town, 'The Sea Symphony', in Byron Adams and Robin Wells, eds., *Vaughan Williams: Essays* (Burlington, Vermont: Ashgate, 2002). Percy M. Young, *Vaughan Williams* (London: Dennis Dobson, 1953), 48–54, is perceptive about the social as well as the musical background.

[5] See Ralph Vaughan Williams, *National Music and Other Essays*, 1963, ed. Michael Kennedy (Oxford: Oxford University Press, 1987).

[6] For Whitman's British reception see M. Wynn Thomas, 'Walt Whitman and Risorgimento Nationalism', in Winnifred M. Bogaards, ed., *Literature of Nation and Region* (St John's: University of New Brunswick, 1996), 1.

Their voices consciously broke away from the class-bound gentility of 'salon music' which they reproached Elgar for writing, in favour of a wider canvas, an engagement with mighty political and cultural concerns. After all, wasn't the greatest playwright and political polemicist of the day, Bernard Shaw, as famous as a music critic? One who had, in Whitmanite style, greeted the music-drama of Richard Wagner as the epic of the capitalist epoch: a position which would later be paralleled by the prophets of literary modernism: T. S. Eliot in *The Waste Land* and James Joyce in *Ulysses*.

The Cambridge critic F. R. Leavis, in *New Bearings in English Poetry* (1932) trying to sum up cultural developments since Tennyson's death in 1892, claimed that poetry ought to be 'at the most conscious point of the race in time'. This reflected in part the wartime Anglicization of academic culture—the eviction of German philology as well as German music—as well as a reaction of the socially sensitive *against* the enforced collectivity of war—and of the provinces against the centre. Pre-war music had been more immediate than poetry, and on a grand civic scale. A war in which avant-gardism was interwoven with action and propaganda, and the recasting of Europe in populist nationalist mode—whether voiced by Apollinaire, Jünger, Sassoon, Mayakovsky, Hašek, or Mann—deserves something more than post-modern miniaturism. Within Britain, the sense of unity that would inevitably be diminished was a sense of nationality borne by music's complex lyric achievement—didactic, programmatic, and collective—the consciousness of the epoch provided by the image of the sea.[7]

The sea figured both in populist, patriotic entertainment—music-hall songs echoing Navy League propaganda and Dreadnought programmes *and* in 'invasion scare' novels like Erskine Childers's *The Riddle of the Sands* (1903)—via John Masefield's 'Cargoes', Henry Newbolt's 'Admirals All', and Rudyard Kipling's 'Big Steamers'. Something more individualist and metaphysical emerged in the works of followers of Meredith and Joseph Conrad. The sea was not just Britain's *mare nostra*; it was also liberator and destroyer in one.

Thomas Hardy seems geographically and temperamentally remote from Whitman, but his canvas was as broad, if less sanguine. Hardy had always acknowledged his Cornish element—'Lyonesse', a Celtic kingdom on the edge of the Atlantic—and the fashioner of the vast *Dynasts*, on the Anglo-French wars of 1793–1815 (1913), claimed kinship with Nelson's Captain Hardy. In the profound self-interrogation that followed the death of his wife Hardy returned to 'old love's domain' and to the sea. In 1912 the *Titanic* figured in 'The Convergence of the Twain', and in 'Channel Firing' of April 1914, the guns of Churchill's Dreadnoughts stressed the hubris of the mechanical age. The poem's haunting close, in which war, civilization, and the sheer age of Wessex combine, is unreassuring:

> That night your great guns, unawares
> Shook all our coffins as we lay,

---

[7] F. R. Leavis, *New Bearings in English Poetry* (London: Chatto and Windus, 1932); see also Chris Baldick, *The Social Mission of English Criticism, 1848–1932* (Oxford: Clarendon Press, 1981), chap. 4. The memoirs and novels of J. B. Priestley (1895–1985) suggest something of the importance of orchestral music for his generation.

And broke the chancel window-squares,
We thought it was the Judgement-day.

And sat upright. While drearisome
Arose the howl of wakened hounds:
The mouse let fall the altar-crumb,
The worms drew back into the mounds,

The glebe-cow drooled. Till God called, 'No;
It's gunnery practice out at sea
Just as before you went below;
The world is as it used to be:

All nations striving strong to make
Red war yet redder . . .
        .        .        .

So down we lay again. 'I wonder,
Will the world ever saner be',
Said one, 'than when he sent us under
In our indifferent century!'
        .        .        .

Again the guns disturbed the hour,
Roaring their readiness to avenge,
As far inland as Stourton Tower,
And Camelot, and starlit Stonehenge.[8]

In the same year Vaughan Williams completed his second symphony, *A London Symphony*. He described it to a friend as 'my social-democratic symphony'. Purely orchestral, but of Mahlerian proportions, this too had a radical literary programme, derived from *Tono-Bungay* (1909) by the notorious H. G. Wells: scientist, novelist, free-lover, socialist: a man conscious that London's recognition of 'industrial' Britain was more than erratic: 'People talk and write about an Industrial Revolution meaning the coming of factories, railways, and the great towns, but these changes were not a revolution; they were a growth!'[9] *Tono-Bungay* was locked into the mobile but complacent Edwardian metropolis; its politics reflecting an 'enterprise' of quack cures, advertising, and yellow press journalism far removed from the puritan craftsmen and traders of Whitman or his more prosaic British contemporary Samuel Smiles (1815–1905). The sea plays a different, more subversive role. In the last chapter of a novel about fraud and pretence, Wells's disillusioned hero George Ponderevo steers a new destroyer he has built down the Thames, 'passing all England in review', and out into the open seas of world commerce.[10]

---

[8] Written April 1914, published in Thomas Hardy, *Satires of Circumstance* (London: Macmillan, 1914).

[9] H. G. Wells, 'Will the War Change England?', *The Daily Mail History of the War: Illustrated* (20 Feb. 1915).

[10] Town, 'The Sea Symphony', 95. See also Simon Heffer, *Ralph Vaughan Williams* (London: Weidenfeld, 2000).

Vaughan Williams conveys this voyage with a quiet modulation portraying the river, perhaps echoing another river and another drama of wealth and moral decay, Wagner's *Rheingold*, almost certainly echoing the last sentences of Wells's friend Joseph Conrad's *Heart of Darkness*:

'We have lost the first of the ebb', said the Director, suddenly. I raised my head. The offing was barred by a black bank of clouds, and the tranquil waterway leading to the uttermost ends of the earth flowed sombre under an overcast sky—seemed to lead in to the heart of an immense darkness.[11]

Over this is heard, in the minor, the notes of Big Ben about to strike the hour. This fixes the scene precisely. But it's not the imperial London of Elgar's marches. Within seconds the tranquillity of the riverscape is shattered by shafts of discord which reveal the dark city of Conrad, of Dickens's *Oliver Twist*, of George Gissing, James Thomson's *City of Dreadful Night*, or William Blake:

> In every cry of every Man,
> In every Infant's cry of fear,
> In every voice, in every ban,
> The mind-forged manacles I hear
>
> How the Chimney-sweeper's cry
> Every black'ning Church appalls;
> And the hapless Soldier's sigh
> Runs in blood down Palace walls.[12]

Vaughan Williams's London is not all 'dreadful night' but a mosaic of quiet parks, shrieking street markets, buses, music halls, bursting with the same vigour that the American Charles Ives would bring to a similarly Whitmanite programme. In the final movement this democracy confronts a ponderous Elgarian march, and the two virtually fight one another to a standstill—the echoes of Sibelius's *Finlandia* are almost explicit. Into the tense diminuendo that follows, the ominous river motif, and the muffled bells, slip again.

Wells himself would remark, only months later, on the real differences between 'Britain' and 'England' and be precise about both. What the industry on its fringe meant would be comprehended only when 'war burns its way through all the

---

[11] Based on Conrad's voyage up the Congo in 1890, this was serially published in 1899. The version quoted is that reprinted in *Conrad: Collected Short Stories* (London: Pickering, 1993).

[12] William Blake, 'London', written 1794, in *Songs of Experience* (self-published, 1794). Far from being fanciful, the linkage of Blake and Whitman would be to Ralph Vaughan Williams's generation quite precise: a 'cluster' which anticipates Lord Justice Vaughan Williams's notion. Both poets were projected to a British audience from an intellectual milieu of London Scots, northern patrons, exiled artists, and industrialists. Blake's biographer Alexander Gilchrist was the son of a Scots Baptist minister, literary editor, and friend of Carlyle. On his premature death his widow, Anna, later Whitman's muse, was assisted by Dante Gabriele Rossetti, whose brother the socialist William Michael campaigned for *Leaves of Grass* (1855). Alexander Gilchrist's kinsmen were the metallurgists Percy Thomas and Sidney Gilchrist Thomas (see Chapter 5). Many of their patrons came from the north and west, including the Liverpool shipowner Frederic Leyland, James McCracken of Belfast, and John Ruskin 'the Scot of Scots' himself.

substance of England'.[13] Ponderevo's farewell was equally tormented, leaving an England consumed by shams, for a commercial, unattached, probably menacing, world which would pay for destroyers and no questions asked.

Vaughan Williams's symphony had been performed only once when, on 4 August 1914, war broke out. Its revised version, premiered in 1918, would be more lyrical, and more serene. Georg Lukacs wrote of the early novels of Thomas Mann—a writer preoccupied by music—that they were 'composed' to subordinate the subject-matter to the bourgeois ideal of the artist's own autonomy. 'RVW' in the inter-war years was a different, less disturbed, and less disturbing figure, within an 'English' tradition that had changed as well.[14]

## II   'THE WRITING AND ACTING OF HISTORY'

Two works of one composer locate and interrogate two 'worlds', in Fernand Braudel's sense, within the state structure of Victorian and Edwardian Britain. The political ethos of the mid Victorians, of John Stuart Mill, Walter Bagehot, or the authors of *Essays on Reform* (1867) had been one of unity or 'nationalization', appropriated from Italy or the USA, rather than one derived from any deep study of the social identity of these nations. This did not keep pace with imperial expansion. The Irish Home Rule crisis in 1886, which ended the concerted political activism of the university liberals, a putative British intelligentsia, became what the Germans call a *Zeitbruch*—a break-in-series. Despite the failure of Gladstone's *démarche*, it swept 'nationalization' away.[15] Subsequent unity was mechanical: centrifugal tendencies were frustrated by a mixture of war and welfare (and after 1919 the absence of mutinous Ireland) which prolonged what James Bulpitt called 'central autonomy' in the 'long first half' of the twentieth century. It ran down, with empire, after the 1950s, though a further *Zeitbruch* in 1979 managed to freeze in the temporary rictus of Thatcherism a national-cultural centrifuge gripping the United Kingdom.

This forced the ideas of *A Floating Commonwealth* into action. With civil society in Northern Ireland broken, the province was ruled from London; the challenge of the *Blaid* and the SNP had been beaten off; the metropolitan establishment—Wells's 'Bladesover'—got a revitalizing slug of North Sea oil. When I started my research, in 1985, myth and Celtic nationalism seemed unfortunate twins. Yet British instability soon reasserted itself. What Walter Scott had once described as 'the deep and smooth river' of the Union began to break into rapids, with the consolidation of the European Union and the break-up of the Soviet monolith complicating an increasingly heterogeneous politics. 'Celtic nationalism' per se still seemed two-dimensional: ideologically thin, economically dependent, too contingent on external forces. This was

---

[13] Wells, 'Will the War Change England?', 20–1.

[14] Georg Lukacs, 'In Search of Bourgeois Man', 1922, in *Essays on Thomas Mann* (New York: Grosser and Dunlap, 1965).

[15] Christopher Harvie, *The Lights of Liberalism: University Liberals and the Challenge of Democracy, 1860–86* (London: Allen Lane, 1976), chaps. 6 and 9.

the conclusion of Joseph Lee's magisterial dissection of independent Ireland, published in 1990: in retrospect an intellectual Caesarian which helped deliver the Celtic tiger-cub.[16] Yet the Atlantic moment seemed different and more powerful, when seen against not just temporal politics but the zones of interaction, Braudel's 'world'—of population, transport, economic activity, urbanism, local government, and their relation to British and anglophone institutions, to social class, and to work.[17] International trade—Britain in 1851 commanded more than half of it—added a third dimension. Cumulatively this seemed to create the two worlds which Vaughan Williams's symphonies had symbolized: the land-based core, centred on the capital, with its 'establishment', its parties and elites, still vividly present in the 1980s, and the commercial, bourgeois, seaborne chord or arc—now ambiguous and shadowed—of 'the West'.

Despite their current academic salience, the differing types of 'national movement' have been imperfectly surveyed in our multi-community culture. 'Great Power patriotism', with its military and imperial ambitions, its economic pressure groups and army or navy leagues, was quite distinct from European ethnic nationalisms, still agrarian-based, or commerce-driven city states or civic republics—though these could overlap, for instance in the German Empire. If two-thirds of Europeans were subject to the Great Powers of Britain, France, Austria, Russia, Germany, Italy, and Turkey in 1900, they had not been so for very long, and experiences differed. Britain and Russia had recently expanded their empires, but the oldest—Turkey, which had lasted over 400 years, and Austria, 200 years—were in decline. France, Germany, and Italy were based on centralized militarism and its success, but political Germany was at least in theory a decentralized federation and Italy in practice one.[18] The peculiarity of the Victorian United Kingdom was that it was a great power which was also a compound of ethnic nationalities *and* had become quite recently an urban society run by public authorities with great autonomy: a structure that combined the modernist hegemony of the state with the existence of 'cultural communities' not distant from those which post-modernists would recognize.[19]

---

[16] J. J. Lee, *Ireland, 1912–1985* (Cambridge: Cambridge University Press, 1989). This remarkable work was foreshadowed by *The Modernisation of Irish Society, 1848–1916* (Dublin: Gill & Macmillan, 1973). Lee's insistence on the primacy of intellectual history was fundamental to my own study of twentieth-century Scotland, *No Gods and Precious Few Heroes: Scotland since 1914*, 1981 (4th edn, Edinburgh: Edinburgh University Press, 1999).

[17] The solidarity of E. P. Thompson, *The Making of the English Working Class* (London: Gollancz, 1965), opened out into a more pluralist, parliamentary and regionally inflected structure in Patrick Joyce, *Visions of the People: Industrial England and the Question of Class, 1840–1914* (Cambridge: Cambridge University Press, 1991), and Eugenio F. Biagini, *Liberty, Retrenchment and Reform: Popular Liberalism in the Age of Gladstone, 1860–1880* (Cambridge: Cambridge University Press, 1992).

[18] See Stanley Leathes, ed., *The Cambridge Modern History, xii: The Latest Age* (Cambridge: Cambridge University Press, 1910), chaps. 5, 6, 8.

[19] A productive quarry for material on ethnic and civic nationality in Europe is Michael Thompson, ed., *Comparative Studies on Governments and Non-Dominant Ethnic Groups in Europe, 1850–1940*, 8 vols. (Aldershot: Dartmouth Press, and New York: New York University Press, 1990–3). I reviewed it in an essay in the *European History Quarterly*, 25 (1995). Most conventional studies, following Stubbs and Dicey, stressed the parliamentary/constitutional element, but the works

This generated elite politics of a curious sort, as they failed to impinge on that phase of the European intellect in which elitism—in the hands of Vilfredo Pareto, Gaetano Mosca, or Max Weber—fell loosely into the category of 'modernism'. One looks in vain in a classic like H. Stuart Hughes's *Consciousness and Society* (1958) for any significant British contribution to 'the reorientation of European social thought, 1890–1930'. Noel Annan attributed this to an archaic devotion to positivism—the atheoretical accumulation of data and sense-perceptions—but he ignored the mismatch between this and the huge contributions of the British physical sciences, literature, and economics. The essential difference was that European modernism was posited on a state structure which extended deep into the socialization process. In Britain not only were politics divided into 'high' and 'low'—parliament's preoccupation with defence, foreign policy, and public finance—and the devolution of the rest to local bodies—but the state itself was divided into four nations, each with its own 'strong' civil society.[20]

These factors constantly influenced each other: British trade and technology were theoretically the least regulated in Europe, but were guaranteed by overseas investments, emigrants, and colonies and the world's largest and most modern battle fleet. Ethnicity, social structure, and religion influenced socialization, notably in education and welfare, so compatible goals were reached by different institutions in the different nations. Social philosophy was centred on the new phenomena of urbanism and class, yet influenced by the values of an earlier rural society. Over the time span from the 1860s to the 1920s, there seemed to be less of a distinction between the nationalities—English, Scots, Welsh, Irish, and Ulster-Scots—than between the evolving industrial littoral and the metropolitan core whose establishment took it for granted. This arc, with its giant ports and their industrial hinterlands, became, though only for a few decades, a 'world' like Fernand Braudel's Mediterranean. Yet a 'Celtic' (Scots, Welsh, and Irish) proportion of the British population which declined from 45.8 per cent in 1831 to 20 per cent in 1911 was already troubling this economic dominance.

Arc and core were united in two discrete, even contradictory, ways: by commerce (trade, democracy, culture, and finance) and by war. These expressed the two great forces of the nineteenth century, industrial capitalism and nationalism, and their

---

of two continental scholars, Emil Boutmy's *The English People: A Study of their Political Psychology*, 1901, trans. E. English (London: Unwin, 1904), and Josef Redlich's *Englische Lokalverwaltung* (Leipzig: Duncker und Humblot, 1901), trans. Brian Keith Lucas as *The History of Local Government in England* (London: Macmillan, 1958), highlighted other sub-national dynamics. And see Patrick Geddes, *Cities in Evolution* (London: Williams & Norgate, 1915).

[20]  See Noel Annan, 'The Curious Strength of Positivism in English Political Thought', Hobhouse Lecture, London School of Economics, 1958 (Oxford: Oxford University Press, 1959), 9. In the 'high'–'low' politics stand-off my indebtedness to James Bulpitt's *Territory and Power in the United Kingdom* (Manchester: Manchester University Press, 1983), is patent, and see Fernand Braudel, *La Méditerranée et le monde méditerranéen à l'époque de Philippe II* (Paris: Colin, 1949), trans. Sian Reynolds as *The Mediterranean and the Mediterranean World in the Time of Philip II* (London: Collins, 1972). For 'strong civil society' see Tom Nairn, 'From Civil Society to Civic Nationalism: Evolutions of a Myth', in *Faces of Nationalism: Janus Revisited* (London: Verso, 1997). The sort of ethnic-derived nationalism identified with Anthony D. Smith, *National Identity* (Harmondsworth: Penguin, 1991), came under question in Thompson, *Comparative Studies*. For an introduction, see my review article in *European History Quarterly* (see n. 17 above).

dynamism gave the semblance, and ultimately after 1914 the reality, of national unity. This was seen, by liberals as well as Marxists, as evolutionary, yet even this 'key word' which dominated the intellectual life of Britain after 1860 advertised its ambiguities. Charles Darwin (1809–1882) and Alfred Russel Wallace (1823–1913) came to the same conclusion about natural selection in 1859, but it was the metropolitan, intellectual-aristocrat Darwin, not the Scots-Welsh socialist Wallace, who christened the 'ism'. The balance of innovation and power was a historical event, dependent on people being in the right place at the right time.[21]

The urgency of analysis came when 'place' stopped having a shared meaning. After 1989–90 and the end of the cold war, 'Europeanization', 'globalization', and domestic devolution put Britain in question. Not for the first time. Little more than a decade after surviving World War II the Suez debacle sparked a debate about Britain's viability: Martin Green, Arthur Koestler, and C. P. Snow would be followed twenty years later by Ralf Dahrendorf and Martin Wiener. The core of this was justifiable worry about the health of manufacturing industry. But when the argument started again in the 1990s this had been displaced by identity and its seductive sister lifestyle, fuelled by the migration of entrepreneurship to the service industries. British Cultural Studies threatened to become a post-modern conceit—of bijou research topics lacking any sort of governing concept—while British History seemed a commercial gamble undertaken by the metropolitan media which had survived Thatcher's strong state and been remoulded by resurgent capitalism.[22]

In 1997 the Conservative Party, the vertebra of the Union State, plunged not simply to defeat but to years of crisis. New Labour conceded autonomy to the culture-nations of Scotland and Wales, but then mishandled English regionalism and industrial reconstruction and the future international orientation of a state which was unclear whether it was part of Europe or in a special relationship with the USA. The irony was that the vestigial arc—driven by or trying to emulate Celtic Tiger Ireland—now tended to be pro-European, while the core had become pro-American where not owned from America.[23] But political dialectic was thin. The Anglo-Britishness of Simon Heffer, the *Spectator*, and the *Salisbury Review*, a

---

[21] See Philip Appleman, William Madden, and Michael Wolff, eds., *1859: Entering an Age of Crisis* (Bloomington: Indiana University Press, 1959).

[22] Martin Green, *A Mirror for Anglo-Saxons* (London: Longmans, 1960), Arthur Koestler, ed., *Suicide of a Nation: An Inquiry into the State of Britain Today* (London: Hutchinson, 1963), and C. P. Snow, *The Two Cultures* (London: Macmillan, 1963), were important to the first stage of the debate, when the challenger was European social-democratic planning. As the Callaghan government tottered, solicitous Americans organized Isaac Kramnick's symposium, the proceedings of which were published as *Is Britain Dying? Perspectives on the Current Crisis* (Ithaca: Cornell University Press, 1979). Martin Wiener, *English Culture and the Decline of the Industrial Spirit* (Cambridge: Cambridge University Press, 1981), R. E. Tyrell Jr, *The Future that Doesn't Work* (Garden City, New York: Doubleday, 1977), and Ralf Dahrendorf, *On Britain* (London: BBC Publications, 1983), reflect a shift to the neo-liberalism associated with Mrs Thatcher. I attempted a critique of the genre in 'Liturgies of National Decadence: Wiener, Dahrendorf and the British Crisis', *Cencrastus*, 21 (1985).

[23] Of the eight major commercial publishers in Britain in 2005 only two—Hodder Headline and Pearson Longman—could be regarded as British-owned. See Silvia Stolzenburg, 'Best Sellers and the Book Market in Britain', PhD thesis, Tübingen University, 2006.

'core' reduced to an US-dominated City of London and its PR penumbra, faced a once-powerful Anglo-Marxism—the successors of Hill, Hobsbawm, Kiernan, Thompson—enfeebled by the earthquake of 1989–90. On these slippery foundations occurred two contradictory developments: collaborative 'national' histories of high quality emanated from the UK constituents, and from the core came a series of rather random attempts to alter the take on the political structure.[24]

Linda Colley, in *Britons: Forging the Nation, 1707–1837* (1992), claimed to ground Anglo-Britain in a robust Protestant imperialism, evolving between the Civil War (now becoming known as the 'War of the Three Kingdoms') and Victoria's accession. Apologizing for past Protestant misdeeds, the New Labour project in its moments of seriousness found the thesis useful. Norman Davies's *The Isles* (1999) thought that such compromise was useless, that the breakup couldn't be avoided, but culled little evidence for this from the modern period. Common to both was an indifference to the new national histories, as well as a lurch into market-driven populism. In a surrender of critical responsibility led by the BBC and compounded by the acumen of the publishing and PR trade, Simon Schama, Niall Ferguson, Roy Strong, and David Starkey made millions out of recycling the old stories of Anglo-Britain. Attempts to provide a political and economic rationale for a decentralized Britain were overshadowed by the privatization and marketing of myth, and by an obsessive managerialism in which the media was the politics, and history was what paid, not what explained.[25]

Yet the themes of this conflict, and indeed its personnel, stemmed from earlier political and cultural relationships. Understanding them, and the varying nature of their bequests, is what this book is about.

## III   THE ATLANTIC MOMENT

In 1859 Thomas Babington Macaulay, Lord Macaulay, historian, poet, and proconsul, died, as old as the century; he was followed in 1861 by the radical poet Arthur Hugh Clough, at 42. Macaulay's ambitious *History of England*, started in 1845, had reached only 1697, a decade short of its goal, the Anglo-Scottish Union of 1707. Clough's mature career, with its remarkably modern poetry, had scarcely begun.[26]

---

[24] W. E. Vaughan, ed., *A New History of Ireland, Ireland under the Union I: 1801–1870* (Oxford: Oxford University Press, 1989), and vi: *Ireland under the Union, II: 1870–1921* (Oxford: Oxford University Press, 1996); Christopher Smout and Jenny Wormald, eds., *The New History of Scotland*, 8 vols. (London: Edward Arnold, 1979–82); Tom Devine, Rosalind Mitchison, Hamish Fraser, Robert Morris, and James Treble, eds., *People and Society in Scotland*, 3 vols. (Edinburgh: John Donald, 1988–92); Kenneth O. Morgan, *Rebirth of a Nation: Wales, 1880–1980* (Oxford: Oxford University Press, 1981).

[25] Linda Colley, *Britons: Forging the Nation, 1707–1837* (New Haven and London: Yale University Press, 1992); Norman Davies, *The Isles* (London: Macmillan, 1999). My own response to these is 'Uncool Britannia', *Times Literary Supplement* (8 Jan. 1999) and a review of Davies in *The Independent* (1 Jan. 2000). I would except Richard Weight's thoroughly researched *Patriots: National Identity in Britain, 1940–2000* (London: Macmillan, 2002) from this stricture.

[26] Besides his writings, Clough served as amanuensis to Florence Nightingale. Although *The Bothie* was a success, his poems were not widely published until 1862, after his death.

But his most famous lines indicated that, after the failure of the revolutions of 1848, his contemporaries and juniors looked west:

> Say not the struggle nought availeth
> The labour and the wounds are vain
> The enemy faints not nor faileth,
> And as things have been they remain.
>
> If hopes were dupes, fears may be liars;
> It may be, in yon smoke concealed,
> Your comrades chase e'en now the fliers,
> And, but for you, possess the field.
>
> For while the tired waves, vainly breaking,
> Seem here no painful inch to gain,
> Far back, through creeks and inlets making,
> Comes silent, flooding in, the main.
>
> And not by eastern windows only,
> When daylight comes, comes in the light;
> In front, the sun climbs slow, how slowly,
> But westward, look, the land is bright.[27]

For all his Whiggism, Macaulay was by descent Hebridean; his grandfather a Gaelic speaker from the Uists, on the edge of the Atlantic. Confronted with the hostility of Toryism to the new age, he was scornful.[28] Clough, from a Denbigh merchant family, had been brought up in Charleston, South Carolina, on the other shore; his most democratic poem 'The Bothie of Toper-na-Fuosich' (1848) was about radical Gaelic Scotland. To both 'England' was a convenient, expansive term, instantly recognizable to foreign customers, but shorthand for something much more federative, complex, and un-English, and extensible to the New World. The latter, sketched by a French liberal aristocrat, Alexis de Tocqueville, in *De la democratie en Amérique* (1838), provided a political prototype which was, spiritually and socially, remote from the reaction which had enveloped Europe. Its influence on a younger generation of Oxbridge liberal constitutionalists and reformers—James Bryce, A. V. Dicey, Henry Sidgwick, T. H. Green—would be given intellectual form in such symposia as *Essays on Reform*.[29]

Yet the 1860s were convulsed by war and *Machtpolitik*: the Franco-Austrian War of 1859, the American Civil War of 1861–5, Bismarck's assaults on Denmark

---

[27] Arthor Hugh Clough, 'Say Not the Struggle Naught Availeth', written in 1849, was first published in *The Crayon* (Aug. 1855). The MS was presented by Scribners to Winston Churchill in 1941. *The Poems of Arthur Hugh Clough*, ed. F. L. Mulhauser (Oxford: Clarendon Press, 1974), 206, 677.

[28] Thomas Babington Macaulay, 'Southey's Colloquies on Society', *Edinburgh Review* (Jan. 1830), repr. in *Critical and Historical Essays*, i (London: Longman, 1874).

[29] See Christopher Harvie, 'Who were Geordie's Neighbours: London or the Clyde?', delivered at Conference on North-Eastern History, 2004. Publication in 2008.

(1863), Austria (1866), and France (1870). Britain remained detached from these, although the American conflict was provoked as much by British trade requirements—for cotton above all—as by the internal breakdown of a federal commonwealth still smaller (25 million in 1861) than the UK in population. This distraction gave West Britain its not-altogether-expected opportunity to draw on technical innovations which made it expand, in partnership with the Americas, for two generations. The American merchant marine was decimated by commerce-raiding and Europe convulsed in great land battles just as engineers from Wales to the Clyde inaugurated the epoch of the British-built-owned-and-fuelled long-distance freight steamer, the 'medium-gauge' railway, and the telegraph network, which effectively brought steam-powered mass production into all branches of manufacturing industry, and all corners of the globe.[30]

Karl Marx ought to have been alert to this. The first volume of his *Capital* appeared in 1867, with its brilliant model of 'machinofacture' in 'The Working Day'. But he took little direct interest in the British industrial regions, visiting his collaborator Friedrich Engels only twice in his Manchester home.[31] Events were already falsifying their *Communist Manifesto* of 1848, whose apocalyptic tone owed much to Thomas Carlyle. Instead, 1865–75 saw the triumph of constitutionalism, which could be managed by conservatives. Universal male suffrage in Germany and the French third republic had their shadow-sides, but the victory of Lincoln's Union over the 'slave power' conserved the democratic ideal.[32] This implied 'a sort of *religion*', rather than scientific materialism, and a uniquely infective culture, whether the hot-gospelling of Moody and Sankey in their crusade of 1873–4, Whitman's secular, Carlyle-derived 'personalism', or the mass-marketed consumer goods, from tinned salmon to typewriters and sewing machines, which were the long-delayed pay-offs of industrial transformation.[33]

In 1870 the Oxford dons James Bryce and A. V. Dicey sailed for America on the Cunarder *Scotia*.[34] Two months' travel, as far west as the Great Plains—hours spent with Emerson and Longfellow, with precinct captains and unchaperoned, opinionated girls—enraptured both men and gave them links which would last for over half a century. Thereafter they filed reports for the New York *Nation* and its Ulster editor E. L. Godkin, and later wrote the key constitutional treatises of both nations: Dicey's *Law of the Constitution* (1885) and Bryce's *The American Commonwealth* (1888).[35] This Atlantic seduction would be important as a background to 'splendid isolation',

[30] See François Crouzet, *The Victorian Economy* (London: Methuen, 1982), chap. 11.

[31] A. J. P. Taylor, 'Marx's Better Half', 1976, in *Politicians, Socialism and Historians* (New York: Stein and Day, 1982), 145.

[32] Edmund Ions, *James Bryce and American Democracy* (London: Macmillan, 1968), 4–5. A. V. Dicey, whose *The Law of the Constitution* (1885) was fundamental for a century, confessed to 'making a religion of my politics'.

[33] The Singer sewing machine, patented in 1851 by an émigré Polish Jew, went worldwide after 1881 with the building of a giant factory at Clydebank, using the labour of female workers from Glasgow's declining cotton textile industries and the wives of shipyard workers.

[34] The *Scotia* was the last paddle steamer built for the Atlantic route.

[35] A. V. Dicey, *Lectures Introductory to the Study of the Law of the Constitution* (London: Macmillan & Co., 1885); James Bryce, *The American Commonwealth* (London: Macmillan, 1888)

but also to an increasingly problematic British internationalism. Gradually Britain was pinned down to a European role, until after 1905 the challenge, and after 1914 the actual clash, of 'the elephant and the whale' or 'the Romans and the Greeks'—the land-based power of Germany versus the seaborne power of Britain—detonated a European crisis which it would take the first half of the twentieth century to resolve.[36]

World War I summoned the business elite of the West to the Westminster core, an exoticism captured by the naturalistic novelist and critic Arnold Bennett in *Lord Raingo* (1926) in his portrait of Andy Clyth, a fictionalized Lloyd George:

Andy was the greatest fighter of them all. He had no scruples, no sense of justice or of decency, no loyalties; his cynicism was dazzlingly intrepid . . . but he could fight and keep on fighting. . . . Not a drop of English blood in him, but there he stood, dominating and bullying hundreds of pure-bred Englishmen.[37]

The longer-term consequences were more ominous, through the transfer of much of British finance to the United States. Partly because of American pressure, the Union State was fractured by the withdrawal of most of Ireland, resulting in a much more conservative structure of British identity. Culturally this would be expressed by a paradox: the centralized cultural-imperialism of the BBC under John Reith, a Clydeside engineer, established in 1923–6 a precedent for public-service radio establishments worldwide, while through private-enterprise cinema Hollywood would become by the 1930s—with everyone from Sergei Eisenstein to Thomas Mann attracted there—arguably the centre of world culture.[38]

Between the crises of 1861–71 and 1914–22, the civil society of the British littoral, from Cornwall to Argyll, was subjected to a sequence of changes, never totally or systematically comprehended, which sustained an intense economic and social dynamism. Nationalism remained persistent, but within limits. In Scotland and Wales it stuck at a cultural level; even in Ireland, though more deeply rooted in the land issue and Catholicism, it tolerated, not altogether derisively, the 'West British': the commercial, urban middle classes. These, in their turn, did not so much challenge nationalism as elide it, through migration and the intermediate institutions of churches, schools, community organizations, and public interventionism, with the quite new phenomenon of the civic conurbation, a term coined by the peripatetic Scots sociologist Patrick Geddes on the eve of the war.[39]

'West Briton!' James Joyce finally left Dublin in 1912, though for other cosmopolitan metropoli: Trieste, Rome, Paris, ultimately Zurich. In 'The Dead', the last and subtlest of his stories in *Dubliners* (1913), Gabriel Conroy, a liberal, early-middle-aged *littérateur*, is, at a shabby-genteel Dublin party, upbraided by the

(thirty-five subsequent editions are listed in the British Library catalogue), and see Harvie, *Lights of Liberalism*, 210.

[36] See Peter Lyon, 'The British Commonwealth', in Michael Howard and W. Roger Lewis, eds., *The Oxford History of the Twentieth Century* (Oxford: Oxford University Press, 1998), 292.

[37] Arnold Bennett, *Lord Raingo* (London: Cassell, 1928), 82.

[38] Peter Gay, *Weimar Culture* (London: Secker and Warburg, 1969).

[39] The definition stems from Geddes's *Cities in Evolution*, 1915; see Robert E. Dickinson, *City and Region: A Geographical Interpretation* (London: Routledge, 1964), 15 ff.

Gaelic nationalist Molly Ivors for reviewing books for the Dublin *Daily Express* and for going to France, Belgium, and Germany for cycling holidays. Gabriel is caught between his anglophone 'progressive' culture—Browning rather than Tom Moore—and the Irish west. This he sees as the seat of Molly Ivors's new, troubling idealism and at the same time of an incalculable *passion*, exemplified by his wife's memory of a boy from County Galway, long-dead, whom she once walked out with, shivering in the rain at their last meeting. This enchantment, Gabriel realizes, he cannot emulate, and the imagery with which Joyce concludes, of snow falling 'on every part of the dark central plain, on the treeless hills, falling softly upon the Bog of Allen and, further westwards, softly falling into the dark mutinous Shannon waves'[40] becomes as symbolic of political intransigence as Yeats's own more resonant verdict in 'Easter 1916':

> Hearts with one purpose alone
> In summer and winter seem
> Enchanted into a stone
> To trouble the living stream.[41]

'West Briton' was a play on 'North Briton', a neologism coined around the time of the Scottish Act of Union in 1707. It drew on James VI and I's decision to use 'Great Britain' for the state formed by the monarchic union of 1603 (avoiding precedence issues between the Scots and the English), reinforced by the Union flag (1607) and the English Bible (1611). Development of the concept was kept at bay by mid-seventeenth-century conflicts and until 1746 the persistence of Jacobitism. Thereafter the idea of 'Britishness' had a particular Scots provenance. *The Briton*, a pro-government paper founded by the Scots novelist Tobias Smollett in 1760, provoked 'North Briton' as a term of abuse by the London radical John Wilkes in his opposition to Lord Bute, George III's prime minister and Smollett's patron.[42] Nevertheless, its use swelled in Scotland during the early nineteenth century, giving its name in 1845 to the main Scottish railway line connecting with the English system. Even then, it was controversial. Slightly over a decade earlier, Sir Walter Scott had attacked London for meddling in Scottish banking affairs: 'In place of canny Saunders you will have a damn'd dangerous North British neighbourhood.' The only real outcome of a brief nationalist revival in the 1850s was its gradual displacement by 'Scots' and 'Scottishness'.[43]

But 'Britain' itself remained opaque in its identity, even at its political centre in London. A constitutionalism still dominated by aristocratic practice, where not (after the 1880s) by actual aristocracy, still had strong anti-national drives. Disraeli thought in terms of an oriental empire centred on the Middle East; Gladstone's last crusade

---

[40] James Joyce, 'The Dead', 1906, in *Dubliners* (London: Cape, 1967). Miss Ivors is claimed by Conor Cruise O'Brien to be a portrait of his mother; see O'Brien, *Memoir* (London: Profile 1998), 6.

[41] W. B. Yeats, 'Easter 1916', written May–September 1916; for background see Roy Foster, *W. B. Yeats: A Life*, ii: *The Arch-Poet, 1915–1939* (Oxford: Oxford University Press, 2003).

[42] George Rudé, *Wilkes and Liberty*, 1962 (Oxford: Oxford University Press, 1972), 20 ff.

[43] Christopher Harvie, 'Scott and the Image of Scotland', in Alan Bold, ed., *Sir Walter Scott: The Long-Forgotten Melody* (London: Vision, 1985).

was to offer 'justice to Ireland' and 'international public right' to the world, even at the cost of British prestige. The bourgeoisie, whose ships and mines and cotton mills propelled the trade that held the nation together, thought only episodically of the state at all, but more about 'their' industry and local commonwealth of town council, port authority, trade or commercial association, railway company, church, community, and/or the high culture of orchestras, university colleges, and art galleries. They could take on national, even international loyalties, but they were not dominated by them. Their politics and culture were almost alarmingly existentialist: they could be philistine but mostly and mysteriously were not. Margot Asquith noted her—almost blasé—expectation that a Clydeside magnate's picture collection, besides stags and highland ragamuffins, would have a Corot or two.[44]

## IV  PERSPECTIVES

Analysing the rise and fall of the West has not got easier with time. As the apparatus of industry vanishes, the centre has ironically inherited the resentments of the nationalities. That sense of external menace all too familiar in Edinburgh and Dublin has transferred to the *sacro egoismo* of Schama's television series *History of Britain* and the BBC's *Great Britons*. In 1914–56 a very tangible Britain had been dominated by European crises where it—or more particularly the industries of the West—rescued democracy and the liberal-capitalist order. War implicitly influenced the high Tory G. M. Young's *Early-Victorian England: The Portrait of an Age* (1932) and the Austrian economist F. E. Schumpeter's *Capitalism, Socialism and Democracy* (1942): intelligent, reflective, but stressing the centre—the City, Westminster, Wells's 'Bladesover', Oxford, and Cambridge—and its compromise with tradition. In the era of the Butler Act, this pervaded school history. Yet an awareness that elite politics had succeeded at the cost of economic dynamism was to increase during the troubled 1960s.[45]

War meant centralization. State machines swelled, the qualities of executive ministers mattered. Economics retreated, since the nature and timing of decisions prevailed over housekeeping. History-writing was both important—think of the immediate need for military history and the huge official records which followed both wars—and framed the task of the historian, even someone as influential and individualistic as A. J. P. Taylor. Taylorian loyalties lay with the Manchester of free trade, pacifism, and radicalism from which Marx and Engels had taken their cue, but these were deflected by the crisis of 1914 and its sequel, his idolization of a dynamic Scots-Canadian, Lord Beaverbrook, whose metropolitan-and-littoral

[44] See *The Autobiography of Margot Asquith* (London: Thornton Butterworth, 1920–2). *Stothers's Glasgow, Lanarkshire and Renfrewshire Xmas and New-Year Annual, 1911–1912* (Glasgow: James Stothers, 1911) captures the image of this 'dead, dicky-bird-watching world' while the portrait of the Hopkinsons of Manchester and Altrincham in Kate Chorley, *Manchester Made Them* (London: Faber & Faber, 1950) gives a sympathetic account of its mentality.

[45] The collection of essays edited by Sir Ernest Barker, *The Spirit of Britain* (Oxford: Oxford University Press, 1948) illustrates this.

intrigues helped create Lloyd George's war machine in 1916.[46] The paradox was that war was about the only time when the British elite thought about technology—obsessed by fire-power, rates of climb, turbines, armour-plate. In peacetime (outside the armed services and a yen for speculative gambling) they forgot about it altogether, with broadsheet papers evicting everything but cars in favour of court, consols, appointments, and test matches. Once wars were won, the cousinhoods of Whig magnates, surveyed by Taylor's rival, the Polish-Jewish Sir Louis Namier, gently gave way to the obsessive genealogy—which its author would have ascribed to his Welshness—of Anthony Powell's emblematic *A Dance to the Music of Time* (1951–73).[47]

But the residue of one important rationalization from industry remained until the 1990s. Industrial Britain had been the laboratory of Marx; the lessons then learned would mark, by emulation and rejection, the twentieth-century world, not least through an Anglo-Marxism which took the United Kingdom as its interpretive sphere. By the 1970s, as industry ebbed, history on the periphery became more nationalist. The economic basis had always inflected the national historical traditions: in Scotland shifting from the anti-metropolitanism of Fletcher of Saltoun to cash-register justifications of Whig Unionism.[48] In Wales the defence of the language community confronted first Whitehall and then the dynamic, cosmopolitan southern coalfield. Irish historians had to explain why nationalist modernization atrophied into clerical sclerosis. In 1975 Michael Hechter attempted to create a general model of core–periphery relationships in his *Internal Colonialism: The Celtic Fringe in British National Development*. This vision of a core systematically exploiting the fringe was enthusiastically seconded by nationalist politicians, until it as well as they was marginalized by the failed referenda of 1 March 1979.[49]

Thereafter the stresses inflicted by the Thatcher experiment exported such insecurity to London. 'The English way' modulated from a prescription to a symptom of national decline, and re-emerged as a commodity. Martin Wiener's *English Culture and the Decline of the Industrial Spirit* (1981) was more than rhetorically important in analysing the ailing British mixed economy: copies were presented by the premier to doubting members of her Cabinet.[50] When neo-liberalism seemed to perish with Thatcher, Linda Colley's *Britons* partly filled the vacuum, trying to contain the centrifuges of the 1990s. The metropolis, the great beneficiary of English print-capitalism, had the least interest in analysing it, even when such an analysis seemed crucial to the state's survival. Although the City of London had the benefit of David Kynaston's four volumes, the technology which it serves and depends

---

[46] See A. J. P. Taylor, *A Personal History* (London: Hamish Hamilton, 1983), 237–8, and Adam Sisman, *A. J. P. Taylor* (London: Sinclair-Stevenson, 1994), 257 ff.

[47] See Christopher Harvie, *The Centre of Things: Political Fiction from Disraeli to the Present* (London: Unwin Hyman, 1991), 210–12.

[48] See Colin Kidd, *Subverting Scotland's Past* (Cambridge: Cambridge University Press, 1993), 31–96.

[49] Gwyn A. Williams, *When Was Wales? A History of the Welsh* (Harmondsworth: Penguin, 1985).

[50] Ralf Dahrendorf, quoted in the BBC's *Dahrendorf on Britain* 1982, and see Dahrendorf, *On Britain*, 18–23.

on—containerization, road haulage, air transport, computers, and international financial services themselves—were, in comparison to banks, railways, and shipping lines, almost unrecorded.[51]

In Scotland, Wales, and Ireland concessions to nationalism bred chronicles of 'rebirth' of these nations—'imagined communities' of more than psychological interest as the morphology of 'Britain' became indistinct. The radical Marxist turned Welsh nationalist Gwyn Alf Williams asked 'When was Wales?' in 1986. If the Welsh made the place totally plastic, in what greater constellation, he asked, did their stadia of national development occur? A similar background was demanded and supplied in Joseph Lee's inquest *Ireland 1912–1985* (1989). Tom Devine's *The Scottish Nation* (1999), published in the triumphal dawn of an autonomous legislature, was also nationalist but, arguably influenced by Devine's own Irish ancestry, emphasized land and people over an industrial experience which an earlier generation of Marxist-influenced historians had regarded as revolutionary.

In the nations and provinces, history became a political act; in the capital it was anchored no longer to the state but to international media-capitalism. In 1800–50 history had drawn on the industrial and constitutional developments of the time, adapting them into metaphors of civic discourse to serve a British liberal order which, propelled by but also fearing trade and enterprise, valued culture as a 'nationalizing' agent. It was a means of recruiting potentially disruptive provincial intellectuals, and thus reinforcing the metropolitan elite, reshaping the landscape in the hands of a Macaulay or a Carlyle. How did it change, and where was it now?

## V NATIONALIZING HISTORY

In *Essays on Reform* (1867), Dicey, Bryce, Leslie Stephen, and Frederic Harrison, pleading for a 'more national policy', squared the ideas of Mill and Mazzini with the wealth and connections of Oxbridge. In the 1950s Noel Annan would see their authors as the fathers of 'the intellectual aristocracy'—of education, the civil service, the 'clerisy' of the reviews and family-owned publishing houses—while in 1968 the New Left historian Perry Anderson accused them of retarding Britain's modernization and Europeanization: a 'traditional intelligentsia', to use Gramsci's term, which had usurped the rational, bourgeois role of the 'organic intelligentsia'.[52]

The essayists' ideas never bridged centre and province. Ireland inevitably split them. Dicey elevated centralization and parliamentary sovereignty into a totem—which it remained for over a century. Bryce (from whom he derived his 'flexible constitution' idea) believed Home Rule was achievable under the American type of federalism, oiled

---

[51] David Kynaston, *The City of London*, 4 vols. (London: Chatto and Windus, 1994–2001); W. D. Rubenstein, *Elites and the Wealthy in Modern British History* (New York: St Martin's Press, 1988), establishes the far greater gains in wealth which accrued to finance and trade, but the attraction of the civic-industrial mode remains to be explained.

[52] Noel Annan, 'The Intellectual Aristocracy', in J. H. Plumb, ed., *Studies in Social History* (London: Longman, 1955), 244–5; Perry Anderson, 'Components of the National Culture', in *The Student Revolt* (Harmondsworth: Penguin, 1968).

by its urban life and political culture. In practical terms both settled for Walter Bagehot's version of the *English Constitution* (1865) as something centralized and determined by a combination of the mechanical and the psychological. Yet these Oxbridge
dons were largely drawn from the provinces: their or their fathers' origins lay in Yorkshire rectories, Liverpool offices, or Scottish universities. Their critics regarded them
as 'more at home in Switzerland or America than in England'. They also represented a
decentralized metropolis, whose intellectual organization rested on two medium-sized
market towns an hour and a half away from London by train.[53]

This group was preoccupied with a 'nation' which had evolved around 1800, and
now 'had to be brought to recognise its true dimensions'. They could do the ideology: the problem was to relate this to geography. What had emerged in the 1800s
was difficult to pin down, and varied its shape when seen retrospectively: a contractual
bourgeois patriotism, whose tropes could simultaneously further British democracy,
national culture, and civic virtue. Robert Crawford records the Scots as creators of
English literature. Colley has shown the bourgeois muscling in on 'patriotic' memorials and celebrations at the expense of the local aristos.[54] Literary unification, propelled
by Wordsworth and Coleridge, would be consolidated by the 'Scotch Reviewers' after
the *Edinburgh Review* started in 1802 and *Blackwood's Magazine* in 1817, with German models of nationality to the fore. These were expanded by wartime finance. Scots
and Welsh entrepreneurs—Loyds, Lloyds, Couttses, Drummonds, Barclays—allied
with such immigrants from Europe as the Schröders, Rothschilds, Barings, Klein-
worts in elaborating 'the Thing' as Cobbett called it, the City establishment which
underwrote Britain's wartime efforts and alliances.[55]

'The Thing' was obviously metropolitan; the argument about it was not. The gen-
erators of 'old corruption' and 'stock-jobbery' were regarded as captiously malignant:
even though they ran Europe's best-ordered financial polity. But arguments about
them, and their sheer unbearableness, provoked provincial print-capitalism into an
articulacy which went beyond political manoeuvre. Utilitarianism *was* Scottish: 'the
greatest good of the greatest number' was coined by the Ulster-Scot Professor Francis Hutcheson in 1745, although it was systematized by Jeremy Bentham after 1776.
These were furthered and publicized by Scots at the India Office and on the *Westminster Review*. Infrastructural improvement—the provision of roads, lighthouses,
docks, and canals—was Scots- or, particularly in matters military, Irish-dominated.
So too was the administration of empire: the Governors-General, the Royal Engineers, the East India Company, the Colonial Office.[56]

What emerged as the concern of print-capitalism wasn't Colley's populist Protestantism, but a loose coordination of several national identities, contrived through

---

[53] Harvie, *Lights of Liberalism*, chap. 1.

[54] Robert Crawford, *Devolving English Literature* (Oxford: Clarendon Press, 1992), 16–44;
Colley, *Britons*, 272–3.

[55] When the banks fell into disfavour in the inter-war period the American Harvey Allen's
*Anthony Adverse* (New York: Farrar and Rinehart, 1933), about the financial world of this period,
became a transatlantic bestseller, particularly favoured by the left.

[56] Michael Fry, *The Scottish Empire* (Edinburgh and East Linton: Birlinn and Tuckwell, 1999),
chap. 4.

commerce and agricultural success as well as war: the Welsh Tory gentry and rising mineral capitalists who paid Edward Williams, 'Iolo Morganwg', to invent a past for them; Scots of the Thomas Campbell generation who deified Robert Burns as the national poet, yet lusted after careers in the Union. Ireland, whose population was five-eights of the English figure in 1801 (Scotland in 1707 had been barely a fifth), brought a problem of an altogether different order, though the career of Tom Moore flourished (what other poet had a prime minister as his biographer?) and the political power of Daniel O'Connell took effect in a specifically British context. The ethos of what William Hazlitt, the Cockney radical, would later call 'the spirit of the age' pro-pelled print-capitalist discourse into a balance of contradictions: Anglo-British hege-mony was made both metropolitan *and* provincial, established *and* Nonconformist, experimental *and* conservative, moralized *and* opportunistic. Few development pos-sibilities were excluded, and technology, finance, and trade would drive these in quite unprecedented directions.

An English patriot could dissent: William Cobbett, the Hampshire farmer, was fierce against 'Scotch Feelosophers' and 'Jew Stockjobbers'. He assaulted a 'Great Wen' which seemed supremely self-preoccupied: the world which Thackeray would later lampoon in *Vanity Fair* (1848), with the conspicuous consumption of the Court at its centre. Yet it was in its way cosmopolitan: its hero was the conservative Irish-man Wellington, for whom the way had been cleared by the conservative Irishman Burke. Its romantic leads were Tom Moore, Walter Scott, and Byron. If its disgrace was the bloodbath which accompanied the divorce of George IV (made into a polit-ical issue by the Scots lawyer Brougham), its compensatory fest was the Royal Jaunt, the attempt by the king to court his Scottish subjects, arranged by Walter Scott in 1822: not surprising, because the Thing's sensational literature was set in Ireland or Scotland. Its dominant contribution to world literary culture would be the Waverley novels.[57]

If England had a moral centre it was unlikely to be Carlton House or Grub Street. It would be rooted in the moral community of the Lake District and the demotic con-servatism of Wordsworth, or the squirearchical Devon of Coleridge, both of which had their own links to Oxford and Cambridge. But would the Lake poets have writ-ten without Burns? Would Burns have written at all without Adam Smith and the Edinburgh literati?[58] Aside from the direction that inspiration and imagination took, this 'imagined community' had an immediate need for technology and marketing and management. This made possible the mass production of printed articles—not just books but newspapers, prints, and caricatures—and their dissemination. Mechanical production of paper, the iron press, the mail coach running on the turnpike road, some degree of authorial protection by copyright, critical publications which pre-cised information about books: all of these were successfully put in place between the 1790s and the 1820s; and where once London's Paternoster Row had ruled, many of these initiatives were provincial. With the Stamp Act the government tried to mould the new channels of information in its own interest, but with little success: imported

---

[57]  Elie Halévy, *England in 1815*, 1913 (London: Benn, 1924), 338–9.
[58]  Liam McIllvanney, *Burns the Radical* (East Linton: Tuckwell, 2002), 212–15.

books and illegal newspapers continually sapped it until it gave the exercise up in the 1850s.[59]

This media landscape, expressed first by print, later by broadcasting and film, was generally metropolitan; but absorbed talent from nations whose educational systems, outrunning their economies, overproduced entrepreneurs, journalists, and manipulators. Against the stabilities of land-based politics and conservative British patriotism, they could invoke the new and incalculable force of industrialism and the provincial, industrial city.

At the beginning of George Eliot's *Felix Holt* comes her superb panorama of the coach journey from London to the north-west, something praised by Henry James (Ulster-Scot in ancestry) for 'a retarding pervasiveness which allows her conjured images to sink slowly into your very brain'.[60] At the end of that trajectory was an English culture far different from the Johnsonian norms of the metropolis, housed in new cities which had scarcely been the size of market towns at the time of the last Jacobite rising. Cardiff went from 2,000 to 164,000 in 1801–1901, Belfast from 25,000 to 350,000, Glasgow from 80,000 to over 900,000. Charles Oakley, a Somerset man, graduating from London University in 1913, was told 'Go North'. He went to Glasgow as an industrial psychologist, a calling which the littoral spun off during its climacteric during World War I. He would later chronicle Glasgow as *The Second City*, but had to stay and fight for his new homeland in unforeseen circumstances.[61]


VI  BASINS


In the bleak uplands of the Brecon Beacons a cast-iron tramway was laid down in 1815–16, from the Swansea Canal near Banwen to Senny Bridge, twenty-five miles to the north. The Crown property of the Brecon Forest was being sold off by Lord Liverpool's government, and the purchaser was an Edinburgh-born merchant, William Christie, who had made his money importing indigo to London from India, combining the Scots preoccupation with the subcontinent with the demand of the expanding cotton-printing industry for dyestuffs. He wanted to develop the agriculture of the region by building large 'Scots farms', and to exploit its coal. His line was, like all of the 200 or so miles of track in South Wales, a cast-iron plateway. It was worked by horses, self-balancing inclines, and gravity, its 3 ft 6 in.-gauge waggons freewheeling down the track, supervised by brakemen. It cost him about £40,000. Christie brought down Borderers for his farms, and the line was laid out by the Scots engineer William Brunton, who as a sideline set up iron- and copper-smelting works, and built steam engines to propel local barges. His descendants would go on to become pioneers of Japanese industry and build the Meiji Empire's lighthouses.[62]

[59] Stephen Koss, *The Rise and Fall of the Political Press in Britain*, i: *The Nineteenth Century* (London: Hamish Hamilton, 1981).

[60] George Eliot, *Felix Holt, the Radical*, 1867 (Oxford: Oxford University Press, 1988).

[61] Charles Oakley, 'Reminiscences', in *Scotland*, 10 (1959).

[62] Stephen Hughes, *The Brecon Forest Tramroad: The Archaeology of an Early Railway System* (Aberystwyth: Royal Commission on Ancient and Historical Monuments in Wales, 1990), 36.

The tramway was a speculation by merchants rich from industry and war finance on the price of grain remaining high, thanks to Lord Liverpool's Corn Law of 1816. It had the dynamic potential of all transport schemes (where cargo is aided to go from A to B, potential is created for other cargo to go cheaply from B to A), but in itself it did not pay. Demand for grain wasn't enough to sustain the high capital investment, and the slump of 1825–6, which would claim the fortune of Walter Scott and almost squash the infant speculator Benjamin Disraeli, bankrupted the Christies. But some of their mines prospered and David Thomas, their overseer at Senny Bridge, used his expertise in the difficult business of mining anthracite—a type of coal very hard though high in energy content—and took it to the United States, where in the 1840s he became the principal developer of the anthracite field of Pennsylvania around Scranton, which developed into America's 'Little Wales'. Other local entrepreneurs along the Swansea Canal coated wrought iron, thin-rolled in local mills, with tin shipped from Cornwall, to produce tinplate for cooking utensils and canning foodstuffs.[63]

The Brecon Forest tramway was an epitome of the early industrialization of South Wales, showing what Patrick Geddes would have called a 'mature eotechnic' transport system: as far and as fast as you could get with cast-iron plates and horses. Because South Wales's investment was congealed in this, it lost out on the advance being made in the north-east: George Stephenson's high-pressure steam locomotive, running on wrought-iron-edge rail and capable of infinite progress in terms of payload and speed. Such patterns of technical advance, consolidation, retardation, and obsolescence would mark the 'paleotechnic' (carbon-powered) littoral. They could be, and were, 'sprung' by floods of surplus capital into infrastructure, viz. the railway mania of the 1840s, or synergies (these days 'clusters') of scientific and engineering progress, viz. the Clyde Valley, 1850–70. But they could also be skewed, or wrecked, by natural disaster, foreign competition, or war.[64]

The Brecon Forest tramway was fairly typical in combining speculative finance, migrating engineering expertise, and Atlantic development, part of a network of sea-connected enterprises which pushed inland from the ports. Most historians have registered modernization in terms of the expansion of land transport systems, from drove-roads and pack-horse trails to turnpikes, navigable rivers, canals, and railways. Yet, from the prehistoric epoch onwards, Barrie Cunliffe among others has concluded, sophisticated seaborne systems of trade developed, running from northern Scotland to the Mediterranean. Industrialization and inland transport improvement didn't diminish these: even in the 1850s a greater tonnage of goods was moving coastwise round Britain than was travelling by the public railways, and much of it was

---

[63] Ibid. 50–3.

[64] The contemporary literature on this is huge, but see Joachim Schwerin, 'The Evolution of the Clyde Region's Shipbuilding Innovation System in the Second Half of the Nineteenth Century', *Journal of Economic Geography*, 4/1 (Apr. 2004): special issue on 'Physical and Organizational Proximity in Territorial Innovation Systems', ed. Kevin Morgan, Claudia Werker, and Christoph Meister; and, in the same issue, Kevin Morgan, 'The Exaggerated Death of Geography: Learning, Proximity and Territorial Innovation Systems'.

making its way to the ports, rivers, and canals by road, river, short canal, and local railway and tramroad.[65]

Once at the coast, such traffic would encounter a decentralized merchant marine. Joint-stock shipping was for the old chartered companies and new, government-subsidized mail-and-passenger steamer lines, and really came in only with the international cargo steamer, the 'liner', at the end of the nineteenth century. Sailing ships tended to be owned where there was a tradition of local trade. In South Wales most of them came from the other side of the Bristol Channel, from the Channel Islands, Devon, or Cornwall, or from the small ports of Cardigan Bay, cut off from the English Midlands by the Cambrian mountains, yet handling huge quantities of slate, lead, and copper from quarries, some worked from Roman times. To the north, around the Isle of Man, people were similarly organized, but reluctant to say what their business actually was, as smuggling may have made up more than half of it. And, until the French wars were at an end, there was a lot of money to be made by 'privateering'—piracy legitimized by 'letters of marque'—which allowed British crews to prey on enemy merchantmen.[66]

South Welsh industry and minerals, as they expanded, drew on Cornwall not just for ships but for copper and later for tin. The Cornish mineral business had expanded through the use after the 1780s of the separate-condenser steam engine of James Watt, which enabled undersea mines to be pumped out. Innovations were made to it by 'imported' Scots such as William Murdoch, also the pioneer of coal gas, and local mine captains such as the endlessly ingenious Richard Trevithick. Murdoch introduced the high-pressure engine, Trevithick developed it—as powerful as the Watt machine but only a quarter of the size—and spread it to South Wales, Shropshire, and the north-east.[67] Industrial novelty, speculative investment, war, and press-gang pressure on communities, and the importation of artisan elites, led to a scramble for innovation along the coasts. After 1815 this went global, both through speculative booms—like the one which took Trevithick and Robert Stephenson mineral-prospecting in South America in the wake of the liberators (besides Simon Bolivar, these included the part-Irish Ferdinando O'Higgins and the Scots radical Admiral Cochrane)—and through the steady build-up of demand for textiles, iron, metals, and slate. Bristol and Liverpool had to re-orientate their commerce with the suppression of the slave trade within the Empire in 1808, while the intensifying French blockade made the Channel dangerous, and pushed commerce to the north and west. Birmingham, where Boulton and Watt had their works, rose from 71,000 to 202,000

---

[65] Barry Cunliffe, *Facing the Ocean: The Atlantic and its Peoples, 8000 BC–AD 1500* (Oxford: Oxford University Press, 2001). For records of coastal shipping I am greatly indebted to the work of the late Aled Eames and the late Lewis Lloyd, in the journal *Maritime Wales*; and see J. Geraint Jenkins, *Maritime Heritage: The Ships and Seamen of Southern Ceredigion* (Bridgend: Gomer Press, 1982).

[66] David Jenkins, *Shipping at Cardiff* (Cardiff: University of Wales Press, 1993).

[67] L. T. C. Rolt, *Victorian Engineering* (London: Allen Lane, 1970), 33.

in 1801–41, but steam-powered cotton propelled Manchester and its port of Liverpool from 157,000 to 551,000.[68]

Throughout, there was a need for huge quantities of labour, for new mineral resources, and for capital equipment: the machinery which converted raw material into trade goods. Although the technology of textile mass production had in principle been around for over a century, the innovations of the next stage of industrialization depended on iron. Severn-side works first used cheap coke to smelt iron ore, and puddling furnaces and rolling mills to transform pig to wrought iron: iron plates, rails, and pillars replaced wood from the 1780s. The use of wood pulp to make cheap paper in the 1790s likewise required complex mechanical engineering, a continual succession of machines, and machines for making them, which had to be painstakingly developed. To facilitate the adoption of steam power, railways, chemicals, and in due course electricity, it was important to replace part of the labour force, to allow it to be retrained, and for the cost of that force to be cut by using unskilled labour to compete with it, liberating funds for investment.[69] A sixpenny steamer trip away, in Ireland, was an answer—and a further, more intractable, problem.

## VII COVENANTS

The success of imperial Britain, commemorated in the textbooks which descended on the new Board Schools after 1870, masked anxieties and uncertainties. These generated ideological responses to the experience of industrialization, when the reality, notably when faced with the crisis of the 1840s, was much more disorganized. Clydeside's survival, for example, seemed problematic, as textiles were prone to severe cyclical depressions, ironworking had expanded erratically during the French wars, and marine engineers tended to make their money by going south. The ideology of 'Improvement' was being questioned by apprehensive literati—in the writings of Thomas Erskine of Linlathen or of Thomas Carlyle, the social gospel of Thomas Chalmers, and the nationalist grumbling of Walter Scott. In 1829 James Beaumont Neilson, manager of the Glasgow gasworks, invented the 'hot blast' furnace whereby gases were reignited to superheat the iron ore. This could smelt the coal in the 'Blackband' ore of the Monklands and produce a very fine pig iron for casting or steam-forging: the basis of the Clyde's dramatic rise as a mechanical engineering centre.[70] Its take-off demanded the same sort of cheap-labour input as slavery had given American cotton in the wake of Whitney's cotton gin (1796). It was confirmed by a classic *Gastarbeiter* influx,

---

[68] J. K. Walton, 'The North-West', in F. M. L. Thompson, ed., *The Cambridge Social History of Britain* (Cambridge: Cambridge University Press, 1990).

[69] Eric Hobsbawm, *Industry and Empire*, 1968 (Harmondsworth: Penguin, 1970), 309–14.

[70] John Hume and Michael Moss, *Workshop of the British Empire* (London: Heinemann, 1977), 4–10.

mainly off the Irish steamers. It met a country where religion, local civic society, and print-capitalism were deployed to contain the tensions of population expansion and ethnic heterogeneity. Social criticism modulated into a positive ideology, through religious and cultural nationalism, not a political-nationalist programme.

The Scottish paradox, embodied in many members of Bentham's entourage, was central. For almost a century, the Scottish intelligentsia or 'clerisy', to use Coleridge's term of 1830, had acquiesced in parliamentary union, yet been granted policy autonomy in socialization, education, law, and social welfare. Scottish 'management', dominated for sixty years by the Dundas family, lubricated the system with military, naval, and imperial patronage, tactfully extended to evangelicals in the Kirk. The problem was the arbitrary and institutionally corrupt electoral basis of this otherwise satisfactory arrangement, particularly when the Scots economy had to diversify away from textiles. This reached a climax in 1842, with the Paisley unemployment crisis, in which Peel's Cabinet had to take on responsibility for the well-being of the country's second-largest textile centre, and when the Church of Scotland submitted its Claim of Right—essentially a demand to live free from parliamentary control. The failure of Peel to resolve the second issue, and the Disruption of the following year, would mark Scottish politics for the rest of the century.[71]

Wales shortly stated its own case. Its revival was even more complex, because of the fusion of revolutionary ideas with 'linguistic romanticism' in the exotic shape of 'Old Iolo' Morganwg, whose imaginative additions to Welsh history and tradition fed a fascination with a 'British' druidic past. Nevertheless, there was a firm imposition of English authority in a country with dynamic pockets of industry and, since 1801, a vital physical linkage with Ireland. The Holyhead Road, with its mighty bridges at Conwy and Menai, was built between 1815 and 1825 by the engineer-educator Thomas Telford: steamers after 1820 completed the link with Kingstown. Industrial unrest was a threat in the new towns. The Merthyr Rising of 1831 was put down with the same ferocity inflicted on the followers of 'Captain Swing' in the English corn-growing areas. The prescription was repeated eight years later at Newport.[72] In 1832, the last independent Welsh institution, the Court of Great Sessions, was abolished. This went generally unremarked by the Welsh, who were concerned with the simultaneous growth of the slate, coal, and iron industries, yet later that decade the Rebecca Riots made patent the fact that, as far as their religious and social views were concerned, the hierarchies of the English establishment no longer applied. After 1810, with the secession of the Methodists, the Anglican Church had been pushed to the margin of Welsh society. In 1848 the attempt of British officialdom to censure Welsh religious belief and language triggered a national cultural revival which lasted until 'American South Wales' exploded into life in the 1890s.[73]

---

[71] I. D. L. Clark, 'From Progress to Reaction: The Moderate Regime in the Church of Scotland', in Nicholas Phillipson and Rosalind Mitchison, eds., *Scotland in the Age of Improvement* (Edinburgh: Edinburgh University Press, 1970).

[72] Williams, *When Was Wales?*, chap. 9.

[73] Ibid., and see Peter Lord, *The Visual Culture of Wales*, ii: *Imaging the Nation* (Cardiff: University of Wales Press, 2000), chap. 7.

The 1840s were for Scotland and Wales adjustments, for Ireland a catastrophe—both unexpected and somehow inevitable, given a union which had arisen
from the bloodbath of 1798, and the crushing of Presbyterian radicalism. But what
about Catholicism? In 1800–15, France—not Catholicism—was the mighty 'other'
against which Britain defined itself: not in the terms of Colley's Protestant–Catholic
conflict, but in a Burkeian, conservative response to a godless, mathematical power
ethic. In *The National Churches of England, Ireland and Scotland* (2001) Stewart Jay
Brown has shown how Evangelicalism made up part of a determinedly unifying ideology, which persisted until the 1830s.[74] Burke himself was an ambiguous prophet,
given his support for tradition, locality, and religion. Far from being execrated, Catholic practice was made welcome during the French wars. Exiled Bourbon supporters and their families were greeted like the Huguenots a century earlier; orders of
priests and nuns were accommodated. The chivalric revival movement of Sir Walter Scott and Kenelm Digby, not to mention Augustus Pugin, was crypto-Catholic,
in Pugin's case not crypto at all: architects and patrons also made it West British. To
this extent there was, as J. C. D. Clark has argued, a prolongation of the *ancien régime*
in the west.[75]

The Union in 1801 imposed London rule much more drastically than in Scotland,
but meant the fall of the Irish *Protestant* parliament. This was followed by the co-
option of a military elite, and then of a military rank and file. Protestants and Catholics were subsidized against atheistic Jacobinism. There was resentment over the failure
to grant Catholic emancipation, until O'Connell secured it in 1829, but over this
period government prescriptions varied, as indeed did O'Connell's approaches. It
was the Conservatives who went furthest in a French direction by creating a national
gendarmerie, the germ of the Royal Irish Constabulary (1814), and a quasiprefect-
orial type of local government by resident magistrate. Under Thomas Drummond,
a Liberal Scottish engineer who was resident under-secretary in the 1830s, Ireland
was governed to a great extent by Irish, or at least by O'Connell's, ideas and the result was tranquillity and fairly rapid modernization. This suited the Catholic Church,
enabling it to impose its control on the National School system. Far from being
nationalist, O'Connell proved only too anxious to demonstrate his Benthamite credentials, and Irish immigrants fought manfully for the Anti-Corn Law League against
the Chartists in the early 1840s. Only in 1848, under the erratic leadership of Feargus
O'Connor, did matters change in a nationalist—and Chartist—direction.[76]

The Convenant ideas which persisted in Scotland melded into the 'federalism'
espoused by the Young Irelanders before 1848. Burns and Scott were read and
repeated stylistically by Tom Moore in his *Irish Melodies* of 1807 and by Gerald Griffin in *The Collegians* of 1829, the latter memorably dramatized by Dion

[74] Stewart Jay Brown, *The National Churches of England, Ireland and Scotland* (Oxford: Oxford
University Press, 2001), chap. 1.
[75] Mark Girouard, *The Return to Camelot: Chivalry and the English Gentleman* (New Haven and
London: Yale University Press, 1981).
[76] See David Fitzpatrick, 'A Peculiar Tramping People: The Irish in Britain, 1801–1870', in
Vaughan, ed., *New History of Ireland* i.

Boucicault as *The Colleen Bawn*. Ireland's problem—like that of the Scottish high-lands—was the commercialization of land. But this happened in the absence of a coordinated capitalist class. Managers and technologists left; the printing business, deprived of protection, migrated wholesale to the USA after 1801. Ireland's role would be to supply the littoral with much of its intellect, its unskilled labour, and its food.[77]

Benthamism and Old Corruption in England came to a concordat in 1832, under Edinburgh-trained politicians such as Lord John Russell, Lord Brougham, and Lord Palmerston: this modernized landed power, underpinned the 'high farming' which persisted until the 1880s, producing 'improvers' across the islands among the Cecils, the Strutts, and the Cavendishes. These were steadily reinforced by professional elites—Engels's *avocati*—recruited through the universities, through Benthamite reforms to government, whether in Britain or in India, and through the annexation of the literati.[78] Thomas Carlyle, born within a day's journey of the Lake poets, would enshrine the values of the arc in calling journalists and writers 'the priests of our new church'. Carlyle himself was 'boosted' by America, principally by Ralph Waldo Emerson after his visit of 1834. The broadcasting of literary-social critiques depended to a great extent on a print-capitalism which was Scottish-Irish-American (and piratically cheap) rather more than it was London-orientated.[79]

Along the littoral human geography debated with intellectual opinion. The boundaries of identity—civic, regional, or national—were movable. Science, transport, education, religion imposed divergent templates, so any formal rationalization from an economic base to an intellectual superstructure is unhelpful. Carlyle's great steam engine kept several force fields—technical innovation, moral conflicts, religious antagonisms—in motion, but always also under continual threat of explosion or entropy.

## VIII MEDIATIONS

Nation states were firm, tangible legal subjects, something confirmed at least in theory by Lloyd George's achievement, the Paris Peace Conference of 1919. Regions and arcs of development were more malleable, given the imperatives of industry and trade. Between the two, the politics of identity, always ambiguous, became more discursive, and divisive, as bourgeois society evolved, while some of the fustier notions about English politics—deference, sectarianism, xenophobia, philistinism—didn't work in practice. Ireland in the 1820s shocked observers like Walter Scott with its poverty and primitiveness. He would probably have been as appalled by the slums of his native Edinburgh, had he ever visited them. Yet O'Connell was part of the Westminster

---

[77] Louis Cullen, *An Economic History of Ireland since 1660* (London: Batsford, 1972).

[78] Friedrich Engels, 'The Chartists', *New York Daily Tribune* (25 Aug. 1852).

[79] Anand Chitnis, *The Scottish Enlightenment and Early Victorian English Society* (London: Croom Helm, 1986).

furniture and the Irish would take over Chartism and its *Northern Star*.[80] This did not however forebode a 'British' revolution of the sort Engels expected in 1844 (he kept quiet about its constitutional outcome, though some sort of devolution, with Tom Moore-ish cultural nationalism thrown in, could be guessed at). Instead the conservative settlement with Ireland's strong farmer and seaport elite penetrated even the statistics on which Britain's liberals prided themselves. Although Ireland entered a customs union in 1801, her statistics were never integrated with those of the United Kingdom (just as if Germany after 1990 had decided to ignore the ex-DDR's statistics). This explains why the British Isles' advance over all other European countries was paradoxically accompanied by low growth rates. Statistics were, as Carlyle insisted, ideological 'spectacles'. To take them off was to encounter a quite different reality.[81]

At the same time the *active* moral ideas and determinations of the disparate nations were not grounded in purely economic interest but in what a later generation would call a 'social gospel' or 'civics'. Theoretically these could lead—given publicity and adaptable social overhead capital—to reconciliation rather than confrontation. The Jacobin Cavaignac gunned down Parisian workers in the June days of 1848, and his Scots contemporary General Sir Charles Napier, in a similar situation, sure-footedly negotiated with Lancashire Chartists, showing them what fieldguns did but getting the government to compromise. In a less visceral way Carlyle, already a best-seller with *The French Revolution*, had published *Chartism* in 1839. He saw disaster as impending but not—given the deployment of reform—inevitable. In 1848 his ideas helped mobilize his friend the young former Quaker W. E. Forster to mediate between masters and men in Bradford. Forster, Matthew Arnold's brother-in-law, would go on to draft the Education Act of 1871.[82]

Sir Arthur Quiller-Couch, the late Victorian novelist and educationalist, called his native Cornwall the 'Dialectical Duchy' and so fixed one characteristic of the western littoral. Promethean, shape-changing capitalism always tended to react to crises in one of three ways: by diversifying, by moving out of industry, or by moving physically to a new investment possibility. Between 1860 and 1914 it did all three; but the civic nexus of the crises meant that the businessmen who had to hold communities together could recruit and deploy enough native literati to keep a reform alliance on the road, in dialogue with forms of religion and ideology which both backed

---

[80] K. T. Hoppen, 'Riding a Tiger: Daniel O'Connell, Reform and Popular Politics in Ireland, 1800–1847', in T. C. W. Blanning and Peter Wende, eds., *Reform in Great Britain and Germany, 1750–1850* (Oxford: Oxford University Press, 1999). Ironically, the dominance of British intellectual history by Americans in the 1950s and 1960s—Hynes, Aydelotte, Koss, etc.—effectively minimized the lively American influence on British provincial pluralism.

[81] François Crouzet attributes the low rate of mid-nineteenth-century British growth (something calculated by economists, Phyllis Deane, Charles Feinstein, etc. only from the 1960s on) to the de-industrialization of Ireland. After 1880 it picked up because the Irish population was dropping towards only 10 per cent of that of the UK. Crouzet, *The Victorian Economy*, chap. 2. See B. R. Mitchell and Phyllis Deane, *Abstract of British Historical Statistics* (Cambridge: Cambridge University Press, 1962).

[82] See T. Wemyss Reid, *Life of the Right Honourable William Edward Forster*, 1888, i (Bath: Adams and Dart, 1970), 233.

and interrogated national distinctiveness. Never was Engels wider from the mark than when he denounced churches as 'faux frais of production'! In Ireland Catholicism shifted under Cardinal Cullen from nationalism to ultramontanism, yet his 'devotional revolution' both served and arraigned secular Britain. Joseph De Maistre, Burke's disciple, had sketched this out in his *Du Pape* (1819): he could never have imagined that this would be both the outcome of Burkeian ideas *and* a type of Irish clerical radicalism.[83]

In this situation there were two possible paradigms. The first lies in the gap that Marx left: what were intellectuals to do in the confrontation of capitalist and worker? If they were 'truly conscious of the historical situation' how much was this worth? Could they not generate more political clout by using their education to mediate between the classes than by throwing their lot in with the workers? The littoral's intelligentsia was remarkably mobile, and became more so as transport and communications improved, thanks to the postal reformer Anthony Trollope's world of telegrams and ambition. This was initially Ireland-centred, where a substantial Protestant intelligentsia was buttressed by a Catholic Jacobin one. If both were undermined by a population implosion, a surplus of teachers, journalists, and clergy was there to be recruited to the metropolis, and to the new industrial regions, in this process helpfully buying off radicalism as well.[84]

Thirdly, in contrast to most European countries of equivalent size, Britain was *politically* monoglot. Germany had three million Poles, France had substantial Basque, Breton, and Provençal-speaking minorities even after she lost Alsace, Italy had no accepted dialect for a national language until Tuscan was imposed after 1870; Spain had the Basques and Catalans. Russia and Turkey were formidably confused, and in Austria-Hungary the elite status of German, numerically the speech of a small minority, became increasingly threatened by a Slav majority. But the English language had by 1860 pressed Scots and Irish Gaelic to the margins. Welsh rode out the industrialization process, with 60 per cent (one million) able to speak or understand the language in 1901, but since the late eighteenth century a fissure had developed within Welsh-speaking society which meant that the 'practical' element of national politics was carried in English.[85]

This political discourse was, implicitly, common to the nations and regions: historical and civic but lacking a formal state system. Its experimental, magus-like nature — from Meredith through to Shaw, Joyce, and MacDiarmid — rose from the displacement of a single and consistent parliamentary tradition by assimilation, civics, localism, political and cultural nationalism, *and* the power of industry, empire, communications, and transport. Was the result a linguistic supercharge akin to the 'heteroglossia' of Mikhail Bakhtin, as literary historians such as Cairns Craig have argued? Or what the English critic F. W. Bateson called the 'métèque' style: exotic, adaptive,

---

[83] See Chapter 4.

[84] Owen Dudley Edwards, 'Trollope the Irish Writer', *Nineteenth Century Fiction*, 38 (1983–4), 3.

[85] See Ieuan Gwynedd Jones, 'Language and Community in Nineteenth Century Wales', in David Smith, ed., *A People and a Proletariat* (London: Pluto Press, 1980).

corrosive?[86] Capable of being the booster of imperial cohesion *and* its most destructive critic?

## IX  L'INVITATION AU VOYAGE

In George Meredith's unfinished novel *Celt and Saxon*, set in the late 1850s, he hauls
his Welsh, Irish, and English protagonists up to the peak of Caer Gybi, above Holyhead, to view the expanse and limits of the inland sea—'the mountain ranges holding
hands about an immensity of space'. It was, he writes of the young English journalist Colesworth, 'one of our giant days to his emotions'.[87] Dissecting this giant yields
the components of trade, technology, capital, language, and religion: the whole being
governed by time. I am not suggesting permanency but arguing that their collective impact created, partly within and partly outside the British domains, a *mentalité*,
aspects of which have not lessened but further problematized national identity. A
right diagnosis of contemporary ills requires an exploration of this heredity, and this
provides the plan of the book.

I begin by examining the vehicles of investigation and argument: vocabulary and
imagery. First we have Adam Smith's 'sympathy', coexisting awkwardly with the language of divisive loyalties and disruption—an image popularized at the very end of
our period by a clever technician and publicist of the Union, John Buchan, as it
strove to remodel itself under pressure of war. The emotive and infectious patriotism
conveyed by song shows, on closer investigation, strong contractual elements, flowing from Scotland to the other nations, both directly and through London. Images
of volcanic power and the boundary between civilization and barbarism, common
throughout the islands, can be traced back to the evolution of arc and core within the
discourse of the enlightenment, and to its scientific as well as literary controversies
(Chapter 1).

Having established the language, who spoke it? *Mentalités* being spatial as well as
cultural, I then try to describe the geography of the arc or littoral, the inland sea and
what Halford Mackinder called the Antechamber of England, its threshold to the
Atlantic, its industrial linkages, and the specialized vocabulary of union and patriotism which the Victorians developed out of their technological triumphs and applied
to it (Chapter 2). As the language of 'thin crusts' made plain, however, this landscape
had its menaces, chiefly its dependence on world markets—rarely stable—and its
unacknowledged exploitation of the poverty which shadowed the scenes of its success,
both in the great port cities and their hinterlands and in Ireland. The response to this
was the conflation of technology and *ethnie*, as evidenced by that Protestant problem-
solver the Scottish engineer: Kipling's MacAndrew (Chapter 3). This prototype, despite its intense energy, managed to escape disaster only quite narrowly, and the result

---

[86] Cairns Craig, *The Modern Scottish Novel: Narrative and the National Imagination* (Edinburgh:
Edinburgh University Press, 1990), 30–1.
[87] George Meredith, *Celt and Saxon* (London: Constable, 1910), 264.

would be a gradual Scottish shift towards a more defensive form of nationalism which aligned the country with a Celtic rather than an Anglo-Saxon identity (Chapter 4).

The reaction to this effervescence would issue in the communitarian qualities of Scots and Welsh religion and the contagious social criticism of Thomas Carlyle, his influence on Marx and Engels and their 'religion of socialism' on one side, and on Catholic social autonomy in Ireland and among Irish emigrant communities on the other (Chapters 5 and 9). In a more subdued way, such autodidact political theory—and its link to the metropolitan centre—drew on a long-lived, if partly fabricated, literary-religious landscape, whereby rural values were given a role which was to prevail far into the epoch of urbanization: the mental worlds of the Scots folk, the Welsh *gwerin*, and their influence on the apparently foreign world of Ireland's 'devotional revolution' (Chapter 6).

The incompleteness of nationality within the arc provoked attempts to reify it, to create new patterns of belief and analysis, and to communicate these: something which broke conventional national frameworks. Two significant reactions to this challenge drew on the inheritance of the enlightenment and tried to marry it to the new democracy. They can be traced back to the dialectic between the 'polite' materialism of Adam Smith and the more cautious, communitarian analysis of his friend Adam Ferguson, who stressed the irrational claims of corporate identity and the rituals whereby enthusiasm—*Spieltrieb*—would unite the polis. In the hybrid polity of the arc, sport and recreation—from the steam yacht and the golf course to the hurling of Celtic Ireland and the soccer of Celtic Glasgow—became technical experiment, big business, agents of community development, unifiers of religion and society, and of the regions against the metropolis (Chapter 7).

There was also the competitor, the outcome of the Smith–Comte–Marx continuum: the creation of a new and liberated post-religious ethos where the society of status would give way to that of scientific system as well as contract, and where human rationality would expand to allow for new capabilities: the mental world of Herbert Spencer and Patrick Geddes. Did this prompt the rise of Supercelt, someone figured forth by the fey revivalist William Sharp, alias Fiona MacLeod, in the 1890s and the practical mystic George Russell 'AE' in the 1900s? The notion of a superior, cosmopolitan reach seems inherent in the literature of these decades, and at its centre was Bernard Shaw, not just a dramatist but a post-Marxian economist at grips with globalizing capitalism (Chapter 8). Through Shaw surged the same complex of themes that his musical contemporaries handled. This time, however, their constellation in retrospect seems pathological: the descent into the crisis of 1914–18, and the impact of this on nationality and culture. In what David Landes has called the period of 'short wind and second breath', the dialogue between nationalism, technology, and literary modernism was complex, at its centre the 'geotechnic city' of Dublin, of Shaw and (albeit in retrospect) of James Joyce. The bourgeois subjects of their discourse would shortly face a crucial challenge: the 'men of push and go' would mobilize the littoral against the Central Powers, not just technologically but morally—with the Covenant of the League of Nations as their tabernacle—and triumph (Chapter 9). Yet they simultaneously contrived, through a barbed and inept dialogue with an unexpectedly violent Irish nationalism, to destroy the unity of the arc. After this catastrophe, what would remain of arc and core would have, in our own epoch, to be embedded in 'New Britain' or 'These Islands' (Aftermath).

# I
# PLACES AND VOICES

# 1

# Sacred Lambencies and Thin Crusts: The Metaphors of Identity

...They went to the window. The fronting heavens were a black purple. The thunder, which had been growling in the distance, swept forward and roared above the town. The crash no longer roared afar, but cracked close to the ear, hard, crepitant. Quick lightning stabbed the world in vicious and repeated hate. A blue-black moistness lay heavy on the cowering earth.

George Douglas Brown, *The House with the Green Shutters*, 1901[1]

If a city hasn't been used by an artist not even the inhabitants live there imaginatively.

Alasdair Gray, *Lanark*, 1982[2]

## I  NATURA MALIGNA

The Atlantic coast was appreciated for the qualities of light and landscape—the soft days of the Irish west, the clarity of Cornwall, the Welsh picturesque at Betws-y-Coed—but Victorian fictionalists encountered a Scotland which seemed irredeemably dour: bleakness of moorland, withered grasses, stunted trees, flailed by a merciless wind; towns and villages slattern and sullen; great cities truly hellish chasms of filthy streets and pandemonian crowds. 'Land of the mountain and the flood' characterizes some of this. The 'Bonnie Briar Bush' of the Kailyarder Ian MacLaren waves outside the window of a talented boy dying of tuberculosis. The same malady kills Cunninghame Graham's returning migrant at 'Beattock for Moffat'. George Douglas Brown in *The House with the Green Shutters* granted himself a couple of sentences of exhilaration, but soon let fly with *natura maligna*.

Ibsen's Norway is no more friendly, but it was *like that*—the drenched fjord towns, the terrific mountains, the seas pounding on Rosmersholm's beach. By contrast, educated Scots—the bellwethers of the Atlantic intellect—made their landscape a metaphysical horror. After the delight in their land's beauty of such Gaelic poets as Duncan Ban MacIntyre and Alasdair MacMaisthir Alasdair (who had otherwise little reason for content), the likes of Alexander Smith, John Davidson,

---

[1] (Edinburgh: Nelson, *c*.1950), 129.    [2] (Edinburgh: Canongate, 1982), 243.

Robert Louis Stevenson, George Douglas Brown, and Lewis Grassic Gibbon wielded sternness and wildness—at best, with bleak tropes of rocks, graves, and peewits—relentlessly. The human geography expertly displayed by Sir Walter Scott stayed quiet until its sensibilities were rediscovered by such regionalists as Neil Gunn and George Mackay Brown in and after the 1930s.[3]

The Scots literati were notable cosmopolitans—the inventors of English literature, in Robert Crawford's thesis, the 'red Scots' of my own *Scotland and Nationalism* (1977)—whose migration contributed crucially to British, and Welsh and Irish, nationality in the Victorian epoch.[4] But the psychological cost was high; symbolized by the inverted sublime of the above as well as by the 'divided self' from James Hogg via Stevenson to R. D. Laing. Were they also deliberately spurning a society bent on what Scott called a 'terrifying and unnatural' urban life, as Andrew Noble has alleged?[5] Imaginative writers don't just interrogate, and recoil from, reality. As the language and symbols of the Victorian Scots came from a literary tradition which was conscious of social semiotics, this equipment could be formidably directive.[6] Two driving metaphors were the result: the psychological metaphor of dualism, and the equally powerful physical-social metaphor of 'the thin crust of civilisation'.

The German scholar Elmar Schenkel, an adept of such post-industrial Celts as the Powys brothers and David Jones, has argued that the speed of change in industrial society makes the ideal of 'completeness'—the overcoming of alienation—affirmable or deniable only through metaphor. The actualities of childhood, the village, the small community have changed so much that invoking them makes them, as it were, metaphors of a metaphor. Schenkel argues that, to escape intolerable reality and unstable metaphor, writers in industrial societies implicitly align themselves with 'green' and 'small-is-beautiful' projects aimed at a non-industrial, utopian *logos*. This provides a bearable trajectory for discourses which in turn condition the history that they survey.[7] I want to trace the linked ways in which a peculiarly influential elite interpreted, and recoiled from, an overtaxing project: the maintenance of human personality in a society in upheaval. The result was what John Buchan called the civilization–barbarism frontier: 'a thread, a sheet of glass', a phrase which Graham Greene in 1941 reckoned as summing up the character of the twentieth century.[8]

G. M. Young, whose subtle *Portrait of an Age* (1936) 'composed' in Lukacs's terms the English establishment's—'Bladesover's'—subjugation of social change to

---

[3] I owe the Stevenson–Grassic Gibbon comparison to Angus Calder.

[4] Robert Crawford, *Devolving English Literature* (Oxford: Clarendon Press, 1992), chap. 1; Christopher Harvie, *Scotland and Nationalism*, 1977 (London: Routledge, 2004), 4.

[5] Andrew Noble, 'Urbane Silence: Scottish Writing and the Nineteenth-Century City', in George Gordon, ed., *Perspectives of the Scottish City* (Aberdeen: Aberdeen University Press, 1985), 70.

[6] See, for example, Rory Watson, 'Carlyle: The World as Text and the Text as Voice', in Douglas Gifford, ed., *The History of Scottish Literature, iii: Nineteenth Century* (Aberdeen: Aberdeen University Press, 1988).

[7] Elmar Schenkel, 'The Poet as Placemaker', in Lothar Fietz, Paul Hoffmann, and Hans-Werner Ludwig, eds., *Regionalität, Nationalität und Internationalität in der zeitgenössischen Lyrik* (Tübingen: Attempto Verlag, 1992).

[8] Graham Greene, 'The Last Buchan', in *The Lost Childhood and Other Essays* (Harmondsworth: Penguin, 1962), 119.

political continuity, had told Greene's generation to 'Go on reading until you can hear people talking'.[9] It was able to sort and structure this within an intellectual as well as temporal dimension because it was still conscious of biblical and classical exegesis. This sort of personal history seemed redundant in the collective ethos of the 1960s and 1970s, which was seen as accelerating the research/learning process.[10] Since then market forces as well as the dwindling of the British state have compelled a reversal to the biographers, military historians, and heritage merchants, suspended between Merchant and Ivory and Sellar and Yeatman, exuding 'the glamour of backwardness'. In Scotland, Ireland, and Wales collectivity still seems stronger: witness the three volumes of *People and Society in Scotland* (1988–92) and the four volumes of the *History of Scottish Literature* (1987–8). But interpretative lacunae remain, most notably concerning the economy and culture of Victorian Scotland.

This is partly because historians tend to interrogate the texts of the period for fact rather than discourse. When argument and symbol are analysed, other preoccupations emerge. In the emerging 'world' of the Atlantic coast—as we shall see—Thomas Carlyle was the 'central singer', but his texts have to be teased out. Did he read James Hutton on geology? Was he influenced, in his idea of political community, by Thomas Chalmers's 'Godly Commonwealth'? The literary scholar is more concerned with aesthetic and emotional impact, the stylistic and ideological imprint of earlier authors. W. B. Yeats, whose 'Meditations in Time of Civil War' (1923) would become an equally emphatic summing-up, called this 'the half-read wisdom of daemonic images'. In a present of precipitate change, with the fragmentation of the traditional Anglo-British context, such images count for so much that interdisciplinarity and intertextuality become unavoidable.

For Ernest Renan, history was the pivot of nationality, and the dialectic between imaginative writing and social change seems crucial to the recent Scottish cultural renaissance, whether in the exploration by William Donaldson and Tom Leonard of Victorian popular literature or, conversely, the 'conjectural history' of Alasdair Gray's novels.[11] In my study of British political fiction *The Centre of Things* (1991) I analysed literary texts, not just to distinguish purpose and historical impact but, through examining language and allusion, to locate writers and politicians' arguments in an evolving series of stylistic and literary 'epiphanies'. This suggested a possible approach to the peculiarly faulted Scotland of the Victorians, analysing the success of their cultural incorporation into the Union State, especially in the 1840s, and its ambiguous psychological and social consequences.[12]

---

[9] G. M. Young, *Today and Yesterday* (London: Hart-Davis, 1948) 112; and see Georg Lukacs, *Essays on Thomas Mann* (New York: Grosset and Dunlap, 1965), p. vi.

[10] See Theodore Roszak, *The Dissenting Academy* (Harmondsworth: Penguin, 1969).

[11] Ernest Renan, 'What is a Nation?', 1882, trans. I. H. Grant in Stuart Woolf, ed., *Nationalism in Europe, 1815 to the Present* (London: Routledge, 1996). See also William Donaldson, *Popular Literature in Victorian Scotland: Language, Fiction and the Press* (Aberdeen: Aberdeen University Press, 1986), and Tom Leonard, ed., *Radical Renfrew* (Edinburgh: Polygon, 1990).

[12] Christopher Harvie, *The Centre of Things: Political Fiction from Disraeli to the Present* (London: Unwin Hyman, 1991), 38–9.

## II   A PATRIOT FOR WHOM?

Nineteenth-century Scots identity has been called British, but it was more complex than that. 'British', if politically accurate, was too cumbersome a formulation for diplomats, merchants, and publicists to deal with. 'English'—eliding language and predominant state—was a sort of default position. The Scots had to live with it, and what they made of it was patent in a key document of Scottish Unionist identity, *The Scottish Students' Song Book*. This was edited in the 1890s for the Students' Representative Councils set up by the Universities (Scotland) Act of 1889 by Prof. John Nichol of Glasgow University, biographer of Robert Burns and the friend of Mazzini and Swinburne. It came hard on the heels of the celebration of the centenary of the Kilmarnock edition of Burns in 1886, stage-managed by the Earl of Rosebery, from which the modern Burns cult essentially dates: one of many celebrations of enlightenment, radicalism, technical progress, and dynastic survival that filled the last quarter of the nineteenth century. David Cannadine has termed the British element of this 'ornamentalism', yet the language of cult and songbook was not uniquely that of empire or ethnic heroism but of commerce and civic choice, or blends of both.[13] Its anthems repay study.

   'God save the King', though figuring in formal ceremonial, did not appeal. Composed around 1740, perhaps by Henry Carey, it took off during the Jacobite crisis of 1745, its fourth stanza instructing God:

> Lord grant that Marshal WADE
> May by thy Mighty Aid
> Victory bring.
> May he Sedition hush,
> And like a Torrent rush,
> Rebellious Scots to crush,
> God save the King.[14]

It was a Tory Party song, customary only in that phase of Churchill-cinema Britishness, from 1939 and 1955. Yet its historical twin 'Rule Britannia', also from 1740, was by James Thomson of Ednam, the Augustan poet, and Thomson was not the last transferred patriot. In 1801, only eight years after Burns's 'Scots wha hae', another Scottish radical, Thomas Campbell, wrote 'Ye mariners of England', and in the 1840s yet another, Charles Mackay, wrote 'Cheer boys, cheer!' and 'England over all!' But Campbell accompanied 'Ye mariners' (he had not actually visited England) with 'An exile of Erin', sympathizing with the Irish rising of 1798, and would die revered by

---

[13] David Cannadine, *Ornamentalism: How the British Saw their Empire* (London: Allen Lane, 2001) deduces from orders, durbars, and jubilees an imperial ethos; Bernard Porter, *The Absent-Minded Imperialists* (Oxford: Oxford University Press, 2004), grants this, at best, only fleeting significance. Elfie Rembold's study of the Glasgow Exhibition and Caernarfon investiture of 1911, *Die festliche Nation: Geschichtsinszenierung und regionaler Nationalismus vor dem ersten Weltkrieg* (Berlin: Philo, 2000), is subtle in assessing the interplay of regional and imperial politics.

[14] David Nichol Smith, ed., *The Oxford Book of Eighteenth Century Verse* (Oxford: Clarendon Press, 1926), 302.

the Poles. MacKay, editor of the *Illustrated London News* and father of the astonishing Marie Corelli, spent his later life campaigning for Gaelic poetry. Did Robert Crawford's Anglo-Scots create, besides English literature,[15] an 'imperial song' which was masculine, positive, and *portable*, compared with a Scottish patriotism—Jacobite songs composed after the Cause was safely dead, or Lady Nairne's post-Flodden *tristesse* in 'The Flowers of the Forest'—gone winsome?[16]

In 1886 Burns was all but unavoidable. 'The aforesaid "old-kind chiel" remains to my heart and brain almost the tenderest, manliest (even if contradictory) dearest flesh-and-blood figure in all the streams and clusters of by-gone poets,' wrote Walt Whitman, in a shrewd, affectionate appraisal, rubbishing his Jacobitism and claiming him for America: 'Without the race of which he is a distinct specimen, (and perhaps his poems) America and her powerful democracy could not exist today—could not project with unparalleled historic sway into the future.'[17] But where did this leave national culture? Not simplified when Burns's key contribution is deconstructed, exclamations, emphases, and all:

> Scots, wha hae wi' WALLACE bled,
> Scots, wham BRUCE has aften led;
> Welcome to your gory bed,—
> Or to victorie!—
>
> Now's the day, and now's the hour;
> See the front o' battle lower;
> See approach proud EDWARD's power—
> Chains and Slaverie!
>
> Wha will be a traitor-knave?
> Wha can fill a coward's grave
> Wha sae base as be a Slave?
> —Let him turn and flee!
>
> Wha for SCOTLAND's king & law
> Freedom's sword will strongly draw,
> FREE-MAN stand, or FREE-MAN fa',
> Let him follow me.—
>
> By Oppression's woes and pains!
> By your Sons in servile chains!
> We will drain our dearest veins,
> But they shall be free!
>
> Lay the proud Usurpers low!
> Tyrants fall in every foe!

---

[15] Crawford, *Devolving English Literature*, 16–44.

[16] William Donaldson, *The Jacobite Song in Scotland* (Aberdeen: Aberdeen University Press, 1993).

[17] Walt Whitman, 'Robert Burns as Poet and Person', in *November Boughs* (Philadelphia: D. MacKay, 1888).

LIBERTY's in every blow!
Let us DO—or DIE![18]

The poem is less simple, and much less ethnic, than it looks. Burns's opening in stanza 1 is a statement of fact, not the rousing command 'Allons, enfants de la Patrie!' which starts the 'Marseillaise'—though it still *sounds* like a command, a Gaelic *slo-gan* or war-cry, calling up martyrs and liberators, anticipating sacrifice before eventual triumph. The comparatively downbeat mood continues in stanza 2; the looming crisis isn't Rouget de L'Isle's 'le jour de gloire est arrivé' but the grimmer 'see the front o' battle lower', with enslavement threatening national pride. Stanza 3 presents a choice: become a traitor, coward, or slave—and in his pre-Bannockburn career Bruce had arguably been all three—by clearing off, or risk death by fighting for the right. Stanza 4 then establishes a social compact in the style of the Declaration of Arbroath of 1320, via Archdeacon Barbour's long narrative poem *The Brus* of 1376. 'Scotland's king & law' will triumph through the strength of freemen fighting for freedom. The alternative is stated in stanza 5: oppression, pain, and slavery will continue until Scotland gains freedom by blood sacrifice. Stanza 6 is the only one to use an ethnic argument. Usurpation by the English transfers guilt to individual English soldiers: 'Tyrants fall in every foe'. These lines, Burns wrote, were taken not from Barbour but from the later and much more aggressively anti-English Blind Hary's *The Wallace* (*c*.1476). The final couplet states that national liberty demands success or death, but by embodying the motto of the Douglases 'Doe or die!' sounds a less-than-reassuring echo of where over-mighty nobles would later get the country.[19]

The song in fact posits choices, not the ascriptive attitude: 'you are Scots, you must do this' as in the ethnic patriotism of 'La Marseillaise'. Rouget de L'Isle composed the latter in April 1792, and it was broadcast after the insurrection of 10 August.[20] Burns wrote 'Scots wha hae' five months after the execution of Louis XVI on 21 January 1793 (the declaration of war on Britain came in February) yet it was not published in, or politically directed at, Scotland. Burns sent it, anonymously, to the London *Morning Chronicle*, a Whig daily, where it appeared on 8 May 1794, when the confrontation between the English Friends of the People and the government appeared imminent.[21] Enthusiasts such as the Whig composer Robert Nares, and in 1841 Thomas Moore, regarded it as 'a song which in a great national crisis, would be of more avail than all the eloquence of a Demosthenes'.[22] Its Scottish identity was more enigmatic.

Burns the enlightenment intellectual was salient in 'Scots wha hae' : the youth who, with other farmers' sons, was privately tutored by John Murdoch, and admired Adam Smith, both the *Theory of Moral Sentiments* (1759) and *The Wealth of Nations*

[18] *The Letters of Robert Burns*, ed. John de Lancey Ferguson, 2 vols. (Oxford: Clarendon Press, 1931), ii, 195.

[19] For Blind Hary's politics see Harvie, *Scotland: A Short History* (Oxford: Oxford University Press, 2002), 40, 65.

[20] For text and background to 'La Marseillaise' see *Grande Encyclopédie Larousse* (Paris: Larousse, 1960–4), vii, entry 6703.

[21] Smith, ed., *The Oxford Book of Eighteenth Century Verse*, 676.

[22] D. S. Low, ed., *Robert Burns: The Critical Heritage* (London: Routledge, 1974), 174.

(1776). Smithian ideas underlie not just the idea of contract and mutuality in 'Scots wha hae', but Burns's sociable principles, as in the 'Epistle to J. Lapraik' (1786):

> But ye whom social pleasure charms,
> Whose hearts the tide of kindness warms,
> Who hold your being on the terms,
> 'Each aid the others.'
> Come to the bowl, come to my arms,
> My friends, my brothers![23]

Smith's 'sympathy' gives a 'composure' to much of Burns's poetry, notoriously present in 'The Cottar's Saturday Night', a near-parodic bit of rustic Augustan about a class which would be dead almost before Burns himself.[24] Elsewhere reality forced itself on him, as in 'To a Mouse', in which the little animal dehoused by the coulter of his plough is compared with the poet's own failure to establish himself on a farm:

> But thou art blest compared with me
> The present only troubles thee
> While oh! I backward cast my 'ee
> On prospects drear
> But forward, tho' I canna see,
> I guess and fear.[25]

Politically, this is untenable self-pity. The Irish critic Luke Gibbons has contrasted Smithian 'sympathy'—a learned drive towards the conscious and rational present-ation of the individual—and the emotional self-degradation of the Greek warrior Philoctetes, who displayed his wounds to excite sympathy: an accusation often lev-elled at the Irish on account of their own anthems 'The Wearing of the Green' (1798) and T. D. Sullivan's 'God save Ireland' (1867).[26]

'To a Mouse' is Burns in Philoctetic mode. 'Scots wha hae', though drawing on patriotic sources, presents a politics of contract. The enemy is not named as English, the breach remains civic, not ethnic. The echoes of the Declaration of Arbroath reflect Bruce's own Anglo-Norman background and concerns common to both countries in 1200–96 when the Plantagenet kings, preoccupied with their French possessions, kept the peace. Proud Edward, the father of the enemy at Bannockburn, had disrup-ted this balance, but it could be rearranged in Whig fashion. The result has a lot in common with 'Rule, Britannia':

> When Britain first, at heaven's command,
> Arose from out the azure main;
> This was the charter of the land,

---

[23] *Robert Burns: Selected Poems*, ed. William Beattie and H. W. Meikle (Harmondsworth: Penguin, 1952), 107, and see Liam McIlvanney, *Burns the Radical* (East Linton: Tuckwell, 2002), 116–19.

[24] *Robert Burns: Selected Poems*, 80–7.     [25] Ibid. 88–9.

[26] Luke Gibbons in Terence Brown, ed., *Celticism* (Amsterdam: Rodopi, 1996), 281, and see Seamus Deane, ed., *The Field Day Anthology*, 3 vols. (Derry: Field Day, 1991), ii, 106, for T. D. Sullivan, 'God save Ireland', originally in *The Nation* (7 Dec. 1867).

And guardian angels sung this strain:
'Rule, Britannia, rule the waves;
Britons never will be slaves.'[27]

Thomson's constitutional patriotism is similar to the contract element—'king and law' in Burns—and is also agnostic about England, although the song originally featured in a play, *Alfred*, in which 'Britain' could only have been a remote notion. The concepts Burns regarded as alien—slavery, autocracy, ill-disposed foreigners, internal weaknesses—are all flayed in Thomson's longer poem *Liberty* (1736):

> . . . Theirs the triumph be,
> By deep *Invention's* keen pervading eye,
> The heart of courage, and the Hand of *Toil*,
> Each conquer'd ocean staining with their blood,
> Instead of Treasure robb'd' by ruffian War,
> Round social Earth to circle fair Exchange,
> And bind the Nations in a golden Chain.[28]

Burns's expansive Whiggery responded to the Scots *menu peuple*, threatened by agricultural improvement and industrialization. His arguments in 'Scots wha hae' parallel those of Sir David Lindsay's John the Commonweal in *The Three Estates* (1544)—plunder by the 'folk above', and the landlords barring the people's right to 'come into the body of the kirk'—and though the play doesn't seem to have been known to him, its ideas almost certainly reached him via Allan Ramsay's *Gentle Shepherd* (1725) and the Tory and Jacobite Robert Fergusson, who had been influenced by Bolingbroke's *Patriot King* (1738). Burns revered the Covenanters, whose sense of democratic struggle he brought out in another short poem:

> The Solemn League and Covenant
> Now brings a smile, now brings a tear,
> But sacred freedom then was theirs.
> If thou'rt a slave, indulge your sneer[29]

This was not the National Covenant of 1638 but by the 1643 agreement between the Scots and English parliaments, which endorsed a 'British' identity similar to Thomson's. Even treason is defined in enlightenment terms. In an earlier ballad, 'A Parcel of Rogues', Burns had attacked the destruction of the Scots parliament in 1707:

> The English steel we could disdain
> Secure in valour's station.
> But English gold has been our bane.
> Such a parcel of rogues in a nation.[30]

But this also fitted into the arguments of Smith and Ferguson that the actual fruits of commerce could lead to 'luxury and corruption'. Populist patriotism was difficult,

---

[27] Smith, ed., *The Oxford Book of Eighteenth Century Verse*, 252–3.
[28] Reproduced ibid.        [29] Quoted in McIlvanney, *Burns the Radical*, 7.
[30] Quoted in *Poems and Songs of Robert Burns*, ed. James Kinsley (Oxford: Oxford University Press, 1968), 643–4.

when the nature of the state was founded not on ethnie but on negotiation. Hence 'England': intellectually with Carlyle himself and his 'Condition of England Question' of 1839, practically with the assumption that the red duster of the merchant marine was a symbol that in everyday business mattered far more than the saltire. Contract inhibited the emotional appeal and the allure of martyrdom. English gold, or French gold, was part of the negotiation and couldn't be wished away. Money—David Marquand's 'universal pander'—meant complexity. Deconstruct 'Scots wha hae' and we find, besides nationalism, Whiggery, Freemasonry, Bolingbrokism: something the hard-headed Edinburgh reviewers of 1802 could live with.[31]

In its religious or federal-covenant form, Burnsian democracy was flexible, and could apply beyond the national community itself. The cost was ambiguity. Take 'Chains and Slaverie' in 'Scots wha hae' or 'the coward slave' in 'A Man's a Man'. In Scotland in 1793 some colliers *were* slaves, a status defended a century earlier by Fletcher of Saltoun with nationalist arguments.[32] Scots pressed for the end of black slavery, but benefited greatly from its products, the tobacco and cotton which commercialized the country. Had Burns settled in Jamaica in 1786 he would have been a part of this.[33] Even the triumph of 'liberal' economics was coupled with the rise of wage-slavery. As Carlyle's 'cash-nexus', its radical interpretation would influence nineteenth-century social criticism and Marxism. Less reassuringly, as Scottish democracy consolidated, wage-slavery became defined racially as a low-cost Irish labour force. Burns died before the Irish rising of 1798, but would probably have sympathized as a Presbyterian radical of the Henry Joy McCracken, William Drennan sort. Yet Ulster Presbyterian radicalism was bribed out of existence, and his own Ayrshire became deeply hostile to Catholicism. Burns's Freemasonry and popularity among Ulster Scots—who continued to quote the Declaration of Arbroath on their banners, but directed it against Dublin rather than London rule—would reinforce their Protestant Unionism.

The Scottish attitude to France was quite different: the optimism of James Mackintosh's *Vindiciae Gallica* (1791) certainly gave way to Burkeian pessimism; but the revolution was regarded as inevitable in John Galt's *Annals of the Parish* (1820), in which he followed many of the literati such as Robertson, Ferguson, and Reid. Carlyle's *French Revolution* (1837) took the same line, seeing with Burns the French King as an indolent fathead who courted his inevitable downfall, much like the Stewarts. This evolutionism was passed on to Engels, typical enough of the radicals who universalized Burns (he liked to believe that his Irish partner, Mary Burns, was a kinswoman) while dismissing Scots exceptionality: an occluded vision bequeathed to the later generation of historians and literary scholars, from Christopher Hill to Raymond Williams, who established Marxism at he heart of the Anglo-British canon.

---

[31] See David Marquand, 'How United is the Modern United Kingdom?', chap. 16 of Keith Stringer and Alexander Grant, eds., *Uniting the Kingdom? The Making of British History* (London: Routledge, 1995).

[32] *Fletcher of Saltoun: Selected Writings*, ed. David Daiches (Edinburgh: Scottish Academic Press, 1979), p. xxiv.

[33] Catherine Carswell, *The Life of Robert Burns*, 1930 (Edinburgh: Canongate, 1990), 150.

## III   AULD SCOTIA—WHO SHE?

Burns's nationality was hard-wired, realistic—influential in Wales and in the Ireland of Tom Moore and Thomas Davis—but it was also emotionally attenuated. What's lacking is national pathos, or more directly, sex: Scotia not only isn't Britannia, *she* doesn't seem to be there at all. Woman-as-nation can personify integrity—the national matron—along with dependence, martyrdom, and liability to rape. With the last comes miscegenation, an attack on ethnic purity. So she is both radical and conservative: Marianne and, alternatively, Marie Antoinette. Seamus Deane has cited Burke on the French Queen as the birth of anti-modern Irish nationalism.[34] Eccentric? Tom Paine was read far more than Burke in Ireland itself, yet Marianne/Marie Antoinette personifies powerful if antithetical images of the nation: the fructifying mother and the symbol of traditional reverence. Both have roots in Catholic cults of the Madonna. Deane rightly sees this as critical: the nation as an aspect of Burke's *sublime*.

Burnsian patriotism has different roots: in the covenanted nature of the Scots state. This also concurs with the 'authoritarian family' detected by the French social anthropologist Emanuel Todd: the Scots family as a contractual, not an affective, unit, underwritten by male actors and political will.[35] The nation of 'La Marseillaise' is female, her subjects are her children; 'Wha for Scotland's king & law . . .' implies no such relationship. Its maleness is further emphasized by Wallace, castrated, beheaded, and quartered, symbolically eradicating the Scottish nation. 'Scots wha hae' involves a rebirth, but the seed is the blood—and cooperation—of warriors. Women do not figure at all.

Scotswomen were mistrusted, even if they actually kept society in existence. In recurrent witch-hunts social solidarity was bought through female sacrifice as the 'authoritarian families', whose various layers and 'estates'—kirk, law, burghs, schools—made up the state, turned on them as scapegoats when things did not work out. The literati responded by engineering a sort of Smithian 'sympathy': adopting 'feeling' of the Henry Mackenzie sort, and incorporating female characteristics which also met certain conservative criteria. A more general status of victimhood could be conferred on Celtic monks slaughtered by the Norsemen, George Wishart and the Calvinist martyrs, and in the late seventeenth century the Covenanters. This was when Scotland's two images, Covenanter and Highlander, confronted each other; Whiggism and nationalism interwove and created extreme psychological pressure. James Hogg seems to have been peculiarly alive to it, in *The Brownie of Bodsbeck* (1815), with insights learned from his friend the pioneer psychoanalyst Professor Andrew Duncan. This got full play in *The Memoirs and Confessions of a Justified Sinner* (1823).[36]

---

[34]  Seamus Deane, 'Irish Nationalism and the Romantic', paper read at Tübingen, July 1997.

[35]  See Emmanuel Todd, *The Causes of Progress: Culture, Authority and Change* (Oxford: Blackwell, 1989), chap. 2.

[36]  See Christopher Harvie, 'The Covenanting Tradition', in Graham Walker and Tom Gallagher, eds., *Sermons and Battle Hymns: Protestant Popular Culture in Modern Scotland* (Edinburgh: Edinburgh University Press, 1990); and see Karin Straub, 'Psychological Disturbance in the Scottish Novel of the Nineteenth and Twentieth Centuries', PhD thesis, Stuttgart University, 2005.

Sado-sexual themes, central to 'the romantic agony', have an uneasy presence in a nation dominated by sublimation and repression.[37] In John Galt's *The Provost* (1821) a pretty, silly teenager is tried, condemned, and hanged for infanticide; Scott has an adulteress immured in *Marmion* (1808), fragile women persecuted in *The Heart of Midlothian* (1816) and *The Bride of Lammermoor* (1819). George Douglas Brown's *The House with the Green Shutters* (1901) ends up with the Gourlay women killing themselves to the accompaniment of 1 Corinthians 13—'for here abideth faith and hope and charity, and the greatest of these is charity'—expressive of all that Victorian Scotland was not. Femininity—or sensitivity in general—became a sort of civic disqualification, to be overcome by becoming 'more like men'. This emotional inflexibility, latent in R. D. Laing's critique of the family, has since had its Scottish roots analysed by such neo-Jungian feminists as Kay Carmichael in *For Crying Out Loud* (1993) and Carol Craig in *The Scots' Crisis of Confidence* (2003).

What does one do in such circumstances? One answer was to re-engineer 'sympathy' to stress tactical victimhood, exile, and loss, even by those who had success in commercial life. The ambitious young Scot Donald Farfrae performs this with a Jacobite ballad in Thomas Hardy's *The Mayor of Casterbridge* (1886):

The singer himself grew emotional, till she could imagine a tear in his eye as the words went on:—

> 'It's hame, and it's hame, hame fain would I be,
> Oh hame, hame, hame to my ain countree!
> There's an eye that ever weeps, and a fair face will be fain,
> As I pass through Annan Water with my bonnie bands again;
> When the flower is in the bud, and the leaf upon the tree,
> The lark shall sing me hame to my ain countree!'

Young Farfrae repeated the last verse. It was plain that nothing so pathetic had been heard at the Three Mariners for a considerable time. The difference of accent, the excitability of the singer, the intense local feeling, and the seriousness with which he worked himself up to a climax, surprised this set of worthies, who were only too prone to shut up their emotions with caustic words.[38]

It was to be in the 1880s that Scots expatriates, under pressure for sharp business practices and energetic colonial activity, were to bind themselves together in Burns clubs and St Andrew or Caledonian societies. R. L. Stevenson would give them yet more pabulum in *The Master of Ballantrae*. En route to America, and the novel's strange climax, the Master, Alexander Durie, trying to win over his steward Ephraim McKellar, launches into 'the saddest of our country tunes, which sets folk weeping in a tavern':[39]

> Now, when the day dawns on the brow of the moorland,
> Low stands the house, and the chimney-stone is cold.

---

[37] Mario Praz, *The Romantic Agony*, 1930 (Cleveland: Meridian, 1965), 120.
[38] Hardy, *The Mayor of Casterbridge* (London: Macmillan, 1886), 60–1.
[39] See Margot Finn, 'Scottish Credit Drapers, Solidarity and Patriotism', in Martin Daunton, ed., *Consumption and History* (Oxford: Berg, 1999), and H. J. Hanham, *Scottish Nationalism* (London: Faber, 1968), 97–8.

> Lone let it stand, now the folks are all departed,
> The kind hearts, the true hearts, that loved the place of old.[40]

Stevenson's image is that of the Clearances—an issue revived by Scottish Land Leaguers in the 1880s—but the Master is a formidably confused character: he and his dour, competent brother suffer not just from national history but from the proto-schizophrenia and post-Darwinian degeneracy which, at the same time, naturalist writers such as Flaubert, Zola, and Nordau were diagnosing in French bourgeois society.

Injections of sentiment provided a sort of charm against the corrosion that 'luxury and corruption' could inflict on the contractual state. Allan Ramsay the elder, Adam Smith, and Henry Mackenzie, the psalmody of the Convenanters *and* the Jacobite songs, washed Scotland into tactical martyrdom by a combination of patriotism and sentiment. A sentimentalized Burns, Jacobite, radical *and* romantic, could revive nationality through song and the fetishizing of exile, blamed on remote landlords, religious rivals, the immigrant 'other'. But acrobatic intellectualism brought disadvantages.

Instrumental Scottishness had to dispense with the precise geography of Hoffmann von Fallersleben's 'Deutschland, Deutschland über alles' (1841), otherwise very Burnsian in its addiction to wine, women, and song, or the linguistic loyalties of the Parry brothers' 'Hen Wlad fy Nhadau' (Land of my Fathers) (1854) which stemmed from defence of the Welsh language against the 'treason of the Blue Books' or the Anglo-Scottish education commissioners of 1848. On the other hand its portability featured in the patriotic democracy of T. B. Macaulay's 'Lays of Ancient Rome' (1842), as much as Samuel Smiles's *Self-Help* (1859):

> And how can man die better, than facing fearful odds,
> For the ashes of his fathers and the temples of his Gods?[41]

Derived in part from Carlyle's *Heroes and Hero-Worship* (1841), this was a calculating commitment to a utilitarian-run Empire which was—unlike the Union or success in trade—more British than English, and friendly to the Scots. The Radical Martyrs of 1793–1820, the victims of the Clearances, the Free Kirkers who lost church and manse: through emigration and democracy in the colonies, all of these could use disruption to transform their status from victim to elite. A century of success followed in which the superman forged in such a mill—from Carlyle via Smiles's engineers to MacDiarmid's Lenin—was Scotland's version of the sublime.[42]

---

[40]  R. L. Stevenson, *The Master of Ballantrae* (London: Longman, 1889), 194.

[41]  T. B. Macaulay, *Lays of Ancient Rome* (London: Oxford University Press, 1932), Stanza xxvii, p. 11.

[42]  It might seem odd to number the grand Whig Macaulay among the instrumental martyrs—and indeed he figures very little in Michael Fry, *The Scottish Empire* (Edinburgh and East Linton: Birlinn and Tuckwell, 1999)—but the Gael in him comes out in his passionate treatment of the Massacre of Glencoe in his *History of England* (1848–55).

## IV   A THIN CRUST

So far, so straightforward. But when in 1914–18 this floating world of contract was damaged by international breakdown, another image became almost pervasive, to be encountered everywhere from thrillers to the essays of J. M. Keynes: 'You think that a wall as solid as the earth separates civilisation from barbarism. I tell you the division is a thread, a sheet of glass.'[43]

John Buchan would become a central figure of Allied propaganda, which Joseph Goebbels would credit with the *Dolchstoß* (stab-in-the-back) demoralizing of Germany. His thriller *The Power-House* (1913) contains his most famous line, given to a Tory-anarchist supervillain, Andrew Lumley. It seemed, Graham Greene later noted, to describe the predicament of twentieth-century man.[44] Did Buchan believe it? Probably not at the time of writing. Political thrillers are usually paranoid, but *The Power-House* is rather complacent. Lumley is seen off by two MPs, Tory and Labour, whose decent inadequacies seem to prove the strength of Westminster constitutionalism, just as the 'very ordinary fellow' Richard Hannay outperforms British as well as German intelligence in *The Thirty-Nine Steps* (1915).[45]

The upheaval of World War I made Buchan reconsider. In *The Three Hostages* (1924) he used his near-professional knowledge of psychiatry to get a medic, Dr Greenslade, to state:

the fact of the subconscious self is as certain as the existence of lungs and arteries [but] with the general loosening of screws they are growing shaky and two worlds are getting ruined . . . you can't any longer take the clear psychology of most human beings for granted. Something is welling up from primeval deeps to muddy it.[46]

Lumley's lines were certainly floating about in the years before 1914, but if they weren't a reaction to actuality, where did they come from? There were earlier sightings in Buchan, in short stories and in the longer political novel *The Half-Hearted* (1900). But as David Daniell has noted, Buchan seemed to make the civilization-barbarism stand-off the point of complication rather than simplification.[47] Not untimely, of course when according to Virginia Woolf, a friend of his wife Susan, the things that had changed human nature in December 1910—post-Impressionism, the Ballets Russes, psychoanalysis—mixed up the savage with the sophisticated in a very public way.[48]

Closer reading however showed up two things. One: in *The Power-House* this line is given to a man whose Nietzschean ambition—'Once concentrate the intellect of the world and the age of miracles will come'—also recalls the doomed project of

---

[43] Buchan, *The Power-House*, 64.      [44] Greene, 'The Last Buchan'.

[45] Christopher Harvie, introduction to Buchan, *The Thirty-Nine Steps* (Oxford: Oxford University Press, 1993), and see Harvie, *The Centre of Things*, 150.

[46] John Buchan, *The Three Hostages*, 1924, in *The Adventures of Richard Hannay* (London: Hodder and Stoughton, 1930), 17.

[47] David Daniell, *The Interpreter's House* (London: Nelson, 1975), p. xix.

[48] Quoted in Noel Annan, *Our Age*, 1990 (London: Harper Collins, 1991), 76.

Stevenson's Dr Jekyll in that classic of Scots dualism.[49] Two: Lumley echoed a similar usage by the thriller's dedicatee, Arthur Balfour. In H. G. Wells's *New Machiavelli* (1911) there's a strange scene, apparently drawn from memory, in which idealistic, priggish Richard Remington tries to convert the Tory Party to his welfare panacea of 'Love and High Thinking'. He dines at a grandee's house, and there endures Mr Evesham (Balfour) presiding with elegant callousness over some nasty baiting. Those assembled discuss the West's rape of Peking. Evesham comments, 'What is civilisation but a mere thin net of habits and associations?' and then they settle on Remington as the entrée.[50]

At the end of the novel, Remington's deserted wife nails his political character:

'You remind me—do you remember?—of the time we went from Naples to Vesuvius, and walked over the hot new lava there . . . One walked there in spite of the heat because there was a crust: like custom, like law. But directly a crust forms on things, you are restless to break down to the fire again.'[51]

Where *did* Lumley stand anent civilization-versus-barbarism? The super-civilized man, able to use barbarism where and when he wanted, to gain 'advanced' ends? How was barbarism to be defined? Buchan knew his *Culture and Anarchy*, where Matthew Arnold's 'barbarians' were the landed gentry, the upper crust of England's 'layer-cake of fine class distinctions'.[52] Lumley brandished pure intellect just when the same gentry were threatening civil war during the Ulster crisis. A threat at first outlandish, given the overfed complacency of Edwardian society—the philistinism of Forster's Wilcoxes, the pedantry of Woolf's Mr Ramsay, the paralysis of Joyce's Dublin—took its place with the near-psychopathic neuroses that George Dangerfield would later diagnose in his *Strange Death of Liberal England* (1934).

Where did the metaphor come from? One source is that omnium gatherum of permissible myth, Sir James George Frazer's *Golden Bough*:

It is not our business here to consider what bearing the permanent existence of such a solid layer of savagery beneath the surface of society, and unaffected by the superficial changes of religion and culture, has on the future of humanity. The dispassionate observer, whose studies have led him to plumb its depths, can hardly regard it as otherwise than as a standing menace to civilisation. We seem to move on a thin crust which may at any time be rent by the subterranean forces slumbering below.[53]

But there is a further, and more political clue. Benjamin Disraeli's last novel, *Falconet*, started shortly before his death in 1881, remained unread until Moneypenny

---

[49] Buchan refers to Nietzsche, trans. into English, 1900–13, by the Scot Thomas Common, in *Greenmantle*, 1917 (London: Nelson, 1942), 252; see Robert Louis Stevenson, *Dr Jekyll and Mr Hyde*, 1885 (London: Cassell, 1907), 72–3.

[50] H. G. Wells, *The New Machiavelli* (London: John Lane, 1911), 529–30.      [51] Ibid. 558.

[52] Matthew Arnold, *Culture and Anarchy*, 1868 (London: Macmillan, 1869), 66; Ralf Dahrendorf's fetching phrase is from *On Britain* (London: BBC Publications, 1982), 55 ff.

[53] *The Golden Bough: A Study in Comparative Religion*, 1890 (London: Routledge Curzon, 2003), ii, sect. 1, pp. 74–5; and see also a similar passage in Frazer's Liverpool inaugural lecture, repr. in *Psyche's Task* (2nd edn, London: Macmillan, 1913), 166–70. See also Christopher Harvie, ' "For Gods are Kittle Cattle": J. G. Frazer and John Buchan', in Robert Fraser, ed., *Sir James Frazer and the Literary Imagination* (London, Macmillan, 1990), 255.

and Buckle published it in *The Times* in 1905. A mystery man appears in English society, with an international conspiracy in tow:

'Society is resolving itself into its original elements. Its superficial order is the result of habit, not of conviction. Everything is changing, and changing rapidly. Creeds disappear in a night. As for political institutions, they are all challenged, and statesmen, conscious of what is at hand, are changing nations into armies.'[54]

As an undergraduate the methodical Buchan had planned to write a biography of Disraeli, despite a shared Conservatism fascinated and repelled by the man's ruthlessness and ultra-intellectualism. Semitism apart, there is a lot of Disraeli's Sidonia in the 'archetypal Buchan villain', the Irishman Dominick Medina in *The Three Hostages*.[55] But what was Disraeli's source?

## V  ENLIGHTENMENT AND UNCERTAINTY

Enter Carlyle, and in particular *The French Revolution* (1837). Robert Blake considers it unclear whether Disraeli ever read Carlyle.[56] Disraeli in fact injected quantities of Carlyle into his novels, and even offered him a knighthood (feelings which were not reciprocated at all). In the 1830s he was writing passable imitations, and would encounter a recurrent Carlyle metaphor of the volcano seething under the crust of society: 'the infinite gulf of human Passion shivered asunder the thin rinds of Habit, and burst forth all-Devouring, as in seas of Nether Fire'.[57] This was from 'Characteristics' of 1831, Carlyle's defence of social science. By 1837, when *The French Revolution* appeared, it roared away *in extenso*:

*IMPOSTURE* is in flames, Imposture is burnt up: one red sea of Fire, wild billowing, enwraps the World; with its fire-tongue licks at the very Stars . . . Higher, higher get flames the Fire-Sea; crackling with new dislocated timber; hissing with leather and prunella. The metal images are molten; the marble Images become mortar-lime; the stone Mountains sulkily explode.

*RESPECTABILITY*, with all her collected Gigs inflamed for funeral pyre, wailing, leaves the Earth: not to return save under new Avatar. Imposture how it burns through generations: how it is burnt up; for a time. The World is black ashes;—which, ah, when will they grow green?[58]

This is not the eternal nay of secular-Calvinist hellfire. To Carlyle the crust is both the necessary 'bands' of society, and also something calcified and rigid. The volcano

---

[54] Printed in George Moneypenny and H. T. Buckle, *Disraeli*, ii (London: John Murray, 1905), 1548 ff.

[55] Janet Adam Smith, *John Buchan* (London: Rupert Hart-Davis, 1965), 80. The commander of the Spanish Armada was the Duke of Medina-Sidonia.

[56] Robert Blake, *Disraeli* (London: Methuen, 1968), 191.

[57] This is from Thomas Carlyle, 'Characteristics', *Edinburgh Review* (1831), repr. in *Scottish and Other Miscellanies* (London: Dent, n.d.), 221; and see Morris Speare, *The Political Novel* (New York: Oxford University Press, 1924), 164–6.

[58] Carlyle, *The French Revolution* (London: Chapman and Hall, 1895), iii, bk 7, chap. 7 (5 Oct. 1795), 322–3.

destroys and renews. To an earlier generation, the evangelical Thomas Chalmers for example, the upheavals after the end of the Napoleonic Wars were 'a glimpse into pandemonium', but Chalmers's then assistant, Carlyle's friend Edward Irving, wrote to him in the year of the Bonnymuir rising, 1819: 'I do not warrant against a radical rising, though I think it vastly improbable. But continue these times a year or two, and unless you unmake our present generation, and unman them of human feeling and Scottish intelligence, you will have commotion'.[59] Carlyle agreed. Far from being Engels's reactionary monster beached by the tide of history, his radicalism carried on up to the 1840s. Carlyle viewed Chalmers the *ci-devant* rationalist with mistrust: religion involved active reason, while Chalmers's defensive dogmatism hinted at a weakness of fundamental religious impulse.[60] But the Chalmersian ideal of the 'Godly Commonwealth' burned fiercely in the younger man, combined with an intense nationalism which was, like that of Burns, intellectual rather than *völkisch*:

A country where the entire people is, or even once has been, laid hold of, filled to the heart with an infinite religious idea, has 'made a step from which it cannot retrograde.' Thought, conscience, the sense that man is denizen of a Universe, creature of an Eternity, has penetrated to the remotest cottage, to the simplest heart.[61]

That poor temple of my childhood is more sacred to me than the biggest cathedral then extant could have been; rustic, bare, no temple in the world was more so; but there were sacred lambencies, tongues of authentic flame which kindled what was best in one, what has not yet gone out.[62]

The plebeian piety of Burns's 'The Cottar's Saturday Night' is visible here. The 'infinite religious idea' is plainly less conventional, but is still compatible with the commonsense theism of the enlightenment, as defined by George Elder Davie:

. . . it is inherent in the nature of the belief in an external world or in the mathematical ideals to envisage facts not contained in the sum of the various elementary experiences involved in the genesis of these items of the common sense, and this peculiar and fundamental fact of self-transcendence is held . . . to be an ultimate irrational mystery.[63]

Carlyle's political interventionism, and indeed his *étatisme*, was in part a *réprise* of the existential civic ideal which Adam Ferguson constructed over this fundamental mystery. As his friend the landowner and modernist theologian Thomas Erskine of Linlathen (correspondent of Madame de Stael, Guizot, and F. D. Maurice) recognized, with Carlyle 'political science . . . [became] one with religious obligation'.[64] Erskine, a scarcely researched figure, was probably the Scot closest to the Christian

---

[59] Letter of 28 Dec. 1819, quoted in J. A. Froude, *Thomas Carlyle: A History of the First Forty Years of his Life* (London: Longmans Green, 1885), i, 77; for Carlyle's later recollections see ibid. 73.

[60] Fred Kaplan, *Thomas Carlyle* (Cambridge: Cambridge University Press, 1983), 48–9.

[61] Thomas Carlyle, 'Sir Walter Scott', *Edinburgh Review* (1838), repr. in *Scottish and Other Miscellanies*, 71.

[62] Carlyle, quoted in Froude, *Thomas Carlyle*, 18.

[63] George Elder Davie, *The Democratic Intellect: Scotland and her Universities in the Nineteenth Century*, 1961 (Edinburgh: Edinburgh University Press, 1961), 275.

[64] Thomas Erskine to his sister, 6 Feb. 1838, quoted in *The Letters of Thomas Erskine of Linlathen*, ed. William Hanna, i (Edinburgh: David Douglas, 1877), 301.

Socialists—Maurice, Kingsley, and company—and, like Carlyle, stressed 'good government' over 'self-government'. Yet Carlyle remained fiercely radical, as in *Sartor Resartus*:

Call ye that a Society . . . where there is no longer any Social Idea extant; not so much as the idea of a Common Home, but only of a common overcrowded lodging-house? Where each, isolated, regardless of his neighbour, turned against his neighbour, clutches what he can get, and cries 'Mine!' and calls it Peace, because in the cut-purse and cut-throat scramble, no steel knives, but only a far cunninger sort, can be employed?[65]

He was equally strongly Scottish. When Goethe wrote at length to him in 1828 about his *Life of Schiller* he specifically dwelt on Carlyle's Scottish identity, and the ways in which national and international identities complemented each other:

The efforts of the best poets and aesthetic writers throughout the world have been directed towards the general characteristics of humanity . . . [but] one must study and make allowances for the peculiarities of each nation, in order to have real intercourse with it. The special characteristics of a people are like its language and currency. They facilitate exchange; indeed they first make exchange possible.[66]

Goethe's Scottish enthusiasm had begun in the 1760s, when the *Sturm und Drang* of Macpherson's Celtic epic *Ossian* was balanced against the secular ethic of 'improvement': militant juxtaposed with market society. In the early 1830s Carlyle swithered between similar but now inverted choices: the history of the Scottish Church and that of the French Revolution: the crust of a developed civil society and the lava of social upheaval. At the same time the political compromise which had underpinned Scots semi-independence broke apart, in the 'Ten Years' Conflict' which preceded the Disruption of 1843; 'sacred lambencies' spluttered into the religious legalisms that he would later denounce as 'Hebrew old clothes'.

Carlyle's failure to establish himself in Scotland, despite the support of education, family structure, and locality, was part of a basic disjunction in his thought between Enlightenment rationalism and millenarianism. The Scots Enlightenment's central metaphysical notion presupposed a similar human system of ratiocination in every state of civilization. Essentially conservative, Adam Ferguson's Society or Adam Smith's Sympathy inhered within human Conscience, Consciousness, or Common Sense. But if these qualities were inherent, how was Common Sense to react to the dynamism of the market, technology, and imperial expansion?

One reaction was to insist that all change implied decay, and oppose it, like the 'hanging judge' Lord Braxfield, who, by insisting that only landed authority counted, represented civic *virtú* at its most conservative.[67] But Carlyle's background in evangelical millenarianism led him to reject this post-enlightenment stasis, and laud the

---

[65] Thomas Carlyle, *Sartor Resartus*, published in *Fraser's Magazine* (1833–4), repr. in *Sartor Resartus and On Heroes and Hero Worship* (London: Dent, 1956), 174. For the philosophical basis of the Christian Socialists see Duncan Forbes, *The Liberal Anglican Idea of History* (Cambridge: Cambridge University Press, 1952), 39 ff.

[66] Quoted in Froude, *Thomas Carlyle*, 414–20.

[67] This conservative view of the enlightenment is strongly put by Bruce Lenman, *Integration, Enlightenment and Industrialisation: Scotland 1746–1832* (London: Arnold, 1981), 113.

'fire and strength' of his Calvinist upbringing: he agreed with 'old Ferguson' as to the strength of society, but he recognized that, under pressure, it could break up and compose itself in new forms. The influence of Henri de Saint-Simon complemented his fading theism, by insisting on social progress, not as a steady continuum but as the alternation of 'organic' and 'critical' periods: the latter called for all the 'sacred lambencies' they could get.

## VI   GALATEA

Saint-Simon also represented social science, and to make this transition, as with so much else, Carlyle needed the stimulus of Goethe. Goethe had absorbed the 1780s debate on the origins of the earth between the followers of the Saxon Abraham Gottlob Werner and those of the Scotsman James Hutton. The Wernerians or Neptunists believed that rocks were laid down by accumulations of marine sediment; the Huttonians or Vulcanists saw them as the results of volcanic activity. To Goethe these explanations symbolized evolution and revolution, concepts which he dramatized in *Faust*, fusing his reactions to the French Revolution with his geological learning. According to Georg Simmel, his interpretation of the debate was symbolic rather than scientific: 'It was not the explosive force that was involved in Vulcanism that counted against it in his eyes, but that this was simultaneously part of the natural order and something that tore the unity of this order apart'.[68] Goethe wrote in his geological commentaries, part of his duties as administrator of the mines of Saxe-Weimar, that the randomness of Vulcanism conflicted with the deistic idea of design: 'What is the whole upheaving of the mountains but fundamentally a mechanical act, without any understanding of the possibility of a purposive effort being involved?'[69]

   This debate, latent in much of *Faust: Part Two*, which Goethe worked on between 1808 and 1831, climaxes at the end of Act II, set in the rocky inlets of the Aegean Sea. The Homunculus, Goethe's symbol for a Frankenstein-like artificial intelligence, born of mechanism and out of his element in the mythic Neptunist realms, is thrust towards the conch of the sea-nymph Galatea, literally in her own element:

> THALES   Homunculus this, whom old Proteus misleads . . .
> And the signs show the longing and will of their master,
> Boding the pangs and the moans of disaster,
> His glass will be shivered against the bright throne,
> Comes in a flash, on the floods he is strown.
> SIRENS   The waves are transfigured with fire-laden wonder,
> They glitter in impact, in flame leap asunder.
> Here's shining and swaying, and spurting of light,
> With forms all aglow in the track of the track of the night.
> And lapping of fire touches all things around:

[68] Quoted in Werner Dunckert, *Goethe: Der mythische Urgrund seiner Weltschau* (Berlin: De Gruyter, 1951), 77.
[69] Goethe, 'Über die Bildung der Erde', notes of 1790, quoted ibid., 78.

Let Eros who wrought it be honoured and crowned!
Hail to the Ocean! Hail to the wave!
The flood of the holy fire to lave!
Waters hail! All hail the fire!
The strange event hail we in choir!
ALL VOICES IN CONCERT    Hail light airs now floating free!
Hail earth's caves of mystery!
Held in honour evermore
Be the elemental four![70]

To Goethe this was the modern crisis: fire symbolizing the liberation of carbon, the holy fire of palaeotechnology, but also the problem of whether it could be controlled: the problem faced, as every child knew, by his 'Sorcerer's Apprentice'.[71] His resolving figure was Galatea, the eternal female, the synthesizer of fire and water, erotic as well as reconciling. Carlyle took on the geological dialectic and made this powerful synthesis another of his repertoire of signifiers.[72] But the erotic as reconciler proved too much for his inhibitions. The man who in the 1840s set out to brand contemporary mores as 'The Phallus and the Money-Bag' ended up as yet another stricken refugee from a Scotland where intellect consistently triumphed over feeling.[73]

Goethe stressed imperative change which disrupted the cyclic pattern of history on which Scots social thought had been founded. Carlyle was caught between two philosophies: a cyclic, civic conservatism, and a millenarianism posited on either Christian or collective beliefs. Any return to the Christian equilibrium in Scotland was implausible, and the utopianism of Saint-Simon and his own sense of crisis drove him, despite Goethe's warnings, into the greater arena of England in the 1830s and 1840s, where his impulses and injunctions were transformed first into positive movements for reform, and then to personal frustration.[74]

But social change also indicated a turbulence verging on what Emil Durkheim would call *anomie*.[75] The menaces that Carlyle warned against became actual when industrialization set Scotland, like the towns affected by the railway in 'Hudson's Statue',

a-dancing, confusedly waltzing, in a state of progressive dissolution, towards the four winds; and know not where the end of the death-dance will be for them, in what point of space they will be allowed to rebuild themselves.

---

[70] J. W. Goethe, *Faust: Part Two*, 1832, trans. Philip Wayne (Harmondsworth: Penguin, 1959), 155–6.

[71] This was written in 1797. It appeared as part of Walt Disney's *Fantasia* with Mickey Mouse in the title role, in 1937.

[72] Carlisle Moore, 'Carlyle and Goethe as Scientist', in John Clubbe, ed., *Carlyle and his Contemporaries* (Durham, NC: Duke University Press, 1976), stresses Carlyle's interest in the *Farbenlehre* (theory of colours), but is unforthcoming on *Faust* or Vulcanism.

[73] Kaplan, *Thomas Carlyle*, 332–3.

[74] K. J. Fielding, 'Carlyle and the Saint-Simonians', in Clubbe, ed., *Carlyle and his Contemporaries*, 35–59, esp. p. 41.

[75] Thomas Carlyle, 'Characteristics', *Edinburgh Review* (1831), repr. in *Scottish and Other Miscellanies*, 221.

... Joplin of Reading, who had anchored himself in that pleasant place, and fondly hoping to live by upholstery and paperhanging, had wedded, and made friends there,—awakens some morning, and finds that his trade has flitted away ... Sad news for Joplin:—indeed I fear, should his sagacity be too inconsiderable, he is not unlikely to break his heart, or take to drinking in these inextricable circumstances![76]

As a vision of *England* this was extreme. The railway only accelerated the urbanization of the canal and turnpike age. Joplin remained reasonably prosperous and sober. In palaeotechnic Scotland, however, the railway-driven industrialization after 1830 *was* volcanic, based on industries which were noisy, lurid, and polluting. The working class was low-paid and appallingly housed; once away from the churches and artisan virtu (which on the whole had it by the tail) it anaesthetized itself with whisky or erupted in pointless violence. The middle class could be traumatized by disasters like the collapse of the City of Glasgow Bank in 1878.[77] If such extremities provoked the synergic work of the Carlyle-influenced Patrick Geddes, they also made a humane reform of Scots social divisions appallingly difficult.[78]

To return to that chronicle of damnation, George Douglas Brown's *The House with the Green Shutters*, set in the 1860s, is to find formless, questionably creative chaos. Brown's purpose had originally been that of Carlyle in 'Hudson's Statue'—personalizing the impact of transport change on Scottish society:

When a man who has been jogging comfortably along, under the old conditions, suddenly finds his world revolutionised, finds that in middle life, perhaps, he must adapt himself to strange and unpleasing ways, his end is often inevitable tragedy ... Such tragedies happened more than once when railways began to push their way along the quiet and sequestered valleys of the south of Scotland. Men of importance in the parish, men who had held their heads high at Kirk and market, grain-merchants, cheese-merchants, who had inherited businesses from their fathers, suddenly found that the ground on which they had stood so long was being taken from beneath their feet.[79]

Brown's final draft gave the death-struggle of male tyranny against economic nemesis a brutal poignancy, and made John Gourlay symbolize the damage that industrial Scotland inflicted on itself. Like Stevenson's *Weir of Hermiston* (published only four years earlier) this involved a *jeté* back to the Scotland of the revolutionary epoch.

Young Gourlay's revolt against his father, undirected by any philosophy, ends in a private reign of terror. The just society appears only as an ironic ghost in the final chapter, when the doomed Gourlay women fruitlessly invoke the Christian charity of 1 Corinthians 13. Brown had worked with David Meldrum on editing John

[76] Thomas Carlyle, 'Characteristics', *Edinburgh Review* (1831), repr. in *Scottish and Other Miscellanies*, 229.

[77] See James Buchan, *Frozen Desire: An Enquiry into Money* (London: John Murray, 1997), chap. 8.

[78] For Geddes see Helen Meller, *Patrick Geddes: Social Evolutionist and City Planner* (London: Routledge, 1990).

[79] George Douglas Brown, Unpublished 'Prologue', in Brown's notebook, National Library of Scotland (NLS MS 8171), quoted in Alistair McCleery, 'The Devil Damn Thee Black: A Note on *The House with the Green Shutters*', *Scottish Literary Journal*, 16/1 (May 1989), 45; compare with Carlyle, *Latter-Day Pamphlets* (London: Chapman and Hall, 1850), 228–30.

Galt, and saw in Galt's 'theoretical histories' the destructiveness of individualism unconstrained by community. The fate of the Gourlays is in fact the working out, in Carlyleian terms, of Galt's pessimism about the future of the polis: something which had resonance in a Wales scarred by coal and slate waste and chemical pollution, and Ireland after famine, sectarianism, and repression.[80] Buchan himself would resume the inquest, scarcely more optimistically, in his greatest historical novel, *Witch Wood* (1928), where the harsh discipline of Calvinism conjures up its devil-worshipping alternative. He wrote *Witch Wood* after reading his way through Scott and Hogg, and was particularly impressed by one little-known Scott work, *The Chronicles of the Canongate* (1827). This makes explicit, in two short stories of self-destruction, 'The Highland Widow' and 'The Two Drovers', the suppressed social tensions of a multinational state based on highland subjugation, and is framed by a long introduction in which Scott's narrator 'Chrystal Croftangry' uses Edinburgh to symbolize the nature of his country:

> A nobler contrast there can hardly exist than that of the huge city, dark with the smoke of ages, and groaning with the various sounds of active industry or idle revel, and the lofty and craggy hill, silent and solitary as the grave; one exhibiting the full tide of existence, pressing and precipitating itself forward with the force of an inundation; the other resembling some time-worn anchorite, whose life passes as silent and unobserved as the slender rill which escapes unheard, and scarce seen, from the fountain of his patron saint. The city resembles the busy temple, where the modern Comus and Mammon hold their court, and thousands sacrifice ease, independence, and virtue itself at their shrine; the misty and lonely mountain seems as a throne to the majestic but terrible genius of feudal times, when the same divinities dispensed coronets and domains to those who had heads to devise and arms to execute bold enterprises.[81]

Arthur's Seat is, of course, an ex-volcano.

For Scotland the turmoil of industrial and social disruption persisted for most of the century after Carlyle's death, albeit with native 'captains of industry' giving way to multinational capital. Because the Victorian crisis was comprehensive, metaphors of 'disassociated sensibility' built up to an awareness of full-blown schizophrenia, from Hogg to Laing.[82] The fundamental tension between 'sympathy', inherently conservative, and individualism, inherently disruptive, became stasis. The thin crust of civilization and whatever was roaring and slurping away underneath it was inorganic, forceful, and male. The customary way out was precisely that, with ready-made contractual equipment to hand, while domestic reform implied compromise with remedial forces which were biocentric, conciliatory, and female. Their germ was visible in two works of Carlyle's disciple John Ruskin, *Unto this Last* (1861) and *Ethics of the Dust* (1872), with their appeal to craftsmanship, woman as conservatrix, and

[80] Brown was himself half Irish, Patrick McGill of *Children of the Dead End* and A. J. Cronin of *The Citadel* wholly so. Regina Weingartner has documented Brown's influence on Caradoc Evans's scathing criticism of Lloyd Georgite Welsh Nonconformity; see *Planet*, 75 (June–July 1989).

[81] Buchan, in his biography *Sir Walter Scott* (London: Cassell, 1932), praised the Turgenev-like 'economy and certainty' (p. 315) of Scott's *Chronicles of the Canongate* of 1827; and see Christopher Harvie, 'Scott and the Image of Scotland', in Alan Bold, ed., *Sir Walter Scott: The Long-Forgotten Melody* (London: Vision, 1983), 31–2.

[82] See Straub, 'Psychological Disturbance'.

piecemeal, sensitive, social reconstruction. These recurred in Patrick Geddes's projects for the Edinburgh Social Union after 1884 and his sociological laboratory the Outlook Tower, and later in the boundless ambitions of Geddes's disciple Hugh MacDiarmid.[83]

MacDiarmid, temperamentally akin to 'volcanic Carlyle', regarded his own creativity as necessarily disruptive: 'I produce heat and light and also a great deal of rubbish.' Yet his celebration of Goethe in 'The Oon Olympian' (1932) also shows him adopting the latter's reconciliatory Neptunist symbolism: water and femininity invoked against nihilistic destruction:

> Consciousness springs frae unplumbed deeps
> And maist o' men mak haste
> To keep odd draps in shallow thoughts
> And let the rest rin waste.
> Quickly forgettin' ocht they catch
> Depends on the kittle coorse
> O' a wilder fount than they daur watch
> Free-springin' in its native force
> Against the darkness o' its source.[84]

MacDiarmid's friend William Power wrote that the nation was the Galatea of the young nationalists of the 1920s, a reconciler, an epiphany of the planned and dignified society. But her appeal would be limited in the empty forges and slipways of the world's former workshop.

[83] The Ruskin–Geddes continuum, and its social as well as aesthetic consequences is sensitively described by Duncan Macmillan, *Scottish Art*, 1990 (Edinburgh: Mainstream, 2000), chap. 15.

[84] Hugh MacDiarmid, 'The Oon Olympian', in *Collected Poems* (London: Martin Brian and O'Keefe, 1985).

# 2

# Garron Top to Westward Ho! The Inland Sea

... my memories are full of enormous skies, as bright as water, in which clouds sailed, bigger than any others; fleets of monsters moving in one vast school up from the horizon and over my head, a million miles up, as it seemed to me, and then down again over the far-off mountains of Derry. They seemed to follow a curving surface of air concentric with the curve of the Atlantic which I could see bending down on either hand, a bow, which, even as a child of three or four, I knew to be the actual shape of the earth.... it was a constant source of pleasure. I can remember jumping on a piece of hard ground, as one jumps on a deck, to test its spring, or simply to enjoy the feel of a buoyant ship beneath me.

Joyce Cary, *A House of Children*, 1941[1]

## I   THE IRISH BOAT

In the summer of 1953 my father and I—then nine—went on a day trip by the Burns Laird steamer *Laird's Isle* from Ardrossan to Belfast: the deck canted over in the wind, grey sea roaring past the open companionways, log-line trailing into the wake. We sat aft of the red-blue-black funnels hot with the exhaust from the antique turbines and that curious shipboard smell of burning oil, steam, rope, and chip-pan fat: feeling not utterly secure, as only six months before, the modern diesel ferry *Princess Victoria* had gone down in a hurricane off Belfast Lough, with 140 drowned. At Carrickfergus we went about and steamed, stern first, up the lough to Donegall Quay. The aircraft carriers *Centaur* and *Bulwark* were building at Queen's Island; Belfast's last trams whined past and black-capped policemen carried revolvers. Years later this came back when reading Joyce Cary's *A House of Children*:

I can recall perfectly my feeling when I sat on the boat deck of a Liverpool–Derry steamer, at about eight years old, wedged firmly between two aunts while they smoked their cigarettes and guarded themselves from flying into the Atlantic at every roll of the ship by nothing better than their shoe-heels hitched against the two-inch gunwale. For we sat behind the boats where there were no rails.[2]

---

[1] (London: Michael Joseph, 1951), pp. 18–19.

[2] Joyce Cary, 'Prefatory Essay' (1951) to *A House of Children*, 5. The *Laird's Isle* had an eventful history. She was built as the *Riviera* by Denny of Dumbarton, became an aircraft carrier in World War I and was a landing-craft 'mother ship' at D-Day. She was scrapped in 1957, 46 years old. The average ship's life seems to be 30 to 35 years, half the human span.

The *Laird's Isle* was an ex-South Eastern and Chatham channel packet, built in 1911 when Cary was just out of his teens and turbine technology even younger; she steamed once a day to Belfast and back. The direct Glasgow boats which I sailed with in 1966 made up a convoy to Dublin, Belfast, and Derry. At Greenock we passed to port the *Queen Elizabeth*, floodlit in the James Watt dock, on her last refit. A year later Queen's Island would finish the *Sea Quest*, almost the first and almost the last British-built oil rig for the North Sea. That small convoy was the end of an itinerary: a mobile working class within a short sea voyage of two habitats, wheeling their barrow of belongings to the boat, from and to the 'single ends' of Clydeside and the 'wee hooses' of Belfast, able to follow the shipbuilding contracts from the Clyde to Belfast Lough and vice versa. A year later the boats had gone, and Scotland's maritime interest was shifting, with the oil, to the east coast. England's had already done so; something confirmed by the entry into the Common Market in 1973, and—despite the Troubles—the effective removal of Northern Ireland from its consciousness.[3]

Such a nexus of fact and feeling may mislead. But the experience suggested understanding the Firth of Clyde as the northern reach of an inland sea, opening into something Protean, problematic, and stimulating: easily understood when you climb Garron Top, a few miles north of Larne, and see Kintyre, Islay, Ailsa Craig, and Arran laid out before you. And when you think, too, about a feeling conveyed by Cary on a similar promontory, of headlands as kinetic places, suggesting the relativities of existence. Whitman saw from Cape Cod that universalism of 'the sea, great ships', and provided a gospel for that moment in the 1880s when the Atlantic coast cities emerged as a technology-articulated confederation of city states, often more closely bound to one another by work and trade than they were to their national hinterlands: the world geography summed up by Cary in his long novel *Castle Corner* (1938). The imperialist geographer Halford Mackinder called the southern approaches, between Cornwall and Wexford, 'the marine antechamber of Britain', but it would probably be more apposite to regard Bristol, Cardiff, Swansea, Liverpool, Dublin, Belfast, and Glasgow, and the waterways between them, as a West British sea. This in its turn was, in Braudel's sense, part of a larger Atlantic 'world'.[4]

Presently, this is a far from optimistic prospect. All of these Atlantic places, to a greater or lesser extent, are problematic; at the same time, they coincide with a crisis in British identity. Their reputation for conviviality battles with endemic high unemployment; their multicultural articulacy and healthy mistrust of the metropolis contend with an incipient tribalism and the abdication of local elites; an inability to conceive of themselves as self-governing regions. Their cultural dialectic has produced unavoidable, sometimes monstrous, international icons: the Beatles, Roald Dahl, Shirley Bassey, Richard Burton, Dylan Thomas, Bob Geldof, R. D. Laing, George Best, Lord Reith, C. S. Lewis, Ian Paisley—associated with challenging

---

[3] See Christopher Harvie, *Fool's Gold: The Story of North Sea Oil* (London: Hamilton, 1994), chap. 1.

[4] Halford Mackinder, *Britain and the British Seas*, 1902 (Oxford: Clarendon Press, 1907), 14–15; and for an overview of geographers' approaches see E. Estyn Evans, *The Personality of Ireland* (Cambridge: Cambridge University Press, 1973), chap. 1.

achievements, social tensions, self-destruction. Of all of these, the long agony of Ulster seemed the most deep-seated and tragic. But Ulster's problems are not *sui generis*. We are dealing with the grandeurs and miseries of a region which, more than any other, changed and was maimed by world history.

## II   'A COUNTRY THE POETS HAVE IMAGINED?'

Cary, born in Derry, has been considered a quintessentially English author. He certainly managed the feat of transferring Lloyd George, in that masterful capture of the man as Chester Nimmo, from Wales to Devonshire. But it is a peculiar sort of Englishness that imagines the country, in *To be a Pilgrim* (1942), as if on an endless voyage, putting up in makeshift lodgings.[5] Cary's contrasting of the English tinker or field-preacher as alive and the gentry mansion house as inanimate skull is not a metaphor used much in these heritage-ridden days. But metaphor, as we have seen, was not a conceit, it was fundamental to the recognition of a changing, risky, transactional 'world' in the age of modernism and its aftermath: the 'myth-kitty' of a highly literate political-literary intelligentsia. These were the people who created and grew up with the *Oxford English Dictionary*, the *Dictionary of National Biography*, the *Cambridge Modern History*, the eleventh edition of the *Encyclopaedia Britannica*, and *Everyman's Library*, housing this culture in great libraries, museums, and universities—and in the part-works, the *Universal Educator* and *Children's Encyclopaedia*, churned out by Sandy Hammerton and Arthur Mee. These achievements throve on the collaboration of core and littoral, facilitated by but also driving far beyond the 1891 copyright treaty with America.[6]

This consciousness was vivid, extending and historicizing the immediate geography with a deeply allusive literary dimension. It was also unstable: optimism and reaction contend in Cary's novels. Failure and self-destruction—as well as fulfilment and exhilaration—lie in wait: the same sort of conditions that contemporary European sociologists like T. G. Masaryk and Emil Durkheim considered underlay suicide. Ten years before *To be a Pilgrim* the Ulster poet John Hewitt had used a similar oceanic image, darkly, in 'Ireland':

> We are not native here or anywhere.
> We were the keltic wave that broke over Europe,
> and ran up this steep beach among these stones:

[5] Joyce Cary, *To be a Pilgrim* (London: Michael Joseph, 1942), 328. The 'Chester Nimmo' trilogy was made up of *A Prisoner of Grace* (1953), *Except the Lord* (1954), and *Not Honour More* (1955), all published by Michael Joseph. See Christopher Harvie, *Centre of Things: Political Fiction from Disraeli to the Present* (London: Unwin Hyman, 1991), 156, 226, 234.

[6] One extreme example of this collaboration is recorded by Simon Winchester in *The Surgeon of Crowthorne* (London: Viking, 1998), between the autodidact Scot who organized the *OED*, Prof. J. A. H. Murray, and the gifted but insane American philologist Edward Trainer, imprisoned in Broadmoor for homicide. I am unashamedly a product of the *Children's Encyclopaedia*, rejoicing like George MacDonald Fraser in a serendipity which moved effortlessly from 'David, the heroic shepherd boy' to 'How string is made'.

but when the tide ebbed, we were left stranded here
in crevices and ledge-protected pools
that have grown salter with the drying up
of the great common flow that kept us sweet,
with fresh cold draughts from deep down in the ocean.

So we are bitter, and are dying out
in terrible harshness in this lonely place,
and what we think is love for usual rock,
or old affection for our customary ledge,
is but forgotten longing for the sea
that cries far out and calls us to partake
in his great tidal movements round the earth.[7]

Hewitt criticized the inturned vision of Catholic nationalism as a 'centre of paralysis' just as James Joyce, another travelling Irishman, had done, elaborating the argument through his voyagers—Irishman and Jew—in *Ulysses*. If this met F. R. Leavis's
requirement of profundity, then 'Ireland' has continuity with the omens of apostasy
and violence, the intellectual threnody for a once-unified sensibility, of Matthew
Arnold's 'Dover Beach' of 1851:[8]

The Sea of Faith
Was once, too, at the full, and round earth's shore
Lay like the folds of a bright girdle furl'd.
But now I only hear
Its melancholy, long, withdrawing roar,
Retreating, to the breath
Of the night-wind, down the vast edges drear
And naked shingles of the world.[9]

The point to grasp, however, is mutability. Tides flow as well as ebb, and Arnold
was ambivalent. A slightly later poem, 'The Scholar Gipsy' of 1853, sees his pastoral
mode, dissecting post-Tractarian Oxford's 'sick fatigue and languid doubt', end up
surprising and exhilarating:

Then fly our greetings, fly our speech and smiles!
        as some grave Tyrian trader, from the sea,
    Descried at sunrise an emerging prow
Lifting the cool-hair'd creepers stealthily,
    The fringes of a southward-facing brow
        Among the Aegean isles;
And saw the merry Grecian coaster come,
    Freighted with amber grapes, and Chian wine,

[7] John Hewitt, 'Ireland', in *The Listener* (18 May 1932), repr. in *The Collected Poems of John Hewitt*, ed. Frank Ormsby (Belfast: Blackstaff Press, 1991), 58.

[8] F. R. Leavis, *New Bearings in English Poetry* (London: Chatto and Windus, 1932), 13.

[9] 'Dover Beach', 1851 in *The Poems of Matthew Arnold*, ed. Kenneth Allott (London: Longmans, 1965), 239.

Green, bursting figs, and tunnies steep'd in brine—
And knew the intruders on his ancient home,

The young light-hearted masters of the waves—
And snatch'd his rudder, and shook out more sail;
    And day and night held on indignantly
O'er the blue Midland waters with the gale,
    Betwixt the Syrtes and soft Sicily,
        To where the Atlantic raves
Outside the western straits; and unbent sails
    There, where down cloudy cliffs, through sheets of foam,
    Shy traffickers, the dark Iberians come;
And on the beach undid his corded bales.[10]

The drowse of pre-Brideshead summers suddenly gives way to the sort of sharp mercantile force that Whitman lauded. But Arnold's imagery awakes other memories, notably of the Scots' Declaration of Arbroath: 'This nation having come from Scythia the greater, through the Tuscan Sea and the Hercules Pillars, and having for many ages taken its Residence in Spain in the midst of a most fierce people, and can never be brought into subjection by any people, how barbarous soever.'[11] A serious radical of the 1840s, Arnold was much better informed than his dilettante style often suggests. His *étatisme* influenced educational reform in Scotland and Wales much more than it did in England.[12] As a student of national movements he would be familiar, if not with the Scots migration myth in their statement of independence of 1320, then with Adam Smith's near-identical description of the origins of trade in *The Wealth of Nations* (1776), an imagery which suggests not rustic escapism or the harmless inspirationalism of the *Lectures on Celtic Literature* (1867), but the commercial energy of the British periphery.[13]

Arnold in fact echoes his friend Arthur Hugh Clough, the agenda of whose *Bothie of Toper-na-Fuosich* (1848)—Scotland, radicalism, and emigration—had to his mind 'the true Homeric ring'. Clough's childhood home, Charleston, South Carolina, built a steam railway in 1832, only two years after its British partner Liverpool, and the comparison between the power of the ocean and the fricative energy of the seaport is something that pervasively, sensually, marks the 'Bothie':

As at return of tide the total weight of ocean,
Drawn by moon and sun from Labrador and Greenland,
Sets in amain, in the open space between Mull and Scarfa,
Heaving, swelling, spreading, the might of the mighty Atlantic;
There into cranny and slit of the rocky, cavernous bottom

---

[10] 'The Scholar Gipsy', in *The Poems of Matthew Arnold*, 343–4.

[11] For the Declaration, its political theory, and its subsequent history, see Ted Cowan, *For Freedom Alone: The Declaration of Arbroath* (East Linton: Tuckwell, 2002), 144–7.

[12] See R. D. Anderson, *Education and Opportunity in Victorian Scotland: Schools and Universities* (Oxford: Oxford University Press, 1988), 82–3.

[13] Adam Smith, *The Wealth of Nations* (Harmondsworth: Penguin, 1982), bk 1, chap. 3, pp. 124–5.

> Settles down, and with dimples huge, the smooth sea-surface
> Eddies, coils and whirls; by dangerous Corryvreckan:
> So in my soul of souls through its cells and secret recesses,
> Comes back, swelling and spreading, the old democratic fervour.

Clough then leads into a picture of a possible civic utopia in the image of a great city—Liverpool, most likely—at dawn:

> So that the whole great wicked artificial civilized fabric,—
> All its unfinished houses, lots for sale, and railway outworks,—
> Seems reaccepted, resumed to Primal Nature and Beauty:—
> —Such—in me, and to me, and on me the love of Elspie![14]

Influenced but not subdued by two great English conservatives, Thomas Arnold and John Henry Newman, and partly liberated by Emerson, Clough took on a critical, angular stance to bourgeois Europe, with *Amours de voyage* (written in 1849 but not published until 1858), his meditation on the failed revolutions of 1848: almost a Victorian anticipation of *Homage to Catalonia* or Louis MacNeice's 'Spain'. *The Bothie* is about salvation through emigration, Carlyle's solution at the end of *Chartism* (1839); set in Scotland, stylistically on the road to *Ulysses* and *The Waste Land*, and the road away from that 'Bladesover' image of England as estate, church, and parliament.

This imagery also accords with the sea-symbolism, as well as the reformist vision, of another 'Celt by choice' and icon of *fin-de-siècle* radicalism, George Meredith (1828–1909). In Meredith's novel of frustrated democracy *Beauchamp's Career* (1875), the sea is everywhere the vehicle of protest and action, the great connector which sustains but will ultimately overwhelm Commander Beauchamp, the backsliding Liberal. At the heart of that convoluted, cosmopolitan prose is the idea—derived from Herbert Spencer and the Positivists—that a complex social and educational reality would in due course incubate a new and advanced citizen, communicating through a sophisticated, allusive literature. Meredith prophesied in *The Ordeal of Richard Feverel* (1859) that the 'new man' would 'as it were, from some slight hint of the straws, . . . feel the winds of March when they do not blow'. Not the least of *Feverel*'s admirers was James Joyce.[15]

In 1881, stimulated by the Land War in Ireland, Meredith tried to dissect the 'matter of Britain'. Set along the axis of Budapest–London–Bangor–Dublin, *Celt and Saxon* was to be a political novel, hingeing on a by-election in the 1850s, in which his loquacious, good-hearted hero Captain Con O'Donnell would stand as a Home Ruler. Against the inclinations of his soldier cousin Philip—'We want all our strength in these days of monstrous armies directed by banditti Councils'—the Captain sees Home Rule as a reconciler: 'Let Ireland be true to Ireland. We will talk of the consolidation of the Union by and by.'

Always a 'Big Navy' man—like the later Home Ruler Erskine Childers—Meredith seems to anticipate the synthesis of a wider, federal sort of union. On the

---

[14] See Arthur Hugh Clough, *The Bothie of Toper-na-Fuosich*, ed. Patrick Scott (St Lucia: University of Queensland Press, 1976), 51–2.

[15] George Meredith, *The Ordeal of Richard Feverel* (London: Constable, 1914), 233–4.

pivotal headland of Caer Gybi, Holyhead, O'Donnell's political plan takes shape. Landing from the Dublin steamer, he recruits a young journalist, Colesworth, to his cause, through his fetching niece, who escorts him to the summit:

...a memorable walk in the recollections of the scribe, because of the wonderful likeness of the young lady to the breezy weather and the sparkles over the deep, the cloud that frowned, the cloud that glowed, the green of the earth greening out from under wings of shadow, the mountain ranges holding hands about an immensity of space. It was one of our giant days to his emotions...[16]

'Holding hands about an immensity of space': Meredith uses the headland to suggest that linkages between the Celts can compensate for John Bull's alternations of pride and panic. At present the Welshman

...gladly ships himself across the waters traversed by his Prince Madoc of tradition, and becomes contentedly a transatlantic citizen, a member of strange sects—he so inveterate in faithfulness to the hoar and the legendary!—Anything rather than the Anglican. The Cymry bear you no hatred; their affection likewise is undefined. But there is reason to think that America has caught the imagination of the Cambrian Celt.[17]

Here, from Caer Gybi, is the prospect of a new synthesis, not just racial, but technological and political. West lies Ireland, and to the north the Cumbrian peaks, the locus of post-revolutionary English patriotism. And somewhere in the centre, the Meredithian future: the new man and new woman.

*Celt and Saxon*, ominously, got no further, though Meredith, almost alone among English imaginative writers, was enthusiastic about Home Rule. The novel's sole completed volume was published in 1910, a year after his death, when this particular constitutional ideal was facing the stormiest of passages. But Meredith's attempt at synthesis does suggest that, even at the zenith of 'West Britain', we are dealing with a complicated, federative phenomenon. It may have been temporary—contingent on a distinct technological and social intersection—but it has left a huge and awkward legacy, not least in helping mould the intelligentsia of that literate, autodidact culture to which Hewitt, Joyce, MacDiarmid, and even Yeats belonged. Arnold's post-1885 Liberal Unionism—with a scheme for four provincial councils in Ireland—was itself far more sophisticated (if foredoomed: one is reminded of the hopeless ingenuity of Shaw's Larry Doyle in *John Bull's Other Island*) than A. V. Dicey dancing before the ark of parliamentary sovereignty, or the opportunism of Carson and Bonar Law in 1912–14.[18]

Far from being the supine colony of Irish legend, West Britain was a productive, busy, inventive place. Its nationalists required an epical culture to homogenize modernity, not to escape from it. Joseph Lee sees this implicit in the political thought of Patrick Pearse; it was quite blatant in Bernard Shaw's *The Perfect Wagnerite* (1898). William Archer remembered that he had first met the red-bearded Irishman under the dome of the British Museum, *Capital* and the score of *Tristan und Isolde* open before him. Maud Gonne, muse of the young Yeats, named her

[16] George Meredith, *Celt and Saxon* (London: Constable, 1910), 264.          [17] Ibid. 240.
[18] Matthew Arnold, 'The Nadir of Liberalism', *Nineteenth Century*, 19 (May 1886).

daughter Yseult by the French politician Auguste Millevoye, also showing that the Ossianic cult was reinforced by the Arthurian 'Matter of Britain'. Arthurianism as imperial epic was revived by Kenelm Digby and Tennyson, but so too was the Tristan romance. The marriage of wilful Irish princess and old Cornish king, the seaborne seduction by the knight Tristan, heroic wounding, and death-in-love engaged Arnold and Hardy as well as Wagner, and had its parallels on the road to the General Post Office. Such epics had their locus in all quarters of the inland sea. A theatrical sensation of 1914–24 was the Arthurian opera cycle, starting with *The Immortal Hour,* that Vaughan Williams's Communist friend Rutland Boughton staged at Glastonbury; the few phrases of hope in T. S. Eliot's *The Waste Land* come from Vedic philosophy and Paul Verlaine on the fateful resolution of the grail quest in Wagner's *Parsifal*: 'O ces voix d'enfants, chantant dans le coupole.'[19]

## III   THE ANTECHAMBER OF BRITAIN

'Holding hands round an immensity of space' suggests a major problem with historiography. Immensities of space, as opposed to dry land, don't get documented. Recourse to the novel and poetry becomes legitimate because the imaginative writer sees something the historian can't. 'The clue to many contrasts in British geography', wrote Halford Mackinder in 1902, 'is to be found in the opposition of the south-eastern and north-western—the inner and outer faces of the land. Eastward and southward, between the islands and the continent, are the waters known to history as the Narrow Seas; northward and westward is the Ocean.'[20] In an age obsessed with strategy, however, Mackinder himself was associated with land-based 'geopolitics': the contest over the 'heartland' of the 'world island'—between the Carpathians and the Caucasus—which led to the Anglo-Russian 'Great Game'. He dropped hints:

But as liberty is the native privilege of an island people, so wealth of initiative is characteristic of a divided people. Provinces which are insular or peninsular breed an obstinate provincialism unknown in the merely historical or administrative divisions of a great plain; and this rooted provincialism, rather than a finished cosmopolitanism, is the source of the varied initiative without which liberty would lose half its significance.[21]

But he didn't follow them up.

But seas have topographies: tidal falls, varying from the near-world-record 15 metres of the Bristol Channel (beaten only by the Bay of Fundy off St John in the Canadian Maritimes) to a modest 3 metres in the Clyde, currents, prevailing winds,

---

[19] T. S. Eliot, *The Waste Land*, iii: 'The Fire Sermon', l. 202 (Eliot's note: V. Verlaine, *Parsifal*), in *Collected Poems 1909–1962* (London: Faber, 1986), 71; Gwyn A Williams, *Excalibur: The Search for Arthur* (London: BBC Books, 1994), usefully sums up the later career of the Arthurian myth. Boughton's choric song 'How beautiful they are, the lordly ones' could be described as the Glasgow Orpheus Choir's greatest hit. The choir itself was an offshoot of the Independent Labour Party.
[20] Halford Mackinder, *Britain and the British Seas*, 1902 (Oxford: Clarendon Press, 1907), 14–15.
[21] Ibid.

varieties of marine life with their more or less predictable habits: hence the positioning of harbours, the need for docks accessed by locks (a Bristol Channel speciality, for obvious reasons), the development of fisheries. The west coast of the British Isles, serrated by estuaries, bays, and promontories, rather than the smooth margin of the east, was the preferred route for traders and invaders, even for those, like the Vikings, coming from across the North Sea. The prevailing south-western winds kept it largely fog-free, powerful tides in the Bristol Channel and Mersey aided ships making for the ports, currents were manageable, and distinctive headlands and landmarks eased navigation before the lighthouse era. Given favourable weather, and the speed of up to 15 knots an hour that a swift sailing craft or oared galley could make, few crossings from its coasts would involve more than a day's sail, and some beaches could also be land routes. As early as the Neolithic Age (and intensifying in the Bronze Age) commerce was being carried on along an arc stretching from the Shetlands to the Bay of Biscay: thus Barrie Cunliffe summates recent archaeological research on the region's prehistory. This continued in the sea-kingdoms of the Scots; marked the campaigns of the Anglo-Scottish wars; and overshadowed the Scoto-Irish MacDonald–MacDonnell Lordship of the Isles, which held out against the Stewarts and Edinburgh well into the sixteenth century.[22]

The sea-realms had long been joined by commerce: along the deeply faulted geology of the west outcropped deposits of workable stone or flint, and useful or semi-precious metals: tin and copper in Cornwall, lead and iron in Cumbria, silver, gold, and copper in Wales, and the timber which could be used to smelt them. Here was an openness to trade, second only to that of the narrow seas of the south-east. These had borne the advanced capitalism, textile-based, of the Middle Ages, powered to a great extent by the hydraulics of the Thames estuary, in which the river current was matched by the powerful tides which could carry vessels almost halfway to and from the ports of the Low Countries. This commerce London increasingly monopolized, ingesting the new 'proto-industrial' techniques of Lombardy, Brabant, and the Hanse. Chaucer's 'Merchant' (observed by a Customs Controller) was as sophisticated a City dealer in shares (sheeldes) as the nineteenth century would evolve:

> He woolde thee see were kept for any thyng,
> Betwixen Myddelburgh and Orwelle.
> Well kould he in eschaunge sheeldes sell . . .

The Atlantic from the seventeenth century on was a different proposition. Contestation with Spain brought its rewards, in bullion, slaves, and eventually plantation goods, but by the end of the seventeenth century the power of a united France threatened London's communications, and enhanced the utility of a passage north of Ireland, a route reinforced by the alacrity with which the Scots took to trade after the Union of 1707.

---

[22] Barrie Cunliffe, *Facing the Ocean: The Atlantic and its Peoples, 8000 BC–AD 1500* (Oxford: Oxford University Press, 2000); significantly, various of the key sites—Skara Brae, Callanish—were being excavated and analysed in the 1850s, by such scholars as the Scot Daniel Wilson and the Irishman George Petrie.

Mackinder's antechamber led into his inland sea, bounded by Bristol, Dublin, Belfast, and Glasgow. Apart from the Atlantic trade, and the notorious 'triangle' of the slave trade from West Africa to the Caribbean—shifting ten million units of cheap labour to the plantations, and killing perhaps five million more—this was a region of short voyages and rich cargoes, mobilized by Britain's expansion in the eighteenth century, which demanded iron for weaponry and construction, copper for sheathing hulls, lead for shot, slate for the roofs of growing cities.[23] Besides the great slaving ports of Bristol and after 1709 Liverpool, trade was oiled by an informal and deliberately obscure economy centred on small and discreet harbours—Garlieston, Silloth, Garstang, Red Bay, Dundalk—and lively businessmen, not bigoted about where their money came from. At the sea's centre was the Isle of Man, controlled by the Murray Dukes of Atholl until 1765. A song still sung by Scots children runs:

> The big ship was leaving Bombay
> To sail to the Isle of Man, so they say . . .

Some of the ducal rights were then bought out for £70,000, when Scottish exports totalled £500,000.[24] This shows something of the scale of the

'running trade' . . . carried on along several stretches of the English and Scottish coasts. The Island's strategic position and its low customs duties made it particularly well-suited for engaging in this traffic, which grew to such proportions during the eighteenth century that the British government took the drastic step of passing the Revesting and Mischief Acts in 1765.[25]

This imposed direct Westminster rule on Man 'and the "smuggling mischief" was gradually brought under control'. Sir Walter Scott, however, noted it as still lively in *Redgauntlet*, which he wrote in 1822.[26] The Curries, Dunbars, Ewarts, and Corries of Dumfries, the Irish Barringtons, the Williamses of Parys Mountain, the Wilkinsons of Wrexham and Cumbria, the Cloughs of Denbigh, preserved a resilient frame for three things—exploitation, migration, and trade—which added up to the 'creative chaos', the brew which in Joseph Schumpeter's judgement powered entrepreneurial evolution. The area saw until the end of the eighteenth century smuggling on a huge scale, illegal distilling, the itinerant commercial culture of Scots and Irish pedlars, drovers, harvesters, fisherfolk, and mercenaries.[27] Gwyn A. Williams has suggested, taking Michael Hechter head on, that minerals—slate, lead, and copper preceding

---

[23] For slave trade statistics see Herbert S. Klein, *The Atlantic Slave Trade* (Cambridge: Cambridge University Press, 1999), and the tables in David Richardson, 'The British Empire and the Atlantic Slave Trade, 1660–1807', in Nicholas Canny, ed., *The Oxford History of the British Empire*, i (Oxford: Oxford University Press, 1998).

[24] E. H. Stenning, *The Isle of Man* (London: Robert Hale, 1956), 383; and see T. C. Smout, *A History of the Scottish People* (London: Collins, 1969), 233.

[25] R. H. Kinvig, in T. W. Freeman, H. B. Rodgers, and R. H. Kinvig, eds., *Regions of the British Isles: Lancashire, Cheshire and the Isle of Man* (Edinburgh: Nelson, 1966), 266, and see Louis Cullen, 'Smuggling in the Irish Sea', *Scottish Economic and Social History*, 1 (1982).

[26] Sir Walter Scott, *Redgauntlet* (Edinburgh: Black, 1871), 292, and Cullen, 'Smuggling in the Irish Sea'.

[27] J. A. Schumpeter, *The Theory of Economic Development* (Cambridge, Mass.: Harvard University Press, 1934).

coal—and coastal trade made Wales central, not peripheral in an industrial epoch.[28] Add fisheries and the Atlantic trade, and similar arguments could apply to Cornwall, Ulster, and Scotland. With legal commerce and mineral expansion trade, tourism and the arts moved in. Thomas Pennant (1726–1798), of a Flintshire merchant slaver family, a disciple of Edmund Burke in the sublime, publicized in the 1770s both the industry and the landscape of Wales and Scotland. His family would marry into the Douglases and become dominant figures in the slate industry.[29]

Even when 'legitimized', this economy was predatory as much as proto-industrial, dominated after 1750 by Liverpool, and slave-harvested sugar, tobacco, and later cotton as inward cargoes. This created a robust polity where success did not just excuse dealing in drugs in Jardine-Matheson's Hong Kong, and swapping whisky for furs in Canada, but used this as a means of destroying the trading monopoly of London's Chartered companies. In the American Civil War there would be a similar indifference to legalism in the supply of blockade-runners and commerce-raiders to the slaveowning Confederacy.[30]

The region was formally imprisoned in pre-Reform politics, with rotten Cornish boroughs, unrepresented cities, grand magnates, and poor land communications. Its wealthy elites and their protégés used London to get official imprimatur for their activities, and then returned to the inland sea. Overheads were less, as were transatlantic distances, and authority was safely remote. The decentralized pattern of Whig government prolonged the fitful control of such grandees as the Dukes of Argyll and Atholl, the Marquesses of Londonderry and Bute. With properties in the four littoral countries, and after the Union of 1707 no particular loyalty to any of them, they pocketed their money and pursued idiosyncratic versions of the old Scottish 'territorial jurisdictions'. They were aided by regular wars with France, which opened the French overseas territories up to exploitation, yet inhibited south-east English ports, through high insurance charges and the Navy's press gangs no less than French warships and privateers.[31] The profits of trade, with both the New World and Europe outside French control—notably east Germany and Poland—were big enough to provide fluid finance for mass production in more industries than linen and cotton, an industrialization which went beyond Marx's paradigm of the move of *manufacture* into *machinofacture* to enhance handcraft trades and imports to take advantage of the market created by the advanced transforming industries.

Something similar was happening, though over a longer time and on a more complex and *national* industrial base, in Scotland. The *Statistical Account* in the 1790s

---

[28] Gwyn A. Williams, *When Was Wales? A History of the Welsh* (Harmondsworth: Penguin, 1985), chap. 7.

[29] Peter Lord, *The Visual Culture of Wales: Industrial Society* (Cardiff: University of Wales Press, 1999), 36–9.

[30] See Michael Fry, *The Scottish Empire* (Edinburgh and East Linton: Birlinn and Tuckwell, 1999), 123, and J. Eitel, *Europe in China: The History of Hongkong* (London and Hong Kong: Luzac, 1895), chaps. 6–9. The ambiguities of nineteenth-century trade are well documented in the Liverpool Maritime Museum.

[31] Henry Hamilton, *The Economic History of Scotland in the Eighteenth Century*, 1937 (Oxford: Clarendon Press, 1963), chaps. 9, 10.

and that of the 1830s recorded the rise of tobacco and linen, and coal exports, from Ayr, Ardrossan, and Fife. Scott in *Rob Roy* (1817) and even more John Galt in *Annals of the Parish* (1821) gave these, and the principles of Adam Smith, a perjink self-confidence. But the high-value production would come two decades later in shipbuilding, engineering, and catering for the capital and consumer goods of unchecked urbanization. Only a few hours' sail from the Ayrshire coalfield lay Belfast, which became an outlier of the Clyde after the 1850s. Its population was 70,000 in 1841, 119,000 in 1861, 350,000 in 1900, out of a total Northern Ireland population of 1.5 million. It had in 1914 the world's largest linen factory, tobacco factory, rope-works, and shipyard.[32]

Follow the 1,300 buff-and-cream tons of Sir Thomas Lipton's yacht *Erin*, steaming south from the Clyde in the 1900s.[33] Born in poverty in Glasgow, of a Monaghan family, and working up from a cabin boy on the Irish boats, Lipton had learned the food retail business in the USA—and the magic of advertising—and opened his first chain store in Glasgow in 1870. Now a millionaire and baronet, he would have Edward VII as passenger. South of Stranraer the *Erin* would pass the colliers headed for Belfast Lough, and to the east the smaller, more specialized industrial centres of west Cumberland (coal, iron, and steel making), Barrow (steel and shipbuilding), and Preston (cotton, electrical engineering, trams). She then steered carefully through the throng of Cunarders, tramp steamers, and sailing ships around the Mersey ports of Liverpool, Runcorn, and Birkenhead (warehousing, soap, chemicals, shipbuilding)—meticulously recorded and later versified by the naval cadet John Masefield—and since 1894 and the opening of the Ship Canal, steaming to 'Cottonopolis' Manchester itself.[34] South lay Flintshire (coal and steel), and interspersed were the fancy piers and pleasure steamers of the north-western resorts, from Blackpool, Southport, and Douglas, Isle of Man, to New Brighton and Llandudno.

Further west were the Welsh slate and granite quarries—great bites out of Snowdonia—with their schooners, private docks, and railways, and then, off Caer Gybi, the Kingstown mailboats and the Guinness coasters and cattle boats bound to and from Dublin. Five hours steaming south, then another Irish packet station at Fishguard, and on rounding St David's Head, the dense traffic of the Bristol Channel: timber, tin, iron ore, chocolate, tobacco, sugar, bananas *in*, to Llanelli, Swansea, Port Talbot, Barry, Cardiff and Newport, Bristol and Bridgwater, and from the Welsh ports, overwhelmingly coal *out*. Britain ended with Cornwall (tin and kaolin). The *Erin* set course south-west to Biarritz and Lisbon, Barcelona, and the distractions of the Côte d'Azur and Palermo.

---

[32] J. C. Beckett and R. E. Glasscock, eds., *Belfast: The Origin and Growth of an Industrial City* (London: BBC, 1967). Samuel Smiles's son ran the rope-works; his grandson went down with the *Princess Victoria* in 1953.

[33] She was built by Scotts of Greenock in 1898, and was sunk ferrying medical supplies to Salonica in 1918.

[34] 'The poet of the sea', Masefield (1878–1967), wanted to be a sailor but on his first and only serious voyage realized he got hopelessly seasick, so his 'The Ships', on the Mersey in the 1890s, is really a celebration of ship-spotting, which, like trainspotting, evolved in that decade. His emergence as a poet was aided by the Yeats brothers, particularly Jack.

Between the British ports, for nearly all of the nineteenth century, the main means of freight haulage was shipping: rail certainly made gains between 1850 and 1880, but steam power enabled the coastal trade to recover, a situation strengthened by the Manchester Ship Canal.[35] Welsh steam coal was so rich in energy and low in ash that it outsold, even in Virginia, the product of America's great Pennsylvania field. It made the valleys north of Cardiff and Swansea the equivalent of today's Saudi Arabia, with tank engines and fifteen-ton trucks standing in for the pipelines, and was the essential sustainer of industry not only along the littoral but for a couple of decades worldwide. Coal exports from Cardiff alone went from 172,000 tons in 1833 to 2.6 million tons in 1911, most of the coal loaded on coastal steamers.[36] Four hundred collieries, a quarter of a million miners, up to four railways in each valley, the harbours packed with tramp steamers: the population of the county of Glamorgan rose from 232,000 in 1851 to nearly a million in 1911, over a third that of Wales: 'American Wales' or what Patrick Geddes called 'Walestown' had become a cauldron of inflowing cultures.

## IV  MONEY AND MIGRANTS

The western ports and their seas united strong economic specializations with supra-regional economic control through the aristocracy, finance, and entrepreneurs, and tapped, in Ireland, highland Scotland, and Wales, a supply of strong and cheap labour. Within this were regional stories of success and failure. Bristol was for centuries the commercial centre for South Wales, but it had ceded its slaving dominance to Liverpool by the 1750s. In 1811 Cardigan was registering more ships, some built in the New Cardigan of the Canadian Maritimes. In turn it fell; by the time the railway reached the place in the 1870s its captains were sailing from Cardiff and Swansea, though the Cardis adapted, and used the line to supply London with milk. By 1914 the west Cumberland coal and iron field had followed Cornwall and the west Wales ports into obscurity. James Brunlees's mile-long iron viaduct of 1869, which had carried its output over the Solway to Scotland, was derelict.[37]

In this development sequence Ireland at first kept up, but was then sidelined. As well placed as Scotland or Wales in textiles, Ireland shared for a time in the liberal moment. No part of Britain responded more enthusiastically to Tom Paine, and Daniel O'Connell qua utilitarian had a public presence far greater than his rather theoretical English allies. Yet repression and metropolitan privilege diminished industry,

---

[35] See A. W. Kirkaldy, *British Shipping: Its History, Organisation and Importance* (London: Kegan Paul, 1914), 529–36.

[36] Philip Bagwell and Peter Lyth, *Transport in Britain: From Canal Lock to Gridlock* (London: Hambledon, 2002), 28.

[37] There were at one time, *c*.1914, 2,000 Cardi dairymen in London. One of the last businesses closed in Islington in 1999. Like William Dargan, Sir John Brunlees is under-recorded. He built the first railway over the Alps, a 3 ft 6 in. Fell railway over the Mont Cenis Pass, with an extra central rail for better adhesion, in 1866–8—it closed in 1872 when the tunnel opened—besides many harbours and railways (along the west coast and in South America) and some of the most ambitious pleasure piers at the resorts.

notably Irish publishing, which had to migrate to America when British copyright law was enforced. The failure to use low-cost labour to develop high-value-added industry was worsened by the rationalization, through famine and emigration, of a two-Ireland identity which for a couple of centuries seemed to endorse the Protestant work ethic of north-east Ulster.[38]

Ireland became an emigration economy, something also evident in industrializing Scotland. By contrast, Wales sucked in settlers, in the period between the conquest of the freight steamer in the 1880s, and the collapse of coal in the 1920s. Roald Dahl, Howard Spring, Eric Linklater, Maurice Edelman, and Dannie Abse were all *South Wales*-born writers.[39] Wales, more than Scotland, was 'so far from God and so near to England', as a Methodist minister once mourned. But separation still counted. Dennis Potter from the Forest of Dean—last of the western Nonconformists?—laughed at himself: 'I always hate the Welsh—inevitably, because I was brought up to. Yet many of my friends are Welsh. But the Race Relations Act cannot touch me here—I'm a border person, and that's the way it is.'[40] Yet the first great miner-writer of the Welsh coalfield, B. L. Coombes, was an immigrant from Gloucestershire, and Potter as regionalist recognized that Dean miners, quite different from Monmouth miners, were nevertheless moving to the new fields. In Scotland and Wales in the nineteenth century, a social-industrial distinctiveness lurched into awkward life, remote both from the metropolis and from traditional, ethno-linguistic nationalism.[41]

The father of John Hewitt spent much of his life in Glasgow, one of many whose careers which straddled at least two out of the three nations, but do not fall into any simple definition: not planter, not evicted victim. Arnold's 'grave trader' may come closer to the mark, particularly for that critical half-century after 1860. Any collective biography of the West British elite would tend to show continuous linkages round the periphery, relatively weak links to the metropolitan elite, and a tendency towards speculation and trade. This would not simply be random: political, economic, and educational connections were deeply enough scored to ensure that population movements followed a certain pattern. Angus Calder has adjured us to study capitalism and imperialism as an interlinked package, and to see 'plantation' as its harbinger.[42] Emmanuel Todd argues in *The Causes of Progress* (1989) for a 'Celtic' pattern of extended 'authoritarian family'—founded on agreement,

---

[38] Irish manufacturing fell from 22.8 per cent of GNP in 1851 to 16.0 per cent in 1881; see H. D. Gribbon, 'Economy and Industry', in W. E. Vaughan, ed., *A New History of Ireland*, vi: *Ireland under the Union, II: 1820–1921* (Oxford: Oxford University Press, 1996), 333, and David Johnson, *The Interwar Economy in Ireland* (Dundalk: Economic and Social History Society of Ireland, 1985), 43.

[39] Respectively, Norwegian, Irish, Orcadian, and Jewish.

[40] Brinley Thomas, 'Wales and the Atlantic Economy', in *The Welsh Economy* (Cardiff: University of Wales Press, 1962) Dennis Potter, interview in *The New Left Review*, 205 (May–June 1994), 133.

[41] This persisted until 2007 in the lack of support given to the SNP and Plaid Cymru in the old industrial areas, where they usually remained pinned behind the 25 per cent barrier, compared with the 50 per cent or more unenthusiastically but regularly donated to Labour. The further south-east you got in Wales, the further the *Blaid*'s vote sank below the Raving Loony level.

[42] Angus Calder, *Revolutionary Empire* (London: Jonathan Cape, 1980), 111 ff.

rather than kinship, nurturing trust and talent—which could adapt rapidly to commerce.[43] Such factors were given additional force by the dynastic changes in 1485 and 1603 which opened England to Welsh and Scots noblemen. Aristocratic families like the Stewarts, Hamiltons, and Stanleys were involved early on in such exploitation, under the 'management' of the Clan Campbell in Scotland, which fused earlier clan networks to aristocratic-mercantile connections. The Vane-Tempest-Stewarts, Marquesses of Londonderry, enriched by Durham mining, owned Plas Machynlleth as well as Mountstewart in Armagh, Garron Tower in Antrim, and Londonderry House in the West End. Another branch of the family, the Crichton-Stuarts, as Marquesses of Bute, would develop Cardiff Docks, and much more, after 1839. Do we have here a fusion between the plutocratic entrepreneurialism of the grand Whigs, and the value of such appanages in imposing the rule of British politics on the turbulent northwest? And what relation does plantation ideology bear to the exploitation of the New World, to Welsh Potosis and Golcondas?[44]

Industrial capital got mobile, as mineral areas developed and declined, but Ireland remained inhibited. The locating power of the bulkiest raw material was critical here: management and labour could move more cheaply than coal. Yeats's Pollexfen forebears moved from once-prosperous copper-mining Devon to Sligo, just as the tin-mining Vivians moved from Cornwall to Swansea. Dublin, in its glory at the end of the eighteenth century, was roofed with Welsh slate; Ireland's sharp and long-lived novelist Maria Edgeworth (1767–1849) sprang from the illuminati of the West Midlands. But Irish technology lacked coal, religious liberty, and free trade. A capital of the 'Atlantic Arc' needed more than a pseudo-parliament for a privileged minority, debarred from determining its own policy. By contrast, Scots industrialization and 'improving' ideology travelled out on the routes established by imperial trade and patronage, settlement, Enlightenment, and early industrialization. Scots and Ulster-Scots showed a brisk interest in plantation and trade, legal or not, along with the establishment of ports, fisheries, and 'improved' agriculture.[45] The Seceders of the Antrim glens were no more exiled from Scotland than their brethren in the Highlands; the Bryces of Killaig were far closer to Glasgow than the Bryces of Wick. The links with the Covenanting tradition of Ayrshire were obvious, and the geographical continuum was manifest in the *absence* of separate Ulster dialect culture, or of a tradition of the settlement. The Belfast Scot Samuel Ferguson (1810–1886) wrote in 1836, 'It is remarkable that the recollection of the mother country is scarcely if at all cherished; yet there is a perfect similarity of habits and disposition.'[46]

Modernization transformed the sea trade on both sides of the pond. Cardigan Bay, remote from good roads and without a rail network until the 1860s, had long been a shipping and shipbuilding centre, with half a dozen small ports. Aberporth,

[43] Emmanuel Todd, *The Causes of Progress: Culture, Authority and Change* (Oxford: Blackwell, 1989), chap. 2.

[44] John Davies, *Cardiff and the Marquesses of Bute* (Cardiff: University of Wales Press, 1981), esp. chap. 7.

[45] Tom Devine, *Scotland's Empire, 1650–1815* (London: Allen Lane, 2004), 74–5.

[46] H. A. L. Fisher, *James Bryce* (London: Macmillan, 1927), 1–11, and Samuel Ferguson, 'Attractions of Ireland: No. 3 Society', *Dublin University Magazine*, 48/8 (Dec. 1836), 663.

Llangrannog, New Quay, Aberaeron, stretching north from the head-port of Cardigan, imported lime and culm (anthracite mixed with limestone, for domestic fuel), traded with Ireland, exported lead and slate, trained seafarers. Two careers show how rapidly things changed: those of Captain Benjamin Morris of Newcastle Emlyn and Captain David Jenkins of Llangrannog. Raised in the coastal and Irish trade (smuggling of cheaper Irish salt lasted to the 1890s) and skippering locally built boats, from smacks of 25 tons to brigs of about 160 tons, they went deep-sea with the rise of Cardiff and coal, often with softwood craft from Maine or the Maritimes. Morris's first voyage, on the 558-ton barque *Onward* of Banff in Scotland, from Newport to Santos (near São Paulo) with coal, and back with grain, took nearly nine months in 1886–7. Twenty years later Jenkins, third mate on the SS *Duffryn Manor* of 2,511 tons, was out from Barry to the River Plate with coal and back to Cardiff with grain in five and a half. As cargo capacity was roughly three times any vessel's deadweight, this meant that it took twelve men to shift 1,500 tons on the first voyage, and six men to shift 7,500 tons on the second.[47]

Morris and Jenkins reflected the changing organization of the industry, from small local partnerships into companies and tramp steamer lines, varying from a single ship to big concerns like the twenty-eight-steamer Radcliffe Line, with offices in Aberporth and Merthyr. The South Wales trade drew in mariners from other traditional seafaring areas, north Devon (the Corys and Tatems), Cornwall (the Hains), the Channel Islands (the Morels and Marquands), and Scotland (the Campbells), not to speak of mainland Europe. Many partnerships had started with cheap softwood sailing ships, but by the 1870s they were buying compound-engined freighters from the Clyde or the north-east, rarely faster than a full-rigged ship, but with far higher capacity and reliability against the wind and a smaller crew. What was needed on the further shore were docks and cranes, coal bunkers, tugs and dredgers, warehouses, railways. Sometimes these came from local enterprise: Montreal rose in the 1870s as the main Canadian trans-shipment port under the Ayrshireman John Young, who planted a statue of Robert Burns in the main square (the French retaliated with a third-size replica of St Peter's). More often the operation was financed in the City or New York, and William Arrol or Weetman Pearson commissioned to build the lot. Local success was secondary. There was no South American merchant fleet before 1914, any more than there was an Indian one.

Tramping in the telegraph age—which girdled the globe in the 1870s thanks to gutta percha for insulation, steel wire for strength, and Isambard Kingdom Brunel's 18,000-ton *Great Eastern* (1859–1895) for cable-laying capacity—meant that the situation of the shore office was not critical. Ships from the east coast, Hartlepool, Whitby, and Newcastle—and Norway—would also be found plying to and from the Bristol Channel.[48] With an efficiency which marginalized the prospects of late

---

[47] J. Geraint Jenkins, *Maritime Heritage: The Ships and Seamen of Southern Ceredigion* (Bridgend: Gomer Press, 1982), 140–4.

[48] David Jenkins, *Shipping at Cardiff* (Cardiff: University of Wales Press, 1993); contrary winds were deadly for sailing ships. In *Youth* Conrad mentions three weeks taken in 1881 to cover the 300 miles from Thames to Tyne, and some tows from the Mersey could last until the Bay of Biscay.

entrants, notably the Irish, coastal shipping outdid rail: between 1908 and 1912 shifting 20 billion ton-miles, against between 13 and 15 billion ton-miles by rail.[49] Most of it was coal. Coal exports fluctuated between 1870 and 1888 at around £10 million per annum; thereafter they climbed steeply: to £19 million in 1890, £38.6 million in 1900, £53.7 million in 1914. Inflated by a 40 per cent devaluation, they still rose to £120.3 million in 1920, though the collapse thereafter would be swift, to £49.2 million in 1930.[50]

## V 'TRAFFICS AND DISCOVERIES'

The mixture of trade, engineering, and affluence along the west coast acted as a forcing-ground for innovation. Economic expansion emphasized the bottlenecks which had to be removed: wealth, culture and patronage accelerated technical remedies. Bristol, the centre of the slave trade, financier of mineral activity in Cornwall and South Wales, had Bath its patrician pleasure-ground; this combination originated the Post Office as a reliable communicator, in the reforms of Ralph Allen (1694–1764)—Henry Fielding's Squire Allworthy in *Tom Jones*—in the 1740s. Allen also launched the *principle* of the horse-worked railway in the 1760s, documenting the line he built to deliver stone to Bath. In the 1780s William Palmer of Bath started running high-speed mail coaches, and after 1808 the Bath turnpike trustees were managed by John Loudon McAdam (1756–1836) from Ayrshire, 'the colossus of roads', who used his cheap consolidated small-stone surface with great success. Both innovations spread Britain-wide. Unsurprisingly, given that the Severn was England's premier navigable river, innovation travelled across it to Wales and up it to Coalbrookdale and the west Midlands, while local entrepreneurs such as Davies Giddy were to patronize the Cornishmen Humphry Davy and Richard Trevithick in the 1800s and the Anglo-French Brunel in the 1830s.

Migration could be intellectually as much as technologically driven. Francis Hutcheson (1694–1746), moving from Dublin to Glasgow in 1729, is usually seen as the first philosopher of the Scottish enlightenment, but Scotland had long been an academy for young Welshmen, who gained Daniel Williams bursaries to study for the Presbyterian ministry in Glasgow, where they shared a similar curriculum with their Ulster and Scottish brethren, and became a motor of the rise of Welsh Methodism. Robert Owen (1771–1859) moved from Newtown (flannel) to Manchester (cotton)—where he shared a house with the Scots-American Robert Fulton—and used his first fortune to buy his famous mills at New Lanark. This was a familiar road, taken by Roebucks and Houldsworths, though Owen added to it with a workforce which was largely Highland, and ended his career by migrating to the United States. Not long after his death there in 1859 Newtown's Pryce Pryce-Jones invented mail order with his Royal Welsh Warehouse; its offspring like Sears

[49] Bagwell and Lyth, *Transport in Britain*, 38.
[50] B. R. Mitchell and Phyllis Deane, *Abstract of British Historical Statistics* (Cambridge: Cambridge University Press, 1962), 302–6.

Roebuck would dwarf conventional retailing in the USA. Mining technology necessarily owed much to the advances that Scots scholars, following James Hutton, had made in developing the science of geology, and this relationship was of mutual benefit, since many of the mining engineers who opened up the Lanarkshire coalfield were Welsh.

When, later in the nineteenth century, the South Wales coalfield boomed, its chief facilitator would be the Second Marquess of Bute, who opened Cardiff's Bute Dock in 1839 to serve the first modern railway, Brunel's Taff Vale, to penetrate into the valleys. In the 1860s the Third Marquess, now fabulously wealthy, converted to Catholicism, remodelled the castle with his exotic architect William Burges, and patronized Scots and Welsh culture. He was not the only link between the countries. Archibald Hood would run both the Lothian and Glamorgan coal companies, and Lewis Gordon built the spectacular east–west Neath and Brecon Railway, with its great iron viaduct at Crumlin. Henry Robertson moved from Banff to develop railways and industry in north-west Wales, ending as a partner of Davies of Llandinam and a landowner in Merioneth and hosting Queen Victoria on almost her only visit to Wales. The MacLarens, later the Lords Aberconway, went from being Edinburgh radicals, with a Manchester connection through John Bright, to the North Wales slate industry (already opened up by the Scots-Welsh Douglas-Pennants and the Scots-Manchester McConnells) and Cornish china clay. One of them, F. S. Oliver, boss of Debenhams and friend of John Buchan, produced a Unionist scheme for 'Home Rule All Round' in 1910.

This was only one example of an ideology developed from a foundation of crisscrossing transatlantic and inter-regional friendships, itineraries, and influences. Keir Hardie went from Lanarkshire to sit for Merthyr Tydfil, bankrolled in part by the coal-owner D. A. Thomas; his son-in-law Emrys Hughes would later take Tom Johnston's *Forward* over in Glasgow: a paper which was always open to American socialist writing, from Jack London to Upton Sinclair. Tom Jones, that prizewinning maker of committees and middle-opinion policies, went from the Rhymney to Glasgow (where he worked with R. H. Tawney) and then to Belfast, then back to Wales and on to Downing Street with Lloyd George.[51] Hugh MacDiarmid went from Scotland to become a journalist on the *Monmouth Labour Leader*, turned up in Liverpool in the 1930s, and acted as an inspiration for R. S. Thomas after World War II.[52]

Relations between Glasgow and Belfast were more direct, given rapid communications and similarity of industries. James Thomson, Lord Kelvin, polymath scientist, engineer, and capitalist, went from Belfast to Glasgow. Edward Harland went from Scarborough via Robert Stephenson's works at Newcastle and Leith to Belfast in 1854, his assistant Gustav Wilhelm Wolff from Hamburg via the north-east to Belfast, using cash from his Liverpool uncle G. C. Schwabe to set up the partnership in 1859–61; Workman and Clark, Clyde engineers, founded Belfast's 'wee yard':

---

[51] E. L. Ellis, *TJ: A Life of Dr Thomas Jones* (Cardiff: University of Wales Press, 1992), chaps. 3, 5, 12; see also Susan Tweedsmuir's novel *The Scent of Water* (London: Hodder and Stoughton, 1936).

[52] See R. S. Thomas, 'Some Contemporary Scottish Writing', *Wales*, 6/3 (1946).

'wee' in comparison only to Harland and Wolff. Lord Pirrie, an Ulster-Scot Unionist, though sympathetic to Liberalism and Home Rule, employed 50,000 around the inland sea in 1910, centred on Belfast's Queen's Island Yard (created by William Dargan when he dredged the Lagan in the 1840s, it was first known as Dargan's Island). At the end of his career in the 1920s Pirrie would dominate the Scots shipbuilding, steel, and coal industries, including John Browns, Colvilles, and the Lothian Coal Company, through a whole series of cartels. Along with the German-Jewish financier Sir Ernest Cassel and J. Pierpoint Morgan of New York, he would devise the hybrid (private-state-cartel) financing of the giant Atlantic steamers which—beginning with the Germans in the late 1890s—led to the *Mauretania* in 1906 and the *Titanic* and her sisters in 1911–12, and involved a cartel with the Hamburg-Amerika and other lines led by another German Jew, Albert Ballin.[53]

Lancashire attracted Scots and Welsh technicians to its cotton mills during its steep rise from the 1770s (its population went from 673,000 in 1801 to nearly 5,000,000 in 1921; its cotton imports from 26,000,000 lb in 1795 to 1,920,000,000 lb in 1905), especially when steam and new equipment forced the building of urban mills. McConnells, Fairbairns, Nasmyths, and Kennedys came from Scotland, Owen and Roberts from Wales. But Liverpool was an even more critical junction, as the greatest Atlantic cotton and passenger port. In the eighteenth century it combined Scottish and Welsh strands. The Gladstones (among a host of Ewarts and Corries and Parkers) came in pursuit of trade on a scale impossible from the cramped, shallow harbours of Scotland. They settled in and around the subordinate arc, from Preston via Liverpool to North Wales, after Liverpool built its first non-tidal dock in 1709, and turnpikes and the Trent and Mersey Canal extended its hinterland. In the 1820s, with a population of nearly 200,000, its merchant elite—the Holts, Booths, Roscoes—seeking an alternative to the Mersey Navigation and the Bridgewater Canal, financed Liverpool and Manchester, the world's first high-performance passenger and freight railway, opened in 1830, with Robert Stephenson's revolutionary 'Rocket'. They floated in the 1840s the passenger-and-mail Cunard line, largely financed from Scotland (which also built and engined its ships), which chose Liverpool as its Atlantic Ferry station. The great Scots theocrat Thomas Chalmers was quite at home in the city's Evangelical milieu.[54] The shipbuilding Lairds went from Scotland to Birkenhead, laid out by the Edinburgh neoclassicist Thomas Hamilton. The Cloughs moved from North Wales, as did Matthew Arnold's forebears on his mother's side. (He would die in Liverpool in 1888, running for a tramcar.) Liverpool's docks, with their complex general traffic, required huge numbers of Irish labourers; it became 'the greatest Welsh city' largely through its building workers. But by 1900, being practically equidistant from London and Dublin, it was also the home base for many Irish National MPs.[55]

---

[53] Kirkaldy, *British Shipping*, 189.

[54] See S. G. Checkland, *The Gladstones: A Family Biography, 1764–1851* (Cambridge: Cambridge University Press, 1971).

[55] See Alan O'Day, *The English Face of Irish Nationalism: Parnellite Involvement in British Politics, 1880–1886* (Dublin: Gill and Macmillan, 1977), 10–31.

There were uncertainties. After 1894 Manchester's new Ship Canal bit into Liverpool's cotton trade. The Mersey tides were deterrents to the increasingly large transatlantic liners, and after the London and South-Western Railway started to modernize the more conveniently sited Southampton (new tidal quay in 1892, graving dock in 1905), much Atlantic ferry trade went south. A mixture of insecurity, civic pride, and religious prejudice generated massive Edwardian projects: the 'Three Graces' (the Cunard, Royal Liver, and Mersey Authority offices on the Quay), an Anglican, and later a Catholic cathedral, respectively by Giles Gilbert Scott and Edwin Lutyens, and a School of Architecture and Town Planning which, under Sir Charles Reilly after 1904 and with the cash of Lord Leverhulme, became one of the world's most influential. Liverpool also housed the leader of organized Nonconformity. The Revd John Watson, known to the Kailyard as 'Ian MacLaren', and minister of Sefton Park Presbyterian Church, was in the 1890s the President of the Free Church Federal Council. The nephew of Samuel Ferguson, who died Sir Samuel, he was close to that pre-eminent literary politician, and marketer of the ethical sentimentalism of the Kailyard—'T. H. Green-and-water'—the Revd William Robertson Nicoll. A. J. P. Taylor rightly said of Nicoll that when in 1922 he abandoned Lloyd George, Lloyd George fell.[56]

John Saunders Lewis, the scholarly founder of Plaid Cymru, was born in Birkenhead, and influenced in the first line by Ireland; behind this lay the ideologues of French nationalism, Maurice Barrès and Charles Maurras in particular. This also went for a number of militant Irish nationalists, and for MacDiarmid in the 1920s. Yet on the Catholic side James Connolly, born in Edinburgh, went to Belfast via the army and America to organize the dock workers, along syndicalist rather than nationalist lines; John Wheatley came from Waterford to become Clydeside's most subtle and innovative socialist. Even when John Hewitt quit Ulster in 1953 to settle in Coventry, he encountered a city—the British Motown?—fertilized by a huge Scots and Welsh as well as Irish immigration. Which Richard Hughes, no less, intended to make the scene of the final volume of his 'Human Condition' trilogy.

## VI   'BUT WESTWARD LOOK!'

The littoral wasn't self-determining, as its economy was dependent on that of the UK as a whole, and thus on London, for most of its banking, insurance, and joint-stock capitalism. It might ignore the establishment, but it had no desire to overthrow it. As a name 'England' was more convenient than 'Britain'—trading partners understood England as meaning Navy and Bank—but this very provinciality meant a complex inter-reaction of intellectual influences. 'British' proudly connoted 'provincial'. The British and Foreign Schools Society (1808) was Nonconformity's counter in

---

[56] See Chapter 5 below, and Christopher Harvie, 'Behind the Bonnie Briar Bush: The Kailyard Revisited', in P. N. Furbank, ed., *Proteus II* (1978); Alice Payne Hackett, *70 Years of Best-Sellers* (New York: Bowker, 1967), 91–2; and T. H. Darlow, *Sir William Robertson Nicoll* (London: Hodder and Stoughton, 1929), chap. 10.

the education contest. The British Association for the Advancement of Science was founded in 1831 by the Scots physicist Sir David Brewster, a radical (his brother, minister of Paisley Abbey, became a leading Chartist), who chose York for its first meeting as 'the most central city in the three kingdoms'. Its annual meetings in the great industrial towns were occasions for self-examination as well as pride. On the model of the British Association, Charles Woodyatt Hastings, a Worcester doctor with an Edinburgh degree, founded the Provincial Medical and Surgical Association in 1832; it became the British Medical Association in 1855. Two years later his son George founded with the veteran Lord Brougham the National Association for the Promotion of Social Science, also dedicated to inspiriting bunfights in Manchester, Belfast, and Glasgow, etc. The Ulster-Scot Gladstonian James Bryce (1838–1922), historian, radical, and traveller throughout the globe, was familiar with this scene. He proceeded from Glasgow to Oxford, became Professor, set up legal studies in Manchester, reached Gladstone's Cabinet and Dublin Castle, and ended up in Washington (1907–13) as Ambassador, retaining views owing much to the Scots commonsense school, Carlyle, and such European libertarians as Mazzini. His pabulum was similar to that of Tom Ellis of Bala, Oxford, and Westminster, who was also directly influenced by two Scots—the railway builder Robertson and the cosmopolitan John Robertson of Barmouth. His Young Wales movement bore the imprint of Thomas Davis, himself of Welsh ancestry, and not a few backhanders from Cecil Rhodes. Davis's colleague Charles Gavan Duffy (1816–1903), of Monaghan and later premier of Victoria, Australia, a thoroughgoing devotee of Carlyle, returned to contribute to the 1890s cultural revival.[57] All three were involved to some extent in moves for 'imperial federation' behind which lay an explicit Atlantic ideal.

These 'lateral' influences deflected official attempts to tie intellectual development to English institutions. The Snell Exhibitions, initially a means of subsidizing the Scots Episcopalian minority, took Glasgow graduates to Balliol College, Oxford. Welsh education was a dedicated function of Jesus College, Oxford. As devices to uphold Anglican Oxford these failed; Exhibitioners like Adam Smith ignored the university's mediocre offerings, though the Anglican Communion in post-revolutionary America had been able to maintain apostolic succession by keeping communion with the Scottish Episcopalians. Likewise Welsh Calvinistic Methodism, the major element in New Dissent, owed more to the Scottish Seceders and Non-Intrusionists than to the conservative and Erastian tradition of mainstream Wesleyanism.

Exiled in Paris after 1897, Oscar Wilde called himself Sebastian Melmoth, after another Irishman, Charles Maturin's, doomed Wanderer. The same peripatetic quality was true of the radical opposition, which fed on his *Soul of Man under Socialism* (1891), and to whom America was a progressive ideal which was also easily accessible. Thomas Davidson of Buchan, his autobiography appropriately titled *Wandering Scholar*, founded the proto-Fabian Fellowship of the New Life in London in 1884, then went westward to be inspired by John Muir and form with William James the American summer-school movement, an Appalachian hotbed of progressive and

---

[57] See Neville Masterman, *The Forerunner: The Dilemmas of Tom Ellis, 1859–99* (Llandybie: Christopher Davies, 1971), 84 ff. These paragraphs are largely based on the *Oxford DNB*.

pragmatist thought. Scots were assimilated rapidly in the USA, and tended to retain only a sentimental residue; the Welsh, as William D. Jones's study of Scranton reveals, were only slightly less ruthless about it, though many accused them of nepotism on the way up. The Irish bore more of a desire to settle the conflict which had driven them thence; yet for all three the essentially civic American experience of liberation was a core round which the vestiges of national identity could be wrapped.[58]

The American example went back to the Revolution. John Paul Jones (1747– 1792), the founder of the US Navy, was from Kirkbean on the Solway, and pressed the point by raiding the estuary in 1778. Irish Volunteers and Scottish 'Associationists', notably Robert Burns, were inspired by the revolution. Robert Fulton, inventor of submarine and steamboat, was from a Scots-Irish family, who moved from Galloway to Kilkenny and then to Lancaster, Pennsylvania. The great inhibitor for radicals was America's 'peculiar institution' of slavery, but after 1865 it was purged of this evil; it had also become a trade partner, rather than an industrial competitor. Its population was still predominantly of north European origin, its discourse English, its government limited enough to make aspects of it appear as examples for European reformers. (Paradoxically, the absence of collectivism and its national peculiarities of organization contributed to American democracy's attractiveness as an abstract idea.) To Painites and Emersonians—and scores of self-taught Whitmanites, not least among them Patrick Geddes, who wrote much of his correspondence in Whitmanite free verse—was added the influence of the American Left, from the Mugwumps of the 1880s, boosted by the Ulster journalist E. L. Godkin in the New York *Nation*, via Henry George's 'single-tax' in the mid 1880s, very popular on the littoral, and James Bryce's enthusiastic *American Commonwealth* of 1889.[59] A later radicalism cottoned on to everything from La Follette progressivism to the International Workers of the World and the De Leonist Socialist Labour Party. Hewitt's friendship with the Ulster-American anarchist radical Alexander Irvine fitted into an increasing 'American' Leftism which would occupy the framework left by American revivalism in the 1870s.[60]

This was the result of a mixture of migration, enterprise, and technical change. European uncertainty induced by Bismarck's wars switched investment abroad just as America calmed down. Canada had to consolidate against the by now mighty power to the south, with confederation under Sir John MacDonald in 1867 and the beginning in 1871 of the Canadian Pacific Railway, financed by Donald Smith and Donald Stephen, later the Lords Strathcona and Mountstephen, from the same tiny county of Nairn, and engineered by (Sir) Sandford Fleming (1827–1915), who had emigrated from Kircaldy in 1845. Accelerated by the opening of the Anglo-French-engineered Suez Canal in 1869, there were similarly rapid rail developments in most

---

[58] William D. Jones, *Wales in America: Scranton and the Welsh, 1860–1920* (Cardiff: University of Wales Press, 1993), chap. 2; Thomas Davidson, *Memorials of Thomas Davidson*, ed. William Knight (Boston and London: Ginn, 1907).

[59] See Philip Boardman, *Patrick Geddes: Maker of the Future* (London: Routledge, 1974), chap. 9. Thanks to Dr Paul Salveson for alerting me to the Bolton Whitmanites of the 1880s and 1890s, headed by a Scots doctor and Scots architect, whose worship rather embarrassed the old lion.

[60] See John Hewitt, *Selected Prose Writings* (Belfast: Blackstaff Press, 1990).

of the imperial territories, associated with the use of steel rail and the adoption of a narrower and more economical 'Cape' gauge of 3 ft 6 in.[61]

The traffic was not one-way. From the United States came the first mass-produced 'CKD' ('completely knocked down': with mass-produced, interchangeable parts) goods, starting with the Colt revolver in the early 1850s and bringing the Remington typewriter and Singer sewing machine in the 1870s. Starting out in an old cotton mill in Bridgeton, Glasgow, Singers moved to a purpose-built factory at Clydebank in 1882–4, the biggest in Europe. The sewing machines of the rag trade's sweatshops would be an unavoidable part of the next migrant generation's experience. And in 1873–4 there arrived at Liverpool the evangelical mission of Dwight Moody and Ira D. Sankey. In their unsectarianism, their 'civic mission', and their grasp of music and spectacle (Moody preached, Sankey sang) they lay behind Gladstone's great Mid-lothian meetings (1879) and William Booth's Salvation Army, not to speak of Keir Hardie's spiritualist radicalism; just as Hardie's political efforts were to be backed by the American soap manufacturer Joseph Fels and by Andrew Carnegie.[62] Other disciples of Moody and Sankey were the explorer and Boys' Brigade pioneer Professor Henry Drummond, and John Sinclair, Lord Pentland. Pentland was subsequently the patron of Geddes, as were Lord and Lady Aberdeen, who as Viceroy and Vicereine of Ireland started the Irish planning movement in 1913.[63]

Behind this was another development of the 1880s: university settlements followed hard on the heels of provincial university colleges, whose roots lay in the evangelical activity of young Oxbridge as well as in civic pride and whose gospel was Newman's Dublin lectures *The Ideal of a University* (1852). The settlements had differing histories on arc and core. Toynbee Hall was founded in 1884, when Oxford sensed the explosive tensions of East End slumdom and casualized dock labour. It was intended by such as James Bryce (then the local MP) and Alfred Milner to educate the would-be ruling class; and got much support once Bloody Sunday put the fear of death into the West End in 1886. In Chicago Jane Addams would found the similar Hull House in 1889. On a different, non-communicating groove, Patrick Geddes founded in 1884 the more altruistic Edinburgh Social Union, with a strong feminist, ecological, and communitarian element, based in the Lawnmarket, whose links were with French sociology and the American summer schools.

These tended over time to converge. A judge for Geddes's Dublin Plan competition was the town planner John Nolen of Boston, pioneer of urban renewal. And influence didn't simply come from North America. Aneurin Bevan's guru, the quasi-existentialist Uruguayan philosopher José Rodo, was one of several voices from South America, when observers counted it as a rival to the USA which seemed likely even to overtake it. The Welsh were fascinated by their colony in the Chubut Valley in Argentina, settled in 1867; the Scottish socialist Roland Muirhead was converted to small

---

[61] This was standard in British Africa south of Egypt, the Malay Peninsula, Japan, New Zealand, and Western Australia and Queensland. To coordinate operations on the Canadian Pacific Railway Fleming introduced the modern system of time zones.

[62] Kenneth O. Morgan, *Keir Hardie: Radical and Socialist* (London: Weidenfeld and Nicolson, 1975), 56.

[63] Lord and Lady Aberdeen, '*We Twa*' (London: Collins, 1925), ii, 188–90.

nationalism by observing Brazilian federalism. Bryce, during his ambassadorial stint in Washington, travelled widely on the Continent and wrote optimistically about it in 1913, though in a pessimistic way the unifying symbolism of two of the three continents could have been provided by the influence of a radical Scots aristo on a conservative Polish sea captain. Sulaco, the city of the plain erected on the exploitation of mineral wealth in Conrad's *Nostromo*, stemmed from his and Muirhead's friend 'Don Roberto' Cunninghame-Graham. Graham Greene and Raymond Chandler ensured that Sulaco was not the last monstrous urbanism.[64]

## VII  CIVIC EMPIRES

One doesn't have to look too closely at Glasgow's George Square, Belfast Town Hall, Liverpool's 'Three Graces', or Cathays Park in Cardiff to realize that, engraved on that pale, florid baroque, were the words 'Britain' and 'Empire'. (Protestant Ulster, still referring to Westminster as the Imperial Parliament, was its last redoubt, attracting the otherwise desponding Brummagen proconsul, Enoch Powell.) Collectively, Glasgow, Belfast, and Cardiff added up to, in Patrick Geddes's term, the 'neotechnic city'. A city of rapid growth, both of immigration and emigration, of worldwide markets but still sustaining a local elite; bound together by, and producing, the technology of the second, transport-based stage of industrialization; advanced in culture, art, and intellectual life. 'Imperial South Wales', Geddes's 'Walestown', had its finest hour after 1905 when it humbled the New Zealand All Blacks, who had beaten the motherland's other nations at rugby. This euphoria was short-lived: the depression of 1907–10 fuelled militancy, only temporarily checked by the record-breaking coal production of 1913–14. By then the miners, along with the railwaymen and the dockers, were preparing their own 'Triple Alliance' against their employers, a challenge that went to the roots of industrial society.

There were differences. In Scotland the bias towards imperial aggression and emigration was far more pronounced than Wales. A characteristic mass organization was the Boys' Brigade, carrying on the Covenanting—or for that matter the Orange—tradition of shooting straight in the Calvinist cause, yet also bound up, through its Moody and Sankey origins, with ecumenicism and tolerance. Most families could count up to a fifth who cleared off to North America, Australia, and New Zealand. Uniquely in Europe, Scotland combined industrialization *and* emigration, and in Ulster intellectual emigration—from Kelvin and Bryce to C. S. Lewis and Tyrone Guthrie—may have been a way by which successive generations of an intellectual elite distanced themselves from a stifling Unionist populism. The frontier idea—particularly popular after Frederick Jackson Turner's famous essay of 1896—provides one way of analysing Scots and Scots-Irish identity. Yet it was ambiguous. It indicated democracy and ingenuity: in America the Paxton boys overthrowing Hanoverian rule; Emerson's inventor of new mousetraps watching the

---

[64] Dai Smith, 'The Culture of Aneurin Bevan', in *Aneurin Bevan and the Culture of South Wales* (Cardiff: University of Wales Press, 1993).

world beating a path to his door; the real Robert Fulton devising canal lifts, submarines, and steamboats, or the environmentalist John Muir gaining early fame in Wisconsin with his Heath Robinson waking-up machine. But it also contained a military, colonizing idea, well established since plantation or Covenanting times. Welsh militarism would be a Lloyd George production; Welsh emigration, in its full flood, was a function of the rapid withering of the economy in the 1920s.[65]

Dynamism couldn't of course conceal inconsistencies. Bristol was based on slavery and tobacco and after a brief stab at mastering the steam age—the Great Western Railway in the 1830s and Brunel's iron, screw-driven *Great Britain* in 1842—went into the shadows and was overtaken by the South Wales ports. These concentrated on narrow specialities—coal, timber, tinplate—with underdeveloped manufacturing and a petty bourgeoisie rather than a skilled working class, at the other end episodically present sailors and casual dockers, and the formidable environmental pest of black dust clouds billowing from the coal chutes. Liverpool was likewise overspecialized in cotton, and with even less industry suffered after 1900 greater competition from Manchester and Southampton. Belfast and Glasgow, on other sides of their inland sea, had markedly different records in managing ethnic coexistence.

The Scottish precedent seems dominant, given the relative advance of urbanism, the sophistication of its social overhead capital, and the persistent lack of Scots interest in the conventional European brand of nationalist politics.[66] Yet how resilient was the Scots sense of *urban* identity? The Atlantic city paradigm ought to detach the city from its hinterland, yet the influence on the Scottish city of the countryside persisted. In part this may have been because the sea and estuaries restricted all four coastal cities' hinterlands to two-thirds, even a half, of an inland city's. No British city replicated the estuarial complexity of New York, which soon needed ferries, underground railways, and massive bridges (often supplied from Britain); but Liverpool and Glasgow had developed such utilities by the 1890s, in their steam undergrounds, Glasgow's cable-worked tube (third in Europe after London and Budapest), and the electric Liverpool Overhead, the American-style 'El' that served the docks. Although some of the Victorian and post-Victorian Scots elite thought of the city as sophisticated, and the country as naive, others—probably more—believed that the countryside produced a more stable society.[67]

---

[65] Frederick Jackson Turner, *The Frontier in American History*, 1893 (New York: Holt, 1962); John Muir, *My Boyhood and Youth*, 1913 (Edinburgh: Canongate, 1987), chaps. 7 and 8; J. T. Flexner, *Steamboats Come True: American Inventors in Action*, 1944 (New York: Fordham University Press, 1992), chaps. 9–12.

[66] Sarah Palmer, 'Ports', in Martin Daunton, ed., *The Cambridge Urban History of Britain*, iii: *1840–1950* (Cambridge: Cambridge University Press, 2000).

[67] See R. J. Morris, 'Urbanisation and Scotland', in W. H. Fraser and R. J. Morris, eds., *People and Society in Scotland*, ii: *1830–1914* (Edinburgh: John Donald, 1990); and Andrew MacPherson, 'An Angle on the *Geist*', in Walter Humes and Hamish Paterson, eds., *Scottish Culture and Scottish Education, 1800–1980* (Edinburgh: John Donald, 1983). More prestigious 'social overhead capital investment' went rural, even in the mid twentieth century, with the North of Scotland Hydro-Electric Board (1943) or the Highlands and Islands Development Board (1965). Of the institutions of socialization, the educational system resulted in the values of rural, or at least small-town Scotland, being imposed on the city.

This was influenced both by the dynamic of urbanization and by the later intervention of economic and political factors. The British pattern was for the working class to move into towns from the surrounding countryside. Less so in Scotland, where the rural working class was notoriously mobile and where, of the population of Lanarkshire (530,073) in 1851, practically one-fifth (89,330) were from Ireland. Much the same thing could be said of Liverpool, and Cardiff was overwhelmingly a 'long-distance' immigrant town. The result was the almost existential politics of controlling a workforce whose conditions frequently resembled those aboard ship: low and precarious standards of life countered by repression, and working-class loyalties which lay outside as well as within the city. How much do we know about the cash sent home by immigrant groups, and the effect that this had on their ambitions, as well as on their purchasing patterns? Oral accounts of Irish migrants and recent studies of *Gastarbeiter* in Germany suggest low expenditure on consumer goods, and that rather than becoming more integrated, the first generation of immigrant workers became less so, as their work relationships lapsed on retirement.[68] They consequently tended to preserve conservative values *after* they had been abandoned in the homeland.

They were not moving from 'stable' rural to 'unstable' urban environments. The Irish and to a lesser extent the Scottish famines of the 1840s were extreme versions of what other rural societies with a fast-expanding population had to endure before the import of mass foodstuffs became possible. A survivor mentality rapidly transferred itself from rural to urban life. The Glasgow working class, especially its less-well-off and most-recently-arrived section, often moved by 'moonlit flit' from tenancy to tenancy and from Glasgow to Belfast and further afield—one advantage of the small size of flats, and furniture limited to mattresses, boxes, and chairs.[69] Big-city community, in this and other ways, was different from the small or medium-sized town.[70] The working class saw it as a menu of possibilities; it was their social superiors who tried to dignify it into a 'civic community' while themselves hankering after the stability of the country and the market town.

The shift of settlement and architectural effort from the city block to the suburban villa was one aspect of this, noisily condemned by Tristram Hunt. But on the littoral the suburb wasn't a betrayal of civics but (given the interruption of the urban space by water and transport) one of the only ways the city could expand.[71] This was strongly encouraged by steamer and railway companies and by the theory of such foreign commentators as the German architect Herman Muthesius. In fact, for the

---

[68] Friederike Hohloch, 'Growing Old in a Strange Land', paper delivered at Freudenstadt conference, 25 June 1994, repr. in Eberhard Bort and Neil Evans, eds., *Networking Europe* (Liverpool: Liverpool University Press, 1999).

[69] David Englander, *Landlord and Tenant in Victorian Britain, 1838–1918* (Oxford: Clarendon Press, 1980), chap. 10.

[70] See Christopher Harvie and Graham Walker, 'Community and Culture', in Fraser and Morris, eds., *People and Society in Scotland*, 344.

[71] Tristram Hunt, *Building Jerusalem* (London: Weidenfeld and Nicolson, 2003).

well-doing, there was no great difference between suburb, holiday resort and second home, and modern-minded architects strove to provide comfortable accommodation which should suit any of these contexts. Charles Rennie Mackintosh, with his villas at Kilmacolm and Helensburgh, is the most famous today but his Scots contemporaries George Walton and M. H. Baillie Scott had more extensive practices serving the west coast. Baillie Scott, who was based on the Isle of Man, best conveyed the message that 'real' organic life could be achieved in the family house set in its garden. Was this, especially when relayed by the likes of Muthesius, implicitly an anti-urban message? Was Ramsay Garden in Edinburgh, Patrick Geddes's attempt to design a residential block which should, as in old Edinburgh, bring the classes together, the end of a tradition, not its renewal?[72] Even his disciples—such as Edgar Chappell in Wales—went for the English 'garden city' approach.

Within the Glasgow conurbation some groups consciously resisted the 'melting pot'. The Irish developed a dense social network based on church, pub, Parkhead Stadium, and Irish nationalist politics, which lasted until World War I, when enfranchisement, the Irish Free State, and the rise of the Labour party forced a realignment.[73] Paradoxically, the essentially Saxon idea of the peasant proprietor claimed their remittances, while they excelled in the urban game of soccer. Rural loyalties were also sustained by many associations and bodies catering for Scottish incomers, such as the Highland Society of Glasgow (1727) disbursing £775 per annum in the 1880s, mainly in subsidizing apprenticeships and running its own school. Unlike the Irish bodies, however, these operated more as means of integration and sentimental nostalgia, although there was a degree of politicization during the 1880s, in the cause of Highland land reform.[74]

Immigrants often came from environments which, though rural, were industrial, in coal, in fishing, and on the railways. This meant that a 'total' urban experience was improbable. The cities, though populous, were physically small, often subdivided into urban villages, and rendered yet more pluralist by immigrant groups. For workers, public transport *to work* became affordable in the 1900s only through municipalized halfpenny trams, but the countryside was usually only a few hundred yards away. The urban–rural division was complex not simple, and became more so in time of crisis. The slump of 1906–8 was not just a foretaste: elements of the economy, notably building, remained unstable thereafter. Edwin Muir in his autobiography *The Story and the Fable* (1940) recorded his move in 1901 from edenic Orkney to sulphurous Glasgow as a personal psychological crisis, and the experience of the economic depression scarred his teenage years. Muir, significantly, was one of those who along

---

[72] Herman Muthesius, *Das englische Haus*, 3 vols., 1908–11 (London: BSP Professional Books, 1987).

[73] See Tom Gallagher, *Glasgow: The Uneasy Peace* (Manchester: Manchester University Press, 1987), chaps. 1 and 2.

[74] *Old Statistical Account* (Edinburgh: William Creech, 1791–9), vii, 321; *New Statistical Account* (Edinburgh: Blackwood, 1840), vi, 186; and see Olive Checkland, *Philanthropy in Victorian Scotland* (Edinburgh: John Donald, 1980), 25.

with Saunders Lewis made a hero of James Connolly, a socialist the roots of whose nationalism were firmly rural.

Do not, however, underestimate the power of 'civic' nationalism. Patrick Geddes, who visited Dublin in 1913 to advise the Viceroy, the Earl of Aberdeen, believed that his plan for Dublin, if adopted, would have obviated the Easter Rising of 1916.[75] The civic had always been, even in the Scottish enlightenment, placed in a rural context, and Geddes reviewed this in his 'valley section'—in which the great river balanced the neotechnic city as regional integrator—an ideology which became manifesto in his *Cities in Evolution* of 1915. Both he and the 'civic' Yeats, who sympathized with the Dublin strikers in 1913, saw the key to the Dublin strike as the resolution of the near-Neapolitan conditions of Dublin's housing; but that if this were overcome, Dublin could become the 'geotechnic' City.[76] Similar efforts were being made by Daniel Leufer Thomas, Edgar Chappell, and others in South Wales with the Housing and Town Planning Association. Would this demand intervention at a state or a regional level? And if by the state, then whose state?

Yeats's civics were part of the phase, centred on his visit to Italy with Lady Gregory in 1908, in which he moved from republicanism to the civic humanism of the Italian Renaissance. Such a frame of mind brought forth a poem like 'The People', in which the balance is struck between the life of high culture and the obligation to political morality:

> . . . I might have lived
> And you well know how great the longing has been,
> Where every day my footfall should have lit
> In the green shadow of Ferrara wall;
> Or climbed among the images of the past—
> The unperturbed and courtly images—
> Evening and morning, the steep street of Urbino
> To where the duchess and her people talked
> The stately midnight through until they stood
> In their great window looking at the dawn.

This is Yeats as the reborn Castiglione, fighting Dublin's philistine councillors for the high, cosmopolitan art of Sir Hugh Lane's collection—and happy to have the support of the trade unions. In this context the 'terrible beauty' of Easter 1916 *is* a relapse: the material inertness of dead idealists troubling the water of the 'living' stream. In his indictment of intellectual nationalism, Maurice Goldring cites the reactionary more than the civic Yeats, to make his point. Yet Yeats himself conceded. Against the reproach (presumably from Maude Gonne): 'Never have I, now or any time, Complained of the people', came his ultimate capitulation:

---

[75] Philip Mairet, *Pioneer of Sociology: The Life and Letters of Patrick Geddes* (London: Lund Humphries, 1957).

[76] See Helen Meller, *Patrick Geddes: Social Evolutionist and City Planner* (London: Routledge, 1990), chap. 11.

And yet, because my heart leaped at her words,
I was abashed, and now they come to mind,
After nine years, I sink my head abashed.[77]

---

[77] W. B. Yeats, 'The People' (written 1914–15, published 1919), in *Collected Poems* (London: Macmillan, 1934), 169–70; and see Maurice Goldring, *Pleasant the Scholar's Life: Irish Intellectuals and the Construction of the Nation State* (London: Serif, 1993), chap. 4, and Roy Foster, *W. B. Yeats: A Life*, i: *The Apprentice Mage* (Oxford: Oxford University Press, 1997), 367–9.

# 3

# MacAndrew: The Engineer
# and the Celtic Fringe

...A scheme for the development of Irish tourist traffic in and around Dublin by means of petrol-propelled riverboats, plying in the fluvial fairway between Islandbridge and Ringsend, charabancs, narrow gauge railways, and pleasure steamers for coastwise navigation (10/- per person per day, guide (trilingual) included). A scheme to connect by tramline the Cattle Market (North Circular Road and Prussia Street) with the quays...

James Joyce, *Ulysses*, 1922[1]

## I 'THE FORGING OF THE ANCHOR'

Leopold Bloom was doing what the Irishman—as much as the Jew—was not supposed to be doing. When Bernard Shaw argued, in *John Bull's Other Island* (1904), that Celts were as good at engineering as the Saxons, if not better at it, he challenged an ideology, evolved between the 1840s and the 1870s, which, along with various dubious bits of anthropological lore, claimed technical ability as a racial endowment.[2] 'Celtic Fringe', a phrase invented by Arthur Balfour in 1907, implied something decorative as well as remote, an Anglo-Saxon attitude queried by the biographer of the Scots-Welsh metallurgist Sidney Gilchrist Thomas, when he wrote that the painstaking inventor of the 'basic slag' method of making steel from phosphoric ore—a breakthrough which caused a European upheaval by making the German-controlled measures productive—'was mainly of Celtic strain, and furnished yet another example of the often unrecognized addition of fame which that great race has brought to the "English" people'.[3]

Techno-Saxonism persisted in such imperial offerings as Kipling's monologue 'MacAndrew's Hymn' (1893), and in his *Puck of Pook's Hill* (1906), where destructive Picts are set against the Roman imperial order:

> Mistletoe killing an oak—
> Rats gnawing cables in two—

---

[1] (London: John Lane, 1947), 679.
[2] For the anthropological argument see L. P. Curtis Jnr, *Anglo-Saxons and Celts* (Bridgeport, Conn.: University of Bridgeport Press, 1968).
[3] R. W. Burnie, *Sidney Gilchrist Thomas* (London: John Murray, 1891), 1.

Moths making holes in a cloak—
How they must love what they do!
Yes—and we little folk too,
We are as busy as they—
Working our works out of view—
Watch, and you'll see it some day![4]

Written in the decadence of British manufacturing, Linda Colley's *Britons* (1992) dismissed industry in favour of Protestantism and war as the propellants of Britishness during the 'long eighteenth century' between 1688 and 1837, and also skated over the incorporation into the United Kingdom of five million, mostly Catholic, Irish in 1801. Had Colley prolonged her period of analysis by a decade, her conclusions would have been less firm: there were good Protestant reasons for Scots and Welsh *not* feeling British in the 1840s.[5] Yet thereafter economic success—in northern England, central Scotland, Ulster, and cosmopolitan South Wales—set against the failure of the Scottish Highlands, rural Wales, and most of Ireland, defined a progressive or civic nationality. The central symbol of this was the engineer: not as a member of an elite but as the citizen of a constitutional state who hammered out the links that held it together. Unsurprising, perhaps, that an icon of Irish Unionism should be Samuel Ferguson's poem 'The Forging of the Anchor', published in *Blackwood's Magazine*, the bible of Edinburgh Toryism, in 1832:

Let's forge a goodly anchor—a bower thick and broad;
For a heart of oak is hanging on every blow, I bode;
I see the good ship riding all in a perilous road—
The low reef roaring on her lee—the roll of ocean pour'd
From stem to stern, sea after sea, the mainmast by the board,
The bulwarks down, the rudder gone, the boats stove at the chains!
But courage still, brave mariners—the bower yet remains,
And not an inch to flinch he deigns, save when ye pitch sky high;
Then moves his head, as though he said, 'Fear nothing—here am I.'
Swing in your strokes in order, let foot and hand keep time;
Your blows make music sweeter far than any steeple's chime:
But, while you sling your sledges, sing—and let the burthen be,
The anchor is the anvil-king, and royal craftsmen we![6]

Seven years later, Longfellow's 'The Building of the Ship' repeated the imagery, in the cause of the American union. Yet, just as Ferguson could also be claimed as a Young Irelander, the subsequent history of the concept was problematic. By 1914 the Scots engineer, as well as the Welsh miner, had come to symbolize labour militancy, open to the siren voices of syndicalism, conveyed along the steamer routes of the Atlantic

---

[4] Rudyard Kipling, 'MacAndrew's Hymn', *Scribner's Magazine* (1893), and 'A Pict Song' from *Puck of Pook's Hill* (London: Macmillan, 1906), in *The Works of Rudyard Kipling* (Ware: Wordsworth, 1994).

[5] Linda Colley, *Britons: Forging the Nation, 1707–1837* (New Haven and London: Yale University Press, 1992); see my review in *Welsh History Review*, 18/4 (December 1997).

[6] Repr. in Samuel Ferguson, *Lays of the Western Gael* (London: Bell & Daldy, 1865).

from Europe and the USA, and also audible to the dockers of Belfast and Dublin. After the Easter Rising of 1916 a blend of industrial *and* nationalist militancy filtered into the Scots and Welsh radical movements. Plaid Cymru's founder Saunders Lewis took the Rising as a symbol of national rebirth; the Communist Welsh miners' leader Arthur Horner had been a soldier in James Connolly's Citizen Army. In Scotland John MacLean, the pedagogue of engineer militancy on the Red Clyde, ended his career as the ally of the Gaelic nationalist Ruaridh Erskine of Mar as well as Lenin, and this bequest was fashioned into an anti-imperial ideology by later Scots communists-cum-nationalists such as Hugh MacDiarmid and Hamish Henderson. In the 1900s that very practical mystic George Russell, 'AE', had set his vision of a technologized New Ireland in competition with the Gaelic revival:

> We would no Irish sign efface,
> But yet our lips would gladlier hail
> The firstborn of the Coming Race
> Than the last splendour of the Gael.
> No blazoned banner we unfold—
> One charge alone we give to youth,
> Against the sceptred myth to hold
> The golden heresy of truth.[7]

In 1916 he was writing:

> Here's to you, Pearse, your dream not mine,
> But yet the thought—for this you fell—
> Turns all life's water into wine.[8]

This episode has contemporary bite, though in an oddly reversed form. 'Celtic Tiger' Ireland and its post-1986 leap into new technology—chiefly pharmaceuticals and software—fulfilled much of Bloom's dreaming, and provoked hopeful if less convincing parallels in Scotland and Wales, where nationalist ideals increasingly powered the political agenda. This accompanied, however, the decline of science and manufacturing in a Kingdom becoming less and less United, while problems incidental to the mechanization of society seem common to both parts of the archipelago.[9] On one side the threat of mechanism—and implicitly the link between Welsh nationalism and greenish philosophy—was stated in one of R. S. Thomas's best-known poems:

> Yes, you should see Cynddylan on his tractor.
> Gone the old roots which held him to the soil.

---

[7] AE, 'On Behalf of Some Irishmen Not Followers of Tradition' (1913?), repr. in Brendan Kenelly, ed., *The Penguin Book of Irish Verse* (Harmondsworth: Penguin, 1970). And see Ruth Fleischmann, 'George Russell (AE): Practical Poet', in *Anglistentag Proceedings*, 16 (Tübingen: Niemeyer, 1995).

[8] Quoted in Ulick O'Connor, *The Troubles: The Struggle for Irish Freedom, 1912–22*, 1975 (London: Mandarin, 1989), 99.

[9] Ireland's gross domestic product was 57 per cent of the UK's in 1976, and equal to it in 1997, though because of repatriated profits its gross national product was less. I owe this information to Prof. J. J. Lee of University College, Cork.

He's a new man now, the lord of the machine,
His nerves of iron, and his blood of oil.[10]

On the other side was the fate of those displaced by technical and economic change: the 20,000 who had in the 1950s worked for Harland and Wolff at Queen's Island, Belfast, had dwindled to under 200 in 2002.

## II  THE USES OF RHETORIC

For Samuel Smiles the excursion trains crossing Robert Stephenson's new Royal Border Bridge at Berwick in 1851, en route to the Crystal Palace, marked the fulfilment of the Union of 1707. His *Lives of the Engineers* (1862) celebrated machines and men:

There is indeed a peculiar fascination about an engine to the person whose duty is to watch and feed it. It is almost sublime in its untiring industry and quiet power; capable of performing the most gigantic work, yet so docile that a child's hand may guide it . . . And it is a remarkable fact, that nearly all that has been done for the improvement of this machine has been accomplished, not by philosophers and scientific men, but by labourers, mechanics and enginemen.

. . . They belonged to the ancient and honourable family of Workers—that extensive family which constitutes the backbone of our country's greatness, the common working people of England.[11]

Smiles, Haddington-born doctor, Unitarian, Chartist sympathizer, railway company secretary, and the first systematic historian of the Industrial Revolution, provided a rhetoric binding together technology, history, economics, and culture. As author of *Self-Help* (1859) he was as adept as Adam Smith at fashioning one of W. B. Yeats's 'monstrous familiar images', a usage which, combining the weird and the commonplace, somehow invokes Smith's pin factory in *The Wealth of Nations* (1776). Was this a real factory, or a powerful metaphor? Getting the rhetoric right—and Smith lectured in the subject at Edinburgh, 1748–51—was an essential part of economic politics, ensuring that concepts convenient to the entrepreneurial elite were brought into play and awkward ones were ditched.[12]

Celts were thin on Smiles's ground; and thinner in H. T. Buckle's positivistic *History of Civilization in England* (1861), where the lowland Scots took centre stage and the Irish were doomed to inertia by cheap potatoes. Matthew Arnold's 1867 notion of an emotional, empathic, but unscientific Celt was a long time in dying, for all Patrick Geddes's commendations of 'geotechnic Dublin' in 1913, in which industry

[10] 'Cynddylan on a Tractor', *c*.1947, in R. S. Thomas, *Collected Poems 1945–1990* (London: Phoenix Giant, 1993).

[11] Samuel Smiles, *Lives of the Engineers* (London: John Murray, 1862), iii, 14, and i, 389. For Smiles's career see Asa Briggs, *Victorian People* (Harmondsworth: Penguin, 1955). For the professional background see R. Angus Buchanan, *The Engineers: A History of the Engineering Profession in Britain, 1750–1914* (London: Jessica Kingsley, 1989).

[12] Adam Smith, *The Wealth of Nations* (Harmondsworth: Penguin, 1982), 109–10. W. B. Yeats, 'Meditations in Time of Civil War', in *Collected Poems* (London: Macmillan, 1934), sect. vii, p. 231.

and environment could complement one another.[13] Perhaps the unending fascination of *Ulysses* (1922) stemmed from a recognition of the multitudinous nature of the city by a writer who was poet, playwright, anthropologist, social historian, would-be technocrat—and also owned a cinema. This, however, reminds us that Geddes's 'palaeotechnic' epoch of steam power had been marked by an Irish technical ingenuity which would have been notable in a *thriving* economy.[14] Robert Fulton wasn't the only Irish submarine pioneer. The Fenian John Philip Holland's craft of 1892 was the first successfully to combine internal-combustion power while on the surface, charging up batteries to operate electric motors while submerged.[15] The Admiralty bought him out, only to see its battleships menaced in 1897 by Charles Parsons of Birr with his revolutionary high-speed yacht *Turbinia*. The Irish got the atmospheric railway to work (for a bit, anyway) between Dublin and Kingstown, which was more than Brunel managed. In the 1880s Irish engineers installed the Lartigue monorail from Listowel to Ballybunion. Billed as a transport panacea, carrying goods at a third the cost of a conventional line, it remained unique, but they ran it for forty years, and a more elaborate gyroscope-stabilized version was patented by Thomas Kearney in 1906. They applied early hydroelectric plants in the same decade to power the Portrush and Bessbrook electric railways. The first petrol and then diesel railcars were on the County Donegal railway, along with pioneer radio signalling. Despite the advertised prejudice of the Church against science, the mathematicians Rowan Hamilton and George Boole found nothing to complain about in their students, and a Dubliner, Ernest Walton, was a central member of the team which in Cambridge in 1938 split the atom.[16] No way was this technological tinkering. Dionysius Lardner (1793–1859) was despite a rackety life the first halfway competent railway economist; Charles Bianconi with his horse cars waiting at railway stations provided a 'coordinated transport system' long before the socialists thought about it. Irishmen like William Mulvany (a protégé of the Parsons family) in the Ruhr and Robert Flanagan in California made fortunes from, respectively, mines and railroads, and the greatest of them all, the engineer and contractor William Thomas Dargan, had achievements comparable with those of Locke, Brunel, and the younger Stephenson.[17]

---

[13] H. T. Buckle, *The History of Civilization in England*, 1861 (London: Longman, 1871), iii; Matthew Arnold, *On the Study of Celtic Literature*, 1867 (London: Kennikat Press, 1970).

[14] By this they meant the technological period in which carbon energy was utilized without being fully understood or incorporated into a tolerable ecology.

[15] See article 'Ship', in *Encyclopaedia Britannica*, 11th edn; Roy Johnston, 'Society and Technology in Celtic Nation-Building', in Cathal ó Luain, ed., *For a Celtic Future* (Dublin: Celtic League, 1983); and John de Courcy Ireland, 'John Philip Holland, Pioneer in Submarine Navigation', *North Munster Antiquarian Journal*, 10/2 (1967).

[16] Prof. Philip Williams has stressed the contribution of the Welsh to pure science, and also its unobtrusiveness in accepted accounts of Welsh history, and noted its debt to the Intermediate Education Act of 1887. A case can surely be made out for the Irish record being similarly misread. Was Catholic dogmatism worse than the 'liberal education' of the English public schools, confined exclusively to the classics?

[17] W. Garrett Scaife, *From Galaxies to Turbines: Science, Technology and the Parsons Family* (Bristol and Philadelphia: Institute of Physics, 2000), 64, 100.

In Ireland the potential and indeed the proof of technical progress existed on a scale as lively as that of Scotland or Wales. Trinity College had an important engineering school, feeding Australia, Canada, and the USA, though frustrated by a complex of factors. This bit deep into literature. Charles Lever's talker Joe Atlee in *Lord Kilgobbin* (1872) has an outlook on Irish politics which anticipates technologist Bloom:

'Great Ireland—no first flower of the north or gun of the sea humbug—but Ireland great in prosperity, her harbours full of ships, the woollen trade, her ancient staple, revived: all that vast unused water power, greater than all the steam of Manchester and Birmingham tenfold, at full work; the linen manufacture developed and promoted—'
'And the Union repealed?'
'Of course; that should be first of all. Not that I object to the Union, as many do, on the grounds of English ignorance as to Ireland. My dislike is, that, for the sake of carrying through certain measures necessary to Irish interests, I must sit and discuss questions which have no possible concern for me.'[18]

Atlee was not alone. Parnell's *froideur* dissolved only when discussing rural railways or mineral schemes for his Roundwood estate, and this sort of ideal reappears in a curdled form in Joyce: from the paranoia of 'the Citizen' about done-down Irish genius and the barroom boasts of 'Skin-the-Goat' to Bloom's burgeoning schemes.[19] Engineering, part of the 'endless crazy dreaming' of Shaw's Larry Doyle, was shared, not just by Joyce and AE, but by the young Free State politicians, only months away from civil war, who commissioned west Europe's biggest hydroelectric scheme in 1924.[20]

## III  BREAKTHROUGH

AE was a critic of conventional nationalism, and with reason, given Ireland's record as part of the industrial littoral. The resources of the 'inland sea' were vitalized by the 'palaeotechnic' division of labour: affordable and mobile artisan engineers mechanized production and, with partners, initiated a continuum of profits and investment. 'Clusters' of innovation, demanding and generating expertise, drew in further artisans, sending the likes of William Murdoch from Scotland to Cornwall and London, the Fairbairn brothers and James Nasmyth from Scotland to Lancashire, Richard Trevithick from Cornwall to Wales, the Midlands, the north, London, and South America, Robert Owen from Wales to Manchester, Scotland, London, and North America, and Richard Roberts from Wales to Lancashire. It was their coincidence with the 'maximum profit phase' of cottons and ironmaking that led to the particular success of the Scots, Welsh, and Lancastrians, also visible in the investment shift from slavery to steamers and slate by Liverpool merchants, from cotton to engineering in

---

[18]  Charles Lever, *Lord Kilgobbin*, 1873 (London: Downey, 1899), i, 100–1; Joyce, *Ulysses*, 318 ff.
[19]  James Bryce, 'Charles Stewart Parnell', in *Studies in Contemporary Biography* (London: Macmillan, 1906), 213; Joyce, *Ulysses*, 310, 609, 679 ff.
[20]  See Aftermath.

Manchester and Glasgow, the rise of iron shipbuilding and engine building on the Clyde, and the transition from iron to steel and tinplate in South Wales.

The Scots claimed the first rank in this process, but was Kipling's Chief Engineer MacAndrew a triumph of Scots PR rather than of fact? The Calvinist work ethic gets us only so far. There had been some early interest in invention—at the time of the regnal union of 1603 both the mathematician Napier of Merchiston and the poet Drummond of Hawthornden devoted a lot of time to improving military weaponry—but for decades technology, from guns and clocks to salt-refining equipment and pumps, was bought in. Scotland's first ironworks (1610) and first railway (1722) at Cockenzie were English-owned and operated, and the 'native' Carron Works of 1760, following the Abram Darby pattern of using a blast powered by cheap coke instead of expensive and dwindling wood charcoal, was founded by an English-led partnership which became Scots only when John Roebuck, the English partner, went bust. Dynamism came in part from trade—the provision of return cargoes for tobacco and sugar imports—and from 'proto-industrial enterprises' such as weaving or fishing as an element of rapid agricultural modernization after 1760. This encouraged architecture and civil engineering (along with metal implements, stock breeding, geology, and surveying) to remedy the country's poor roads and treacherous coasts. The Union provided a wider market for such expertise—John Smeaton's Eddystone lighthouse (1756–9), John Rennie's Waterloo Bridge in London (1817). John Loudon MacAdam revolutionized the turnpike trusts from Bath after 1808, and Thomas Telford's canal- and road-building career began in Shropshire in the 1780s. Telford, in fact, made the real breakthrough. A decent man: warm, generous, a would-be poet and dedicated teacher, with a sense of drama in his compositions, he took—with his Conwy, Menai, and Craigellachie bridges, Chirk and Pontcysyllte aqueducts, and the Gota Canal in Sweden—the lead in European transport technology from the French.[21]

The Parliamentary Select Committee on Technical Education in 1865 praised 'the superior primary instruction of the artisans' and foundations like the Watt Institute in Edinburgh or the Andersonian in Glasgow. Medicine, too, was important, as Scotland transformed medical education from sawbones' blood and guts, and the refined quackery of many physicians, into a theoretically sound instruction which extended to such critical areas as public health and educational reform, through Edinburgh-trained activists, while the radical Glasgow professor James Anderson left the town the cash to found a technical and medical university (later the Royal Technical College and now Strathclyde). The educators Andrew Ure and George Birkbeck had a medical background, as had Dr Samuel Smiles and the pioneer Manchester social and later educational reformer Dr James Phillips Kay.[22]

---

[21] Buchanan, *The Engineers*, 34. Telford went only briefly to Sweden, leaving construction to the Swedish army, but the canal resulted in the Motala ironworks, and gave a chance to the brilliant engineer John Ericsson (1803–1889).

[22] See Anand C. Chitnis, *The Scottish Enlightenment: A Social History* (London: Croom Helm, 1976).

William Symington's technically successful paddle tug *Charlotte Dundas* in 1803 and Richard Trevithick's Pen-y-Darren locomotive in 1804 marked the birth of 'palaeotechnology', though Scotland had only twenty-one Watt engines in 1800, and Symington's remarkably advanced horizontal engine was as overambitious a step as Trevithick's for his compatriots. From the 1800s to the 1830s Scots engineering really got its chances in the south. The Fairbairns built stationary steam engines for the expanding cotton mills of Lancashire, and London manufacturing plants. James Nasmyth's steam hammer—essential for forging accurate piston and propeller shafts—was developed at Patricroft in Manchester. David and Alexander Napier, with yards on both the Clyde and the Thames, the Lairds at Birkenhead, and John Scott Russell in London were particularly impressive trainers of marine engineers. Admiral Thomas Cochrane, the Ayrshire sailor of fortune, commissioned the first British steam warship *The Rising Star* in 1821 for a war of liberation in South America, but had it built in London.[23] The breakthroughs in technology transfer came through advances in screw and lathe technology—that absolute accuracy of reproduction which in Marx's view enabled 'machines to make machines'—achieved by such English engineers as Joseph Bramah, Henry Maudsley and Joseph Whitworth, yet even in 1842 Brunel built his *Great Britain* at Bristol, quite remote from any metallurgical centre. In 1850 Scotland still had only 169 steamships out of a fleet of 3,700, 72,000 tons out of a total of over 550,000.[24]

The critical Scots inputs were natural and labour resources rather than technology. 'The whole stock of an engineering or machine establishment might be summed up in a few ill-constructed lathes, and a few drills and boring machines of rude construction' wrote Peter Fairbairn as late as the 1840s.[25] The transformer was the rich 'blackband' coal-and-ironstone of the Monklands, which became important in the 1820s. Several factors impacted together: James Beaumont Neilson of the Glasgow Gasworks devised a way—the hot blast—of smelting the ore; railways were built into the field and Watt's primitive Monkland Canal modernized; an influx of unskilled Irish labour both cheapened the price of coal and enabled a generation of Scots workers to be given new skills at relatively low cost. Foundry masters used Monklands pig to make pure castings, suitable for machining on the new lathes and planing machines and about two-thirds cheaper than anything in the south. The trouble was the lack of a reliable wrought-iron works in Scotland. In the critical decade of the 1850s—the change from wooden to iron hulls: building two-thirds of UK iron tonnage in 1850–1—the Clyde needed the haematite fields of west Cumberland and Cleveland. But profits were high enough to secure the resources to take the river ahead, first in iron screw shipbuilding and then, in the 1860s, in compound marine engines. Locomotives, carriages and waggons, and structural engineering advanced in parallel. In 1858 the young Professor William MacQuorn Rankine of Glasgow

[23] Richard Coston, *Steam at Sea* (Newton Abbot: David and Charles, 1970), 60.
[24] Henry Hamilton, *The Industrial Revolution in Scotland* (Oxford: Clarendon Press, 1932).
[25] Anthony Burton, *The Rise and Fall of British Shipbuilding* (London: Constable, 1994), 86.

University wrote the standard textbook *The Steam Engine*. Only a year ahead of *The Origin of Species*, it was as significant in its milieu, and in the same year the firm of Randolph and Elder of Centre Street Works, Broomielaw, equipped the SS *Propontis* with a compound engine.[26]

Rankine's book was only one part of a remarkable intellectual catching-up on artisan progress—in some ways a parallel to the James Watt–Joseph Black synergy of the 1760s. It foreshadowed the theory of William Thomson, later Lord Kelvin, on thermodynamics, in his commercial laboratory and the 'floating laboratory' of his yacht, and James Clerk Maxwell on energy and electromagnetism in the 1860s, which both reinforced technical advance and incorporated it into theory, a late flowering of the Scottish enlightenment, linked to the contemporary philosophic work of such as J. F. Ferrier on epistemology. 'Work', indeed, changed from a Carlyleian exhortation to a calibration of physical energy. The cultural consequences were more ambiguous: materially, because secularized Oxford and Cambridge were expanding science—along with South Kensington—by the early 1870s, and intellectually because thermodynamics, in Clerk Maxwell's schema, linked work and life itself to energy, but also posited the issue: what happened when energy declined? Towards the condition of entropy, cooling, ultimately death. Perhaps more vividly even than Darwin, this cast its shadow on the Scottish intellect at the mid century.[27]

The crucial decade was the 1860s, when Britain's main maritime competitor, the USA, was beset with the Civil War (aggravated by British yards supplying the Confederacy with blockade-runners and commerce-raiders), and the central fact was the marine steam engine. In the 1840s still low-pressure and huge, it used salt water in the absence of reliable condensers; over long distances steamers could pay their way only with high-value, high-subsidy, business like prestige passengers and mail. Even so, for Charles Dickens crossing the pond on the Cunarder *Britannia* in 1842 was a purgatory of cramped 'staterooms' and bad food. In fact, the real revolution in ship construction had not been steam, but the redesign of the hull and rigging of the sailing ship to transform it from the slow bluff-bowed 400-ton merchantman to the ten-knot 1,500-ton clipper. The testing of hull shapes in tanks marks this period, and their 'composite' construction (using metal frames and wood planking, as with the Dumbarton-built *Cutty Sark* of 1869); and not least the use of steam tugs to get these comparatively huge ships in and out of port (a tow, searching for suitable winds, could last several hundred miles). These made high-speed, long-distance runs possible.[28]

The thoroughbreds in the tea and wool trades flagged up the Scottish yards, though the mass of tonnage still consisted of cheap 'softwood clippers' built in the Canadian

[26] See John R. Hume and Michael Moss, *Workshop of the British Empire* (London: Heinemann, 1977); John Butt, 'Manufacturing', in Irene Maver and Hamish Fraser, eds., *Glasgow, 1833–1912* (Manchester: Manchester University Press, 1999); John Thomas, *The Springburn Story* (Newton Abbot: David and Charles, 1974), chap. 1.

[27] See Christopher Harvie, 'Timberlands', in *Travelling Scot* (Colintraive: Argyll, 1999), and *The Lights of Liberalism: University Liberals and the Challenge of Democracy, 1860–86* (London: Allen Lane, 1976), chap. 4, 'The Tests Agitation'; and Michael Sanderson, ed., *The Universities in the Nineteenth Century* (London: Routledge, 1975), chap. 6.

[28] Anthony Slaven, 'Scottish Shipbuilders and Marine Engineers: The Evidence of Business Biography 1860–1960', in T. C. Smout, ed., *Scotland and the Sea* (Edinburgh: John Donald, 1992).

Maritimes and the north-east USA. These even prompted a westward migration of Scots and Welsh shipwrights. But then the work of Rankine, Randolph, Elder, and Thomson came into play. Provided the water supply was pure, 'compounding' allowed high-pressure steam (of around 150 pounds per square inch) to be used in a small cylinder, and then reused in one or more larger, lower-pressure ones (triple- or quadruple-expansion). Thomson's work on surface condensers assured the recycling of pure water, minus the salts which had wrecked earlier experiments. The size of the engine, which in Brunel's *Great Eastern* (1859) had along with its bunkers filled about a quarter of the hull, fell to about a tenth. In 1867 the firm of Scott of Greenock built, for the Holt Line of Liverpool, the freighters *Agamemnon*, *Ajax*, and *Achilles*, which could, on one bunkering of coal, sail 8,500 miles. The 'Blue Funnelers' were still rigged as three-masters, since coal supplies couldn't be guaranteed, but within fifteen years sails and rigging had disappeared from new vessels. The age of the tramp steamer had begun.[29]

Its conquest wasn't immediate: taking over two decades, as modern sailing ships, snapped up by other countries, notably the Norwegians, provided low-cost competition—but by 1900 it was complete. Britain had about half of world tonnage, of which 60 per cent consisted of tramps. Hardly a steamer flew the flag of any South American state, instead up to 60 per cent of the ships loading or unloading at Buenos Aires in 1913 were British.[30] Trade was driven by coal exports to rapidly industrializing port cities (Singapore, for example, had 220,000 tons for bunkering in 1888), expanding railway networks, and profitable return cargoes: grain from the Americas and the Black Sea, cotton from New Orleans, timber (for pit-props and railway sleepers) from the St Lawrence or the Baltic. Certain facilities had first to be in place: modern non-tidal docks, coaling stations, telegraph links. Another sub-proletariat emerged to crew the steamers—Lascars from India and Afro-Americans from the Caribbean.[31]

The tramp-steamer age foregrounded Wales, and not just the huge southern coalfield. The building of the Cambrian Railway by David Davies into the mountainous central district came later than the Irish system, in the 1860s and 1870s, but had a similar effect, making possible the transfer of labour to the growing coalfield, something that accelerated with the onset of agricultural depression. John Williams has written that Wales resembled South America rather than west Europe: 'the really striking feature of the nineteenth century Welsh economy was the extent to which it was dominated by primary production—agriculture, coal, lead, slate.' Manufacture

---

[29] Scotts of Greenock, *Two Centuries of Shipbuilding* (London: Engineering, 1920), 38–42, and see L. T. C. Rolt, *Victorian Engineering* (London: Allen Lane, 1970). The 3,500-ton P & O liner *Thames* in 1888 burned fifty tons a day on its eight-week trip from London to Singapore, coaling at Brindisi, Aden, and Bombay. Of its 150 crew 50 deck officers and leading seamen were British, 20 stewards were Goanese Christians, and the rest Lascars and Chinese. See Hywel Gwyn Evans, *Sons of the Rock* (Swansea: Maesgwyn, 1996).

[30] Robert Greenhill, 'Shipping, 1850–1914', in D. C. M. Platt, ed., *Business Imperialism, 1840–1930* (Oxford: Clarendon Press, 1977), 119.

[31] Simon P. Ville, *Transport and the Development of the European Economy, 1750–1918* (London: Macmillan, 1990), chap. 4, 'The Shipping Industry'.

was 'virtually unchanged' at 23 per cent of the labour force in 1871 and 1911.[32] It was also largely limited to the steel and tinplate trades, while the rapid settlement of the mining valleys didn't overlay pre-industrial modes of life: the language and religious loyalties survived, while the public face of 'imperial South Wales' supplying coal to the world was effectively an integrated and loyal one. In the test of World War I, which broke the Anglo-Irish union, the Welsh would be almost fanatical patriots.

A second spasm of innovation and enterprise united Manchester and North Wales in the 1860s. Both areas had developed general engineering to service cotton and slate. The latter had grown relentlessly with the cities, and the export boom which Hamburg's great fire of 1842 had started. In its wake came artisan engineers devising hoists, ropeways, drills, splitting and sawing machines. Manchester's situation was then put in hazard by the cotton blockade of 1862, which cut demand for textile equipment and forced a diversification of investment. Some of it went into Wales. John Bright put money into Ceredigion lead mines; the MacConnells bought Bryn Eglwys quarry near Tywyn; the Hollands invested in slate in Blaenau Festiniog. One of the fruits of this would be the modernization of the 2-foot (600 mm) Festiniog Railway in 1863 and the deployment of the first narrow-gauge steam engines. This coincided with a more general rail crisis. Up to that date, most railways had been standard gauge or broad gauge (4 ft $8\frac{1}{2}$ in. or 1,435 mm), expensive to construct and unsuited to the mountainous territory encountered in Scandinavia or South America. Then in the late 1850s the Norwegians settled on a gauge of 3 ft 6 in. (1,067 mm) for a line from Trondheim to Christiania, and the German-born Carl Beyer of Beyer Peacock, Manchester, who was designing light bogie locomotives for the sharp curves of London's Metropolitan Railway, introduced a similar machine for the narrower gauge. Demonstrated both in Norway and on the Isle of Man system, built after 1872, this influenced other engineers and entrepreneurs, notably the landowner and coalmaster the Duke of Sutherland, who was contemplating projects which could be linked up by steamship and telegraph. The first line in Ecuador opened on the 3 ft 6 in. gauge in 1861. Then in 1869 the Festiniog Railway unveiled the first narrow-gauge articulated locomotive, designed by the Scots engineer Robert Fairlie. By distributing weight over four axles a high tractive effort could be accommodated on a narrow track, and the same principle went for bogie carriages and freight trucks.[33]

The result was a cheap, flexible transport system which could itself be transported in a few shipments. It coincided with the introduction (from the USA: the first British line was in Birkenhead, 1861) of the street railway, or tramcar, and after the adoption of steel rail in the later 1860s, the narrow gauge became used for mineral, agricultural, military, and contractors' lines, which gave British railway builders and civil engineering firms a boost similar to that given by the compound marine engine.[34]

[32] John Williams, 'Was Wales Industrialised?', in *Essays in Modern Welsh History* (Llandysul: Gomer, 1995), 21, 19.
[33] Akira Saito, 'Why did Japan Choose the 3′6″ Narrow Gauge?', *Japan Railway and Transport Review*, 31 (1999).
[34] Tramway expansion was slow until an act of 1871 set up Tramway Commissioners. Thereafter most large towns acquired horse (and occasionally steam) trams of standard or 3 ft 6 in. gauge,

The creation of 1,000 mm and 1,067 mm systems in Japan, New Zealand, Queensland, Western Australia, and Africa south of the Sahara, and of a secondary 1,000 mm Indian system, followed with great rapidity in the 1870s and 1880s. Most of Cecil Rhodes's 'Cape to Cairo' would be built to the 'medium gauge'.[35]

The timing of Welsh expansion further disadvantaged Ireland, which lacked its own merchant marine and was crippled by the famine of the 1840s. In the 1850s the Lagan Valley developed rapidly, building up an iron shipbuilding industry supplied from the Clyde and Cumberland, and financed from Liverpool and Glasgow. The rest of the island exported cheap labour, lowering the cost of British artisans while enabling them to be trained to new technologies. As elsewhere in Europe, 'catching up' was accompanied by 'breaking down', with successful regions inflicting social damage on less advanced neighbours, and abstracting from these the low-skill, low-wage labour they needed. Demoralization—the mass alcoholism of much of the Carpathian area, pogroms in Russia, institutionalized criminality in southern Italy—was merely the obverse of the recruitment of low-status immigrant groups to the Ruhr, the Borinage, Lombardy, and, above all, Britain.[36]

Ireland's fightback was more calculated than the 'Railway Mania' which saved Britain from the doom gleefully predicted by Marx and Engels. There were fewer miles of railway in Ireland in 1845 than in Britain in 1825, but following an 1839 report by Thomas Drummond, 1,000 miles were built between then and 1855, 600 of them by William Dargan, a man badly in need of a biographer, who created, besides, the harbour of Belfast (Queen's Island was originally Dargan's Island), and the Dublin Exhibition of 1853. He was brought down by the slump of 1866, and the failure of his attempt to revive Irish textiles: he died only a year later, a disaster of more than personal significance.[37] His statue stands outside Dublin's National Gallery, which he endowed. Its other bronze benefactor, Bernard Shaw, would have saluted him. Dargan had given Ireland, in terms of social-overhead capital, the densest railway network in Europe proportionate to population, and without any military motive. Yet despite this, and the large markets of Dublin and Belfast, the manufacturing take-off came only in the north-east.

This was partly because railways—a 'flutter' always appealing to the aristos' gambling instincts—did little for the masses until the 1870s, when competition among English companies and government intervention combined to 'democratize' their clientele. Who in 1850 could afford 13s. 9d. (70p, €1) for a third-class single from Cork to Dublin (ten hours in an unheated wooden box)? Certainly a lot fewer than could cross by 5s. steerage from Dublin to Liverpool in the same time.[38]

which were electrified and expanded after the mid 1890s. The municipal system in Glasgow had worldwide influence in the 1900s. See Bernard Aspinwall, *Portable Utopia: Glasgow and the United States* (Aberdeen: Aberdeen University Press, 1983).

[35] For the spread of the system in the imperial period see A. C. O'Dell and P. S. Richards, *Railways and Geography* (London: Hutchinson, 1956), 96 ff.

[36] W. L. Langer, *Political and Social Upheaval* (New York: Harper, 1969), 10 ff.

[37] See the obituary of William Thomas Dargan (1799–1867) in *The Times* (8 Feb. 1867), and the entry in the *DNB*; another Telford pupil was the Highland Railway's engineer Joseph Mitchell.

[38] *Bradshaw's Railway Guide* (1 Mar. 1850).

Railway tickets were markedly cheaper in Scotland, where skilled workers regularly travelled by rail to install and maintain machinery, helping spread technology after the 1850s.[39] But the railway could also annihilate local handcraft industry, and as the fivefold increase of Irish rail freight between 1850 and 1870 was mostly imports, it proceeded to do so.[40] By exaggerating Ricardo's law of product specialization the railway encouraged pastoral agriculture and a few associated trades. It conveyed emigrant labour which remitted cash home, and kept a Catholic agrarian-clerical elite in power. So even if Irish capitalism had managed to stabilize itself by the 1870s—had the likes of Dargan not foundered—it would still have found manufacturing in the southern counties disadvantaged.

This was further aggravated by the international implications of improved transport—cheap foodstuffs from North America and east Europe—which undermined agricultural incomes. John Stuart Mill's remark in 1866 that Ireland's peasantry kept her in the mainstream of European social evolution would become only too true after his death in 1873.[41] The 'machinery' of politics in the Catholic south was more susceptible to the Europe-wide move towards a defensive nationalism, headed by an intelligentsia of the clerico-ethnic sort.[42] Confronted with this, Joe Atlee's or Leopold Bloom's progressivism was likely to become self-parodic.

The railway had another conservative impact. The first major locomotive-building factories had been in commercial towns, mainly Newcastle and Manchester, but the lines' operating centres tended to be sited at central points (Wolverton on the London and Birmingham, Swindon on the Great Western, Crewe on the Grand Junction) where early engines had to take on fuel and water. The spate of investment which followed rising passenger and freight business in the 1850s—a bad decade for rail strikes—and the need for constant improvements in engines and rolling stock also seems to have been accompanied by a conservative paternalist programme of encouraging rural 'company towns' instead of expanding existing industrial centres, using the convenience of the railway to diffuse the danger of a compact, skilled, and aggressive proletariat. There was a comforting precedent in the naval and military towns—Woolwich, Chatham, Portsmouth, Plymouth—and their well-heeled Tory deference, and the on-board life of the great ships, 'involving periods of living within a highly disciplined work environment, separated from family and social responsibilities'.[43] While private locomotive manufacturers were urban, of twenty-five major railway company works in 1900, only four were near, let alone in, big port towns.

---

[39] See *The Diary of John Sturrock, Millwright, Dundee, 1864–65*, ed. Chris Whatley (East Linton: Tuckwell Press, 1996).

[40] See R. W. Comerford, 'Ireland, 1850–1870', in W. E. Vaughan, ed., *A New History of Ireland*, v: *Ireland under the Union, I: 1801–1870* (Oxford: Oxford University Press, 1989), 374; Liam Kennedy and Philip Ollerenshaw, *An Economic History of Ulster, 1920–1940* (Manchester: Manchester University Press, 1985), chap. 3.

[41] John Stuart Mill, *England and Ireland* (London: Longmans, 1867), 26.

[42] Tom Garvin, 'Great Hatred, Little Room: Social Background and Political Sentiment among Revolutionary Activists in Ireland, 1890–1922', in D. G. Boyce, ed., *The Revolution in Ireland, 1879–1923* (London: Macmillan, 1988).

[43] Sarah Palmer, 'Ports', in Martin Daunton, ed., *The Cambridge Urban History of Britain*, iii: *1840–1950* (Cambridge: Cambridge University Press, 2000), 148.

Even a Tory like the Swindon blacksmith Alfred Williams found the works' atmosphere stifling and reactionary, a sharp contrast with the artisan culture of Glasgow or Manchester.[44]

## IV  MENTALITIES OF SUCCESS AND FAILURE

This template suggests a situation which is less industrial than imperial: not a smooth process of accumulation and investment leading to take-off, but much more a process of key turning points and chances seized. The 'Scotch engineer' portrayed by Kipling's MacAndrew shows something more than a calculating realism like Scotland's consenting role in the Union; he is also 'bound to the wheel of Empire'. When he has an offer of a humane, sensual existence, MacAndrew sacrifices it for his accustomed rigidity:

> 'Your mither's God's a grasping deil, the shadow o' yoursel',
> Got out o' books by ministers clean daft on heaven an' hell.
> They mak' him in the Broomielaw, 'o Glasgie cauld an' dirt,
> A jealous, pridefu' fetish, lad, that's only strong to hurt.'

MacAndrew isn't economically competent, makes (like the Irish) nothing out of his inventions, but manages to aggregate the specialisms and the peculiar shortsightedness which formed the Scots 'imperial lieutenant class'. What Charles Lever called the 'national absurdities' common to Irish and English intellectual nationalism made both more sceptical of 'modernization'. In *John Bull's Other Island*, one part of Bernard Shaw's engineer Larry Doyle wants to be like Shaw's cockney engineer 'Enry Straker in *Man and Superman* (1905), a mechanical wizard and philistine, another is bound up in the Ruskinian madness of Father Keegan.

Yet there's also a parallel with AE, mystic *and* cooperator, or with the romantic Yeats, who mastered double-entry bookkeeping and fretted about how being technically competent affected his muse:

> The fascination of what's difficult
> Has dried the sap out of my veins, and rent
> Spontaneous joy and natural content
> Out of my heart . . .[45]

As much as Yeats or Eliot, Shaw anticipates the cultural recuperation of modernism, and its Celtic roots. But the Irish experience was 'frozen' by a political rhetoric which reinforced a two-community identity with the firmly subordinate Celtic character conferred by Ernest Renan and by Matthew Arnold in the 1860s, a period

---

[44] Alfred Williams, *Life in a Railway Factory*, 1913 (Newton Abbot: David and Charles, 1969). The Caledonian's St Rollox and the North British's Cowlairs were in Glasgow, the Great Southern and Western's Inchicore in Dublin, and the Great Central's Gorton was in Manchester. Given the events of Glasgow and Dublin in 1916, management had a point. See also Thomas, *Springburn Story*, 75–104.
[45] W. B. Yeats, 'The Fascination of What's Difficult' (1910), in *Collected Poems*.

when market-driven 'improvement' was being queried by democratic demands, by the beginning of an ecological critique, and by a series of horrendous, technologically driven wars.

Arnold's concept of regional tributaries to the central culture, blending publisher's acumen with an evaluation of the unconscious and habitual (extending to mystic hocus-pocus), was still warbling away in T. S. Eliot's *Notes Towards the Definition of Culture* (1950). It was also unerringly carried on to Yeats's ritual anathematization of the world of Huxley–Shaw–Bastien–Lepage 'mechanism' in *Autobiographies* (1913). Patrick Pearse's call for the reification of Ireland through overthrow of the educational 'murder machine' and willed self-sacrifice owes much to Scottish rhetoric, whether Carlyle or that other classic, J. G. Frazer's *Golden Bough* (1890). Even the *Manchester Guardian* Liberal J. L. Hammond attributed Gladstone's commitment to Irish Home Rule, in defiance of the intellectual establishment, from Tyndall and Huxley to Arnold and Sidgwick, to a turn of mind which was essentially theological rather than scientific.[46]

This deflection of outlook reflects a gloomier attitude to mechanism and its human consequences than that which had greeted the early railways and steamers: something analysed in Francis Klingender's Marxian thesis *Art and the Industrial Revolution* (1948). This surfaces in Thomas Hardy, in that episode of *Tess of the D'Urbervilles* when Tess and her fellow harvesters are forced to work to the rhythm of the steam thresher. Here the engineer appears as someone, almost *something*, totally alien:

By the engine stood a dark, motionless being, a sooty and grimy embodiment of tallness, in a sort of trance, with a heap of coals by his side: it was the engine-man. . . . What he looked he felt. He was in the agricultural world, but not of it. He served fire and smoke; these denizens of the fields served vegetation, weather, frost and sun . . .

His fire was waiting incandescent, his steam was at high pressure, in a few seconds he could make the long strap move at an invisible velocity. Beyond its extent the environment might be corn, straw or chaos; it was all the same to him. If any of the autochthonous idlers asked him what he called himself, he replied shortly, 'an engineer.'[47]

This alienated being seems to relate directly to Carlyle's notorious passage on the Irish in *Chartism* (1839):

The Giant Steamengine in a giant English Nation will here create violent demand for labour, and will there annihilate demand. But, alas, the great proportion of labour is not skilled, the millions are and must be skilless, where strength alone is wanted; menials of the Steamengine, only the *chief* menials and immediate *body*-servants of which require skill.[48]

Another aspect of Carlyle comes into play here: the heroic. Carlyle—particularly in *Chartism*—could be seen as straightforwardly anti-Irish; his Anglo-Saxonism was one reason why he pervaded British elite ideology. But he was also to be influential on Young Ireland and the quest for a revolutionary Celtic hero. The drive towards this accumulated the Ossianic paraphernalia that Yeats and Pearse subsequently

---

[46] J. L. Hammond, *Gladstone and the Irish Nation* (London: Longmans, 1938), 523–52.
[47] Thomas Hardy, *Tess of the D'Urbervilles* (London: Macmillan, 1891), chaps. 67–8.
[48] Thomas Carlyle, *Chartism* (London: Chapman and Hall, 1839), 27–33.

welcomed, and took on some of the character of Matthew Arnold's empathic Celt.[49] It was strengthened as the social disadvantages of market society became increasingly apparent in the 1860s and 1870s, not least through the Catholic sociology, community-conservationist in direction and in due course influential on Patrick Geddes, of such as Fréderic Le Play, David Urquhart, and Robert Monteith.[50]

The input *into* Carlyle was twofold: his belief in the fundamental quality of community stems from the Scottish enlightenment, and particularly from Adam Ferguson's *Essay on the History of Civil Society* (1767); this came both directly and via Ferguson's influence on German writers, Schiller and Goethe in particular.[51] The second influence was the Frenchman Henri de Saint-Simon (1760–1825) and his 'evolutionary' alternation of periods of 'organic' stability and 'critical' change: the latter being what Carlyle saw in his *French Revolution* (1837). The outcome was the notion of the 'hero' as the charismatic figure—both actual and a metaphor for the possibilities before the individual—who could secure a new organic settlement.[52] This acted on Irish intellectuals, indirectly as well as directly. Carlyle's 'progressivism' influenced American culture in Emerson and Whitman, returning to Ireland via such Irish Whitmanites as Thomas Sigerson, Standish O'Grady, and indeed Shaw himself.

Carlyle was read in one way by Young Ireland, and in another in Britain and Ulster. Things don't come more heroic than Macaulay's *Lays of Ancient Rome* (1842) which appeared only a year after *Heroes and Hero-Worship*, and its republican-demotic tropes embedded themselves, certainly in Scotland, for the better part of a century. Taken along with his *History of England* (written 1839–48) and his critique of the Tory ruralism of Robert Southey, his ideas seemingly spelt out the battle of rationality (implicitly Roman-Protestant) against Tuscan-Milesian superstition and deference. Yet Macaulay the hebridean claimed his Roman republican epic as part of an international demotic *epos* shared by, inter alia, the Celts.[53]

This Protestant hero, applying himself to steady empirical improvement, went beyond Samuel Smiles's 'industrialism', which climaxed with *Lives of the Engineers* in 1862. His moralistic *Self-Help* had appeared in 1859, the same year as an invasion panic created the Volunteer Movement of amateur soldiering. Smiles thoroughly approved of it, but its pedigree also cast back to the 1780s and would foreshadow Ireland after 1910. Smiles was no devotee of urbanization, indeed he commended the rural origins of most of his engineers, 'brought up mostly in remote country

---

[49] See Owen Dudley Edwards, 'Irish Nationalism', in *Celtic Nationalism* (London: Routledge and Kegan Paul, 1968), 123 ff.

[50] Bernard Aspinwall, 'David Urquhart, Robert Monteith and the Catholic Church: A Search for Justice and Peace', *Innes Review*, 31 (1980), 72.

[51] Ralph Jessop, in *Carlyle and Scottish Thought* (London: Macmillan, 1997), stresses Carlyle's debt to Reid and the commonsense school but doesn't mention the connection with Ferguson. Fania Oz-Salzberger, *Translating the Enlightenment* (Oxford: Clarendon Press, 1995), shows the influence of Adam Ferguson on German thought, which would return via Carlyle to Thomas Davis. See Eileen Sullivan, *Thomas Davis* (Lewisburg: Buckness University Press, 1974), 49.

[52] See Hill Shine, *Carlyle and the Saint-Simonians: The Concept of Historical Periodicity*, 1941 (New York: Octagon Books, 1981).

[53] Thomas Babington Macaulay, introduction to *Lays of Ancient Rome*, 1842 (Leipzig: Tauchnitz, 1851), 8.

places, far from the active life of great towns and cities'.[54] There are elements in this both of Adam Ferguson's ideas of the 'militant' community and of reconciliation between capital and labour: something inherently more possible in Ulster, where capital at least troubled to stick around, than in the South, where it was blatantly absent. Moreover, community in Adam Ferguson and Carlyle *was* created by conflict—by violent games, military clashes, fear of 'the other', not least by tirades against landlords: 'a selfish, ferocious, famishing, unprincipled set of hyenas, from whom at no time and in no way has the country derived any benefit whatsoever'.[55]

A hero, like Michael Davitt, to the young David Lloyd George, the radical Carlyle prophesied individual liberation, from landlordism as much as from conventional religion. The later conservative, however, reacting against the democratic movement—and his mirror image Walt Whitman—stressed 'work and question not'. He was, in this uncomplicated form, ingested into the politics of Andrew Bonar Law and the literary *oeuvre* of Kipling in 'Captain/Soldier of Industry' mode. Through this Ulster built technological superiority into its Unionism.[56]

Yet 'work as prayer' did not just contribute to Cromwellian dogmatism (still audible in the discourse of Ian Paisley), it also promoted in Catholic Ireland, via *Past and Present* (1843), the equally demotic Catholicism of the 'plain people'. Seamus Deane has argued that conservative Irish nationalism took its cue from Burke's assault on the modern in his apotheosis of Marie Antoinette: the aggression—sexual, democratic, mechanistic (what is the guillotine if not a machine?) on 'traditional sanctity and loveliness'. Carlyle found the Jacobins and their *Zeitbruch* inevitable. At the same time he had a fundamental pessimism (again inherited from Adam Ferguson) about what technology, market society, and wealth would imply, which has survived into a world in which the steam engine (or these days the computer) is still 'changing his shape like a very Proteus; and infallibly, at every change of shape, oversetting whole multitudes of workmen . . .'.[57]

Not optimistic. But note that the world of the 'chief menials', the engineers, was almost exclusively male . . .


## V   WORK AND QUESTION NOT

This element emerges when we examine another technologist, Joseph Conrad's Ulster steamer captain MacWhirr in *Typhoon* (1903), in more detail, remembering incidentally that this is a Protestant seen by a Catholic (yet a Catholic who, as a Polish

[54]  Smiles, *Lives of the Engineers*, ii, 292.

[55]  Quoted by Tom Johnston in *Our Scots Noble Families* (Glasgow: Forward Publishing, 1909), 23.

[56]  For Bonar Law see Robert Blake, *The Unknown Prime Minister* (London: Eyre and Spottiswoode, 1955), chap. 1; and for Kipling see Charles Carrington, *Rudyard Kipling*, 1955 (Harmondsworth: Penguin, 1970), 69, 74.

[57]  Carlyle, *Chartism*, 33.

aristocrat, was similarly worried about peasant masses of another faith—the Orthodox Russians). If affectionate, it's also ironic: MacWhirr is so unimaginative he runs the *Nan-Shan* into the typhoon; he's not prepared to waste coal steaming away from it; and so unimaginative that he gets out again. The typhoon could be Edmund Burke's 'sublime', something that had its working-out in the novel of Gothic fantasy. There's nothing of fantasy about Conrad's description of what the typhoon does to the steamer—which is all the more effective because he doesn't describe its passage *from* the typhoon's eye, when MacWhirr subsequently admits he lost hope. The *Nan-Shan* and its complement survive because of a rough-and-ready discipline—lashing the coolies' boxes, dividing their cash—imposed by what is charisma of a sort.

Note that the ship is what Foucault would call a 'total' institution, all-male, like a Catholic abbey or seminar, with MacWhirr as its abbot. Mrs MacWhirr is almost like a Madonna, an indifferent, materialist one, whose comfort is nonetheless the reason for her husband being there. This provokes two thoughts: one, that the paradigm of the ship—living and working conditions reduced to the minimum tolerable, authoritarian command, sexual separation—moved from sea to land, in the organization of workers' lives *outside* small houses, in male workplace, male pub, male sport.[58] Two: social overhead capital humanized this without disturbing it. A mid Victorian elite persisted in power—in industrial Scotland and Wales, as much as Belfast—partly because of old constituencies and a restricted electorate surviving urbanization, but also because of the continuing power of pre-industrial structures of social organization, and the application of industrial-style organization to them.[59]

The Catholic analogue to industrial order was the reorganization of the Church by Cardinal Cullen and his successors,[60] but agriculture was weak after the 1870s, dependent on British demand and on the authoritarian materialism of *John Bull's Other Island*'s Father Dempsey, who would have been at home in the France of Balzac or Stendhal.[61] Shaw—indeed most modernizing Irish nationalists—argued that Ireland could escape agrarian-clerical stasis only through Ulster. Recreating the Scottish enlightenment-inspired liberalism of the 1790s, Ulster would cancel out a Catholic authoritarianism only too prone to pal up with the Tom Broadbents of British capitalism. Arthur Griffith saw a Belfast-built Irish merchant marine as an equal unifier with his dual monarchy. Shaw's Ireland couldn't exist without Ulster, and he assured the Protestants that they would pretty quickly be running the whole show.[62]

Given the Home Rule politics of Lord Pirrie, boss of Harland and Wolff, there may have been grounds for optimism—for a time. But Orangeism and Unionism were themselves total institutions which aimed at bridging rural and industrial, Anglican and Nonconformist. They provided a form of ethnic-sectarian insurance against a

[58] See Palmer, 'Ports'.

[59] Ieuan Gwynedd Jones, 'Glamorgan Politics, 1884–1918', in *Glamorgan County History*, vi (Cardiff: Glamorgan History Trust, 1988).

[60] J. J. Lee, *The Modernisation of Irish Society* (Dublin: Gill and Macmillan, 1973), 42 ff.

[61] Shaw, 'Preface to the Home Rule Edition of 1912', in *John Bull's Other Island*, 3–12.

[62] Patrick Colum, *Arthur Griffith* (Dublin: Browne and Nolan, 1959), 87 ff.; Shaw, *John Bull's Other Island*, 'Preface of 1929'.

global market which in the mid 1900s was looking unwontedly fragile—the 1906–8 period on the Clyde saw output slump by 50 per cent.[63] Shaw's 1912 preface to *John Bull*, equating capitalist instability and speculation with imperialism, was timely enough, and interpretations which see the *Titanic* tragedy of 1912 as a projection of Ulster angst are not totally wide of the mark.[64]

The Welsh inflection of this formula was a hybrid. Firstly, the central industry of coal mining was manual rather than mechanized, so aspects of the heroic persisted within the working day, instead of being smoothed off into Marxian 'machinofacture'. A moderate mining trade unionist like 'Mabon' (William Abraham) could combine the charisma of chapel, labour aristocrat, and cultural priest, as indeed could David Davies, 'top sawyer' of Llandinam, in his route via railway contracting to coal-owning. This reflected the speed of the transition to the mineral valleys, with communities bringing along their language and rural *Gwerin* traditions, memories of the land struggle and slate quarry strikes, good for at least one generation; and individuals often returned at weekly, monthly, and yearly intervals to rural Wales, as sailors had done before them.[65] If the impact of organized socialism in the South Wales valleys dates from 1898, and caused great tensions in the established society of the chapels, it also saw the climax of a migratory stream which brought into South Wales a new, secular radicalism. The product of this was labour militancy and Noah Ablett's syndicalist *The Miners' Next Step* of 1912.

Hard on its heels came, along the littoral, 'scientific management', following Frederick Winslow Taylor's treatise of the same year. The instrumentalizing of time by capital had been growing since 'railway time' was imposed in the 1840s and 'international time' (by the Scots engineer Sandford Fleming) in the 1880s in Canada.[66] Industrial time-discipline pervades the homiletic poems that Kipling wrote for C. R. L. Fletcher's *History of England* (1911):

> But remember please the Law by which we live,
> We are not built to comprehend a lie,
> We can neither live nor pity nor forgive.
> If you make a slip in handling us you die![67]

This might have its origins, too, in Carlyle. The impression-clotted prose of *The French Revolution* anticipated the post-Einstein discourse which cut across the traditional linearity of English prose, in Bergson, Proust, Mann, and even Wells; and also the more uncompromising syndicalist and futurist political culture of the time—the

[63] Christopher Harvie, *No Gods and Precious Few Heroes: Scotland since 1914*, 4th edn (Edinburgh: Edinburgh University Press, 1981), 1.

[64] John Wilson Foster, 'Imagining the *Titanic*', in Eve Patten, ed., *Returning to Ourselves* (Belfast: Lagan Press, 1995).

[65] Brinley Thomas, 'A Cauldron of Rebirth: Population and the Welsh Language in the Nineteenth Century', 1962, in Geraint Jenkins, ed., *The Welsh Language and its Social Domains* (Cardiff: University of Wales Press, 2000).

[66] Christopher Turner, 'Conflicts of Faith? Religion and Labour in Wales, 1890–1914', in Deian R. Hopkin and Gregory S. Kealey, eds., *Class Community and the Labour Movement: Wales and Canada, 1850–1930* (Cardiff: Llafur and Canadian Committee on Labour History, 1989).

[67] Kipling, 'The Secret of the Machines', 1911.

latter explicitly mechanistic—advertised by the likes of George Sorel and F. T. Marinetti.[68]

In 1911 there died in Liverpool 'Robert Tressell', who had just finished, in the holiday resort of Hastings, *The Ragged Trousered Philanthropists*. Under the pseudonym lay two identities. The Irish nationalist signwriter Robert Noonan, shifting in South Africa from Fenianism to Marxism, and under him a member of the ascendancy Croker family, descended from Disraeli's oily intriguer J. W. and the great folklorist Crofton. Hastings was just about the most reactionary town in England, and Tressell wrote about hand-craftsmen, but nowhere was the swelling conflict between skilled men and management more mercilessly depicted. This was predictive of the situation only two years later, when Dublin—Tressel's birthplace and Geddes's 'Geotechnic City'—would become in 1913 the battlefield of the Irish Transport and General Workers' Union, headed by James Larkin, and the dock and tramway concerns of the former Nationalist MP and colonial contractor William Martin Murphy.

## VI   PRUSSIANS AND ASIATICS

Anglo-Saxon artisan technology was ideologically established by Carlyle and Smiles. The Continent was different. Institutional growth was fostered by the French Saint-Simonians and Prussian or Württemberg bureaucrats, the Perières, Beuths, and Steinbeises, along with the military leadership. This produced something closer to what Thorstein Veblen would, in the 1890s, christen 'technocracy'. Its natural *habitus* was the North Atlantic, where it received an American extension through the Civil War and the era of massive economic expansion that followed.[69] In this a crucial figure was Andrew Carnegie, whose holdings in the United Steel Corporation—effectively a cartel—amounted to £100 million in 1900 (Scottish gross output in manufacturing was in that year £159 million).[70] In Germany something analogous happened with the rise of the Krupps and Thyssens through Bismarck's wars of conquest. The Great Power, the cartel, and the military-industrial complex displaced the liberating ideal of the travelling artisans.

This was, however, masked in the 1870s and 1880s by the synergies of steam communication, proceeding from individual ships and railway projects via the telegraph network, the Suez Canal (1869), and the coal trade, to a steamer-based civilization. A torrent of innovations, as well as the propellant of Welsh steam coal in vast quantities, surged in to fill gaps and open out bottlenecks in the system. Dynamic entrepreneurs like Edison or the Siemens brothers drew on new knowledge and experiments to adapt and exploit telephones, hydraulics, lifts, electrical circuits, sewage purification, power steering, optics. Out of this emerged applied electrics: photography and

---

[68] See Stuart Hughes, *Consciousness and Society*, 1958 (London: Paladin, 1974), chap. 5, and *Futurismo, 1909–1919* (Newcastle: Northern Arts, 1972).

[69] This treatment owes much to David S. Landes, *The Unbound Prometheus* (Cambridge: Cambridge University Press, 1969), 231 ff.

[70] 'Carnegie, Andrew', in *Encyclopaedia Britannica*, 11th edn; output table in Harvie, *No Gods*, 36.

telegraphy combining in picture transmission and reproduction (1907), bringing in turn more possibilities of emulation, and the expansion of high-value-added service industries. At the same time national patronage and policies of 'picking winners'—or selecting the best from several systems—provided means of cutting corners. Meiji Japan in its modernization progress took technical education from Scotland, practical experience from the shipyards and engineering works of the English north-east, where the Japanese navy was built, and organization from Prussia. By 1893 a perceptive Anglo-Australian politician Charles Henry Pearson, a 'Reform Essayist' back in 1867, was sketching in *National Life and Character* what Werner Sombart would later call 'the Asiatic mode of production', in which technological specialization, authoritarianism, and a workforce habitually unquestioning was more 'modernizable' than one inspired by Western individualism.[71]

The cost of this process was its militarization, and with this the imposition of a deeply conservative compromise, yet Pearson's popularity—both Bryce and Theodore Roosevelt commended the book—coincided with enthusiasm for 'general staffs' and the geopolitics of Alfred Mahan's *The Influence of Sea Power* (1890–2). Technology could coexist with military dictatorship, as in South America: the optimism with which that continent had once been regarded was fast evaporating. Bryce, who had regarded it as a potential Positivist utopia, curbed this view when he visited it in 1911.[72] Joseph Conrad and his friend R. B. Cunninghame-Graham were, in *Nostromo* and *Progress* (both 1905), much bleaker.

Technology could take a benign form: the creation of an innovation-driven consumer market or a collectivist utopia like Edward Bellamy's *Looking Backward* (1890). This provided a rationale for contemporary 'revisionist' social democrat theory: Eduard Bernstein, and following him J. A. Hobson, Wells, and Veblen himself. Cheap consumer goods marketed by consumer cooperatives partly realized the 'paper utopias' previously advanced by the likes of Robert Owen, also being rediscovered at this time. He wasn't just the proto-Fabian in Frank Podmore's lengthy biography of 1906; the Motherwell architect Alexander Cullen, in his *Adventures in Socialism* (1910), made him the forerunner of the town's 'municipal socialism', which was balanced between Colville's steelworks and the Dalzell Co-op, the second largest in Scotland.[73] Elsewhere a downturn in prosperity made Hobson, Wells, and colleagues attribute imperialism to underconsumption on the part of a working class which had been looted by a conservative capitalist order.[74] The wealth of the latter—and its supportive technology: typewriters, telephones, cars, lifts, central heating—seemed more and more to be secured at the expense of the masses whose efforts at political organization had been severely suppressed during the 1890s. The evolution of capitalist

---

[71] Charles H. Pearson, *National Life and Character* (London: Macmillan, 1893), 132 ff., and Harvie, *Lights of Liberalism*, 232–5.

[72] James Bryce, *South America* (London: Macmillan, 1912), chap. 16.

[73] See Robert Duncan, *Steelopolis: The Making of Motherwell* (Motherwell: Motherwell District Council, 1991).

[74] See Jules Townshend, *J. A. Hobson* (Manchester: Manchester University Press, 1990), esp. 137 ff.

industry seemed firmly towards 'helotry' with the introduction of 'Taylorism' following labour disputes in the 1890s, such anti-union legal decisions as Lord Halsbury's judgment in the Taff Vale case (1900), and the creation of an ideology of conservative modernization most notably in Kipling's writings.

It was at this point that the west-coast industries felt the cost of concentration on capital goods. They were not just bypassed by the new electricity, chemical, and motor-car industries, but found that Smilesian 'enthusiasm' was ebbing from them. Not just towards socialism or nationalism. Consumer technology relocated. Innovations like Meccano, Hornby model railways, 'Hobbies' fretwork sets, Bassett-Lowke model engineering, were market- and 'lifestyle'-driven, using many of the techniques of modern publicity and global organization (until 1914, most 'British' model railway equipment was built in Germany), and were sited close to the middle-class market, in the south-east of England. The crucial publicity backing for it, which the Scots of the Samuel Smiles generation had mastered via the literary reviews and the local press, now came, both in Britain and the United States, through the cheap, lower-middle-class national press: newspapers such as Harmsworth's *Daily Mail* (1899) and Pearsons's *Daily Express* (1903).

Consider powered flight. This was a Scottish breakthrough but would it *réprise* the marine steam engine? Alexander Graham Bell, of telephone fame, did much work on aerodynamics with kites. Percy Pilcher, an English engineer at Glasgow University, carried out crucial experiments in parallel with Otto Lilienthal in Germany, building a 4 h.p. triplane, untested when he was killed in a gliding accident in 1899. A Dundee pilot, Robert Watson, may even have taken to the air in a petrol-driven biplane before the Wright Brothers in 1903. R. B. Haldane, War Minister (1906–10), was sympathetic and knowledgeable and even flew as co-pilot on one occasion. Scotland arguably led the world in this technology, becoming the centre of aircraft building in World War I, which saw aircraft numbers grow from 200 to over 20,000, and provided in William Weir the first Air Minister. So, why did it not take off? Powered flight was rather like steam at sea in the 1840s—expensive and uncommercial. The difference was that, unlike the admirals in the case of steam, the generals (Douhet, Trenchard, Mitchell: ex-cavalrymen, looking for a new offensive weapon) were bitten by the bug. Aeroplanes were almost purely of military importance, and remained such until a cheap workhorse, the Douglas DC3, appeared in 1937: mass civilian use came only after World War II. Farnborough, next door to Aldershot and Sandhurst, not Cathcart or Dumbarton, became the development centre. Secondly, the small, affluent commercial market depended, for development, on a publicity-driven machine, and this was inevitably London-centred.

So while Scots often controlled the new technologies—Weir in aircraft and John Reith at the BBC were preceded by the expatriate *New York Times* proprietor Gordon Bennett in motor racing—their field of action was far remote from Scotland itself. There the conditions of success for the capital goods industries—a relentlessly contested terrain between stroppy labour aristocrats and conservative management—inhibited the rise of consumer-goods industry, and even the investment profits necessary to develop it. This situation would be radically exacerbated by the impact of World War I.

The post-1906 slump was an omen, particularly in Glasgow and Belfast. The impact of the Russo-Japanese War on France and Russia hit exporting industries sharply, just at the moment when profits and lively markets were essential to boost investment in new industries. As wages fell along Clydeside, so too did rentier income from the workers. The building market never recovered: among its casualties was the architect Charles Rennie Mackintosh, whose order book dried up after 1909. The downturn ate into much of the market for consumer goods, at a period when the surviving Scots suppliers of these were under increasing pressure from English and foreign competitors. Expansion into the motor industry and diesel engines had to be financed out of shrinking profits, while combines like the new North British Locomotive Company, faced with railway rationalization and electrification (notable on the English North Eastern Railway under Eric Geddes, its Scots General Manager), never achieved the targets they had set.[75] The Clyde's major attempt at diversification, the Argyll Car Company, was technically far in advance of Ford (setting up in Cork and Manchester) but its investment programme was unsustainable, and it collapsed in 1912. The increases in shipbuilding tonnage which the region managed in the immediate pre-war period, reaching record levels in 1913, were based on unsustainably low prices and on government commissions for warships. This unpromising outlook led the bosses to demand sweeping changes in working practices, to the point where a destructive confrontation seemed inevitable.[76]

These divergences, however, remained essentially economic ones, influenced by international trade. What people did not expect were the consequences of the realpolitik of World War I, which turned pacific internationalism on its head, ushering in nationalism, immigration control, and protectionism—and a quite different range of technologies, often state-sponsored. On top of this came a post-war recession which swept across the ocean, vividly captured by William Carlos Williams, of Welsh-Spanish descent, in his long poem *Paterson* (1946–58). The great industrial community became the 'soulless city' condemned by Lewis Mumford, its sense of exfoliating energy frozen into bickering stasis: 'Missing was the thing Jim had found in Marx and Veblen and Adam Smith and Darwin—the dignified sound of a great calm bell tolling the morning of a new age . . . instead, the slow complaining of a door loose on its hinges.'[77]

---

[75] See the tables in J. Cunnison and J. B. S. Gilfillan, eds., *The Third Statistical Account of Scotland: Glasgow* (London: Collins, 1958), 188; R. H. Campbell, 'The North British Locomotive Company between the Wars', *Business History* 20/2 (July 1978), 204.

[76] William Kenefick and Arthur McIvor, eds., *Roots of Red Clydeside, 1910–1914?* (Edinburgh: John Donald, 1996), particularly Arthur McIvor, 'Were Clydeside Employers More Autocratic?'

[77] William Carlos Williams, *Paterson* (Manchester: Carcanet, 1992), 80.

1. Trade emblem of the Amalgamated Society of Engineers, Machinists, Millwrights, Smiths, and Pattern Makers, engraved by James Sharples 1852. © Trades Union Congress, London/Bridgeman Art Library. This is the world of the west-coast skilled engineer. Note the 'factory', with smiths, millwrights, patternmakers, engineers and boilermakers, their products—beam engines, mills, trains, and Brunel's steamer *Great Western*—and their ideals: peaceful progress (Mars on left getting the brush-off from a smith; Peace giving a treaty to the engineer) and solidarity (one stick breaks, the bundle doesn't). The varying fortunes of James Watt, centre (worthily successful), Richard Arkwright on right (unreasonably successful), and Henry Crompton (a genius who ended in poverty) tell moral tales.

**2.** John Patrick Crichton-Stuart, Third Marquess of Bute. National Portrait Gallery, London. Bute's conversion to Catholicism in 1867 inspired Disraeli to write his fanciful *Lothair* (1870), a reprise of the more original *Tancred* (1846), in which he had speculated on a British Empire centred in the Middle East. Bute got his money from South Wales coal and docks, and was a Tory, medieval scholar and Scottish nationalist.

**3.** Mount Stuart, Isle of Bute, the west front, photograph by H. B. Lemare, 1904. Reproduced courtesy of the Royal Commission on the Ancient and Historical Monuments of Scotland. Designed by Sir Robert Rowan Anderson, this huge Florentine-gothic castle near Rothesay (Glasgow's Blackpool) reflected Bute's fastidious medievalism as much as his famous Welsh buildings by William Burges: Cardiff Castle and Castell Coch.

4. Cathays Park, Cardiff: postcard of 1930. Author's collection. Bought from the Butes, this became after 1900 the administrative centre of 'American South Wales' and indeed resembled Washington or the Chicago World's Fair, with town hall, university, national museum, courts, and, in the middle, the Scottish architect Ninian Comper's War Memorial (1926): in effect a tombstone to the region's prosperity.

5. The Glasgow Stock Exchange, May 1908. Reproduced courtesy of the Mitchell Library, Glasgow. 500 men in bowler hats whose deals determined the world price of pig iron. Not a shaven lip or a woman in sight, and an odd commentary on the 'creative chaos' which was supposed to propel capitalism. Andrew Bonar Law, future Conservative premier, must be here somewhere.

**6.** The Three Donkeys. Author's collection. Punch's Phil May was a radical in a conservative cartooning profession which catered for the metropolitan and provincial bourgeois. His style, forced on him by awful Australian newspaper printing, influenced two of the greatest cartoonists of the period to 1950, Will Dyson and David Low, also Australasian.

PAT (*shouting after Tommy Atkins*). 'Who shtole the cat?'
TOMMY. ''Oo stole yer bloomin' country?'

**7.** Jack Butler Yeats (1857–1951), The Greater Official. © The Estate of Jack B. Yeats/DACS, London 2007. Photo © The National Gallery of Ireland. In one of a fine series of illustrations from George A. Birmingham's *Irishmen All*, this grandee off the train from Dublin looks very like James Bryce, MP, Ulster-Scot Liberal, political scientist, and Irish Chief Secretary 1905–7, on a provincial tour, at a time when Home Rule, which both the brothers Yeats and Birmingham (Canon J. A. Hannay) believed in, seemed only a matter of time.

**8.** Pushing and Going. National Library of Wales. A still from Maurice Elvey's *The Life of David Lloyd George,* made in 1918 but never released and rediscovered only in 1996, shows the real Prime Minister (played elsewere by Norman Page) apparently celebrating victory in November 1918 but in fact receiving the Freedom of Neath.

**9.** Sean Keating, *Night's Candles are Burnt Out* (1929). Reproduced courtesy of the Gallery Oldham. Sean Keating's painting of the Shannon power scheme, 1927, took its title from Juliet's vision of the dawn in Shakespeare's *Romeo and Juliet.* It was one of a series of semi-surreal visions of Irish society in transition, he hoped, from war to progress.

**10.** 'Work as if you lived in the early days of a better nation'. © Trustees of the National Library of Scotland. Frontispiece of book IV of Alasdair Gray's 'Life in Four Books' *Lanark* (1982), forced into print by the Scottish devolution debacle of 1979. It combines political criticism (of Hobbesian absolute sovereignty), with a meticulous Patrick Geddes-style camera-obscura-like view of central Scotland.

# II
# OURSELVES TOGETHER

# 4

## Anglo-Saxons into Celts: The Scottish Intellectuals, 1760–1930

I realised for the first time that Medina might be damnable, but was also great. Yes, the man who had spat on me like a stable-boy had also something of the prince. I realised another thing. The woman's touch had flattened down the hair above his forehead, which he brushed square, and his head, outlined in the firelight against the white cushion, was as round as a football. I had suspected this when I first saw him, and now I was certain.

John Buchan, *The Three Hostages*, 1924[1]

### I  ENLIGHTENMENT AND DECEPTION

John Buchan's most commanding villain, Dominic Medina, was already something of an antique when he made his appearance in *The Three Hostages* (1924). Richard Hannay's description represented the 'brachycephalic' (round-headed) Celt, out of the phrenological anthropology of seventy years earlier. Medina was Irish, but despite the 1919–21 conflict which had resulted in the Free State, the notion of a racially programmed Celtic conspiracy against Britain seemed far in the past (but see Aftermath). Still, the scientistic style of the nineteenth century, when applied to race, left a long shadow. The violence of the suppression of 'ninety-eight'—in which the British killed between 10,000 and 30,000 Irish—and the end of Irish autonomy came only a year before the end of the serfdom of the Scottish colliers.[2] This liberation—and probably the connection between the two events—was seen as a sort of nationalism, notably in areas such as Ayrshire and Lanarkshire, with a strong Protestant identity.[3]

---

[1] In *The Adventures of Richard Hannay* (London: Hodder and Stoughton, 1939), 980.

[2] For 'Phrenology' see *Encyclopaedia Britannica*, 11th edn; Peter Collins, ' "Who fears to speak of '98?": Historic Commemoration of the 1798 Rising', in Eberhard Bort, ed., *Commemorating Ireland: History, Politics, Culture* (Dublin: Irish Academic Press, 2004).

[3] See Alan Campbell, *The Lanarkshire Miners* (Edinburgh: John Donald, 1979), 44, 279; and see Christopher Harvie, 'The Covenanting Tradition', in Graham Walker and Tom Gallagher, eds., *Sermons and Battle Hymns: Protestart Popular Culture in Modern Scotland* (Edinburgh: Edinburgh Uuniversity Press, 1990), and L. P. Curtis Jnr, *Apes and Angels: The Irishman in Victorian Caricature* (Newton Abbot: David and Charles, 1971), 11–12, 96–7. For background see Roy Foster, *Modern Ireland* (London: Allen Lane, 1988), 280.

Scotland was the prime example of 'enlightenment' along the littoral, but like both Wales (until the 1920s) and Ireland (until the 1980s) it could also claim even in the mid twentieth century to be a highly religious country. As late as 1951 59 per cent of Scots were church members, against only 23 per cent in England and Wales; the comprehensive piety of Catholic Ireland was almost matched by the northern Protestants. 'The secularization of the European mind', something taken as axiomatic by liberal academics, including not a few Scots, Irish, and Welsh, failed quantitatively to grow along with industry, and didn't show up before the economic crisis of the 1920s. So a central theme of this and the following two chapters is the hybridity of religious and national feelings, with the former offering, in all three countries, an inflected idea of nationality which also could have an imperial currency.[4]

The re-imagining of Scots identity was also mixed up with pseudo-science as propaganda and efforts to improve on the legacy of history. Deception in the cause of the nation remains under-researched, despite its continual recurrence: James MacPherson and *Ossian* (1761), Iolo Morganwg and the Druids, the affair of the Könighöfen Manuscripts (1817), an alleged Czech *Nibelungenlied*. There seems to be a pattern to this, since the exposure of forgery, usually by another nationalist—Thomas Stephens at the Welsh National Eisteddfod in 1859, T. G. Masaryk in the 1880s—ultimately strengthens the national cause.

Are scientism and its controversies, forgery and its exposure, not *both* essential to national movements? Members of the 'traditional' intelligentsia first create an instant identity and a vivid past which fits into the dominant historical discourse (analogous to the tariffs behind which fledgling firms are founded): usually some sort of national epic which can be set against the cosmopolitan classicism of the aristocracy, or a flawless ethnic-heroic symbol. Then, once the native 'scientific' movement has crawled out from under the aristocratic shadow, the exposure of this 'ideal type' tests the maturity of organized nationalism. This partly subverts the 'symbolic appropriation' thesis of the likes of Malcolm Chapman: that the native was there as a sort of quarry for the 'improver'. The Highland Society (1780), which first sustained MacPherson and then diplomatically sidelined him, was emphatically an 'improving' organization. Edward Williams, 'Iolo Morganwg' (1746–1826), was, as remembrancer of the Druidic past, deeply influenced by *Ossian*.[5] Yet his invented rituals—the Druids, the Gorsedd, the revived Eisteddfod—ran alongside his own radical politics and 'modernizing' intentions for South Wales, and continued after his wilder innovations had been exploded.[6] Iolo reflected the influence of a Scots intellect which refereed the dialectic between the rationality of the enlightenment and the emotional impulse towards the old order: appealing to conservatives as well as to progressives and secularists. If the Whig judge and unofficial historian of late enlightenment Scotland Henry

---

[4] See William Knox, *Industrial Nation: Work, Culture and Society in Scotland, 1800–Present* (Edinburgh: Edinburgh University Press, 1999), 266–7; Owen Chadwick, *The Secularization of the European Mind in the Nineteenth Century* (Cambridge: Cambridge University Press, 1975) is notably unforthcoming on non-English Britain.

[5] Gwyn A. Williams, *When Was Wales? A History of the Welsh* (Harmondsworth: Penguin, 1985), 164 ff.

[6] Emyr Humphreys, *The Taliesin Tradition*, 1983 (Bridgend: Seren Books, 1989), 106–14.

Cockburn (1779–1856) lauded the popularity of Adam Smith among his generation, on the Continent attitudes were different, as Bernard Aspinwall has written: 'Scotland . . . stimulated the quest into the mystery of human origins, into primitivism and the picturesque . . . By dispensing with the exaggerated individualism of the contractual theory, Ossian restated the organic view of society.'[7]

This was an egg-dance for a Scots intelligentsia which was, in Gramsci's terms, 'traditional' in its origins (academics, clergy, lawyers) but performed the modernizing tasks he associated with the 'organic' intelligentsia of industry and commerce.[8] Its status was derived from a *Scots* civil society (or more precisely, a distinctive fusion of society and local state), which had over the centuries with almost unique success fused five ethnic groups—Briton, Pict, Gael, Angle, and Viking—into a nation. It wanted to be considered European, but was now politically allied to England, and with the decline of Latin, was firmly within the field of the English language. Hence, it had to be defensive about national institutions *and* inventive about 'English Literature'.[9] The Scot of Burns and Scott's time understood himself as an English writer no more and no less than the Genevan Rousseau understood himself as French.

This dualism helps explain the Scots' ambiguity about Celticism. The term didn't imply the inferior status that W. J. MacCormack, following Edward Said on 'orientalism', has identified in Ireland. By the 1920s it was regarded as positive, a culture which distinguished Scotland from England. But the Scottish Celts were a component of nationality, not the whole of it—and the word (with a soft C) meant, for 99 per cent of the male population, Glasgow Celtic Football Club, founded in 1888 and directly identified with Catholic Irish immigrants. Sport—with its heroes, partisans, and dramas—meant the same sort of engagement that came with *Ossian* in the 1760s, and will be dealt with in Chapter 7. Besides the cultural defensiveness over the 'retrieved epic', *Ossian* had stirred European interest in the country for non-commercial reasons, typified by the tour to the Hebrides by the arch-sceptic, but crypto-Jacobite, Samuel Johnson in 1773. Johnson reverencing Flora MacDonald, or pensive in the ruins of Iona—'perhaps, in the revolutions of the world, Iona may be again the instructress of the Western nations'—implied a cultural recognition of Scotland which balanced its political integration with England.[10]

How was distance to be kept? Writing of Victorian Wales, Ieuan Gwynedd Jones has stressed the need for the social overhead capital that converted the urban into the civic, and also fashioned common ground for differing religious groups. The symbolism congealed in universities, town halls, banks, and railway stations was much more than decorative. It also provided a bridge between the elements of *Gemeinschaft*, or

---

[7] Henry Cockburn, *Memorials of his Time* (Edinburgh, 1856), quoted in David Craig, *Scottish Literature and the Scottish People* (London: Chatto and Windus, 1961), 15; and Bernard Aspinwall, 'Some Aspects of Scotland and the Catholic Revival in the Early Nineteenth Century', *Innes Review*, 26 (1975), 6–7.

[8] Antonio Gramsci, *Prison Writings*, ed. Simon Nowell-Smith (London: Lawrence and Wishart, 1971), 18.

[9] Robert Crawford, *Devolving English Literature* (Oxford: Clarendon Press, 1992), esp. chap. 1.

[10] Samuel Johnson, *A Journey to the Western Isles of Scotland* (1775), quoted in Hugh MacDiarmid, *The Islands of Scotland* (London: B. T. Batsford, 1939), 193–4.

community (family, street, chapel), which were intimate but archaic, and *Gesellschaft*, or industrial society. But it also projected the civic on to an international stage, where the temptation to convert integration to assimilation was powerful.

In Scotland the driving force of socialization was the Presbyterian religion, which had control over the Poor Law, education, and social discipline. Consideration of its imaginative world, in 'The Folk and the *Gwerin*', will make up Chapter 5. But Presbyterianism was increasingly riven by theological litigation, culminating in the Disruption of 1843. Hence the importance of national symbols as compensating factors: circumspect, self-conscious 'sympathies' in Adam Smith's terms, which sheltered the contractual basis of the Scottish nation.

The *Ossian* episode is, for Malcolm Chapman, an exotic condiment to mechanistic enlightenment.[11] Luke Gibbons highlights MacPherson's debt to the Adam Smith of the *Theory of Moral Sentiments* (1759) and marks him as an 'end of history' man, drawing a line under the 'militant' epoch and reinforcing Smith's 'sympathy' as a means of moralizing the grey approaching age of secular calculation.[12] Part of *Ossian's* allure, however, surely stemmed from the basically conservative premises of Scottish enlightenment social thought, which regarded solidarity both as intuitive and as bound up with the 'militant' state. The Gaelic-speaking Adam Ferguson on the ancient Greeks in his *Essay on the History of Civil Society* (1767) was as inventive as MacPherson on the third-century Gaels.[13] But the Celts had to be incorporated within the realm of the civilized. The literati's support for MacPherson's claims went along with the belief that society was based on something more than contract, even on an indulgent attitude to Celtic tradition.[14] Some contemporary scholars, like Murray Pittock, have argued for more than 'symbolic appropriation': the positive, popular attachment to the Jacobite tradition, projected by Allan Ramsay (1686–1758) and Robert Fergusson (1750–1774).[15] Pittock overstates his case, but Chapman's view of the manipulated Celt ignores the improving areas—Glasgow, Inverness, Ayrshire—which were partially Gaelic-speaking, and the managerial dominance up to the 1750s of the Inveraray-based Campbells. *Ossian's* heroics fitted the efforts of conservative neo-Machiavellian 'civic humanists' to protect community from 'commercialism' and 'corruption' by rediscovering the moulding forces of the past.[16]

The interest in defending existing *Gemeinschaft* waned as highland elites lost their 'heritable jurisdictions' in 1746, and as post-Smithian economics—transposing the motor of social action from the individual (and so theoretically unchanging)

---

[11] See Malcolm Chapman, *The Gaelic Vision in Scottish Culture* (London: Croom Helm, 1975), 28; and the same writer's *The Celts: The Construction of a Myth* (London: Macmillan, 1992), *passim*.

[12] Luke Gibbons, in Terence Brown, ed., *Celticism* (Amsterdam: Rodopi, 1996).

[13] Adam Ferguson, *An Essay on the History of Civil Society* (Edinburgh: Edinburgh University Press, 1966), 197; and see Duncan Forbes in the introduction, esp pp. xvii ff.

[14] John Robertson, *The Scottish Enlightenment and the Militia Issue* (Edinburgh: John Donald, 1985).

[15] Murray G. H. Pittock, *The Invention of Scotland: The Stuart Myth and the Scottish Identity, 1638 to the Present* (London: Routledge, 1991), esp. chap. 3. Colin Kidd, 'Race, Empire and the Limits of Nineteenth Century Scots Nationhood', *Historical Journal*, 46/4 (2003), has argued almost the opposite.

[16] See J. G. A. Pocock, *The Machiavellian Moment* (Princeton: Princeton University Press, 1975).

conscience to the invisible hand of blind market forces—marginalized the militant community. Many lowlanders—the intemperate historian John Pinkerton (1758–1826) was not utterly eccentric—vilified the defeated: 'The Irish Celts were savages, have been savages since the world began, and will be forever savages, mere radical savages, not yet advanced even to a state of barbarism.'[17] Such prejudice lived on in the histories of Henry Grey Graham (1846–1906), *The Social Life of Scotland in the Eighteenth Century* (1899) and *Scottish Men of Letters in the Eighteenth Century* (1902), who popularized the idea of the enlightenment a century later.[18] But a counter-discourse conflated the Highland problem with social relationships elsewhere in Scotland. Burns as a 'moral sentiment' Smithian transformed the small farmer's attachment to a dying order into Jacobitism *and* Jacobinism.[19] Others made the hospitality and solicitousness of the highland order—embodied, say, in Flora MacDonald—part of the 'politeness' with which they sought to moralize market society.[20]

By 1815 the fictive epic gave way to a historical fiction which tried to present an 'ideal-typical' account of the nation. Sir Walter Scott (1771–1832) is altogether more complex, and not only as a dominant literary-political presence in Europe for over a century, but as a founding father of Benedict Anderson's 'print-capitalism' at its most imaginative.[21] Emotionally Jacobite and practically an integrationist Whig, Scott wished to compose, in Georg Lukacs's terms, a cultural unity for his country which would withstand the likely consequences of a fulfilled Union. Hence his desire to depict, as well as the evolution of its society, its various regions and cultures in his novels and poems—Orkney in *The Pirate* (1821), Angus in *The Antiquary* (1816), Lanarkshire in *Old Mortality* (1816), and so on.[22] Among Linda Colley's Protestant-imperial-bourgeois forgers of the nation, Scott's literary business, supplying a whole canon of books to a mass audience, fits in. But he was also entrepreneur and innovator—publisher, landlord, gas company and railway director—aiming at unity through industry, a factor that Colley underplays.[23]

Scott did not rise to the romance of the Highlands, already publicized by *The Scottish Chiefs* (1810) by Jane Porter (1776–1850) and by Christine Johnston's *ClanAlbin: A National Tale*, published just after *Waverley*. He found the theme difficult to handle, principally because as Buchan put it, he 'knew next to nothing' about it.[24] In most of the novels, such as *Waverley* (1814) and *Rob Roy* (1818), where it appears, Celtic Scotland was laggard in social evolution; its individuals anthologies

---

[17] John Pinkerton, *History of Scotland from the Accession of the House of Stuart to that of Mary* (London: Nicholls, White & Herbert, 1794).

[18] Laurence Gourievidis, 'The Image of the Clearances in Scottish History', PhD thesis, St Andrews University, 1993, 17.

[19] Pittock, *The Invention of Scotland*, 79–84.

[20] See John Mullen, 'The Language of Sentiment', in Andrew Hook, ed., *The History of Scottish Literature*, ii: *1660–1880* (Aberdeen: Aberdeen University Press, 1987), 275.

[21] Benedict Anderson, *Imagined Communities* (London: Verso, 1983), esp. chap. 5.

[22] Georg Lukacs, 'In Search of Bourgeois Man', 1992, in *Essays on Thomas Mann* (New York: Grosset and Dunlap, 1965), 24–5.

[23] Linda Colley, *Britons: Forging the Nation, 1707–1837* (New Haven and London: Yale University Press, 1992).

[24] John Buchan, *Sir Walter Scott* (London: Cassell, 1932), 85.

of social dislocation, fecklessness, violence, and primitivism. Yet Scott's impulse to commit it to the social dustbin was constrained by the effect on him of the highland clearances *and* the new instabilities of commercial society. In 1816 he sponsored the harper and bilingual poet Alexander Campbell, author of a huge, ill-versed, but heavily documented diatribe against the Clearances, *The Grampians Desolate* (1804), to tour the Highlands collecting folk songs, and he later supported him when he fell into poverty.[25] With many friends among 'improving' highland landlords, notably the Sutherlands and MacDonnell of Glengarry, Scott was reluctant publicly to condemn them, but the indictment of his chief that he put into the words of the old highland soldier More MacAlpin in *A Legend of Montrose* (1819), on being evicted from his native glen, show someone deeply disturbed by what Campbell recorded: 'I cannot curse him . . . I will not curse him; he is the descendant and representative of my fathers. But never shall mortal man hear me name his name again.'[26]

In 1822 the Highlands starred in Scott's organization of George IV's visit to Edinburgh. The King forewent improvers for 'a gathering of the Gael': investing him with the Jacobite tradition, which Scott formally buried in *Redgauntlet* (1824)—'Then, gentlemen, the cause is lost FOREVER!'[27] Almost immediately afterwards, he was himself destroyed both as print-capitalist and as moderate integrationist by the slump of 1825–6 and the fall of Dundas rule in Scotland. The attempt at composure disappeared, as he created self-destructive Highlanders in his short stories 'The Highland Widow' and 'The Two Drovers', published in *The Chronicles of the Canongate* (1828). In this, his last great work, plot and outlook are grim. In 'The Two Drovers' two friends, one English and the other Highlander, dispute over some grazing land in the Carlisle area; after being (unfairly) humiliated in a wrestling match, the highlander borrows a knife and stabs the Englishman, and is himself executed. This not only is a projection of Scott's own troubled identity, after the collapse of his publishing empire, but takes up the theme of mutual tribal destruction in the feud of the pig farmers in the *Tain bo Cuailnge*.[28] Scott the conservative cultural nationalist conveys the unconstrained, destructive force which would be released by the Whigs' dissolving of society's constraints—something vividly borne in on him both by his interest in Irish folklore, and by his traumatic journey to Ireland in 1825.[29]


## II  THE USES OF ETHNOLOGY

In his last years, Scott like Burns added emotion to his contractual nationality, but apprehensively. He feared that liberal reform and assimilation would release social

[25] Gourievidis, 'The Image of the Clearances', 6.

[26] Walter Scott, *A Legend of Montrose*, in *The Waverley Novels* (Edinburgh: Adam and Charles Black, 1879), v, 146.

[27] Christopher Harvie, 'Scott and the Image of Scotland', in Alan Bold, ed., *Sir Walter Scott: The Long-Forgotten Melody* (London: Vision, 1983), 31.

[28] Ibid. 37 ff.

[29] Scott was acquainted with Crofton Croker, whose *The Fairy Legends and Traditions of the South of Ireland* appeared in 1825. See Sidney Lee, 'Thomas Crofton Croker, 1798–1854', *DNB*.

anomie: 'Instead of canny Saunders, they will have a very dangerous North British neighbourhood'.[30] Yet reform in fact reinforced a radical 'Scottish' tradition, neglected by Chapman and Pittock, which was anti-Celtic: the legacy of the Calvinist Covenanters who in the late seventeenth century saw themselves as bulwarks against the anarchy and Catholic credulousness represented by the Stewarts and the Highlands. They became part of the mythology of the middle-class evangelical movement against landowner patronage in the Kirk. The appropriate 'moment' for Protestant memory was out of Scottish rather than Ulster history, the defence in 1690 of Dunkeld by a scratch Cameronian force under the poet William Cleland after the Jacobites had defeated General MacKay (at the cost of their leader, Graham of Claverhouse) at Killiekrankie. This had a presence like the Boyne and the siege of Derry, but with significant differences. In James Hogg's *The Brownie of Bodsbeck* (1817) and John Galt's *Ringhan Gilhaize* (1823), both deliberate ripostes to Scott's anti-Covenanting *Old Mortality* (1816)—and in the cult of Alexander Peden and the histories of Robert Wodrow and Thomas McCrie—this employed much of the symbolism that Chapman associates with Celticism, but in the service of lowland, Low Church Presbyterianism.[31]

In the 'Ten Years' Conflict' over lay patronage, from 1833 to 1843, this could have developed into a Scottish variant of full-blown Anglo-Saxonism. The sectarian impulse was bound up with racial stereotypes derived from evolutionary science: James Burnett, Lord Monboddo (1714–1799), equated, in *The Origins and Progress of Language* (1773–87), the 'lower forms of man' with the orang-utans. Cranial measurement was popularized by the success of phrenology through George Combe's activities in the Edinburgh area, where it had a strong alignment with radical Protestantism.[32] 'Scientific' racism was notorious in the anatomist Robert Knox, the employer of Burke and Hare in 1829, and his *The Races of Mankind* (1850).[33]

Ethnological stereotypes also informed the development of archaeology in Scotland, which under (Sir) Daniel Wilson (1816–1892) had strongly 'patriotic' inclinations: commentators were precise as to the 'brachycephalic' (round-headed: 'Celtic') or 'dolichocephalic' (long-headed: 'Danish') skull types of skeletons discovered in burial mounds, and vague about specifying what they meant by 'Celtic'.[34] Until the 1840s the Society of Antiquaries of Scotland catalogued every find that was not Roman as 'Danish'.[35] Something of this semi-scientism was also to be found in the neutral attitude of lowland Scotland to the Clearances of the 1810s and the 1840s, its general hostility both to highland and to Irish immigration, and a popular Protestantism which cultivated its Ulster connections. The socialist historian Tom Johnston

---

[30] Entry for 14 Mar. 1826 in *The Journal of Sir Walter Scott*, ed. John Guthrie Tait and W. M. Parker (Edinburgh: Oliver and Boyd, 1950), 133.

[31] Harvie, 'The Covenanting Tradition'.       [32] Curtis, *Apes and Angels*, 11–12, 96–7.

[33] See Owen Dudley Edwards, *Burke and Hare* (Edinburgh: Polygon, 1978).

[34] D. V. Clarke, 'Scottish Archaeology in the Second Half of the Nineteenth Century', in Alan Bell, ed., *The Scottish Antiquarian Tradition* (Edinburgh: John Donald, 1981), 130.

[35] R. B. K. Stevenson, 'The Museum: To 1850', in Bell, ed., *The Scottish Antiquarian Tradition*, 109.

(1881–1965), in his fierce chapter 'The Clearances' in *The History of the Working Classes in Scotland* (1920), still talks of 'the general disposition of the time to regard the Highlanders as a wild, hungry, thievish race, whose extermination would be a national gain'.[36]

Thus, lowland Protestant opinion had some similarities to Marx and Engels's denunciation of the Celts as

> ...a remnant-people, left over from an earlier population, forced back and subjugated by the nation which later became the repository of historical development. These remnants of a nation, mercilessly crushed, as Hegel said, by the course of history, this 'national refuse', is always the fanatical representative of the counter-revolution and remains so until it is completely exterminated or de-nationalised.[37]

Given sweeping Irish and highland in-migration to industrial areas, often tapped for cheap labour and strike-breaking, why did the Scots not move, as in Ulster, further towards a British identification?[38]

## III 'AN INFINITE RELIGIOUS IDEA'

There were two major individual interventions. The first was Thomas Carlyle, whose influence in the 1830s and 1840s was as profound on Scotland as on the English intelligentsia. Engels's views and thus Marx's owe much to Carlyle on the Irish in *Chartism* (1839), but Carlyle was never a down-the-line Anglo-Saxonist.[39] The 'heroic', in a man claimed by John Mitchel as 'royal and almost Godlike', is more of a Celtic trait inherited, like his condemnation of 'mechanism' and the 'cash-nexus'—his own variant on Arnold's 'despotism of fact'?—directly from the Gaelic-speaking Adam Ferguson; and his relationship to the Young Irelanders became almost avuncular.[40] When he wrote about the character of Scotland, in his essay on Scott in 1838, he stressed qualities which were quite un-Anglo-Saxon: 'Thought, conscience, the sense that man is denizen of a Universe, creature of an Eternity, has penetrated to the remotest cottage, to the simplest heart.'[41]

---

[36] Tom Johnston, *The History of the Working Classes in Scotland*, 1922 (4th edn, Glasgow: Unity Publishing Co., 1946), 189.

[37] Friedrich Engels, 'The Magyar Struggle', *Neue Rheinische Zeitung* (13 Jan. 1849), trans. in David Fernbach, ed., *Karl Marx: The Revolutions of 1848*, ed. David Fernbach (Harmondsworth: Penguin, 1973), 221–2; and see Kriszta Fenyö, *Contempt, Sympathy and Romance* (East Linton: Tuchwell, 2000).

[38] See Campbell, *The Lanarkshire Miners*, 74–5, 277–81.

[39] K. J. Fielding, 'Ireland, John Mitchel, and his "sarcastic friend" Thomas Carlyle', in Joachim Schwend, Susanne Hagemann, and Hermann Völkel, eds., *Literature in Context: Festschrift for Horst W. Drescher* (Frankfurt: Peter Lang, 1992).

[40] For Carlyle's debt to Adam Ferguson compare the argument in Carlyle, 'Characteristics', *Edinburgh Review* (1831), repr. in his *Scottish and Other Miscellanies* (London: Dent, n.d.), esp. 194–9, with Ferguson's *Essay on the History of Civil Society*, 16–19; for his relations with Young Ireland see Owen Dudley Edwards, 'Ireland', in *Celtic Nationalism* (London: Routledge and Kegan Paul, 1968), 123–4.

[41] Thomas Carlyle, 'Sir Walter Scott', *Edinburgh Review* (1838), repr. in *Scottish and Other Miscellanies*, 71.

The sense of the prior claims of society, belief, and art over the economic mechanism would, through Carlyle's disciples John Ruskin and Patrick Geddes, have an effect on the Celtic revival of the 1890s. But, writing in 1847, the geologist and journalist Hugh Miller (1802–1856), himself deeply influenced by Carlyle, distinguished between the intellectual bent of the Scots and the amiable but undemanding English: 'The preponderance of enjoyment lies on the more credulous side . . . I never yet encountered a better-pleased people . . . Unthinking, unsuspicious, blue-eyed, fair-complexioned, honest Saxons.'[42] Miller raises a second radicalizing element as the leading publicist of the Free Church movement. This was not simply Evangelical in inspiration, but owed something to the mysticism of MacLeod Campbell and Edward Irving; some of its leaders were on friendly terms with the Tractarians.[43] Miller, himself half-Gael, was also led by his own frontier background (he came from Cromarty, a lowland town only a dozen miles from the highland line, with its own immigrant Gaels) into following Crofton Croker's Irish folklorism in *Scenes and Legends of the North of Scotland* (1834). His strong anti-Clearance line in the 1840s reflected the religious revolution which gave overwhelming support to the Free Church in the Highlands.[44]

The Free Kirk had its own element of populist mysticism in the role of the 'Men', who looked like pirates in their bandanna scarves and combined the roles of lay preachers and seers, and the frequent transfer of supernatural powers from old mythology to new evangelicalism.[45] But it also, for the first time, provided a cause equally popular in urban Scotland and in the Highlands, just when internal migration was making the Scots population more homogeneous. William Ewart Gladstone (1809–1898), Liberal leader from 1867, from the same 'mixed' east-coast highland-line background as Miller (father lowland Scots, mother a Celt from the clan Donnachaidh), would ultimately provide the political leadership of this movement, partly by stressing the highland continuity provided by his episcopalianism with its Jacobite background, and his linkages to the Free Church.[46]

## IV REVIVALS

Gladstone, the Free Church, and the land reform movement were to exert influence in the 1880s, but the mid century period 1850–80 was one of setbacks to Scottish identity, culminating in the 1860s. Buckle's *History of Civilisation in England* devoted its second volume to an attack on the Scottish deductive philosophical tradition, and in 1865, a year after his election as Lord Rector of St Andrews, John Stuart Mill gave

[42] Hugh Miller, *First Impressions of England* (London: John Johnstone, 1847), 45–6.
[43] See Robert Calder, 'A School of Thinking: Realism and the Revival of Learning', unpublished MS, 1994.
[44] For Miller's political journalism see George Rosie, *Hugh Miller: Outrage and Order* (Edinburgh: Mainstream, 1980).
[45] See Donald Meek, 'Celtic Christianity' in Brown, ed., *Celticism*.
[46] See Christopher Harvie, 'Gladstonianism, the Provinces, and Popular Political Culture', in Richard Bellamy, ed., *Victorian Liberalism* (London: Routledge, 1990), esp. 164–5.

'common sense' the *coup de grâce* with his *Examination of Sir William Hamilton's Philosophy*. In 1867 Matthew Arnold's *Celtic Literature* put the Highlands—with the Welsh and the Irish—in their soulful, a-scientific place. The Free Church stimulated radical journalism, and its ministers criticized the landowners more than their 'Established' predecessors.[47] But the split in the Kirk destroyed it as a semi-independent political institution and paralysed attempts at a liberal nationalism.[48]

Into this vacuum flowed two forces. The imperial or at least transnational artisanry of the MacAndrews we have already met: agnostic about nationality, it was no more British than it was Scots. The other was a conservative romanticism which owed much to the example of Scott, and was represented by the authors around *Blackwood's Magazine*. W. E. Aytoun's *Lays of the Scottish Cavaliers* (1848) had run into twenty-nine editions by 1883; John Wilson, 'Christopher North', provided an opinionated, sub-Johnsonian link with the weekending English clerisy of the Lakes; he and Theodore Martin wrote the lively *Bon Gaultier Ballads*, and Martin later interested himself in the Welsh language, Samuel Ferguson emulated Aytoun in Ireland with his *Lays of the Western Gael* (1865). The technical skill of this group was considerable—as was their apparent openness to the Scots and to other traditions—but they deployed this in such a way as to anaesthetize the development in Scotland of an authentically liberal politics. Wilson, according to Andrew Noble, 'created a flatulent rhetoric of national feeling as an antidote to either true national consciousness or will. He exploited nationalism and religion in order to pursue class politics.'[49]

This eased the way for the decorative, politically impotent Celtic revivalism spawned by the industry of the brothers Sobieski Stuart, and the patronage of the Royal Family after they had discovered Balmoral Castle, significantly enough in 1848. The retreat of the Scottish Conservative nobility from government after 1826—though not from administration or the military—influenced the recovery of folk tradition and the outright invention of much highland custom, such as pipe bands, highland dances, and highland games, not to speak of literally hundreds of 'baronial' mansions, rearing up everywhere from suburbs to desolate glens, much of their inspiration stemming from the Londoner R. W. Billings's *Baronial and Ecclesiastical Antiquities of Scotland* (1845–52).[50]

Important here was the applied antiquarianism which recovered Celtic patterns of dress and decoration. The creation of Victorian tartan has been the subject of a fine pasquinade from Lord Dacre; one can modify his notion of the tartan being an English eighteenth-century invention, on the grounds that the metropolitan development of post-industrial folkways was the rule in Europe, not the exception. The work of the

[47] William Donaldson, *Popular Literature in Victorian Scotland: Language, Fiction and the Press* (Aberdeen: Aberdeen University Press, 1986), 17–18.

[48] I. G. C. Hutchison, *A Political History of Scotland, 1832–1924* (Edinburgh: John Donald, 1986), 60–2.

[49] Andrew Noble, 'John Wilson (Christopher North) and the Tory Hegemony', in Douglas Gifford, ed., *The History of Scottish Literature*, iii: *The Nineteenth Century* (Aberdeen: Aberdeen University Press, 1988).

[50] See Valerie Fiddes and Alistair Rowan, *David Bryce* (Edinburgh: Edinburgh University Fine Art Department, 1976).

indefatigable Sobieski Stuart brothers in ascribing weaves to particular clans helpfully coincided with Balmoral, the heroics of the Crimea and Indian Mutiny, mechanized wool weaving, and the impact of aniline dyes to create that lurid assault on the senses which is modern highland dress.[51] It also encouraged the militarism and imperialism which distinguished Scottish Celticism—radical and conservative—from its pacifist Welsh and rebellious Irish contemporaries.[52]

As significant, perhaps, at a time when art and architecture were loaded with political significance was the renaissance of Celtic ornament, out of use since the eighth century, revived in the seventeenth, and then forgotten.[53] This was a reflex of the neo-Jacobite and antiquarian movements. General David Stewart of Garth (1772–1829), founder of the Edinburgh Celtic Society in 1820, produced his Jacobite *Sketches of the Character, Manners and Present State of the Highlanders of Scotland* in 1822. James Logan's *The Scottish Gael* came out in 1830, followed by the Sobieski Stuarts' *Vestiarium Scoticum* in 1842, and their *Costume of the Clans* in 1844. Drawing, more legitimately, on the antiquarians, James Stuart's *The Sculptured Stones of Scotland* appeared in two volumes, in 1856 and 1867. This was just after the Scottish rights movement of the early 1850s, and offered timely monumental designs.

Celtic monumentalism took on throughout the 'periphery'. The Welsh eccentric and Chartist Dr William Price (1800–1893) had already erected round towers to guard his estate at Llantrisant in the 1830s. Similar monuments were raised to commemorate the Battle of Largs (1863) and, in Dublin's Glasnevin Cemetery, Daniel O'Connell (1867). Daniel Maclise, of Scots ancestry, created in London huge tableaux of the Irish past, such as *The Marriage of Strongbow and Eva* (1854), full of torcs and knotwork. With even greater ambition but notably inferior talent, David Scott tried something similar for Scotland. His brother the Pre-Raphaelite artist William Bell Scott (1811–1890) raised a Celtic cross in Glasgow to his memory in 1860. The Scots-Irish painter George Petrie used his artistic as well as his linguistic skills to promote a more scientific recovery of the Irish past through his work with the Irish Ordnance Survey, a project of the Scots engineer-turned-Irish Under-Secretary Thomas Drummond. By the 1860s knotwork and Celtic crosses were appearing as jewellery, testimonials, and advertisements. Often, because of a scaling-up of Celtic motifs from illuminated manuscripts, this produced memorably awful distortions, as a glance at many a highland cemetery will show. 'We saw the Celtic cross put up to the late Duke of Athole,' wrote Queen Victoria in 1873, intriguingly enough at Adam Ferguson's Logierait. A decade later, another was raised over the graves of the Sobieski Stuarts at Eskadale in Strathglass.

While architecture was in this way 'open', the Gaelic revival movement in Scotland—*An Comunn Gaidhealach* and the *Mod* (1892)—remained, unlike its equivalents in post-Parnellite Ireland and Liberal Wales, firmly in Conservative, landed

[51] Hugh Trevor-Roper, 'The Highland Tradition of Scotland', in Eric Hobsbawm, ed., *The Invention of Tradition* (Cambridge: Cambridge University Press, 1984).

[52] Hugh Cunningham, *The Volunteer Force: A Social and Political History* (London: Croom Helm, 1975), 46–7.

[53] Lloyd Laing, *Celtic Britain* (London: Routledge, 1979), 177–81.

hands.[54] The 1870s and 1880s had been boom years for historical associations: out of forty-nine founded since 1780, twenty dated from these two decades, and the four largest categories of members of the oldest group, the Society of Antiquaries of Scotland, in 1878–9 were 'gentlemen', landowners, lawyers, and English residents.[55] Paradoxically, individual wealthy men had a more radical impact. Various national-ist and historical causes in Wales and Scotland received donations from the Third Marquess of Bute (1847–1900), the *Lothair* of Disraeli's 1870 novel, living off the vast wealth of his Cardiff properties. Libraries, universities, and the Catholic Church benefited from his benefactions, he kept the Paisley publishing firm of Alexander Gardner going reprinting Scottish titles and bankrolled the *Scottish Review*, which perished at his death.[56] The further Celticizing of the Carlyleian 'heroic' style owed much to an unreconstructed Herderian, Professor John Stuart Blackie (1809–1895), who for over a decade campaigned for a Chair of Celtic at Edinburgh, ultimately founded in 1882. An opponent of reform in 1867 on lines not far from those of Carlyle's *Shooting Niagara* (1866), Blackie nevertheless pronounced the clan sys-tem in a pamphlet of 1880 'the best possible system that has ever been or ever will be devised, with its admirable social steam and social cement . . . bound together by strong ties of moral esteem and regard'.[57]

   Secondly, and aligned more with the Free Church tradition, a small farmer-settler radicalism grew up in the areas settled by emigrants, chiefly in Canada, Australia, and New Zealand, and then reacted on the political tradition of the mother country. After 1873 this combined with agricultural depression to borrow from the Irish example of Michael Davitt and the Land League, and to give an impulse to the Crofters' War of the early 1880s, when crofters forcibly resisted eviction in Skye.[58] Out of these upheavals and the granting of the rural household suffrage emerged in the mid 1880s the Crofters' Party, which swept the Highlands in 1885 and influenced the early home rule and socialist movements. An important input here was W. F. Skene's *Celtic Scotland: A History of Ancient Alban* (1876–1880), the work of a son of one of Scott's entourage and the brother of George Skene, who had in 1847 felled the Sobieski Stuarts in the *Quarterly*. Skene's description of surviving communal control of land revived the ideal of Celtic communism, and was timely for the Napier Com-mission's inquiry into highland land tenure. The government, however, settled for a type of 'dual ownership' along the lines of the Irish Land Act of 1881.[59]

   [54] F. G. Thompson, 'Gaelic in Politics', *Transactions of the Highland Society of Inverness*, 47 (1972), 81.
   [55] C. S. Terry, *A Catalogue of the Publications of Scottish Historical and Kindred Clubs, 1780–1908* (Edinburgh: HMSO, 1909); Society of Antiquaries of Scotland, *Annual Report* (Edinburgh: Society of Antiquaries of Scotland, 1880).
   [56] H. J. Hanham, *Scottish Nationalism* (London: Faber, 1969), 83–5, 88; 'Stuart, John Patrick Criton, third Marquess of Bute', *DNB* (by John Horne Stevenson).
   [57] J. S. Blackie, *Gaelic Societies, Highland Depopulation, and Land Law Reform* (Edinburgh: Gaelic Society, 1880), 5.
   [58] James Hunter, 'The Politics of Highland Land Reform, 1873–1895', *Scottish Historical Review*, 53 (1974).
   [59] See Clive Dewey, 'Celtic Agrarian Legislation and the Celtic Revival: Historicist Implications of Gladstone's Irish and Scottish Land Acts, 1870–1886', *Past and Present*, 64 (1974).

The highland land-and-order problem propelled the bipartisan restoration of the Scottish Secretary in 1885—largely against the inclinations of Edinburgh's power brokers.[60] In terms of resources and authority a twenty-year succession of minor Tory noblemen scarcely challenged great urban magnates like Sir James Marwick, Town Clerk of Glasgow, but the fact that they derived their authority from highland issues—fisheries, communications, lighthouses, as well as land—meant that they could both pre-empt Scottishness and 'pro-Irish' (and often carpet-bagging) Liberalism and avoid the class tensions of urban Scotland. This enjoyed some success, with a succession of celebrations (Burns in 1886, the Royal Jubilee in 1887 and 1897, Edinburgh Exhibitions in 1886, 1890, and 1908, Glasgow Exhibitions in 1888, 1901, and 1911) at which national unity could be made to count. The Unionists actually won 38 out of 72 Scottish seats in 1901, only to fall to the Liberal revival, partially nationalist-driven by the Young Scots, in 1906, when only 12 survived.[61]

By the 1880s much of the hostility to the Scottish Celt had evaporated, not least because so many had migrated south and intermarried with the lowland population. But it was still difficult, after a century of economic and social upheaval and urbanization, to see any unifying vision of the cultural traits of the country. Douglas Gifford has suggested that the dualism of Robert Louis Stevenson's vision in *The Master of Ballantrae* (1889), his tale of the two feuding Durie brothers, one Jacobite, imaginative, and evil, the other Hanoverian, conscientious, and dull—yet both doomed to be degraded—can be taken as a metaphor for the whole troubled society: divided individuals in a divided family in a divided nation.[62]

## V  GEDDES AND SYNERGY

After 1885 the radical movement came to use the land issue as a more positive metaphor. The Clearances were seen not just as highland history but as a symbol for the exploitation of the Scottish people.[63] Celtic communism revived as a putative type of socialist organization. Yet both Gaelic conservatives and radicals lacked the powerful impulse of the Scottish lowland or Welsh-language weekly press and its promotion of writing in the vernacular. Gaelic, unlike Welsh, had failed to make a timely transition to print-capitalism: only sixty-seven books were published in the language in 1750–1800, and 1,000 in the nineteenth century, two-thirds of them religious works.[64] There was no Gaelic equivalent of Thomas Gee's weekly *Baner ac Amserau Cymru*, founded in 1859, which carried serial novels and commentaries on British and foreign politics, and no novel in the language until 1912.

---

[60] H. J. Hanham, 'The Creation of the Scottish Office, 1881–87', *Juridical Review,* 10 (1965), 209.

[61] For national celebrations see Elfie Rembold, *Die festliche Nationen: Glasgow Exhibition 1911, und Carnarfon Investiture 1912* (Berlin: Philo, 2002).

[62] Douglas Gifford, 'Myth, Parody and Dissociation: Scottish Fiction, 1814–1914', in Gifford, ed., *History of Scottish Literature,* iii, 248–9.

[63] Gourievidis, 'The Image of the Clearances', 282 ff.

[64] Derick Thomson, *The Companion to Gaelic Scotland* (Oxford: Blackwell, 1983), 245; D. Maclean, *Typographia Scoto-Gadelica* (Edinburgh: Grant, 1915).

In Scotland by the 1890s, however, the print-capitalism of the Lowland vernacular was weakening, under the impact of the Kailyard, English-style sensation journalism, and mass-spectator sport.[65] Welsh radicalism was deeply puritan and deprecated sport—until Wales beat the All Blacks in 1905, when the chapels gave rugby their blessing. In Scotland the revival of Gaelic sports made modest progress after the codification of the rules of shinty in 1877, and the founding of the Strathglass shinty team in 1879 by Captain Chisholm of Strathglass, Catholic, radical, and land reformer, friend of the pan-Celtic radical John Murdoch (and, one wonders, of Strathglass's other prodigies, the Sobieski Stuarts?).[66] But the movement lacked the political input which bolstered the Gaelic Athletic League, and shinty was in the 1890s rapidly outpaced by the growth of professional soccer, largely because the Glasgow Irish used the professionalism of Celtic (and former shinty) players after 1888 to beat the Scots at their own game.[67]

Still, by the third quarter of the nineteenth century, certain aspects of a Celtic Scottish social ethos were beginning to be constructed: a respect for the small community and its constitutive habits and myths, and a desire to subordinate market forces to it; a scepticism about the claims of national political units; a notion, as Harold Laski later put it, of the 'essential federalism of society'; a sensitivity to the natural world, a preference for an imaginatively extensive rather than a hard-and-fast style of argumentation, of the sort characterized by Sophie Bryant's 'correction by expression, not suppression'.[68] This ideology provided a notable Celtic slant to the social overhead capital with which the country was increasingly provided, symbolized by the subtle interplay of functionalism, art nouveau, and the vernacular in the Glasgow School of Art, 1896–1909.

Carlyleian and Ruskinian ideas had already contributed to the setting up in the 1880s of university settlements and social unions in the cities, which sought a basis for a new cooperative ethic. This linked with an advertisedly Celtic literary and artistic renaissance. George MacDonald (1824–1905) wrote as both realist and fabulist, and Neil Munro (1864–1930), alias Hugh Foulis, and William Sharp (1856–1905), alias Fiona MacLeod, actually created separate Scots and Celtic literary personalities. By the 1890s, with the painters John Duncan, Robert Burns, and the Dublin-born Phoebe Anna Traquair (1852–1935), the 'Glasgow Boys' and the architectural *ensemble* around Charles Rennie Mackintosh (1868–1928), of a Tiree family, the Celtic renaissance was strongly under way, largely encouraged by Professor Patrick Geddes (1854–1932).[69]

---

[65] Donaldson, *Popular Literature in Victorian Scotland*, 149.

[66] Roger Hutchinson, *Camanachd! The Story of Shinty* (Edinburgh: Mainstream, 1989), 112 ff.

[67] W. F. Mandle, *The Gaelic Athletic Association and Irish Nationalist Politics, 1884–1924* (London: Christopher Helm, 1987).

[68] See, for example, Harold Laski's pluralist study 'The Political Theory of the Disruption', in *Studies in the Theory of Sovereignty* (Princeton: Princeton University Press, 1917); the career of Andrew Lang as a social anthropologist, covered inter alia by Richard Dorson in *The British Folklorists* (London: Routledge, 1968), 206–20; Sophie Bryant, *The Genius of the Gael* (Dublin: Hodges, Figgis, 1913), quoted by Luke Gibbons, in Brown, ed., *Celticism*.

[69] Duncan Macmillan, *Scottish Art, 1460–1990* (Edinburgh: Mainstream, 1990), 272–5, 291–301; Elizabeth Cumming, *Phoebe Anna Traquair* (Edinburgh: Scottish National Portrait Gallery, 1993), 11–13.

Born a soldier's son in Ballater, Geddes studied under Huxley and went through a phase of religious Positivism, but became Professor of Botany at Dundee in the 1880s. Reading Carlyle, Ruskin, and Le Play, incidentally one of the Catholic conservatives enthused by Ossian, turned him into a pioneer sociologist; he created the Edinburgh Social Union in 1885, and in the 1890s operated from the imaginative art nouveau university settlement 'Ramsay Garden' that he built around Allan Ramsay's house near Edinburgh Castle, dominated by its Outlook Tower.[70] Geddes equated his 'Celtic revival' with ecological sociology and a bio-centric approach to town planning, and seemed uncannily successful in picking up funding from sympathetic and above all wealthy Liberals. Sir Robert Pullar made him a star of the Paris Exhibition of 1900, and Lord Pentland, Secretary under Asquith, took him to India; Lord Aberdeen, Viceroy of Ireland, let him commission the competition for the Dublin plan of 1913. Geddes developed ways of thinking, intuitive and yet dialectically precise, which he claimed were 'Celtic'. He had lost his memory in Mexico in the 1890s and reconstructed it by means of 'thinking machines', an ancestor of programmed learning. His 'sociological laboratory' at the Outlook Tower was to have a huge though diffuse impact on twentieth-century geographical and social studies. His ideal of 'Sympathy: Synopsis: Synergy' seems to fit Sophie Bryant's discourse snugly:

The sorely needed knowledge, both of the natural and the social order, is approaching maturity; the long-delayed renaissance of art has begun, and the prolonged discord of these is changing into harmony; so that with these for guidance men shall no longer grind on in slavery to a false image of their lowest selves, miscalled self-interest, but at length as freemen, live in Sympathy and labour in the Synergy of the Race.[71]

Geddes interested himself in Irish developments and tried to incubate a 'literary renaissance' cognate with that of Yeats and Lady Gregory in Ireland. The short-lived *Evergreen* magazine (1896–98), named after Ramsay's journal, and *Lyra Celtica: An Anthology of the Lyric Poetry of the Gael*, with an introduction by William Sharp (Fiona MacLeod), which Geddes published in 1896, were the results, before Geddes—aided by Andrew Carnegie, who commissioned a social study of Dunfermline in 1903—pursued synergy into his studies of urban organization and city planning.

## VI  'THE GENIUS OF THE GAEL'

Elsewhere Sharp, rather unfairly pigeonholed as a sentimentalist, argued that Celticism was not nationalistic: its strength was that it dispensed with nationality in favour of cosmopolitan openness. Geddes was a more orthodox home ruler, but his Celtic quality seems to have been the expansiveness of his ideas. He did not shift out of one field to another, but incorporated the results of his research into his 'three Ss'—coupled with a methodical and disciplined quality about their arrangement which had conscious parallels with triads, the Welsh disciplines of strict-metre verse and the complexities of Celtic ornament.

---

[70]  Helen Meller, *Patrick Geddes: Social Evolutionist and City Planner* (London: Routledge, 1990).
[71]  Quoted in Macmillan, *Scottish Art*, 272.

Whether there was as strong a connection between Geddes's Taliesin-like shape-changing and the Celtic politics of the linguistic revivalist and 'Celtic communist' notions of another well-heeled enthusiast, Ruaraidh Erskine of Mar (1869–1960), is more debatable. Erskine had been taught Gaelic by his nurse, and published his bilingual review *Guth na Bliadha* between 1904 and 1925, pursuing the much more aggressively Herderian line of 'no language—no nation'.[72] After 1918 Erskine influenced the Clydeside Marxist John MacLean (whose family came from Mull in the Inner Hebrides) to combine his Marxism with an idiosyncratic Scottish proletarian nationalism based on 'Celtic communism': 'When I stand true to my class, the working class, in which I was born, it is because my people were swept out of the highlands.'[73]

Also co-opted was the memory of James Connolly, born in Edinburgh in 1866, and active there as a local socialist before he migrated to North America and later Ireland in 1896.[74] Connolly was *Forward*'s Irish correspondent, and although the Glasgow Independent Labour Party folk could not understand his course of action in 1916, he was assumed to represent a Celtic socialism, and remained a significant influence on the Scottish left in the inter-war period.

All four—Geddes, Erskine, MacLean, and Connolly—were important influences on Hugh MacDiarmid, who was also, at Langholm, a near neighbour of, and deeply influenced by, Carlyle.[75] MacDiarmid conceived of his Lallans revival in the early 1920s as a dialectical stage in the capture of Scotland by the 'Gaelic idea', something which had by the 1930s modulated into a kind of mystic materialism. This could be cited as evidence of that intellectual *folie de grandeur*—'He kept his genius but lost his talent'—which Norman MacCaig mourned, but in the 1930s MacDiarmid's Gaelic enthusiasm still spurred Sorley MacLean, the greatest Gaelic poet since the eighteenth century, into writing. In the 1930s, too, a cognate impulse of Celtic 'organicness', confederalism, and social reform, stemming from another independent-minded and rather authoritarian socialist, led the Revd George MacLeod to pick up Dr Johnson's challenge, and create the Iona Community, a monastic, ritualistic community dedicated to social reform and the restoration of the abbey.[76]

It was MacDiarmid's desire to provoke the 'Caledonian Antisyzygy', a perpetual, fricative unrest, and also to 'see Scotland whole', to produce some great synthesis of the nation. The Gaelic idea was invoked to this end. But was 'Antisyzygy' at all compatible with the 'synergy' that Geddes had counselled? Edwin Muir, in *Scott and Scotland* (1936), took a strictly Herderian line, dismissed Gaelic as impossibly decayed, regarded lowland Scots as limited to the emotions, and feared that his countrymen had no alternative to limping forward in English.[77] MacDiarmid was

---

[72] See Ruth Drost, 'Die schottische Nationalbewegung von 1886 bis 1928', MA dissertation, Munich University, 1990, 127–32.

[73] Quoted in Gourievidis, 'The Image of the Clearances', 353.

[74] Hanham, 'The Creation of the Scottish Office', 134–40.

[75] Hugh MacDiarmid, *The Company I've Kept* (London: Routledge, 1966), 81 ff.

[76] George MacLeod, 'Religion', in David Cleghorn Thomson, ed., *Scotland in Search of its Youth* (Edinburgh: Oliver and Boyd, 1932).

[77] Edwin Muir, *Scott and Scotland* (London: Routledge, 1936), 113 ff.

virulently hostile to this, but in *The Islands of Scotland* (1939) could only show a mosaic of different and incompatible cultures. Recently, Ursula Kimpel, a German critic, has suggested that it is precisely in this multiplicity—always latent in MacDiarmid—that the character of Scottish culture lies, as the situation has got no more straightforward since then.[78] Neither the cosmopolitan Celt William Sharp nor the nationalist Celt Patrick Geddes would disagree with that. In the 1970s the imaginative work which most affected Scottish politics was John McGrath's *The Cheviot, the Stag and the Black, Black Oil* of 1973, a folk drama which drew together highland history, the Clearances, and lowland and Gaelic culture: unity being provided by the fact—now common to all Scots—of being exploited by external powers. McGrath's play ended with the lines of Mary MacPherson, from the 1880s:

> Cuimhnichibh ur cruadal
> Is cumaibh suas ur sroill,
> Gun teid an roth mun cuairt duibh
> Le neart is cruas nan dorn
> Gum bi ur crodh air bhuailtean
> 'S gach tuathanach air doigh,
> 'S na Sas'naich air fuadach
> A Eilean Uain a' Cheo.

> Remember that you are a people and fight for your rights—
> There are riches under the hills where you grew up.
> There is iron and coal there, grey lead and gold there—
> There is richness in the land under your feet.

> Remember your hardships and keep up your struggle
> The wheel will turn for you
> By the strength of your hands and the hardness of your fists.
> Your cattle will be on the plains
> Everyone on the land will have a place
> And the exploiter will be driven out.[79]

The 'embassy' of that odd pair, MacDiarmid and Erskine to Dublin, to view the revived Tailteann Games in August 1924 and meet Yeats, AE, de Valera, and Gogarty, was critical in establishing the Celtic credentials of Scottish literary and political nationalism.[80] That much, at least, is fact. And Scotland beat Ireland at hurling...

---

[78] Ursula Kimpel, 'Modern Scottish Poetry: Beyond the "Caledonian Antisyzygy"', in Lothar Fietz, Paul Hoffmann, and Hans-Werner Ludwig, eds., *Regionalität, Nationalität und Internationalität in der zeitgenössischen Lyrik* (Tübingen: Attempto Verlag, 1992).

[79] John McGrath, *The Cheviot, the Stag and the Black, Black Oil* (Broadford: West Highland Publishing Company, 1974), 33.

[80] Alan Bold, *MacDiarmid: Christopher Muray Grieve: A Critical Biography* (London: John Murray, 1988), 233.

# 5

## The Folk and the *Gwerin*

We were a tribe, a family, a people.
Wallace and Bruce guard now a painted field,
And all may read the folio of our fable,
Peruse the sword, the sceptre and the shield.
A simple sky roofed in that rustic day,
The busy corn-fields and the haunted holms,
The green road winding up the ferny brae.
But Knox and Melville clapped their breaching palms
And bundled all the harvesters away,
Hoodicrow Peden in the blighted corn
Hacked with his rusty beak the starving haulms.
Out of that desolation we were born.

Courage beyond the point and obdurate pride
Made us a nation, robbed us of a nation.
Defiance absolute and myriad-eyed
That could not pluck the palm plucked our damnation.
We with such courage and the bitter wit
To fell the ancient oak of loyalty,
And strip the peopled hill and the altar bare,
And crush the poet with an iron text,
How could we read our souls and learn to be?

Edwin Muir, 'Scotland 1941'[1]

## I  THE PERSISTENCE OF FAITH

In 1941 the poet Edwin Muir, exiled from Scotland and by Nazism from central
Europe, wrote bitterly about the impact of religion on his native country. His background was secular and socialist, although, like his contemporaries W. H. Auden
and T. S. Eliot, he would return to a qualified form of religious belief. This move
seemed against the post-World War I trend, which had seen the dramatic decline of
Nonconformity. This had been 'the real religion' of England, and in Wales it was
personified in the *gwerin*—the Welsh image of popular democracy—in Prys Morgan's definition, 'a classless society, progressing rapidly yet retaining a closeness to

---

[1] In *Collected Poems* (London: Faber, 1960).

the soil, educated, religious, cultured, keen to own its own land and property, hard-working and methodical, law-abiding, temperate in drink, respecting the sabbath, and an example to the world . . .'.[2] Muir came from the Scots, or more properly Orcadian, version of such a world, but it had declined since Thomas Carlyle's 'sacred lambencies'. Muir indicted Calvinism with the destruction of the Scottish sense of community and humane belief: it 'made us a nation, robbed us of a nation'. The parallels were uneasy. Religious enthusiasts could find Carlyle as disturbing and even infidel as he was stimulating; Muir handled urban Scotland as apprehensively as any *gwerinwr* confronted by 'cosmopolitan South Wales'. The great industrial city, like Calvinism, was an unbudgeable but unwelcome intrusion on his ideal of nationality.[3]

In Scotland, something close to the *gwerin* both preceded and followed its flowering between the years 1880 and 1914. Translated as 'a man of the commonalty', the ideal goes back to the archetype of 'John the Commonweal' in Sir David Lindsay's *The Thrie Estaitis* (1540). The Scots peasant who embodied the popular impulse which led to the Scots Reformation evolved into the nation's sense of itself as a 'covenanted people', and the use of its twin, the word 'commonwealth', by James Bryce to describe his universal democratic ideal in the later nineteenth century.[4] Despite different languages, commonalities of religious culture reinforced such connections: the influence of the Free Kirk's Thomas Chalmers on Methodist doctrine and culture; the Sixth Marquess of Bute bankrolling Scottish nationalist and Catholic publications and groups out of his Cardiff income; Keir Hardie as MP for Merthyr, continuing to live in Cumnock; the young Tom Jones going from Rhymney to the Glasgow University of Edward Caird and Sir Henry Jones; the young Hugh MacDiarmid imbibing the class struggle while a cub reporter on the *Monmouthshire Labour News*.[5]

As MacDiarmid, as much as Muir, would suggest, the mix is powerful, but united by myth—by uncalculated assumptions and habits—as much as by facts. Yet as we have seen, myth works to impose ideological order on a reality which is itself often contradictory. Robert Anderson, Welsh by birth and the historian of French as well as Scots education, takes the latter's ideology seriously. Myth, defined pedagogically as a projection of potential, also contributes to policy:

The belief that Scottish education was peculiarly 'democratic', and that it helped to sustain certain correspondingly democratic features of Scottish life, formed a powerful historical myth, using that word to indicate not something false, but an idealization and distillation of

[2] Prys Morgan, 'The *Gwerin* of Wales—Myth and Reality', 1967, rev., trans., and repr. in I. Hume and W. T. R. Pryce, eds., *The Welsh and their Country* (Llandysul: Gomer Press, 1986), 139.

[3] Edwin Muir, *Scottish Journey* (London: Heinemann, 1935), 102–3, quoted in G. F. A. Best, 'The Scottish Victorian City', *Victorian Studies*, 11 (1967–8), 330. Muir in 1948 became the first Principal of Newbattle Abbey College, which was consciously modelled on Coleg Harlech.

[4] David Jenkins, *The Agricultural Community in South-West Wales at the Turn of the Twentieth Century* (Cardiff: University of Wales Press, 1971), 35; and see Thomas Kleinknecht, *Imperiale und internationale Ordnung: Eine Untersuchung zum Gelehrtenliberalismus am Beispiel von James Bryce, 1838–1922* (Göttingen: Vandenhoeck und Ruprecht, 1985), esp. 59 ff.

[5] H. J. Hanham, *Scottish Nationalism* (London: Faber, 1969), 83–5; Thomas Jones, *Welsh Broth* (London: W. Griffiths, 1951), 1–80; Kenneth O. Morgan, *Keir Hardie: Radical and Socialist* (London: Weidenfeld and Nicolson, 1975), 112 ff.; Alan Bold, *MacDiarmid: Christopher Murray Grieve: A Critical Biography* (London: John Murray, 1988), 63–7.

a complex reality, a belief which influences history by interacting with other forces and pressures, ruling out some developments as inconsistent with the national tradition, and shaping the form in which the institutions inherited from the past are allowed to change.[6]

The popular-democracy myth was between 1920 and 1980 arraigned by the dialectical materialism of Scots and Welsh industrial radicalism as at best a dubious *faux frais* of production. Gwyn A. Williams saw the *gwerin* as the 'pseudo-nation of Welsh dissent', whereby the elitist disremembered both the sweeping population movements of the period and the industrial proletariat who were the true bearers of historical change. Matthew Price's academic task in Raymond Williams's *Border Country* (1961) was to correct this and instead to 'measure the distance' between this new democracy and the Welsh-language tradition.[7] But by the 1960s materialism was under challenge, as two-party class-based politics declined and—through the influence of Ralf Dahrendorf, John Vincent, and Peter Clarke's re-animation of the 'new Liberalism'—economic class-consciousness was seen as neither inevitable nor dominant; in Clarke's phrase 'classes are essentially groups in conflict about power'.[8] In this retrospection, Labour's rise had more to do with the malfunctions of ideology and organized politics than with any dramatic change of grass-roots allegiance.

In the late 1980s this reappraisal was boosted by two apparently contradictory phenomena: the Marxian political order in Eastern Europe collapsed, reinstating 'civil society'; at the same time patterns of political behaviour in Scotland and Wales had to transcend the economic decline of class politics and the challenge of Thatcherite individualism. The miners marching back to Mardy Colliery in the Rhondda in 1985 with their banners flying had lost an industrial conflict but won new communitarian loyalties. The same could be said of their Scottish comrades under Mick MacGahey. The recovery from the devolution debacle of 1979 and from the miners' strike echoed not just the symbolism of 1926—as potent in Scots as in Welsh culture—but the Crofters' War of 1884–5 and the Penrhyn quarrymen's strike of 1900–03, becoming the rallying point for a wider radicalism.[9]

Behind the activists, and the geographical similarity of anti-Thatcher Britain to Gladstonian Britain, stood more complex social reasoning. When David Marquand attempted to define the 'principled society', he cited the Scots theologian and philosopher Alasdair McIntyre's revival of Aristotelian politics against dogmatic individualism: 'On the traditional Aristotelian view such problems do not arise . . . There is no way of my pursuing my good which is necessarily antagonistic to you pursuing

---

[6] R. D. Anderson, *Education and Opportunity in Victorian Scotland: Schools and Universities* (Oxford: Oxford University Press, 1988), 1.

[7] In Morgan, 'The *Gwerin* of Wales', 146; Raymond Williams, *Border Country*, 1961 (Harmondsworth: Penguin, 1964), 333.

[8] John Vincent, 'The Political Feelings of the People', in *Poll-Books: How Victorians Voted* (Cambridge: Cambridge University Press, 1967); and P. F. Clarke, 'The Electoral Sociology of Modern Britain', *History*, 57 (Feb. 1972), 43.

[9] See R. Merfyn Jones, *The North Wales Quarrymen* (Cardiff: University of Wales Press, 1981), 267–84; a fascinating light is shed on the differences in national *mentalités* from an English Conservative standpoint by Maurice Cowling in his two volumes of *Religion and Public Doctrine in England* (Cambridge: Cambridge University Press, 1981, 1986).

yours because *the* good is neither mine peculiarly nor yours peculiarly—goods are not private property . . .'.[10] If the Mardy and Edinburgh rallies seemed uncannily *gwerinol* in spirit, they also conjured up the young Ramsay MacDonald, whose biographer Marquand was, and that great Aristoteleian W. E. Gladstone himself.

The Scots equivalent to the *gwerin* was as politically active, identified by one of its articulate enemies, the Tory John Buchan, in a pasquinade against a 1900s Liberal:

> I have never listened to any orator at once so offensive and so horribly effective. There was no appeal too base for him, and none too august: by some subtle alchemy he blended the arts of the prophet and the fishwife. He had discovered a new kind of language. Instead of 'the hungry millions', or 'the toilers', or any of the numerous synonyms for our masters, he invented the phrase, 'Goad's people'. 'I shall never rest,' so ran his great declaration, 'till Goad's green fields and Goad's clear waters are free to Goad's people.'[11]

Along this road lay sentimentality and exploitation—a popular radicalism modulating into Tom Nairn's great tartan monster of the Kailyard—Lloyd George's shift from chapel piety to existential power politics, 'rooted in nothing' as Keynes put it. One might even add, in a Catholic inflection, Myles na cGopaleen's reworking of Daniel Corkery's *Hidden Ireland* (1925) into the comically reactionary 'Plain People of Ireland'. If a rhetoric lacks any lodging in the process of production, it can degenerate into the value-Free State vacuity of the sort Myles condemned (Fianna Fáil, when you think about it, could be rendered as 'the *gwerin* of destiny'). What we are dealing with *could* be a resilient alliance of cultural con men, religious bigots, and would-be local oligarchs. So we have to interrogate it both through comparison and by assessing mutual contributions: in particular the influence of the Scots on the Welsh, through the vehicle of the religious and print-capitalist politics that they were the first to capture.

Following Prys Morgan's definition, the *gwerin* presents the following main aspects: it is (1) progressive, (2) educated, (3) religious, (4) cultivated, (5) classless, (6) law-abiding, (7) linked to the soil, and (8) temperate. These dispute the gradations of English society—Dahrendorf's 'layer-cake of fine class distinctions'—but they also interdict the notion of a proletariat, whose self-definition situates itself on the line of economic division.[12] What did the *gwerin* generation themselves see as the key functions of religion and education? How did they expand into a consideration of the ways in which the economic and social evolution of the two societies was affected by institutions of civil society, and by the state? And what role did religion play in separating Catholic and Protestant in what was otherwise a parallel economic situation: that of the localized political community?

---

[10] Quoted in David Marquand, *The Unprincipled Society* (London: Fontana, 1988), 215; and see also Craig Beveridge and Ronald Turnbull, *The Eclipse of Scottish Culture* (Edinburgh: Polygon, 1989), 99 ff.

[11] John Buchan, 'A Lucid Interval', in *The Moon Endureth*, 1912, repr. in *The Best Short Stories of John Buchan*, ed. David Daniell (London: Michael Joseph, 1982), 30.

[12] See Ralf Dahrendorf, *On Britain* (London: BBC Publications, 1982), 51–79.

II   STATE, RELIGION, PEOPLE

'Tis true that her *gwerin*
Own not an inch of her land,
The Welsh are only pilgrims
Upon the earth of beloved Wales,
The arrogant conquered her,
How often has she groaned!—
The people which dwelled in her
Live in dark deep captivity.[13]

John Morris-Jones's *Cymru rydd* ('Free Wales') of 1892 has a language powerful in its imagery, consonant with Welsh tradition and deeply and ambiguously affected by an English religious and political discourse. The image of the landless pilgrim (later to be used so effectively by Lloyd George) relates to Williams Pantycelyn's great hymn of 1772: 'Guide me, o thou great Jehovah, Pilgrim through this barren land'—and of course to John Bunyan (published in Scotland only two years after 1676 and first translated into Welsh in 1699). But the 'dark deep captivity' also suggests the passage in Ralph Lingen's education report of 1847, of their language trapping the Welsh: 'Equally in his new as in his old home his language keeps him under the hatches . . . his superiors are content simply to ignore his existence. He is left to live in an underworld of his own, and the march of society goes completely over his head.'[14] The Welsh Nonconformist elite accepted that while 'Welsh was the language of religion, English was the language of science, business and commerce, philosophy and the arts.' Scottish Presbyterians in the 1700s similarly accepted that the survival of their church required the Treaty of Union with England.[15] The pilgrim's politics were circumspect integration, coupled with the retention of the 'marrow' of national identity (never so strictly defined that it eliminated getting on well elsewhere): the sort of thing which Nicholas Phillipson has described as the 'semi-independence' of eighteenth- and early nineteenth-century Scotland.[16] Morris-Jones's and Sir John Rhys's Jesus College in Oxford was not a stone's throw from Lingen's—and Edward Caird's and A. D. Lindsay's—Balliol.

The pilgrim became, through John Bunyan, central to the Protestant culture of post-Civil War England. The Irish had a quite different memory. But whatever a pilgrim was, he was unlikely to be found in his parish pew, touching his hat to a squire

---

[13] Quoted in Morgan, 'The *Gwerin* of Wales', 137.
[14] Quoted by Saunders Lewis in 'The Fate of the Language' (1962), trans. in *Planet*, 4 (Feb.–Mar. 1971), 19.
[15] Ieuan Gwynedd Jones, 'Language and Community in Nineteenth Century Wales', in David Smith, ed., *A People and a Proletariat* (London: Pluto Press, 1980), 61. The essay by Kenneth O. Morgan in the Festschrift for Prof. Gwynedd Jones explores the political element in this: 'Tom Ellis versus Lloyd George: The Fractured Consciousness of Fin-de-Siècle Wales', in Geraint Jenkins and Beverley Smith, eds., *Politics and Society in Wales, 1840–1920* (Cardiff: University of Wales Press, 1988).
[16] Nicholas Phillipson, 'Nationalism and Ideology', in J. N. Wolfe, ed., *Government and Nationalism in Scotland* (Edinburgh: Edinburgh University Press, 1969).

with a pass degree. Hugh Miller—the stonemason, geologist, and journalist whose Free Church *Witness* was a model for the Welsh *Tyst* and Thomas Gee—wrote in his *First Impressions of England* (1847), 'The merry unthinking serfs, who, early in the reign of Charles the First, danced on Sabbaths round the maypole, were afterwards the ready tools of despotism. The Ironsides, who in the cause of civil and religious freedom bore them down, were staunch Sabbatarians.'[17] The English may have originated Puritanism, but the Scots, and later the Welsh, were better at it, being wired directly into the society of the Old Testament Israel, as in the great song of Scots radicalism, from the Covenanters to the Red Clydesiders, Psalm 124:

> Now Israel
>> May say, and that truly,
> If that the Lord
>> Had not our cause maintain'd;
> If that the Lord
>> Had not our right sustain'd,
> When cruel men
>> Against us furiously
> Rose up in wrath
>> To make of us their prey,
> Then certainly
>> They had devour'd us all . . .

Sung on the moors in the 1680s, it also rang out at St Enoch's Station when the Glasgow Orpheus Choir saw off Maxton, Wheatley, and company to Westminster in 1922.[18] Escape from the elite of the periphery—from Jacobite, laird, or Sir William Weir—came, not just through national efforts, but through a complex cultural diplomacy, of which religious dissent was a major factor. It forged a direct link between Scotland and Wales, which intriguingly flattered the Scots. 'The chapels spoke as one,' Kenneth Morgan writes; Wales's Nonconformity, which underpinned the notion of the *gwerin*, was 'a kind of unofficial established religion'.[19] But although Calvinistic Methodism theologically resembles Scottish Presbyterianism, the notion of any 'unofficial' establishment—a religion stemming directly out of the voluntary collaborations of civil society—was foreign to the Scots. In Scotland Church–state relations were central, and in the mid Victorian epoch, as before, *divided* Presbyterianism in three ways.

First there was the Established Church. In Wales the overwhelming of episcopalianism by Nonconformity was deemed 'progressive'; in Scotland the struggle over a formally Presbyterian body was a different matter: about controlling it according to the letter of the Act of Union of 1707, through congregations and not landlords. This struggle, headed by Chalmers and Miller, was lost in 1843. Although the creative treatment of the Disruption by those whose defeat made them into Free Churchmen

---

[17] Hugh Miller, *First Impressions of England* (London: John Johnstone, 1847), 45–6.
[18] Iain. S. McLean, *The Legend of Red Clydeside* (Edinburgh: John Donald, 1983), 98–9.
[19] Kenneth O. Morgan, *Rebirth of a Nation: Wales, 1880–1980* (Oxford: Oxford University Press, 1981), 17.

presented this as a victory for the Scots religious impulse, it really meant the end of a distinctive devolution of education and social welfare to the assemblies of the Church, and the transfer of this power to an English-style bureaucracy.

The Disruption was also seen as a radical, anti-landlord act, although the conflict between the 'landlords' men' and the 'Godly Commonwealth' was not an overall phenomenon. William Alexander (1826–1894) was the Scots journalist-novelist counterpart to Wales's Daniel Owen (1836–1895); his *Johnnie Gibb of Gushetneuk* (1871) (subtitled 'a study of parish politics') rapidly became a Scottish classic, running into several editions by 1900. The eponymous crofter hero, fighting the 'muckle fermers' in the 1840s for his own livelihood and religious freedom, shows many *gwerin*-like characteristics, yet in the Aberdeenshire in which the novel is set, the 'Auld Kirk' continued to command general allegiance (at least 70 per cent of the population) in an area where Liberals and radicals were politically supreme.[20]

For much of the nineteenth century, moreover, both the 'Auld Kirk' and the Free Church were 'united' in favouring the *principle* of establishment—something quite foreign to the Welsh tradition. They were strongly opposed by 'the Voluntaries', who attacked the state connection, yet even they stemmed from legalistic disputes about religious control. The Auld Licht Anti-Burghers, whom J. M. Barrie satirized in his *Auld Licht Idylls* (1886), a strong influence on Caradoc Evans's *My People* (1915), were such a 'secession'. But where Evans's Methodists represented a Nonconformist oligarchy, Barrie's Auld Lichts could be safely dismissed as an absurd remnant of eighteenth-century Calvinist extremism.[21]

'Dissent' could unite the non-Anglican *gwerin*; in Scotland for much of the century it divided the Presbyterians, creating the bitter, nit-picking politics that the secularist and Liberal politician J. M. Robertson despised—'the inherent reactionary bias of the ecclesiastical system had turned back the hands of the social clock'.[22] Yet this highly 'political' agenda linked religion closely to law and to some extent with statecraft, creating the possibility of a more intellectual, less disputative theology which could venture out from Calvinism and create a discourse broad enough to bridge the Church–government divide—something evident in the theology of Thomas Erskine of Linlathen, the friend of F. D. Maurice, Carlyle, and Guizot, and figures like Patrick Geddes, John Baillie, and John MacMurray in the twentieth century.[23]

Chalmers's influence on the Welsh was notable. Lewis Edwards (1809–1887) studied under him at Edinburgh and went on to found Bala College and, in 1843, *Y Traethodydd*, which, consciously modelled on the *Edinburgh Review* and *Blackwood's*

[20] For a masterly study of Alexander in his literary-political context see William Donaldson, *Popular Literature in Victorian Scotland: Language, Fiction and the Press* (Aberdeen: Aberdeen University Press, 1986), 101–34.

[21] Regina Weingartner, 'The Fight against Sentimentalism: Caradoc Evans and George Douglas Brown', *Planet*, 75 (June–July 1989).

[22] J. M. Robertson, *The Perversion of Scotland* (London: Freethought Publishing Company, 1886), 215.

[23] See *The Letters of Thomas Erskine of Linlathen*, ed. William Hanna, 2 vols. (London: David Douglas, 1877); and see Beveridge and Turnbull, *The Eclipse of Scottish Culture*, 91–111.

*Magazine*, devoted much attention to Chalmers's theology and social projects. One of its leading contributors, Owen Thomas (1812–1891), whose *cofiant* of Chalmers's contemporary and equivalent John Jones Talysarn is reckoned by some the best biography in Welsh, was also an Edinburgh graduate. Their contribution reflects the power and contradictions of Chalmers's approach: the commitment to economic individualism *and* to the idea of community; to scriptural inspiration, but also to scientific sophistication; to the 'select' nature of their own nationality, and to a cosmopolitan world-view. Chalmers has been dismissed by historians of a Fabian turn as a Tory arch-individualist (with saving graces in the social casework line); but Stewart J. Brown rightly sees his project of a 'Godly Commonwealth' achieved through parochial revival as something peculiarly Scottish.[24]

The concentration of the Nonconformist intelligentsia—Lewis Edwards, Michael D. Jones, later O. M. Edwards and Tom Ellis—was around Bala, its Nonconformist colleges and linking position between rural mid Wales and the rapidly developing slate-quarrying north. But Bala made an un-Chalmersian modulation of the parochial ideal. Farmer- and minister-dominated Welsh Poor Law unions, though stingy with their poor rates, but were also notorious for rarely applying the workhouse test.[25] Communitarianism won out over classical economics, providing a basis for *gwerinol* 'classlessness'. But the Free Church also provided precedent for the Welsh confrontations of the 1850s and 1860s: in its defiance of the landlords, its closeness to Gaelic Scotland (over 20 per cent of its clergy were Gaelic speakers), and the democracy of the kirk session, the Scottish equivalent of the Welsh *seissyn*.[26] Coming after Rebecca, the 1848 riots in Glasgow, and the depredations of the 'Scotch Cattle' (did this mysterious movement echo Scottish secret societies like the 'Horseman's Word'?), it presented a reassuring populist legalism.

In Scotland the evangelical revival was not, as H. T. Buckle stigmatized it, a reaction against enlightenment, although it unquestionably mobilized some notable throwbacks to seventeenth-century bigotry, such as the social reformer, nationalist, and ultra-Protestant the Revd James Begg.[27] It was more of a continuation of the theistic, socially conservationist element in the enlightenment represented by the 'common sense' philosophers Thomas Reid and Adam Ferguson, whose position George Davie has described:

it is inherent in the nature of the belief in an external world or in the mathematical ideals to envisage facts not contained in the sum of the various elementary experiences involved in

---

[24] Stewart Jay Brown, *Thomas Chalmers and the Godly Commonwealth in Scotland* (Oxford: Oxford University Press, 1982), esp. 118 ff.

[25] Anne Digby, 'The Rural Poor Law', in Derek Fraser, ed., *The New Poor Law in the Nineteenth Century* (London: Macmillan, 1976), 158 ff.

[26] See Derick Thomson, ed., *The Companion to Gaelic Scotland* (Oxford: Blackwell, 1983), 87; John Rhys and David Brynmor-Jones, *The Welsh People* (London: T. Fisher Unwin, 1900), 589.

[27] H. T. Buckle, *The History of Civilization in England*, iii, 1861 (London: Longmans Green, 1872); I deal with Begg, inter alia, in an essay entitled 'The Covenanting Tradition' in Graham Walker and Tom Gallagher, eds., *Sermons and Battle Hymns: Protestant Popular Culture in Modern Scotland* (Edinburgh: Edinburgh University Press, 1990).

the genesis of these items of the common sense, and this peculiar and fundamental fact of self-transcendence is held . . . to be an ultimate irrational mystery.[28]

Yet the *étatisme* of Scots religion emphasized a further, social-psychological, difference. In Scots Calvinism conflicts between the churches, and between 'members' and 'adherents', detracted from that intense sociocultural hegemony exercised by religious bodies in rural and small-town Wales. The Scots equivalent of the *llythyr canmoliaeth* (a letter of introduction to a remote congregation) and sanctions against adulterers or loose women, for example, seems to have waned long before the kirk sessions lost power over parish relief after the passage of the Poor Law (Scotland) Act in 1845. With such a broad palette of religious options on offer, the Scottish religious consumer was sovereign.

In part this can be put down to earlier industrialization and population change; in part to the fact that the Kirk was part of a pluralistic political system. Thus in Scotland a pagan, hedonistic culture of dancing, storytelling, singing, drinking, and bawdry coexisted with the Calvinist 'unco guid'—even in those areas dominated by the Free Church at its most fundamentalist, such as the Western Isles (still, notoriously, an area famed for record-breaking commitments to pietism *and* alcohol). The national consumption of 2.55 gallons *of spirits* per head per annum in the 1830s was evidenced in terrifying detail in Dean Ramsay's best-selling *Reminiscences of Scottish Life and Character* (1857). The Kirk was not spared, with tales of presbyteries knocking the bottoms off their glasses before starting on an evening of serious drinking.[29] Rural Wales had a limited spirituous culture—as demonstrated by the brief and inglorious career of the country's only distillery and generally low sales of high-alcohol drink, even before the passage of the Welsh Sunday Closing Act (1881).[30] Scotland preceded Wales both in a popular temperance movement (strongly connected with moral-force Chartism) and in the legal enforcement of temperance, with the Forbes-MacKenzie Act of 1857, but illegal distilling continued on a huge scale in the Highlands and Islands, part of the 'bad weather culture' of a north European people, and an involvement with fishing, inshore and deep-sea, which with its dangers and spasms of relaxation was quite different from farmers and quarrymen with their relatively settled lives. J. M. Robertson wrote accusingly in 1886, 'Austerity and joyless gloom on the one hand produce their natural corrective in dissolute mirth and defiant licence on the other . . . A moral duality, so to speak, runs through past Scottish life in a way that seems at times perplexing.'[31] The same year saw this dualism unforgettably dramatized in *Dr Jekyll and Mr Hyde*. This unrespectable culture, which the Church only fitfully reached, had dimensions which astonished those who penetrated through to it—like the schoolmaster Gavin Greig and the minister Robert Duncan,

---

[28] George Elder Davie, *The Democratic Intellect: Scotland and her Universities in the Nineteenth Century* (Edinburgh: Edinburgh University Press, 1961), 275.

[29] T. C. Smout, *A Century of the Scottish People* (Glasgow: Collins, 1986), 135.

[30] W. R. Lambert, *Drink and Sobriety in Victorian Wales, c.1820–c.1895* (Cardiff: University of Wales Press, 1983), 7.

[31] Robertson, *Perversion of Scotland*, 211.

whose Carnegie-funded researches in 1900 into folk song in Buchan were virtually swamped by the material they provoked.[32]


## III 'GODLY COMMONWEALTHS'

The *gwerin* was never as seriously troubled by psychological dualism, although it was unquestionably *there*, in the two-home, two-identity biographies of O. M. Edwards, head of Welsh education, and of Lloyd George. Welsh Nonconformity exercised this sort of comprehensive cultural hegemony because it implied a counter-culture to the British state, whereas Scots Calvinism had been statutorily incorporated into it. Queen Victoria worshipped in the Auld Kirk in Scotland (Crathie Church was specially built for Balmoral in 1896, but the royal family had patronized the local kirk since 1854) instead of the Episcopalian chapels of the nobility, but was generally regarded as hostile to a country which as Queen she visited only once, in 1889.[33] The Scots, moreover, differed from the Welsh in their attitude to the military role of the state. The *gwerin* ideology was fundamentally pacifist, an importation into Wales of the values of 'militant' Old Dissent, via the Liberation Society and Peace Society, triumphing in 1868 with the election as MP for Merthyr in 1868 of the Revd Henry Richard, 'the Apostle of Peace'.[34] In Scotland the reverse was the case. The Liberation Society had no influence on Scottish politics, and from the 1850s on the Volunteer Force gained remarkable support. Hugh Cunningham has calculated that it involved 5.5 per cent of the adult male population in Scotland in 1881 (against 2.6 per cent in Wales and 2.8 per cent nationally).[35] This was not simply a reflex of the belligerency of the Crimean War, 'Thin Red Line' period. The issue of a 'militia', an embodiment in arms of the Scottish people, had been a fixture of Scots political argument since the days of the Covenanters and Andrew Fletcher of Saltoun.[36] This military ethos seems to have affected the Free and Voluntary churches as much as the Church of Scotland; indeed its most enduring traces were in the Boys' Brigade movement, founded by a Free Church elder and Volunteer officer, William A. Smith, in 1883, with the assistance of the scientist, preacher, and Liberal Professor Henry Drummond. It

---

[32] Trefor M. Owen, 'Community Studies in Wales: An Overview', in Hume and Pryce, eds., *The Welsh and theis Country*, 110; see also Ian A. Olson, 'Scottish Traditional Song and the Greig–Duncan Collection: Last Leaves or Last Rites?', in Cairns Craig, ed., *The History of Scottish Literature*, iv: *The Twentieth Century* (Aberdeen: Aberdeen University Press, 1987); and Hamish Henderson, 'The Ballad, the Folk and the Oral Tradition', in Edward Cowan, ed., *The People's Past* (Edinburgh: Polygon, 1980).

[33] She stayed with the Scots-born railway magnate Henry Robertson at Palé, near Bala. See Sidney Lee, *Queen Victoria* (London: Smith Elder, 1904), 516–17, and John Davies, 'Victoria and Victorian Wales', in Jenkins and Smith, eds., *Politics and Society*.

[34] Ieuan Gwynedd Jones, 'The Liberation Society and Welsh Politics', in *Explorations and Explanations* (Llandysul: Gomer Press, 1983).

[35] Hugh Cunningham, *The Volunteer Force: A Social and Political History, 1859–1908* (London: Croom Helm, 1975), 46–7.

[36] See John Robertson, *The Scottish Enlightenment and the Militia Issue* (Edinburgh: John Donald, 1985).

had acquired forty-four companies (twenty-five in Glasgow, four in England, none in Wales) by 1886.[37]

Seventeenth-century Scottish Calvinism, as Arthur Williamson has pointed out, concentrated more on its civic mission—'the Godly Commonwealth'—than on the millenarian and imperial appeal of being a 'protestant nation' that fixated the contemporary English.[38] In the nineteenth century this modulated into a myth of settler democracy: a small-farmer, radical-democrat, religious-dissenting ethos of the F. J. Turner pattern, often strongly moulded by the 'gloomy memories' of persecution in and eviction from their native land, and given a powerful thrust by Carlyle's *Chartism* of 1839.[39] Scotland's was more of an emigrant than an immigrant culture, and although they lacked a Madoc myth, Scots settlements were fairly thick on the ground, particularly the Gaelic-speaking colonies in Cape Breton Island, the Free Church's settlement in Otago after 1848, centred on Dunedin and Port Chalmers, and the mission settlements on Lake Nyasa.[40] The 1850s seem to have been something of a turning point, when after a brief upsurge of romantic Scottish nationalism and associated Scots–English sparring in the newspapers, the Crimea, the Indian Mutiny, and the enormous success of David Livingstone as missionary hero. The volunteers also contrived to implant an imperial enthusiasm which remained at least until the Boer War.[41]

Wales, as a Royalist enclave, had not been subject to the seventeenth-century debate on Protestant destiny, and although a form of Welsh imperialism certainly developed in the nineteenth century, it was overshadowed by the successful and radical Welsh emigration to America.[42] Imperial enthusiasm existed, in the Methodist community and in the effusions of mid-century bards like 'Ceiriog'; there was no political unity in Wales over responses to the Boer War, despite Lloyd George's position.[43] But a wholehearted commitment was lacking, perhaps because too close a linkage with English expansion was seen as inimical to the language. The Welsh colony in Patagonia had an ideological presence out of all relation to its size, while Ulster—'the most successful Scots colony of all time'—was something Scots radicals wanted (and still want) to forget about.[44] Imperialism's role was continually to reconfigure Scotland's contracts of identity at the margin, and to produce the diffusion

---

[37] Olive Checkland, *Philanthropy in Victorian Scotland* (Edinburgh: John Donald, 1980), 56–7.
[38] Arthur Williamson, *Scottish National Consciousness in the Age of James VI* (Edinburgh: John Donald, 1983), 35.
[39] Thomas Carlyle, *Chartism* (London: Chapman and Hall, 1839), esp. chap. 10.
[40] Thomson, ed., *Companion*, 215. There were 34,000 Gaelic speakers on Cape Breton in 1900, and of their thirty-five ministers, twenty-nine preached in Gaelic; Keith Sinclair, *A History of New Zealand* (Harmondsworth: Penguin, 1959), 90 ff.
[41] H. J. Hanham, 'Mid-Century Scottish Nationalism: Romantic and Radical', in R. Robson, ed., *Ideas and Institutions of Victorian Britain* (London: Bell 1967); and see H. C. G. Matthew, *The Liberal Imperialists* (Oxford: Oxford University Press, 1973), 289.
[42] Compare Gwyn A. Williams, *The Search for Beaulah Land: The Welsh and the Atlantic Revolution* (London: Croom Helm, 1980) with Gordon Donaldson, *The Scots Overseas* (London: Robert Hale, 1966), 34–44.
[43] For Ceiriog see Tony Bianchi, 'An Englishman and Something More', *Planet*, 69 (June–July 1988); Morgan, *Rebirth of a Nation*, 45.
[44] Donaldson, *The Scots Overseas*, 29.

of loyalties which so impressed the Free Churchman John Buchan when he became Governor-General of Canada in the 1930s.[45]

The path of the pilgrim had some unusual—but not impossible—termini. No less ambiguous, and longer-lasting, was the educational impulse, something which was central—effectively a religion-surrogate—not only to the generation of John Rhys, O. M. Edwards, and Tom Ellis in Wales, but to Scottish cultural politics. In some ways the Scottish nationalist revival of the late twentieth century stemmed intellectually from the publication of George Davie's *The Democratic Intellect* in 1961. Even in the 1980s the educational sociologist Andrew MacPherson could write that the essential module of Scots education in the *twentieth* century was the rural, all-ability secondary school, and something similar still appertains in contemporary Wales.[46] The rural bias of the *gwerin* was perhaps understandable, given that in 1880 the great urbanization of Welsh society had still to occur. But Scotland had had the most rapid urbanization rate in eighteenth- and early nineteenth-century Europe, so an ideal of progress based on a rural or small-town community seems paradoxical.[47]

Yet both tally with the ideals of 'improvement' which marked the Scottish enlightenment. Francis Hutcheson, in his *Address to the Gentlemen of Scotland* (1735), had seen the defence of Scottish identity as resting in its educational system, and charged the gentry of the country with its development.[48] Adam Ferguson (a Gaelic speaker) and Adam Smith both stressed the essentially agrarian basis of society, and warned against the large-scale urban and industrial unit as something which could destroy the ideal of community, or Smith's vaguer 'social sympathy'. To both Ferguson and Smith, social progress came about by a dialogue between the market and the community, in which the excesses of the former—the automatism of the division of labour or of an individualistic arrogance—was compensated for by an ideal of the collective, by martial valour (hence the importance of the militia issue), and by access to public education.[49]

John Mullen has, for instance, attempted to explain the success of the bland and tautologous but enormously influential *Man of Feeling* (1771) by Henry Mackenzie:

the compensatory assurance of a potential for social solidarity was required by a culture which was learning to describe the effects of competition and self-interest. In Scotland, a nation whose propertied class had to find a substitute in politeness and intellectual cohesiveness for the political identity it had lost with the Act of Union, the ideal of sociability was particularly alluring and difficult.[50]

---

[45] Janet Adam Smith, *John Buchan* (London: Rupert Hart-Davis, 1965), 422 ff.

[46] Andrew MacPherson, 'An Angle on the *Geist*', in Walter Humes and Hamish Paterson, eds., *Scottish Culture and Scottish Education, 1800–1980* (Edinburgh: John Donald, 1983); and see Tony Bianchi, 'R. S. Thomas and his Readers', in Tony Curtis, ed., *Wales: The Imagined Nation* (Bridgend: Poetry Wales Press, 1987).

[47] T. M. Devine, 'Urbanisation', in T. M. Devine and Rosalind Mitchison, eds., *People and Society in Scotland*, i: *1760–1830* (Edinburgh: John Donald, 1988).

[48] 'George Elder Davie, 'Hume, Reid and the Passion for Ideas', in Douglas Young, ed., *Edinburgh in the Age of Reason* (Edinburgh: Edinburgh University Press, 1967), 25 ff.

[49] Duncan Forbes, 'Adam Ferguson and the Idea of Community', ibid. 46.

[50] John Mullen, 'The Language of Sentiment', in Andrew Hook, ed., *The History of Scottish Literature*, ii: *1660–1800* (Aberdeen: Aberdeen University Press, 1987), 275; and see Ian Campbell, *Kailyard* (Edinburgh: Ramsay Head, 1971), 18 ff.

In Scotland education was more than an instrument of socialization or an expression of nationality; it was something central to the institutions of the country's polity. As such it had its parties, its patronage, its own politics. Robert Anderson regards Davie's distinction between Scots and Anglicizers as something which oversimplifies all the various intersecting interests—bureaucracy, teachers, curriculum, class interests, politicians—which went into educational legislation and its enforcement.[51] With the Welsh, creating a system more or less from scratch made for a more homogeneous approach. It would have been inconceivable for a Tory to have provided it with a central rationalization, as was the case in Scotland, where 'democratic intellectualism' was the coinage of Walter Elliot, Secretary of State in 1935–8 and in some ways the Scots' answer to Tom Jones.[52]

In both countries education presented continuing political challenges during the nineteenth century: Anglicizing assaults—in Scotland in the 1820s, in Wales in the 1840s—stimulated a 'national' agitation (but with an eye on the greater partner), then the 'acceptable'—but still mortal—compromise.[53] Did the Welsh take over the myth of the indispensable links between Scottish education and the democratic nature of Scottish society, besides the overvaluing of the 'improving' strengths of Scottish civil society and undervaluing of cruder factors like mineral wealth and low wages?[54] The Welsh national movement devoted itself with great energy—there is no one in Scotland comparable to Sir Hugh Owen (1804–1881)—to acquiring an educational system cognate with the Scots', and achieved success in 1889 with the Intermediate Education Act. Owen's contemporary Cardinal Cullen would be no less effective in Ireland (see Chapter 6). Owen put Wales ahead, as its new educational establishment was more progressive than its Scots equivalent: the radicalism of O. M. Edwards (1858–1920) and the high Toryism of Sir Henry Craik (1846–1931) were reflected in the history books that both wrote.

More generally, we can use education as a paradigm of Ieuan Gwynedd Jones's useful approach—who was providing social overhead capital, and under what terms was it applied? In rural Wales this was crystallized in chapels, schools, halls, *eisteddfodau*, and the 'People's University', a 'from the ground up' business, with the occasional lucky break from a businessman of the David Davies sort.[55] In Scotland much of this capital was already in place: donated by an 'improving' aristocracy which, on account of this, survived as a factor in Scottish politics and educational and cultural life. R. B. Haldane, of a gentry-lawyer family which had been leaders of dissent in the eighteenth century, patronized the Fabians, promoted higher education, and chaired the Welsh University Commission, 1916–18.[56] John Sinclair,

[51] Anderson, *Education and Opportunity*, appendix 1.

[52] Davie, *Democratic Intellect*, preface; and see Colin Coote, *A Companion of Honour: The Story of Walter Elliot* (Glasgow: Collins, 1965), 16.

[53] See Anderson, *Education and Opportunity*, chap. 2; and Donald Witherington, 'Scotland a Half Educated Nation', in Humes and Paterson, eds., *Scottish Culture*.

[54] See Smout, *A Century of the Scottish People*, 109 ff.

[55] Jones, 'Language and Community', 50–1.

[56] Eric Ashby and Mary Anderson, *Portrait of Haldane at Work on Education* (London: Macmillan, 1974), 123–32.

Lord Pentland (1860–1925), of the family which had earlier organized the massive *Statistical Accounts*, became both a popular Scottish Secretary (1906–12), and along with the Earl of Aberdeen the patron of the polymath sociologist, regional planner, and Celtic nationalist Patrick Geddes.[57]

Both countries were subject to increased social tensions as new urban areas expanded at the end of the nineteenth century, particularly with the growth of port and commercial communities with their more cosmopolitan workforce. In Scotland this expansion was poured into a long-lived and sophisticated urban tradition—the Convention of Royal Burghs had its origins in the thirteenth century—but in South Wales this was only vestigial. The 'urban' or employer-paternalist type of town predominated over the 'civic' or political-corporate type until quite late in the century. The commercial provision of social utilities arrived with state action, in the shape of the Cathays Park complex, hard on its heels.[58] In this sense Wales seems to have followed Scotland, which had generated a civic movement comparable with that of America by the 1890s, but the ruralism and puritanism of the *gwerinwr* spoke against developments such as the establishment-backed revival both of local ceremonies (Up Helly Aa! in the Shetlands and the Border Common Ridings in the 1870s), and the enormous expansion in Burns clubs from the 1880s on.[59]

In Scotland the civic was patent in the ambitious town planning schemes of the enlightenment period, replicated on a smaller scale in country burghs and landlords' model villages. The continuation of this tradition may owe something to the relatively greater fortunes made in Scotland in property, trade, brewing, and banking. Major museum, art gallery, and technical education projects were under way from the 1830s, financed in part by the Board of Manufactures created in 1727 as a consequence of the 1707 Act of Union. The universities expanded after 1861: student numbers doubled to 6,798 in 1890, in a combination of state action with private philanthropy. The same factors supplemented the benevolence of Andrew Carnegie (who made his millions at a safe distance from Scotland) in providing opulent public libraries in seventy-seven Scottish towns by the 1900s, and extensive grants to students in higher education.[60] Was this populist or elitist—or a contradictory combination of both?

Two major critiques have been made of such educational movements: one, that they elevated religion and culture above technical innovation; two, that they promoted ambitions which could not be bound by the national unit.[61] The former charge

---

[57] Lady Pentland, *Lord Pentland: A Memoir* (London: Methuen, 1928); Lord and Lady Aberdeen, *'We Twa'* (London: Collins, 1925), 188–90; for Geddes's influence on social studies in Wales see David Michael, 'Before Alwyn: The Origins of Sociology in Wales', in Glyn Williams, ed., *Crisis of Economy and Ideology: Essays on Welsh Society, 1840–1980* (Cardiff: Social Science Research Council and British Sociological Association, 1983), 24.

[58] Neil Evans, 'The Welsh Victorian City: The Middle Class and Civic and National Consciousness in Cardiff, 1850–1914', *Welsh History Review*, 12/3 (June 1985), 351–2.

[59] Christopher Harvie and Graham Walker, 'Community and Culture', in Hamish Fraser, ed., *People and Society in Scotland, 1830–1914* (Edinburgh: John Donald, 1990).

[60] See Checkland, *Philanthropy in Victorian Scotland*, 142–3; Anderson, *Education and Opportunity*, 350–1 for statistics, 287 ff. for Carnegie.

[61] In 1900 the University of Wales conferred 60 degrees in arts and only 10 in science; in 1913 the figures were 114 and 27. See G. W. Roderick, 'Education, Culture and Industry in Wales in the 19th Century', *Welsh History Review*, 13/4 (Dec. 1987), 443.

cannot fairly be laid at the door of the bureaucracy: both the Scottish Education Department and its Welsh equivalent tried to promote modern studies and technical education, only to run into opposition from working-class bodies which suspected that they were being sold a lower-grade product.[62] The latter charge was guiltily evident in hackneyed Scottish jokes about all London Scots being inaccessible since they were 'aa' heids o' depairtments'. Both Scots and Welsh ran into unfriendly fire from the pen of T. W. H. Crosland at about the time of Lloyd George (the tradition of English aggression towards the non-Irish Celts deserves rather more attention than it's been given).[63] But this notion of the university as graduate factory also damaged the fabric of working-class communities, as another Scoto-Welsh witness, Jennie Lee, wrote.[64] The positional goods nature of Scottish education was to come under fierce attack—'a land of second-hand thoughts and second-rate minds'—from G. M. Thomson and A. S. Neill, among many others, in the 1920s.[65]

## IV   RELIGIOUS REBELS

Their relationship to the enlightenment caused major problems for *gwerin* and Godly Commonwealth. An ethos of conviction, social solidarity, and educational idealism sought to embrace scientific progress and the extension of higher education. At the same time their leaders feared the break-up that would be caused by the impact of the division of labour, scientism, and mass literacy. Thomas Chalmers was emblematic. He had been reared in the rationalism of Edinburgh, which had stimulated his interest in science and economics; his later career attempted to equate this with evangelical Christianity.[66] Chalmers's *Christian Revelation and Astronomy* (1846), translated into Welsh the same year, was really the last of Welsh-language borrowings from Scots Calvinist theology, and few Scottish secular writers made this transition, probably because their works were summarized in periodicals like *Y Traethodydd*.[67]

The language issue is, of course, the major divergence. In both societies the eighteenth century saw a revival in native poetry and the native language, though for different reasons: Duncan Ban MacIntyre, William Ross, and Alexander MacDonald in Scotland were shocked into lyrics of outstanding quality by the collapse of the clan society which had housed them. Goronwy Owen, Richard Price, and Williams

---

[62] Anderson, *Education and Opportunity*, 191; and see the opposition to O. M. Edward's plans for technical education in the South Wales valleys, in K. S. Hopkins, ed., *The Rhondda: Past and Future* (Cardiff: Rhondda Borough Council, 1976).

[63] See T. W. H. Crosland, *The Unspeakable Scot* (London: Grant Richards, 1900), and *Taffy* (London: Grant Richards, 1910).

[64] Jennie Lee, *This Great Journey* (London: Macgibbon and Kee, 1963), 89.

[65] G. M. Thomson, *Caledonia or the Future of the Scots* (London: Kegan Paul, 1926), p. 47; Owen, 'Community Studies in Wales', 113.

[66] See Brown, *Thomas Chalmers*, chap. 5.

[67] The popular devotional works of Thomas Boston—*The Fourfold State of Man, The Crook in the Lot*, and *The Covenant of Grace*, were translated between 1769 and 1824. *Y Traethodydd's* index shows rather more substantial entries on Carlyle, Chalmers, Sir William Hamilton, and David Hume than on 'Iesu Grist'.

Pantycelyn in Wales reflected a language which had ridden out attempts at acculturation and made peace on its own terms with 'vital religion', Atlantic identity, and print-capitalism. The daring achievements in cultural construction of James 'Ossian' MacPherson (1736–1796) in Scotland and Iolo Morganwg (1747–1826) in Wales reflected this divergence. MacPherson's exploitation of the juxtaposition of Gaelic and lowland society—the 'militant' and the 'industrial'—helped 'sell' the enlightenment in Continental Europe, *in English*.[68] Iolo, obviously deeply influenced by MacPherson's success, and by the patronage of English romantics like Southey whom 'Ossian' enthused, achieved his enlightened ends in Welsh.[69] Politically, MacPherson wrote a threnody for a Scots Gaelic battered by political collapse, eviction, and dispersal, whose literary witness would ultimately decline to the inconsistent genres of martial poetry, pietism, and social protest.[70]

These proved only too easy to adapt to a sporting-and-tourism-based culture of tartanry, sedulously fostered by the monarchy and the surviving, and surprisingly resilient, Scottish Tories.[71] Only in 1892 was a body similar to the National Eisteddfod Committee, An Comunn Gaedhealach, set up. Although this followed the Crofters' Revolt of 1884–5, which surely contributed precedents to the Welsh tithe war of 1887–8, its role was purely literary and aesthetic. Being largely under the control of the Conservative, Anglo-Gaelic gentry of the Highlands, it could even be seen as an attempt to check the radicalism which had followed the third Reform Act. Lowland prejudice against the Highlanders, which had been almost as widespread earlier in the century as prejudice against the Irish, was diminished by migration into the cities and sympathy with the victims of landlordism, but by that time Gaelic had suffered the fate that, according to Brinley Thomas, Welsh would have suffered in an non-industrial Wales. The numbers of Gaelic speakers slumped from over 20 per cent of the Scots population in 1800 to about 5 per cent in 1900.[72]

William Donaldson has argued for the continuing validity of lowland Scots as a vehicle of intellectual discourse—in local discussion circles, in the local press, and in the realist novels of such as William Alexander. But even he sees this tradition

---

[68] Murray H. Pittock, *The Invention of Scotland: The Stuart Myth and the Scottish Identity, 1638 to the Present* (London: Routledge, 1991), 73–84.

[69] See Gwyn A. Williams, *When Was Wales?: A History of the Welsh* (Harmondsworth: Penguin, 1985), 164 ff. None of the standard works on Southey refer to Iolo, and only Jean Raimond, *Robert Southey: L'Homme et son temps, l'oeuvre, le rôle* (Paris: Didier, 1966) draws attention to his interest in Ossian.

[70] Derick Thomson, 'Gaelic Poetry in the Eighteenth Century: The Breaking of the Mould', in Hook, ed., *History of Scottish Literature*, ii; John MacInnes, 'Gaelic Poetry in the Nineteenth Century', in Douglas Gifford, ed., *The History of Scottish Literature, iii: The Nineteenth Century* (Aberdeen: Aberdeen University Press, 1988); sixty-seven books in Gaelic were published between 1750 and 1800, compared with over a thousand in Welsh (Thomson, ed., *Companion*, 245; Rhys and Brynmor-Jones, *The Welsh People*, 533).

[71] Andrew Noble, 'John Wilson (Christopher North) and the Tory Hegemony', in Gifford, ed., *History of Scottish Literature*, iii.

[72] Brinley Thomas, 'A Cauldron of Rebirth: Population and the Welsh Language in the Nineteenth Century', 1962, in Geraint Jenkins, ed., *The Welsh Language and its Social Domains* (Cardiff: University of Wales Press, 2000) and see James Hunter, 'The Politics of Highland Land Reform', *Scottish Historical Review*, 53 (1974).

in eclipse by the end of the century, overshadowed by the commercialism of the Kailyard, which transmitted a sanitized and sentimentalized Scotland to London and (particularly significant) to the USA after the copyright agreement of 1891.[73] 'Ian Maclaren's *Beside the Bonnie Brier Bush*, the quintessential Kailyard product, was the first book to lead the American best-seller list, established in 1895. 'MacLaren' hid the identity of the Revd John Watson, Presbyterian minister in Liverpool, *the* strategic Scoto-Welsh junction, and President of the Free Church Federal Council, who was promoted by that other luminary of the Nonconformist general staff, the Revd William Robertson Nicoll, Lloyd George's hotline to the free churches he had long since left in spirit.[74]

The Kailyard had plenty of Welsh imitators among the authors of chapel prize books. But one Scottish voice, however, remained significant and disturbing in the areas of religion and education for most of the second half of the nineteenth century: Thomas Carlyle. His impact on the generation of Disraeli and Dickens was vast, but by the time the Welsh national movement got going in the late 1860s his anti-democratic sourness had lost him the metropolitan literati.[75] Not so in Scotland and Wales, whose younger generation accepted Whitman's more generous estimate of Carlyle's epic qualities.[76] In Geraint Goodwin's *The Heyday in the Blood*, a key work of the 1920s Anglo-Welsh literary revival, his young writer rediscovers the books of his father as 'one of the Young Men of Wales. In his dark, bitter, fuming, eyes, his long narrow face, his lean spindle body, one glimpsed the passion that was to devour him. He came at a time when the country was turning anxiously, as though in sleep . . .'. The father had been a Methodist minister whose faith migrated from church to nation, something reflected in his library: 'Theological commentaries jostled one another along the shelves, political tracts, modern-day heresies. There was Locke and Spinoza, Hazlitt and William James, Cromwell's letters and speeches, a whole shelf of Carlyle . . .'.[77] Advancing out of his books, the dead father plucks young Llew from fags and football and sets him down on his writing desk. Something very similar happened to the young Henry Jones at Bangor and to David Lloyd George. As Frank Owen wrote, conflating Carlyle and Bunyan, 'It was Carlyle's *Sartor Resartus* which began to lead him back by a broad track from Doubting Castle to his own rather highly personal view of the Delectable Mountains (for it describes a man who made a similar journey).'[78]

Little of Carlyle was translated into Welsh but despite the risk that religious unorthodoxy would keep him well out of the Calvinist-Methodist main line, he features prominently among the contents of *Y Traethodydd*. The 'devouring passion',

[73] Donaldson, *Popular Literature*, 146–9.

[74] See Christopher Harvie, 'Behind the Bonnie Brier Bush: The Kailyard Revisited', in P. N. Furbank, ed., *Proteus II* (1978).

[75] See Christopher Harvie, *The Centre of Things: Political Fiction from Disraeli to the Present* (London: Unwin Hyman, 1991), esp. chap. 2.

[76] Walt Whitman, *Democratic Vistas*, 1871 (London: Nonesuch, 1938), 708–9.

[77] Geraint Goodwin, *The Heyday in the Blood* (London: Cape, 1936), 134–42.

[78] Henry Jones, *Old Memories* (London: Hodder and Stoughton, 1924), 94; Frank Owen, *Tempestuous Journey: The Life of David Lloyd George* (London: Hutchinson, 1954), 32.

the radical and anti-aristocratic spirit of his most popular writings must have made an impact:

Did a God make this land of Britain, and give it to us all, that we might live there by honest labour; or did the Squires make it, and—shut to the voice of God, open only to a Devil's voice in this matter—decide on giving it to themselves alone? This is now the sad question and 'divine right' that we, in this unfortunate century, have got to settle![79]

This resounded along the debateable lands of the anglophone border—and in Keir Hardie's Merthyr—with an impact similar to that which Carlyle had on Young Ireland or Giuseppi Mazzini on the radical dons of *Essays on Reform*. Both in turn would exercise their influence on Tom Ellis's generation.[80]

## V  THE PEOPLE'S WILLIAM

The 'message' of Carlyle was essentially that of Adam Ferguson—the necessity of society: 'It is in Society that man first feels what he is; first becomes what he can be. In Society an altogether new set of spiritual activities are evolved in him, and the old immeasurably quickened and strengthened.'[81] A comparison of religion and education suggests the centrality in both countries of *structure*: the 'bands of society' mould into which politics has to be poured (see Chapter 1, Section V). The Scottish religious settlement partook more of the state, and this gave it a flexibility which could ride out the inconsistencies of 'vital religion', and resist the blandishments of the English elite, that beguiling mixture of goodwill, condescension, vague ethnic generalization masking tough metropolitan realpolitik, that is Matthew Arnold in *Celtic Literature*.[82] Preoccupation with a strategy which accepted Arnold's statism, but tried to adapt it to the sort of compromise visible in Scotland, informed the Oxford-centred *Cymdeithas Dafydd ap Gwilym* generation, whose national and intellectual programme was a Welsh version of *Essays on Reform* (actually edited by Albert Rutson, out of Liverpool and private secretary to Lord Aberdare) struggling against the autocratic and hostile Principal Hugo Harper of Jesus College—and in an immediate political crisis, Gladstone's declaration for Irish Home Rule, which was overwhelmingly rejected by the Oxbridge and metropolitan Liberal intelligentsia.[83]

---

[79] Thomas Carlyle, 'Baillie the Covenanter', 1841, in *Scottish and Other Miscellanies* (London: Dent, n.d.), 141.

[80] For Carlyle and Young Ireland see Owen Dudley Edwards, 'Ireland', in *Celtic Nationalism* (London: Routledge and Kegan Paul, 1968), 123–4; Neville Masterman, *The Forerunner: The Dilemmas of Tom Ellis, 1859–99*, (Llandybie: Christopher Davies, 1971), 16–19; Morgan, *Keir Hardie*, 22.

[81] Thomas Carlyle, 'Characteristics', *Edinburgh Review* (1831), repr. in *Scottish and Other Miscellanies*, 194.

[82] Matthew Arnold, *On the Study of Celtic Literature*, 1867 (London: Kennikat Press, 1970), esp. 13.

[83] Ibid., chap. 8; and see G. Hartwell Jones, *A Celt Looks at the World* (Cardiff: William Lewis, 1946), 34 ff.

Indeed, if the *gwerin* and the folk have a common political begetter, his name must be W. E. Gladstone. To Gladstone, the Scots Episcopalian, the Free Church 'Godly Commonwealth' of Thomas Chalmers was a reality, no matter how difficult it might be to square evangelical (or for that matter patristic) theology with scientific progress.[84] It showed the possibility of involving the laity in church government and, by analogy, in constitutional politics. This laity was the 'men' of the Scottish Highlands; it could also be the 'fianna' of Celtic antiquity—masses, but also *convinced, empowered* masses.[85] The 1860s was not a good decade, in terms of calculable support, for Gladstone. High Church Oxford rejected him in 1865; his backsliding on the American Civil War and reluctance over reform stigmatized him in the eyes of metropolitan radicals; English urban constituencies were insecure. One senses therefore that the popular mobilization in 1868 of Liberalism in Wales came to him as, literally, a godsend. A constituency existed which could be relied upon to back him, and for some time he paid it careful court.

Ieuan Gwynedd Jones has written eloquently of the groups mobilized at this time, about their cultural ambiguities and their political resolution. Such executive committees of the *gwerin* could—like Gladstone himself—dissolve potential (and indeed actual) intellectual contradictions in activism and in the common experience of struggle against landlords, Tories, and clergy.[86] They were a major input into that dramatic initiative on the Eastern Question, which saw Gladstone first articulate his 'classes versus masses' theme. Thereafter, however, Gladstone, though geographically resident in Wales at Hawarden, realized that Scotland provided greater crowds, an English-language press, greater malleability in terms of issues, and in Lord Rosebery a wealthy and hard-working patron.[87]

Cruder statistics of political calculation were—with Gladstone and the increasingly centralized party over which he presided—apt to take over, and thereafter did. *Gwerinol* ideology, after the 1884 Reform and Redistribution Act and the brief efflorescence of *Cymru Fydd*, was in the cultural and social overhead capital sphere successful, but politically—as the famous Newport confrontation of 1896 between rural and coalfield Liberalism made brutally clear—it was upheld by an archaic political structure which might be tolerable to the Liberal Party but failed completely to cope with demographic change in Wales.[88]

In Scotland the population of the three industrial western counties—Lanarkshire, Renfrewshire, and Ayrshire—was 21 per cent of the Scots total in 1801, 27 per cent in 1831, and 46 per cent in 1911. These counties then returned twenty-two

---

[84] W. E. Gladstone, 'The Theses of Erastus and the Scottish Church Establishment', *Foreign and Colonial Quarterly Review* (1844), repr. in *Gleanings of Past Years*, iii (London: Murray, 1879), 38.

[85] See Christopher Harvie, 'Gladstonianism, the Provinces, and Popular Political Culture', in Richard Bellamy, ed., *Victorian Liberalism* (London: Routledge, 1990).

[86] Ieuan Gwynedd Jones, 'Merioneth Politics in the Mid Nineteenth Century', in *Explorations and Explanations*, 159.

[87] See Michael Fry, *Patronage and Principle: A Political History of Modern Scotland* (Aberdeen: Aberdeen University Press, 1986), 92–3.

[88] Morgan, *Rebirth of a Nation*, 118.

(31 per cent) of the seventy territorial MPs. Between 1881 and 1911 the population of the two South Wales counties of Glamorgan and Monmouth doubled, while that of the rest of Wales rose only by 7 per cent. Although Wales's electorate had been before 1832 more representative than that of Scotland—where scarcely 5,000 could vote—the proportion of electors to population in the new industrial areas lapsed badly by 1867 (from 8 per cent to 4 per cent in Cardiff, for example).[89] Later demographic change worsened matters, since it occurred *after* the last major redistribution of seats, in 1884. By 1910 the political map was grotesque. The single MP for Cardiff represented 186,000 people; the MP for Merioneth scarcely 20,000. Glamorgan and Monmouth, with 63 per cent of the population, had only eleven (or one third) of the Welsh seats (five of which were Labour).[90] This *was* a reflection of real divisions in Welsh politics, marked by growing confrontation in the mines and on the railways, but the counties of the centre and north (and two 'grouped boroughs') were the Liberals' very own pocket borough.

In Scotland not only had population growth been more consistent, with the phases of industrial development—linen–cotton–iron–engineering—dovetailed fairly neatly into one another. The major industrial area remained in the west of the central belt, and the electorate was a fairer reflection of the society. Although fewer working people were enfranchised than in England, Scottish politics were more sensitive to industrial and political change, to imperialism and tariff reform. But if an earlier urbanization produced relatively stable politics by the 1880s, it also bequeathed the appalling social problem of cramped and unsanitary housing: patrolled and kept from crisis by the 'municipal socialism' of the towns, but never overcome. In the 1900s Labour's major issue in South Wales was the issue of control of the work process, as in *The Miner's Next Step* (1910); in Scotland it was housing, whether handled by John Wheatley's schemes on Glasgow City Council or by the Royal Commission that the Scottish Secretary, MacKinnon Wood, granted in 1913 as the result of pressure from the miners in particular.[91]

How much was the raw, confrontational quality of labour relations in the South Wales coalfield the result of the inequities of the degree of parliamentary representation then available? How much was it the result of memories of struggles with landlords, parsons, or quarrymasters being imported from rural Wales?[92] At any rate, in South Wales housing was not the powder-keg it was in Scotland. Welsh 'by-law' housing was unimaginative but on the whole adequate. In Scotland words failed the

---

[89] Ieuan Gwynedd Jones, 'Franchise Reform and Glamorgan Politics in the Mid-Nineteenth Century', *Morgannwg*, 2 (1958).

[90] Ibid., 'Franchise Reform and Glamorgan Politics, 1869–1921', in *Glamorgan County History*, iv (Cardiff: University of Wales Press, 1988).

[91] See McLean, *The Legend of Red Clydeside*, 165 ff.; Ian S. Wood, *John Wheatley* (Manchester: Manchester University Press, 1990), 36 ff.; Joseph Melling, *Rent Strikes: People's Struggle for Housing in West Scotland, 1890–1916* (Edinburgh: Polygon, 1983), esp. chap. 1.

[92] Hywel Francis and David Smith, *The Fed* (London: Lawrence and Wishart, 1980), see the Welsh-speaking element among the miners as conservative (p. 19) but also report some chapels as radical nurseries (p. 10).

Commission of 1917, trying to describe conditions which were, for a start, five times more overcrowded than in England and Wales:

unspeakably filthy privy-middens in many of the mining areas, badly-constructed, incurably damp labourers' cottages on farms, whole townships unfit for human occupation in the croft-ing counties and islands . . . gross overcrowding and huddling of the sexes together in the con-gested industrial villages and towns, occupation of one-room houses by large families, groups of lightless and unventilated houses in the older burghs, clotted masses of slums in the great cities.[93]

Housing sounded a class note in Scottish politics, which the Wheatley act of 1924 made into a class interest (see Chapter 6). Public control of housing and subsidized rents were to remain pillars of Scottish Labour politics until the 1960s.[94]

## VI   LEGACIES

The mid Victorian Scottish Liberal consensus was dissolving as the *gwerinwr* were getting into their stride. The split over home rule in 1886 went deeper than expec-ted, revived the unionist right, and drove Liberals to favour well-heeled southerners as candidates. A trading in votes by interest groups began. The Unionists gave as good as they got, and in 1900 even won a majority of Scottish seats.[95] This reflec-ted the fracture between an empowered people and Liberal organization, but by then *Cymru Fydd* had shot its bolt, while the Scots could now leapfrog ahead, headed by the Young Scots, a body organized explicitly on Welsh lines.[96] But not for long. The fate of both would be sealed by war, the boosting of one *gwerin* leader to world lead-ership, the mobilization of the Welsh and Scottish industrial elites, and a post-war slump which knocked over the ideological and social supports of Liberalism. This cast Calvinism itself into question—an essentially corrosive ideology which had des-troyed an earlier communal 'sympathy'—while in Wales the redistribution of 1918, granting Glamorgan and Monmouth twenty-four seats, would have finished the old Liberal order, even without the havoc wrought by Lloyd George. The war took a savage toll in the rural areas of both countries, further wounding a Welsh pacifism already compromised by its acceptance of 'Lloyd George's Welsh Army'. The con-sequences of this dominate the last chapters of this book but in overview they may explain the limited triumph of class-consciousness over regional loyalties. Proletarian Scotland, and to an even greater extent proletarian Wales, had eclipsed the *gwerin* only to be eclipsed themselves.[97]

   The post-war political-intellectual response was broadly similar in the two coun-tries. A flow from Liberalism into weak home-rule movements, and younger intel-lectuals rejecting nationalism for a combination of Spengler and politicized French

---

[93] *Report of the Royal Commission on the Housing of the Industrial Population of Scotland* (London: HMSO, 1917), Cd 8731, p. 102.

[94] Smout, *A Century of the Scottish People*, 52 ff.

[95] See I. G. C. Hutchison, *A Political History of Scotland, 1832–1924* (Edinburgh: John Donald, 1986), 209–12.

[96] Ibid. 232 ff.        [97] See Harvie, *The Centre of Things*, 156–9.

Catholicism, with Saunders Lewis, or, for Communist internationalism, with Lewis Grassic Gibbon—or, as in the case of Hugh MacDiarmid, for *both*.[98] Edwin Muir's juxtaposition of medieval (and thus Catholic) fruitfulness and Calvinist barrenness, in *Scottish Journey* (1935) and 'Scotland 1941', was something he had in common with Saunders Lewis, as did Compton MacKenzie and Fionn MacColla, who were also more involved in Gaelic, Catholicism, and a conservative corporatism.[99] Yet, as much as Muir and MacColla, MacDiarmid himself stemmed from, and celebrated, a rural Scotland whose experience was a reality to less than a quarter of the population.[100]

The new nationalists were unsparing about the *gwerin*'s political inadequacies. Yet the politics of post-1945 Scotland and Wales were essentially the creation of nationally inclined 'progressives', who had matured in the *gwerin* period: Tom Johnston (one of Sir Henry Jones's pupils at Glasgow University) in 1940s Scotland; James Griffiths in 1960s Wales.[101] 'It is a heritage', wrote Walter Elliot in 1932,

wherein discipline is rigidly and ruthlessly enforced, but where criticism and attack are unflinching, continuous, and salt with a bitter and jealous humour. It is a heritage wherein intellect, speech and, above all, argument are the passports to the highest eminence in the land. These traditions we should study, and their histories are the annals of the parishes, their ministers, and their elders.[102]

This is the *gwerin* talking. But Elliot was a Tory, and able to cite a religious tradition which was far healthier in Scotland after 1918. *Gwerin* hegemony in Wales had been too dependent on political good fortune and the health of Nonconformity. The irony is that both traditions continued to be hypnotically effective, in a Kailyard populism. Thomson-Leng's *Sunday Post* was founded in 1931: its famous comic strip 'The Broons' preserves a small-town-big-family Scotland even then all but extinct. Richard Llewellyn's *How Green was My Valley* (1939) became iconic, though it simplified and sentimentalized the *gwerin* past the limits of caricature. As a doctor in Tredegar, the Scots Catholic author A. J. Cronin gave a character to medical reform almost as vivid as its MP Aneurin Bevan himself.[103]

---

[98] Hugh MacDiarmid, *Albyn, or Scotland and the Future* (London: Kegan Paul, 1927), 11.

[99] Mackenzie's 'Jacobite' political credo is given at great length in the first chapter of *The North Wind of Love* (London: Rich and Cowan, 1945).

[100] Emlyn Sherrington, 'Welsh Nationalism, the French Revolution, and the Influence of the French Right, 1880–1930', in Smith, ed., *A People and a Proletariat*; and see MacDiarmid, *Albyn*, p. i.

[101] For Johnston see Graham Walker, *Thomas Johnston* (Manchester: Manchester University Press, 1988), chap. 1; for Griffiths see Morgan, 'The *Gwerin* of Wales', 150.

[102] 'Scotland's Political Heritage', in *A Scotsman's Heritage* (1932), quoted in Coote, *A Companion of Honour*, 16.

[103] For the Dundee Press, tartanry, etc., see Tom Nairn, 'Old and New Scottish Nationalism', in *The Break-Up of Britain* (London: New Left Books, 1977), esp. 160 ff.; for Llewellyn see John Harris, 'Not Only a Place in Wales', *Planet*, 76 (Aug. 1989). My thanks to David Yendoll, stepson of Bevan's agent Archie Lush, for motoring me around the country associated with Bevan and Cronin.

## VII   SCHOOLS AND SCHOOLMASTERS

The paradox and peril of the mindset figures in a writer frequently featured in
*Y Traethodydd*: Hugh Miller, whose autobiography *My Schools and Schoolmasters* was
published in 1854. Miller was born in 1802 in Cromarty in Easter Ross, a seaport
on the highland line, but his shipowner father drowned and Hugh had to start as a
stonemason, later working himself up to a bank official and journalist. He was psy-
chologically torn by cultural tensions. As editor of the Free Church's *Witness* after
1839 he had to be a moderate Liberal; as a gifted geologist he was hamstrung by his
fundamentalism. Yet the vitality of his career in a changing Scotland comes through;
viewed by a man on the edge of so many divides: of the highland line, the sea, the oral
tradition, the working class, of sanity itself.[104]

Compare Miller not only with Matthew Arnold in *Celtic Literature*, but with Tom
Hughes—the Doctor's disciple. *Tom Brown's Schooldays* (1857) makes plain the
ascriptive ethos of English class society, while Miller's open commitment to experience and change conveys the sensuality of knowledge, the excitement of acquiring it,
the near-inebriated condition of the adept. Both books value childhood, but where
Hughes foresees a life governed by the rules of team games (parliament itself being an
obvious example) Miller's voyage is towards an unknown region, possibly exciting,
possibly (as in his own case) disastrous. Many Welshmen must have written, in their
own language, like this:

'You Scotch are a strange people,' said one of the commercial gentlemen. 'When I was in
Scotland two years ago, I could hear of scarce anything among you but your church question.
What good does all your theology do for you?' 'Independently altogether of religious consid-
erations,' I replied, 'It has done for our people what all your Societies for the Diffusion of
Useful Knowledge, and all your penny and Saturday magazines, will never do for yours: it has
awakened their intellects and taught them how to think.'[105]

By the 1900s the scientific element—and even the crudely economic element—had
in Scotland won out. The Kailyard, that blend of couthy anecdote and T. H. Green-
style moralizing, had spread south, with the Revd Robertson Nicoll and his press
empire equally centred on *The Bookman* and the *British Weekly* and the success of
the Revd John Watson in 1896 in heading up both the new Free Church Council and as 'Ian MacLaren' the first American best-seller list with *Beside the Bonnie
Briar Bush*. Imperialist and social reformer, like his friend Hugh Price Hughes, Watson ministered to the wealthy of Sefton Park in Liverpool. He wrote about the modern Church, but it was a *douce* bourgeois world of soirées, women's guilds, choral

---

[104] For an introduction to Miller see George Rosie, *Hugh Miller: Outrage and Order* (Edinburgh:
Mainstream, 1980); and see Miller, *First Impressions of England*, 16, 46; and see Christopher Harvie,
'Hugh Miller and the Scottish Crisis', in Lester Borley, ed., *Hugh Miller and Early Victorian Scotland*
(Cromarty: Cromarty Society, 2003).
[105] Ibid. 11.

and rambling societies, and fund-raising, with the Council its political arm, eyeing Westminster from the heavily baroque Methodist Central Hall.[106]

By now nationality, along with temperance, had to protect against the beguilements of liberal Anglicanism.[107] In 1901 the Free Kirk and the United Presbyterians amalgamated to form the United Free Church. They were challenged in the courts by the Free Church (Continuing) or 'Wee Frees' on the grounds that the commitment of the new body to disestablishment betrayed the founding principles of 1843. The 'Wee Frees' won after a prolonged court case, in 1904 (counsel for the defence was the reverent agnostic R. B. Haldane, KC MP, whose Hegelian enthusiasms led to almost complete unintelligibility), only to see the United Free and Established churches begin the business of reunification, ultimately carried in 1929. Young Harry McShane, engineer and a future shop-floor militant, noted that around 1905 'controversial divinity' evaporated from the soapboxes on Glasgow Green, and socialism replaced it.[108]

Does this complex of disruption, disfranchisement, and respectability explain the fervour which struck Wales in 1905? The last great revival had only slight Scottish parallels. The solid roman-classical blocks of Horebs and Bethels and Sions had been thirty or more years in place when a 25-year-old miner, Evan Roberts, underwent conversion in September 1904. He started preaching and, backed up by missioners and singers, notably young women, his mission spread throughout the coalfield, then to the North and the Welsh communities in English cities. It was remarkable for its emotionalism and distance from traditional sectarian theology, and in this sense akin to the impact of Moody and Sankey in Scotland thirty years earlier. The link between them was the Essex-born evangelist Rodney 'Gypsy' Smith, who had been a Salvationist captain and was tutored in America on a visit in 1889 by Dwight Moody. Smith spoke English, but—a warm personality, proud of his race, and a fine singer—was winning converts in Wales.[109]

Roberts, from Loughor near Llanelli in the western part of the coalfield, spoke Welsh. The near-scary emotionalism he provoked had probably been pre-cooked by Lloyd George's intemperate campaign against Balfour's 1902 Education Act, which

[106] This male-dominated world was largely female-run. In *The First Hundred Years* (n.p., 1984), his history of a fairly typical Glasgow suburban church, Greenbank, Clarkston, the economist Charles Munn found that it was kept above water in the 1900s by special collections and sales of work run by the women of the congregation (pp. 14, 18). In 1985 Greenbank had yet to elect a woman elder.

[107] William Knox, *Scottish Labour Leaders, 1918–1939: A Biographical Dictionary* (Edinburgh: Mainstream, 1984), shows their overwhelmingly religious and teetotal nature.

[108] Interview with Harry McShane, Nov. 1986.

[109] The revival is still kept alive by conservative Christian websites and clergy trained in Swansea Bible College, such as Martyn Lloyd-Jones and Reinhard Bonnke. An evangelical group in Tübingen (of all places) had in 2002 its mission fronted by a display entitled 'How God saved a nation!' My Llanbadarn neighbour Sophia Thomas, born in 1905, remembered Smith preaching to big Methodist congregations during World War I; his autobiography and hymn books, from the mid 1890s on, surface in many local second-hand sales.

abolished school boards (on which Nonconformists had a majority) in favour of county councils, yet preserved Church schools, and the campaign he subsequently led to disestablish the Anglican Church in Wales. The 'damn'd little Welsh attorney' always had an ear for the popular voice, and was on hand when Roberts, moving almost like an automaton—'Do I believe in *anything*?'—possessed by he knew not what, came to Caernarfon and Ynys Mon.

Roberts's emotionalism, 'not just interdenominational but antidenominational' in Ieuan Gwynedd Jones's words, reacted as virulently as his direct contemporary Caradoc Evans to the douce bureaucracies of the chapels from which the Word had fled, without really knowing what to put in its place: charisma, socialism, or sociology? There was a political earthquake in the winter, which wiped the Tories off the face of Wales. There was a spin-off, but this time into the labour movement, with several 'boy preachers', including Arthur Horner and A. J. Cook, ending up as trade union militants. This was aided by a sudden, fierce depression in 1907–11, and by the latter year the chapel hymns were being drowned out by riots in Tonypandy and a general strike in Cardiff, and the worst of all colliery disasters, with 439 dead, at Sengenydd.[110] Roberts himself burned out, fell silent for forty years, and died forgotten in 1951. There was, thanks to Lloyd George's residual belief, the enactment of disestablishment in 1914 (frozen, like Irish Home Rule, for the duration). And, thereafter?

---

[110]  Neil Evans, 'A Tidal Wave of Impatience: The Cardiff General Strike of 1911', in Jenkins and Smith, eds., *Politics and Society*; Morgan, *Rebirth of a Nation*, 134–5.

# 6

# Contrary Heroes: Catholicism, Carlyle, and Ireland

I would show you...with great eloquence that all Ireland's failures have been due to her incapacity for believing in success or happiness—for talking like Lefanu whilst Irishmen are going out into all lands and putting them on as a shepherd putteth on his garment. As long as Ireland produces men who have the sense to leave her, she does not exist in vain.

George Bernard Shaw to Charlotte Payne-Townshend
4 November 1896[1]

How many divisions has the Pope?

Stalin

## I  MEASURING DISTANCES: IRELAND, INDUSTRY, AND THEORY

In 1921 Viscount Bryce got a begging letter from Arnold Haultain. Haultain had been for years the amanuensis of Goldwin Smith, Professor of History at Oxford and Cornell, unflinching free trader, liberal publicist on both sides of the Atlantic, and towards the end of his long life a successful speculator in Toronto real estate. When he died he got eight pages in the *DNB*. Haultain had been left not the property in downtown Toronto, but Smith's copyrights. These were now worthless.[2] No one read Smith, any more than they read Frank Newman, the rationalist brother of the cardinal, or the Positivists, the last of whom, Frederic Harrison, would die in 1923. Smith would have considered his neglect an Irish Catholic plot, the revenge of superstition for his fervent assault on Gladstonian Home Rule in and after 1886.[3] He would not be the last. Yet 'Totgesagte leben länger' as the Germans say; Bryce

---

[1] Quoted in *Bernard Shaw: Collected Letters, 1874–1897*, ed. Dan H. Lawrence (London: Max Reinhardt, 1965), 691.

[2] Bryce MS, Bodleian Library, Oxford: Haultain-Bryce, n.d. (1921); and see Christopher Harvie, *The Lights of Liberalism: University Liberals and the Challenge of Democracy, 1860–86* (London: Allen Lane, 1976), chap. 7.

[3] See Christopher Harvie, 'Ireland and the Intellectuals', in Owen Dudley Edwards, ed., *The Committed Historian: Essays for Victor Kiernan* (Edinburgh: EUSPB, 1976).

as much as Smith could not have expected the Papacy to see off Soviet Communism in 1989–91. The perspective may give Church–state relations in Ireland under the Union new relevance.

Nationalism and materialism contended for the soul of industrial Europe. The latter was divided into free-market internationalism and Marxism, but boundaries were vague and in the pragmatic British islands far from schematic. Only in the troubled 1960s did 'the peculiarities of the English', in E. P. Thompson's formula, feature, along with revisionist self-interrogations by Irish, Scots, and Welsh. T. C. Smout's *A History of the Scottish People* (1969) and Kenneth O. Morgan's *Wales in British Politics* (1963) tried to relate national experiences to European social evolution and Britain's exemplary role in it. After 1989–91 disrupted both cold war historiography and Anglo-Marxism, British identity itself became problematic. This meant, in Raymond Williams's phrase, 'measuring the distance' between the archipelago's historical discourses.[4] If, after the 1840s a successful free-trading Anglo-Saxonism faced an apparently failing Celticism, in the Linda Colley pattern, in a mirror image the arch-revisionist Conor Cruise O'Brien, in *Ancestral Voices* (1994), saw Catholic dogma, personified by Cardinal Paul Cullen (1803–1878), fusing the secular *ressentiments* of Young Ireland with the ultramontane counter-enlightenment.[5] O'Brien's Ireland seems sometimes like a large Dublin family pitching into each other after a heavy lunch — Joyce's *Portrait* gives the general idea — scattering sparks among the groundlings, yet there is a correlative to this. The 1840s argument about revolution, though it fed in Ireland two patterns of socio-economic development, and drove them further apart, *had* a common language and 'myth-kitty', both vectored through Thomas Carlyle.

The arch Anglo-Saxonist? Confederate of J. A. Froude and Buckshot Forster? Carlyle seems a non-appearer in both 'remembrancer' and 'revisionist' accounts, yet his influence on Young Ireland was explicit, fulminating away on the road to the Post Office, and close reading of most 'nationalist' texts in *any* of the British countries will yield dozens of sightings. If one Carlyle-inspired production, the Communist Manifesto (1848), was lobbed — slow-fused — into world history, and another, Disraeli's *Sybil* (1844), helped form Victorian Toryism, Carlyle also affected those who hoped that the 'sweetness and light' of Celtic and Anglo-Irish literary cultures would curb the 'fire and strength' of Protestant Unionist and ultramontane Catholic alike. The complexity of his relationship to social upheaval — part symptom, part diagnosis, part cause — helps account for this ambiguity. But his underrated influence on Catholicism helps explain why Ireland after the 1840s moved socially in a different direction

---

[4] To cite two metropolitan accounts of the subject-matter of this chapter, in Anthony D. Smith's *National Identity* (Harmondsworth: Penguin, 1991), the treatment of Irish nationalism is brief and 'pre-revisionist'; in Owen Chadwick's *The Secularization of the European Mind in the Nineteenth Century* (Cambridge: Cambridge University Press, 1975), Ireland (surely the great exception to Chadwick's thesis) doesn't appear at all. For the complexities of nationalism, 1850–1940, see Michael Thompson, ed., *Comparative Studies on Governments and Non-Government Ethnic Groups in Europe, 1850–1940*, 8 vols. (Aldershot: Dartmouth Press, and New York: New York University Press, 1990–3), and see my review in *European History Quarterly*, 25/2 (1995).

[5] Conor Cruise O'Brien, *Ancestral Voices* (Dublin: Poolbeg Press, 1994), 10.

to the rest of Britain, while still influencing and being influenced by its social and ideological evolution.[6]

The 1840s saw two themes, active since the 1780s, become synergically intertwined: puritan revolution and the millennium.[7] Carlyle was embroiled in both, as the biographer of *Oliver Cromwell* (1845) and the acolyte of Edward Irving and Henri de Saint-Simon. Edward Caird, archetypal Balliol-Scot home ruler, celebrated his 'Puritanism idealised, made cosmopolitan, freed from the narrowness which clung to its first expression'.[8] In Ireland at a time of demographic disaster, his ideas and language helped catalyse a Catholicism struggling from incoherent doctrine and secular control into its own polity. This involved three things and two remarkable men: the fate of the *ancien régime*, the impact of technology, and Ireland's 'slave role' in British industrialization; Carlyle himself and his near-contemporary Cullen. Carlyle anticipated the transport-based phase of industrialization, and the counter-thesis of 'mechanized' human responses and the loss of social equilibrium. Even after *Latter-Day Pamphlets* (1850) diverted him from Ireland, his influence led to a re-orientation of social thought: a Protestant Carlyle evolved on the mainland and in Ulster, and a Catholic Carlyle in the south. The subsequent working-out of this reaction would share many common factors and milieus, not least the British Empire itself.

## II    'CREATIVE CHAOS': VICTIMS AND *GASTARBEITER*

The notion of mainland unity prevailing in 1837 is misleading. The Disruption in 1843 and the 'brad y llyfrau gleision' (Treachery of the Blue Books) in 1848 made Scots and Welsh feel very un-British by 1850.[9] Ireland would be diverted by the 'famine years' to a completely different terminus: a nationalism racy of the soil, religious and sacrificially heroic but civically weak.[10] This outcome was part of

---

6 There is no reference to Carlyle in Ciaran Brady, ed., *Interpreting Irish History* (Dublin: Irish Academic Press, 1994); a brief sighting in F. S. L. Lyons, *Culture and Anarchy in Ireland* (Oxford: Clarendon Press, 1979), 12, and likewise in the Field Day Theatre Company's *Ireland's Field Day* (London: Hutchinson, 1985), in Declan Kiberd, 'Anglo-Irish Attitudes', ibid., 86, and in Seamus Deane, *Celtic Revivals* (London: Faber, 1985), 30. Malcolm Brown, *The Politics of Irish Literature* (London: Allen and Unwin, 1972), 117–19, takes the 'Anglo-Saxonist' line on him, but Owen Dudley Edwards, 'Irish Nationalism', in *Celtic Nationalism* (London: Routledge and Kegan Paul, 1968), 123 ff., seems fair and perceptive; for Carlyle's influence on the literary intelligentsia see Christopher Harvie, *The Centre of Things: Political Fiction from Disraeli to the Present* (London: Unwin Hyman, 1991), 18–21.

7 See Sheridan Gilley, 'Edward Irving: Prophet of the Millennium' and Raphael Samuel, 'The Discovery of Puritanism, 1820–1914', in Jane Garnett and Colin Matthew, eds., *Revival and Religion since 1700* (London: Hambledon Press, 1993).

8 Edward Caird, 'The Genius of Carlyle', in *Essays on Literature and Philosophy*, i (Glasgow: Maclehose, 1892), 234. Curiously, another Thomas Carlyle was responsible for making Irving's Catholic Apostolic Church popular in Wilhelmine Berlin.

9 Compare Linda Colley, *Britons: Forging the Nation, 1707–1837* (New Haven and London: Yale University Press, 1992) with the studies in Alexander Grant and Keith Stringer, eds., *Uniting the Kingdom* (London: Routledge, 1995), and my review article about both books in *Welsh History Review*, 18/4 (1997).

10 Lyons, *Culture and Anarchy, passim*; see Deane, *Celtic Revivals*, 18.

the European *Zeitbruch* of 1848, which reformulated nationalism as Tom Nairn's 'modern Janus': constructing consensual economic development *and* histories of ancient wrong, something aggravated by the waves of migration which broke over the industrial areas.[11] In Ireland the famine meant that the secular industrialism-and-federalism goal of O'Connell *and* Young Ireland was split. The masses encountered industry by emigrating or settling in Ulster alongside a touchy planter majority.[12] The winners, the poet-priest-peasant conduits, had nationalism without development, their termini the Committee Room of Joyce's 'centre of paralysis', or Fluther Good's 'terrible state of chassis'.[13]

In the second phase of industrialization, the Irish, lacking capital or market for manufacturing, apart from the small north-eastern enclave, provided foodstuffs and *Gastarbeiter*: essential but unprivileged.[14] This two-Ireland identity lasted over a century, and low growth rates stemming from an agrarian economy and subsequent republican austerity in the south seemed to endorse Protestant success in Ulster.[15] European experience showed that this wasn't unique: one region's advance could require another's decline, with the unsuccessful becoming servitors—Braudel's 'fabriques d'hommes a l'usage d'autrui'—to developed areas which carried off the booty of raw material and low-skill, low-wage labour.[16] Misery in Poland and the Carpathians, pogroms in Russia, and criminality in south Italy propelled hard-working peasants to drink, to America or the Ruhr, the Borinage, and Lombardy, just as starvation drove thousands from Ireland to Britain.[17]

[11] Tom Nairn, 'On Studying Nationalism', in *Faces of Nationalism: Janus Revisited* (London: Verso, 1997), 1–20. See W. J. McCormack, *Ascendancy and Tradition in Anglo-Irish Literary History, from 1789 to 1939* (Oxford: Clarendon Press, 1985), chap. 5. Oliver MacDonagh contributes fruitfully to this theme in 'Ambiguity in Nationalism: The Case of Ireland' (1980), repr. in Brady, ed., *Interpreting Irish History*.

[12] Charles Gavan Duffy, *Short Life of Thomas Davis* (London: Unwin, 1895), 180 ff.; Edwards, 'Irish Nationalism', 123: J. J. Lee, *The Modernisation of Irish Society 1848–1916* (Dublin: Gill and Macmillan, 1973), 49–53.

[13] See James Joyce, 'Ivy Day in the Committee Room', in *Dubliners*, 1913 (London: Cape, 1967), 132–52; in Sean O'Casey, *Juno and the Paycock*, 1924 (London: St Martin's Press, 1960), the last lines of Act III could, cleverly, mean either chaos or stasis.

[14] Cormac O'Grada, *Ireland: A New Economic History, 1780–1939* (Oxford: Clarendon Press, 1994), 347–8. David Fitzpatrick, 'A Peculiar Tramping People: The Irish in Britain, 1801–70', in W. E. Vaughan, ed., *A New History of Ireland*, v: *Ireland under the Union, I: 1801–1870* (Oxford: Oxford University Press, 1989), 623–60.

[15] Norman Vance, *Irish Literature: A Social History* (Oxford: Blackwell, 1990), 140, writes of mid Victorian Ireland being 'subjected unevenly to the industrialising process', but in net terms Ireland was deindustrialized. If the Lagan Valley were removed from the statistics, the fall would be even steeper. For the twentieth century see David Johnson, *The Interwar Economy in Ireland* (Dublin: Institute of Economic and Social History, 1985), 43.

[16] Fernand Braudel, *La Méditerranée et le monde méditerranéan à l'époque de Philippe II* (Paris: Colin, 1966), 46. Ya-Fe Hsu, 'Regions in the Development of Historic Capitalism: A Comparison of Scotland, Baden-Württemberg and Taiwan', PhD thesis, Tübingen University, 1999, stresses the deliberate quality of 'unequal development': agricultural crises, for example, being instrumentalized to provide labour for industry elsewhere. For the arrival of the Irish in industrial Scotland see Tom Gallagher, *Glasgow: The Uneasy Peace* (Manchester: Manchester University Press, 1987), chap. 1.

[17] Gearóid Ó Tuathaigh, *Ireland before the Famine* (Dublin: Gill and Macmillan, 1972), 140 ff.; W. L. Langer, *Political and Social Upheaval* (New York: Harper, 1969), 10 ff. Jeffrey Williamson, in

This migration into key unskilled-labour markets—mining, weaving, dock labour, navvying—helped the littoral to move between 1845 and 1865 from textile- to transport-based capital-goods industry *and* to gain civic 'legitimacy' through roads, water supply, sewage systems, gas works. In Lancashire and Scotland, textiles gave way to a dominance in engineering and heavy industry. Wales made the transition from minerals and iron to tinplate and steam-coal export: not just a national but a world-dominating success. The process of socialization was local—Tom Nairn's 'synthetic regionalism' model is useful here—and was calibrated by an evolving British state and flexible intelligentsia which amalgamated Gramsci's 'organic' and 'traditional' types. Its ethos and habitation was, ironically, Irish-inspired: Burkeian sublimity and conservatism transplanted to the Lake District of Wordsworth, Coleridge, and Thomas Arnold. But post-famine Ireland had to create its own elite from those who had served the winners of a damn-close-run economic miracle. A putative Irish bourgeoisie had either to manoeuvre against the flow of British 'policy' or reject a competitive structure which was loaded against it. Comforting parallels with eighteenth-century Scotland didn't work.

The 'railway mania' bought off the doom predicted by Marx and Engels, helping create a new capital-goods-based economy, but in Ireland its impact was, as we have seen, at best ambiguous.[18] The collapse of William Dargan in the slump of 1866 exemplified the problem of a country flooded by imports.[19] Manufacturing outside Ulster was thin and got thinner—22.8 per cent of the workforce in 1851 and 16.0 per cent in 1881.[20]

Irish tariffs against British goods were a prospect which worried Liberals who opposed Gladstonian Home Rule in 1886. With reason: there *was* an Irish protectionist tradition. The railway as economic regenerator, the German economist Friedrich List argued in his *National System of Political Economy* (1841), needed tariffs to protect fledgling manufactures as well as to aid state-sponsored construction. Protectionism went back to the Grattan parliament of 1786–1800. Matthew Carey, one of its leading advocates, left for the United States, where as a Philadelphia publisher, he preached it after 1819. His ideas were taken up by List, exiled from Tübingen, in his *Outlines of American Political Economy* (1827) and refined by Carey's son Henry as *The Principles of Political Economy* (1839). List was taken up by the Hungarian improvers István Széchenyi and Ferenc Deák. Parnell's protectionism in the 1880s thus had Irish-American ancestry, and List's economics would return to Ireland in

---

'The Impact of the Irish on British Labour Markets During the Industrial Revolution', in Sheridan Gilley and Roger Swift, eds., *The Irish in Britain* (London: Pinter, 1989), disagrees, but I find the earlier orthodoxy borne out by regional examples in Lanarkshire and South Wales. See Alan Campbell, *The Lanarkshire Miners* (Edinburgh: John Donald, 1979).

[18] Eric Hobsbawm, *Industry and Empire*, 1968 (Harmondsworth: Penguin, 1970), 109 ff.

[19] Obituary of William Dargan, *Times* (8 Feb. 1867); his *DNB* entry, by G. C. Boase, rev. in *Oxford DNB* by Steve Chrimes, is thin, and he doesn't make Vaughan's list of the Irish great (Vaughan, ed., *New History of Ireland*, v, 794–800). A biography is badly needed.

[20] H. D. Gribbon, 'Economy and Industry', in W. E. Vaughan, ed., *A New History of Ireland*, vi: *Ireland under the Union, II: 1870–1921* (Oxford: Clarendon Press, 1996), 333 ff.

Arthur Griffith's *The Resurrection of Hungary* (1908). But by then the Irish economy had crawled for half a century.[21]

The upshot was the inflected 'modernism' of Ireland. In Charles Lever's late and (for him) sombre novel *Lord Kilgobbin* (1872) his would-be modernizer Joe Atlee remarks that 'Scotland has no national absurdities: she neither asks for a flag or a parliament. She demands only what will pay'.[22] The centrality of nation, land, and church to Ireland had, however, consequences which were neither absurd nor remote from British intellectual concerns. Since Burke the Irish had been close enough to the English critical tradition to share its doubts about progress. The famine was followed by a general sense of dislocation in the 1860s which seemed to commend the reflective 'Celtic culture' of Ernest Renan and Matthew Arnold. Market-driven improvement had been challenged by democratic agitation in 1848, by financial crisis in the mid 1850s and mid 1860s, and by the first ecological critique, Stanley Jevons on the coal question, in 1865. The mid-century bloodbath from the Crimea to the commune contradicted tendencies towards Goldwin Smith's dream of peace and contract. To Arnold and Renan as 'revisionist' 1848ers, regional tributaries to the central culture could help combat materialism, socialism, and militarism.[23] This mission blended with print capitalism—the Macmillan brothers, who published Arnold and later Yeats, were Scottish Celts turned Christian Socialists who scooped the university market—and with a growing appreciation of the unconscious and habitual.

So much Irish literary history consists of the projection-back of the literary renaissance of the early twentieth century, its world reputation, and its controversies, that IreLit evicted earlier, more awkward loyalties, as firmly as EngLit had stamped out Teutonic philology during World War I.[24] Conor Cruise O'Brien registers chapbook patriots, addresses from the scaffold, street ballads, and prison journals. But could these really propel by themselves? Scotland outdid Ireland in print-capitalist nationalism—Scott-and-Burns Jacobitism, the record of a long and articulate period of independence, religious and land grievances, some quite up-to-date martyrs—but her people didn't move.[25] To look at the reading-matter of the youthful Davis and Duffy, Charles Kickham, and later on Michael Collins or Eamon de Valera is to see activism kindled by the friction between an elective Irish nationalism and social criticism bred from British print-capitalism.[26]

---

[21] For Matthew Carey (1760–1839) and his son Henry Charles (1793–1879), also America's leading publisher, see *The Dictionary of American Biography*, iii (New York: Scribners, 1929), and for List (1800–1846: an American citizen after 1827) see *Deutsche allgemeine Biographie*, xiv (Berlin: Duncker und Humblot, 1985).

[22] Charles Lever, *Lord Kilgobbin* (London: Downey, 1899), ii, 18.

[23] McCormack, *Ascendancy and Tradition*, 219 ff.

[24] Ibid. 250; Chris Baldick, *The Social Mission of English Criticism, 1848–1932* (Oxford: Clarendon Press, 1981), chap. 4.

[25] McCormack ascribes this to the effectiveness of the Clearances (*Ascendancy and Tradition*, 246), neglecting the considerable cultural output covered by William Donaldson, *Popular Literature in Victorian Scotland: Language, Fiction and the Press* (Aberdeen: Aberdeen University Press, 1986).

[26] See Thomas Flanagan in Vaughan, ed., *New History of Ireland*, v, 490 ff. Owen Dudley Edwards, *Eamon de Valera* (Cardiff: GPC Books, 1997), 32. De Valera read Macaulay and Goldsmith as well as Kickham, and considered himself a monarchist, getting interested in the

Bernard Shaw's clever *John Bull's Other Island* (1904) has his Irish progressive Larry Doyle aim at an essentially Scots future, yet be seduced, and paralysed by, mad Father Keegan, who combines both the 'ideal' of Ireland and the critique of industrialism.[27] Keegan is Irish, yet he summates British nineteenth-century social criticism, and is traumatized by imperialism. The Englishman Tom Broadbent compares him to Carlyle and Ruskin in his own half-remembered critical canon. But imperialism has made Keegan mad—a logical man thrown together with an oriental whose indifference to Western values subverts his own Christianity:

KEEGAN This world, sir, is very clearly a place of torment and penance, a place where the fool flourishes and the good and wise are hated and persecuted, a place where men and women torture one another in the name of love; where children are scourged and enslaved in the name of parental duty and education; where the weak in body are poisoned and mutilated in the name of healing, and the weak in character are put to the horrible torture of imprisonment, not for hours but for years, in the name of justice. It is a place where the hardest toil is a welcome refuge from the horror and tedium of pleasure, and where charity and good works are done only for hire to ransom the souls of the spoiler and the sybarite. Now, sir, there is only one place of horror and torment known to my religion; and that place is hell. Therefore it is plain to me that this earth of ours must be hell, and that we are all here, as the Indian revealed to me—perhaps he was sent to reveal it to me—to expiate crimes committed by us in a former existence.

Keegan might be Ruskin; being mad, he is Sweeney running in the woods, after absolute triadic values which stand apart from the economic Wasteland of Broadbent and Doyle.

Shaw wrote after Robertson Smith and J. G. Frazer, as well as Arnold and Renan: in a social-psychology context that would later be elaborated by Freud and Jung, Durkheim and Weber, Eliot and Joyce.[28] Keegan's combative mysticality marked George Russell, AE, cooperator and spiritualist, Yeats the theatre manager who mastered double-entry bookkeeping, Patrick Geddes, and even Shaw himself. This was part of an anti-positivist 'cultural recuperation' project within modernism which anticipates, say, J. L. Hammond's interpretation of Gladstone's commitment in 1886 to Home Rule—in defiance of the intellectual establishment, the Tyndalls, Huxleys, and Sidgwicks—as epic-theological rather than scientific-rational, Celtic rather than Saxon. Gladstone *was* both lowlander and highlander.[29]

---

Gaelic literary movement only on his marriage. Richard Ellmann, *James Joyce* (New York: Oxford University Press, 1959), 31, 45, notes Lamb, Tennyson, Meredith, and Hardy among his reading. According to Bernard Aspinwall, Patrick MacGill, 'the first self-conscious, Catholic, working-class writer', read no Irish writers at all ('Patrick MacGill, 1890–1963: An Alternative Vision', in Diana Wood, ed., *The Church and the Arts, Studies in Church History*, 28 (Oxford: Blackwell, 1992), 499).

[27] See Bernard Shaw, *John Bull's Other Island* (London: Constable, 1907), p. vii.

[28] Ibid., Act III; in his interesting discussion of the play in 'Myth and Motherland', in the Field Day Theatre Company's *Ireland's Field Day*, Richard Kearney puzzlingly leaves Keegan out. See William Robertson Smith's *Lectures on the Religion of the Semites* (London: A. & C. Black, 1889) and J. G. Frazer's *The Golden Bough: A Study in Comparative Religion*, 1890 (London: Routledge Curzon, 2003); and Stuart Hughes, *Consciousness and Society*, 1958 (London: Paladin, 1974), 33–67.

[29] J. L. Hammond, *Gladstone and the Irish Nation* (London: Longmans, 1938), 523–52.

   This epic element was also carried on by Standish James O'Grady—directly
influenced by Carlyle and Whitman—and his researches on the *Táin*.[30] It figures
in Yeats's ritual anathemas against 'Huxley-Shaw-Bastien-Lepage . . . mechanism' in
*Autobiographies* (1913) and persists, albeit more politely, in T. S. Eliot's *Notes towards
the Definition of Culture* (1948). This was one end of the scale; at the other was
Pearse's call for the reification of the Irish mind through the overthrow of the 'murder
machine' of English-language, Church-run education, not least by the agency of
poetic self-sacrifice. The drive towards this had accumulated Ossianic as well as
Arnoldian accents, but much of the fire imagery that Pearse conjured up at Bodenstown in 1914 is pure Carlyle.[31]


## III   MACHINES AND HEROES

The fusion of academic Philocelticism with the English critical tradition produced an
'other' fearsome enough to evict or at least qualify earlier enthusiasm for railways and
steamers. As in Hardy's *Tess* (1891), the engineer could be seen as 'chief menial of the
Steamengine'. One way of comprehending this assault was naturalism, recording the
surrender of man before the inexorable pressure of heredity and environmental con-
ditioning. Epitomized by Zola's *Rougon-Macquart* sequence (1873–95), this influenced Ireland through the Dublin–Paris conduit and became patent not only in the
Anglo-Irish career of Zola's closest English-language disciple George Moore, but in
the autodidact 'proletarian realism' of *The Ragged Trousered Philanthropists* by 'Robert
Tressell' and Patrick MacGill's *Children of the Dead End*, both published in 1914.[32]
   The other Irish reaction was the heroic. Though the Carlyle of *Chartism* could be
seen as anti-Irish, and his Anglo-Saxonism was one reason for his influence on the
British literary-political elite in the mid nineteenth century, this was the man who
insisted:

The Sanspotato is of the selfsame stuff as the superfinest Lord Lieutenant. Not an individual
sanspotato human scarecrow but had a life given him out of Heaven, with Eternities depend-
ing on it; for once and no second time. With immensities in him, over him and around him;
with feelings which a Shakespeare's speech would not utter; with desires as illimitable as the
Autocrat's of all the Russias.[33]

Carlyle's 1841 lectures *On Heroes and Hero-Worship* acted on Young Ireland—the
Catholic Gavan Duffy and the Protestants Thomas Davis and John Mitchel in

---

[30] Lyons, *Culture and Anarchy*, 32–5.
[31] Edwards, 'Irish Nationalism', 123; and see the quote from Pearse's Bodenstown speech,
starting with a quote from Ruskin, and climaxing with fire imagery which might be from the end
of *The French Revolution*, repr. in Deane, *Celtic Revivals*, 72. See also Priscilla Metscher, 'Patrick
Pearse and the Irish Cultural Revolution: The Significance of Pearse as an Irish Educator', in Heinz
Kosok, ed., *Studies in Anglo-Irish Literature* (Bonn: Bouvier, 1982).
[32] 'Robert Tressell' [sic], *The Ragged Trousered Philanthropists*, 1911 (London: Grant Richards,
1914) and Patrick MacGill, *Children of the Dead End* (London: Grant Richards, 1914); and
Aspinwall, 'Patrick MacGill, 1890–1963'. The ODNB entries are very useful.
[33] Thomas Carlyle, *Chartism* (London: Chapman and Hall, 1839), 22.

particular—moving them to postulate a revolutionary Celtic hero, able to take on Luther and Cromwell. Owen Dudley Edwards sees this tradition propelling militant nationalism up to the period of Pearse and Griffith.[34]

Irish *ressentiments*, laid low by political failure and the famine, were plainly waiting to be animated and organized. But by whom? What was needed was a doctrinal impetus different from hedge-priests, seminarians from Douai, or shrill Repealers, which could inspire the broad loyalty that in their various ways Tom Paine, Scots Free Kirkers, and in his time O'Connell had enjoyed. There were political contenders of kaleidoscopic variety—R. W. Comerford shows their continual regroupings in 1848–70, responding to English, European, and American political changes, but creating only a fitful momentum and in comparison to the militancy of Italy, Germany, France, and the USA, and their hecatombs of dead, a distinct aversion to bloodshed—and there was the Catholic Church, under Archbishop, later Cardinal, Paul Cullen.[35]

Cullen's upbringing has been misread, not least by Conor Cruise O'Brien, the devotee of Edmund Burke. He was a 'strong farmer's' son from Kildare, where his father, Hugh, had 700 acres. In Scotland, from where the term perhaps came, the 'muckle farmers' were capitalist entrepreneurs paying large rents. The Cullens had little reason to like the British—an uncle was shot in 1798—but from 10 to 14, the vital years of schooling, Paul enjoyed a liberal Quaker education at Ballitore, Burke's alma mater. He rose by patronage in the Church, but he might have been an Irish version of the diffidently ambitious young Scot in Sir David Wilkie's 'The Letter of Recommendation'. At Rome he coincided with the impact of De Maistre's *Du Pape* (1821), demanded a philosophical, not a theological training, and effectively entered the civil service of the Vatican. Close to Pio Nono and hostile to revolution, he returned to an Ireland wounded by a social catastrophe and in a political vacuum.[36]

This didn't encourage pluralism but a devotion to Rome as firm as any Benthamite's commitment to the Greatest Happiness. The 1850s would be a critical decade. Following Protestant campaigns in the 1830s, and attempts to exploit the Famine, the Scottish Disruption of 1843 had spawned a parallel Ulster movement, and had energized the evangelicals, with missions at the top of their list. Thomas Chalmers, temperamentally Conservative (and below that deistic?), was inclined to coexist with Catholics. His fiercer colleagues Thomas Guthrie and James Begg—and in Ulster

---

[34] Edwards, 'Irish Nationalism', 123.

[35] R.V. Comerford, 'Ireland, 1850–1870', 'Churchmen, Tenants and Independent Opposition', 'Conspiring Brotherhoods and Contending Elites', and 'Gladstone's First Irish Enterprise, 1864–7', in W. E. Vaughan, ed., *A New History of Ireland*, v: *Ireland under the Union, I: 1801–1870*, 420 ff. Comparing the casualties of Irish unrest with Europe's wars and the American Civil War is pointless, but the fact that more were killed in the 'policing' of the *Mezzogiorno*, 1860–7, than in all the campaigns of Garibaldi is surely significant.

[36] For Cullen's biography see Desmond Bowen, *Paul Cardinal Cullen and the Shaping of Modern Irish Catholicism* (Dublin: Gill and Macmillan, 1983), and B. MacSuibhne, ed., *Paul Cullen and his Contemporaries*, 5 vols. (Naas: Leinster Leader, 1950–65). These show the sort of secular inputs one would expect from a family with substantial business connections in Liverpool: access to literary reviews, banking connections, and so on.

Henry Cooke—were more nationalistic, social reforming, and bigoted. The Ulster revival of 1859 would present a real challenge. Against them the Catholic hierarchy in Britain was aristocratic and rather weak: and the two routes out seemed dangerous—politicized post-O'Connellite Catholicism, embodied by Bishop McHale of Tuam, or the ecumenical success of the Capuchin temperance crusader Father Theobald Matthew. Cullen manoeuvred, though under-resourced. His Catholic University in Dublin started in 1852, the year of a very qualified Oxbridge reform, under the greatest modern recusant, Father Newman. Lack of resources impeded it, but the tourist could reflect that many of Ireland's grand gothic churches were the work of the Pugins, creator of England's Vatican, the Palace of Westminster, and in the hands of the teaching orders (monks cost a lot less than married ex-dons) the extension of secondary education between 1850 and 1880, from twenty to sixty schools, was more remarkable than that of England. The 'devotional revolution' that Cullen inaugurated at the unprecedented Provincial Synod of Thurles in August 1850, when 'the old passivity and timidity in face of British power was generally replaced by confidence and even, in many cases, by truculence', would by the time of his death in 1878 grant his church a social and political presence which was the envy of any secular leader and which, all too appropriately, Joseph Lee compares with the powers of the greatest of nineteenth-century politicians.[37]

O'Brien's judgement on Cullen thus seems fundamentally wrong, because Cullen's world was that of Rome, not of Ireland. And of Rome instructed, through De Maistre, by Burke, O'Brien's hero and the greatest of Irish conservatives. This was more ambitious, perhaps more prescient—did Pope John Paul II's strategy, for Poland, for the Catholic universe, differ greatly?—than any Irish 'Gallicanism' (national Catholicism) but in terms of the matter of the nation it was ambiguous, and in terms of civil society and gender politics, disastrous. Shaw's Father Keegan was a shrewd shot at psychoanalysing this troubled state.

Like Carlyle, the 'devotional revolution' responded to puritan and millennial concerns but behind both, and the interweaving of the 'spirit of ninety-eight', was the social thought—and in particular social *control*—of the Scottish enlightenment. We will discuss Carlyle's 'Signs of the Times' and *Past and Present* later, but Carlyle encountered Adam Ferguson's *Essay on the History of Civil Society* (1767), with its conservative insistence on social cohesion and *Spieltrieb* (enthusiasm), both directly and via Ferguson's influence on German writers, Schiller and Goethe in particular.[38] Secondly, like many Catholic social thinkers, Carlyle was influenced by the French sociologist Henri de Saint-Simon (1760–1825) and his concept

---

[37] Lee, *Modernisation*, 29. *Whitaker's Almanac* cites only twenty-one Headmasters' Conference schools opening over this period, and even if we throw in older endowed schools which were then 'upgraded' under the Taunton reforms after 1867 the Irish achievement is remarkable.

[38] Ralph Jessop, in *Carlyle and Scottish Thought* (London: Macmillan, 1997), stresses Carlyle's debt to Reid and the commonsense school but doesn't mention the connection with Ferguson. Fania Oz-Salzberger, *Translating the Enlightenment: Scottish Civic Discourse in Eighteenth Century Germany* Oxford: Clarendon Press, 1995), shows the influence of Ferguson on German thought, which would return via Carlyle to Thomas Davis. See Eileen Sullivan, *Thomas Davis* (Lewisburg: Buckness University Press, 1974), 49.

of social evolution through the alternation of periods of 'organic' stability and 'critical' change. Such a *Zeitbruch* Carlyle saw in his *French Revolution* (1837). In this, for good or ill, the entire old order is volcanically blown apart, with no possibility, save that provided by some sort of spiritual rebirth, of it being pieced together again.[39]

The concentration of Saint-Simon and his disciple Auguste Comte on social evolution attracted British empiricists, yet the British Comtists, or Positivists—headed by Richard Congreve, Frederic Harrison, and Professor E. S. Beesly—became known as 'secular Catholics'. They were sympathetic to Irish nationalism, and included John Kells Ingram of Trinity College, Young Irelander, and author of 'Who Fears to Speak of Ninety-Eight?' For a time Ingram's friend Patrick Geddes might have become their 'pope'.[40] Carlyle's historical dialectic resembled theirs in having the 'hero' as charismatic figure, both actual and as a metaphor of individual possibilities, who could secure a new organic settlement.[41] This ideal, 'bold, modern and all-surrounding and kosmical' in Whitman's words, influenced America through Emerson, who, moved by 'Signs of the Times' visited Carlyle in 1833, and launched 'transcendentalism'. Through Emerson's friend Whitman it later returned to Ireland via his Irish disciples Thomas Sigerson, Standish James O'Grady, AE, and Shaw himself.[42] The epical Carlyle, boosted by Macaulay, was 'read' in this way by Young Ireland. But the interpretations of him were different in Britain and Ulster, where the conservative individualism of Bonar Law's, Kipling's, and Ulster's view of its technological good fortune as God-ordained ethnic superiority had evolved from Cromwellian dogma via the Anglo-Saxonist 'captain/soldier of industry' paradigm. Samuel Smiles (whose son became a prominent Belfast Unionist) typified this.

This parallelism showed up in 1859. In response to a French invasion scare, volunteer corps of amateur soldiers were raised in mainland Britain.[43] Ireland was deliberately excluded from this. Her nationalists were initially pro-French, buoyed up by the success of Napoleon III's Marshal MacMahon against the Austrians, but faltered when Rome's secular power was threatened. An unofficial Catholic volunteer movement evolved, directed at defending the Pope as an Italian ruler, and opposed to British enthusiasm for Italian secular liberalism.[44] On the mainland the Volunteers

---

[39] Thomas Carlyle, *The French Revolution*, 1837 (London: Chapman and Hall, 1895), Pt III, bk VII, chap. 8, 'Finis'. The key Saint-Simonian work was his *Nouveau Christianisme* of 1825.

[40] G. K. Peatling, ' "Who fears to speak of politics?": John Kells Ingram and Hypothetical Nationalism', *Irish Historical Studies*, 31 (Nov. 1998); and see T. R. Wright, *The Religion of Humanity: The Impact of Comteian Positivism on Victorian Britain* (Cambridge: Cambridge University Press, 1986).

[41] See Hill Shine, *Carlyle and the Saint-Simonians: The Concept of Historical Periodicity*, 1941 (New York: Octagon Books, 1981).

[42] Walt Whitman, *Democratic Vistas*, 1871 (London: Nonesuch, 1938), 708–9; for the Irish Whitmanites see Thomas Flanagan, 'Literature in English', in Vaughan, ed., *New History of Ireland*, v, 484.

[43] For Bonar Law see Robert Blake, *The Unknown Prime Minister* (London: Eyre and Spottiswoode, 1955), chap. 1; and for Kipling see Charles Carrington, *Rudyard Kipling*, 1955 (Harmondsworth: Penguin, 1970), 69, 74.

[44] Comerford, 'Conspiring Brotherwoods and Contending Elites', 420–1.

were Protestant and particularly strong in Scotland; their peak was during the Fenian
emergency of 1867 (when Fenians managed to infiltrate the Volunteer Corps in Liverpool).[45] Yet the idea of 'volunteering' cast back to Grattan's Ireland of the 1780s.
In the 1860 episode the Catholic Church anticipated events in Ireland after 1910.[46]

   Carlyle's influence within the Catholic-Nationalist tradition seems to negate
Seamus Deane's argument about Burke, the Sublime, and Marie Antoinette. The
Irish people had applauded 'Godless France' in 1789–98, and in O'Connell's Catholic League, far from rejecting the Revolution, they improved on its clanking mechanisms of Supreme Beings and reformed calendars to produce a powerful and resilient
clerico-political populism. But Carlyle was quite remote from this, regarding landlords as 'a selfish, ferocious, famishing, unprincipled set of hyenas, from whom at no
time and in no way has the country derived any benefit whatsoever'.[47] A hero, like
Michael Davitt, to the young David Lloyd George, and to the Fenian John O'Leary,
the radical Carlyle demanded liberation from landlordism as much as from conventional religion.[48]

   He could, though, be interpreted favourably by Catholic-tending churchmen.
Newman in 1840 'hoped he might have come round right' and regretted he 'settled
the wrong way',[49] and he would later appeal more directly to Irish Catholics through
the neo-medievalism of Abbot Samson of Bury St Edmunds in *Past and Present*
(1843). John Mitchel, the most Carlyleian of nationalists, was Protestant, but Charles
Gavan Duffy, reared in a Monaghan environment almost as Scottish as Ecclefechan,
became a central supporter of Cullen's 'devotional revolution', while remaining a
continuing Irish friend.[50] Carlyle was directly influential on the Catholic fiction of
Father Patrick Sheehan, and close reading of sermons and clerical memoirs (a forbid-
ding enterprise) would detect consistent echoes and symbols, as in Don Byrne's 1930s
memoir of Maynooth in the 1890s:

To see the oak stalls in the College Chapel, darkening a little with the years, is to think of all
who have been students there, before my time and since. With no effort I can slip from the
moorings of Past and Present, and see in this moment all rolled in one. The slowly-moving
line of priests down through the Chapel is never-ending; it goes into the four provinces of
Ireland; it crosses the seas into England and Scotland, and the greater seas into the Americas
and Australia and Africa and China; it covers the whole earth . . .[51]

   [45] Hugh Cunningham, *The Volunteer Force: A Social and Political History, 1859–1908* (London:
Croom Helm, 1975), 81–2.
   [46] Jonathan Bardon, *A History of Ulster* (Belfast: Blackstaff Press, 1992), 345–7.
   [47] Quoted by Tom Johnston in *Our Scots Noble Families* (Glasgow: Forward Publishing, 1909),
23.
   [48] John O'Leary, *Recollections of Fenians and Fenianism*, 1896 (Shannon: Irish University Press,
1969), 47.
   [49] Newman to Mrs J. Mozley, 25 Feb. 1840, in John Henry Newman, *Letters and Correspondence*
(London: Longmans, 1891), 299.
   [50] Sir Charles Gavan Duffy, *My Life in Two Hemispheres*, 1898 (Shannon: Irish University Press,
1969), 9, 52.
   [51] See Lyons, *Culture and Anarchy*, 90–1; Terence Brown, 'Canon Sheehan and the Catholic
Intellectual', in *Ireland's Literature* (Mullingar: Lilliput, 1988); quote from Don Boyle, *I Remember
Maynooth* (London: Longmans Green, 1937), 28–9.

Whatever this is, it's not Burkeian conservative. Indeed, in Carlyle's *The French Revolution* there is but one reference to Burke, intriguingly framed:

Great Burke has raised his great voice long ago; eloquently demonstrating that the end of an Epoch has come, to all appearance the end of Civilised Time. Him many answer: Camille Desmoulins, Clootz Speaker of Mankind, Paine the rebellious Needleman, and honourable Gaelic Vindicators in that country and in this: but the great Burke remains unanswerable; 'the Age of Chivalry is gone,' and could not but go, having now produced the still more indomitable Age of Hunger. Altars enough, of the Dubois-Rohan sort, changing to the Gobel-and-Talleyrand sort, are faring by rapid transmutations to—shall we say, the right Proprietor of them? French Game and French Game-Preservers did alight on the Cliffs of Dover, with cries of distress. Who will say that the end of much is not come?[52]

Forget the plumage, in other words: wise up to the resilient nastiness of the landlord and the Big House. The message is hammered home in the closing pages, where the heart of Carlyle's matter stops being France and becomes the Irish peasant:

But what if History somewhere on this Planet were to hear of a Nation, the third soul of whom had not, for thirty weeks each year, as many third-rate potatoes as would sustain him? History, in that case, feels bound to consider that starvation is starvation; that starvation from age to age presupposes much; History ventures to assert that the French Sansculotte of Ninety-three, who, roused from long death-sleep, could rush at once to the frontiers, and die fighting for an immortal Hope and Faith of Deliverance for him and his, was but the second-miserablest of men! The Irish Sans-Potato, had he not senses then, nay a soul? In his frozen darkness, it was bitter for him to die famishing; bitter to see his children famish. It was bitter for him to be a beggar, a liar and a knave. Nay, if that dreary Greenland-wind of benighted Want, perennial from sire to son, had frozen him into a kind of torpor and numb callosity, so that he saw not, felt not,—was this, for a creature with a soul in it, some assuagement or the cruellest wretchedness of all?[53]

Carlyle found the Jacobins and their *Zeitbruch* unavoidable. The Revolution had killed the past stone dead. Burke may have created English Toryism, but Ireland became European—and as such, potentially menaced by Jacobinism.

More important than his overt Anglo-Saxonism was Carlyle's gift for embodying the sense of crisis—and new beginning—in a powerful symbol, which then took on a momentum adjusted to demotic nationality. Transcendentalism might otherwise have been a reheated hash of Unitarianism and Scots deism; Smilesian technocracy the Panglossery of an Andrew Ure. Carlyle implied that in the simultaneous crises of Catholic Church and Irish people the former could take the lead. Not only does *Past and Present* confront the collision of the cash-nexus with medieval Catholic solidarity, but its climax is an extraordinary passage in which the fate of the Papacy literally embodies the menace of the machine. Carlyle describes how the ancient, reactionary Pope Gregory XVI (1765–1846) literally became 'an automaton':

The old Pope of Rome, finding it laborious to kneel so long while they cart him through the streets to bless the people on *Corpus Christi* day, complains of rheumatism; whereupon

---

[52] Carlyle, *French Revolution*, 62.
[53] Ibid. 368.

his cardinals consult;—construct him, after some study, a stuffed, cloaked figure, of iron and wood, with wool or baked hair; and place it in a kneeling posture. Stuffed figure, or rump of a figure; to this stuffed rump he, sitting at his ease on a lower level, joins, by the aid of cloaks and drapery, his living head and outspread hands; the rump with its cloaks kneels, the Pope looks, and holds his hands spread; and so the two in concert bless the Roman population on *Corpus Christi* day, as well as they can.[54]

This may suggest Carlyle at his most Luther-like, but he counters this by praising the heroism of Jesuits battling cholera, and claims that the situation of the puppet-Pope is no different from that of post-1789 Europe:

This poor Pope,—who knows what is good in him? In a time otherwise prone to forget, he keeps up the mournfulest ghastly memorial of the Highest, Blessedest, which once was; which, in new forms, will have to be again. . . . He will ask you, What other? Under this my Gregorian chant, and beautiful wax-light Phantasmagory, kindly hidden from you is an Abyss of Black Doubt, Scepticism, nay Sansculottic Jacobinism; an Orcus that has no bottom. Think of that.[55]

With this Carlyle combined his machine metaphor with his fundamental pessimism about what the fusion of technology, market society, and wealth would imply. In a world in which the steam engine was 'changing his shape like a very Proteus; and infallibly, at every change of shape, oversetting whole multitudes of workmen' the nation became a flawed, demagogue-prone instrument.[56]

Carlyle's alternative was collegiate, paternalist, authoritarian. It was confounded almost immediately by the railway-mania-driven recovery, and his worked-out remedies in the inappropriately apocalyptic *Latter-Day Pamphlets* were scorned. By 1851 his radicalism was waning as fast as his Irish interests, after their brief kindling in 1849, and he turned back to his study and to the authoritarian enlightenment in the shape of Frederick the Great.[57] By contrast, at his thriving Irish college in Santa Agata dei Goti, the 46-year-old Father Cullen, one of the manipulators of the feeble old Pope, had evolved a response to Carlyle's challenge which, in 1849, he would be able to put into practice. Cullen's correspondence is remote from that of Newman or even Bishop William Ullathorne: untheological, untheoretical even, often rather petty and superstitious, but it is that of a man who understood how his own society cohered, as soundly as Abbot Sampson: 'Paul the Prudent' was the hero as churchman.[58]


## IV   THE ULTRAMONTANE OPPORTUNITY

Under Cullen as Archbishop of Armagh after 1849, Irish Catholicism moved towards the sort of theocratic politics from which Carlyle's Scotland had exited in 1843, after

---

[54]  Thomas Carlyle, *Past and Present*, 1844 (London: Dent, n.d.), 132.
[55]  Ibid. 133–4.          [56]  Carlyle, *Chartism*, 33.
[57]  See Morse Peckham, 'Frederick the Great', in K. J. Fielding and Rodger L. Tarr, eds., *Carlyle Past and Present* (London: Vision, 1976).
[58]  Lee, *Modernisation*, pp. 42–51.

the split in the Kirk destroyed its educational and poor-relief role. But there was a crucial difference. After Pio Nono's brief liberal phase ended in 1848 the days of the Pope as a secular ruler were numbered. From would-be Italian unifier he was now a religious despot with dubious claims to benevolence. Prussian Protestantism in Germany, after 1859 anti-Papalism in France, instability in Iberia, and subordination to Habsburg dynasticism in Austria, meant that he had to cast about for new allies, and Ireland—coupled, however awkwardly, with the British Empire—stood to hand.[59] After famine and diaspora, the 1851 'Papal aggression' agitation over the restoration of the English hierarchy, disputes over Italian unification, and the Garibaldi riots of 1864, the Catholic Irish mainstream, once the followers of O'Connell, found in ultramontanism a form of semi-independent identity.[60] Irish bishops were a tenth of the Vatican Council of 1869, but because of their American and imperial connections—by 1910 every seventh Canadian, every fifth Australian was Catholic—Ireland grew in importance within the Catholic world, even winning in 1879 the praise of J. A. Froude: 'Roman Catholicism, which grew sick and stagnant in power and prosperity, has in Ireland been braced in vigour by calamity. Like the myth Monster, it has been in contact with the hard soil of fact, and has gathered fresh life from it'.[61] Today, in 2008, the links, long accepted, between modernization and secularization look weaker than they did in 1908: Pope John Paul II had his divisions, which helped subvert if not defeat those bequeathed by Stalin. Cullen's cognate strategy ensured that Irish Catholicism did not decline, any more than Presbyterianism did in Scotland. Instead it combined the devotional revolution with the principles of the industrial revolution.[62] Cullen's synod came to Thurles in 1850 just after the railway, and in the same year an Irish priest in Canada, Aeneas MacDonnell Dawson, translated Joseph de Maistre's manifesto *Du Pape* (1821) into English as *The Pope: Considered in his Relations with the Church, Temporal Sovereigns, Separated Churches, and the Cause of Civilisation*: the full title is telling.[63] With one of Burke's pupils at his back, Cullen started to remake a shattered country into an exclusivist yet modernizing society comparable to, but more united and centralized than, Chalmers's schism-ridden Presbyterian Scotland. If Cullen wasn't a captain of industry he could actually behave more like Carlyle's ideal of one—as could Moltke or Bismarck—than a Lancashire mill owner subject to market forces. Not only were Church and army similarly authoritarian, but both reacted to Carlyle's 'Abyss of Black Doubt,

[59] The political religious narrative here is based on R. W. Comerford's four chapters (chaps. 20–3) on religion and politics, 1850–70, in Vaughan, ed., *New History of Ireland*, v.

[60] Bowen, *Paul Cullen*, 209–10. For overseas activity see Kenneth Scott Latourette, *Christianity in a Revolutionary Age*, iii: *The Nineteenth Century Outside Europe* (London: Eyre and Spottiswoode, 1961), 58.

[61] J. A. Froude, 'Romanism and the Irish Race in the United States', *North American Review*, 129 (1879), quoted by Owen Dudley Edwards in 'The Irish Priest in North America', in W. J. Sheils and Diana Wood, eds., *The Churches, Ireland and the Irish* (Oxford: Ecclesiastical History Society and Blackwell, 1989).

[62] Lee, *Modernisation*, 42 ff.

[63] *Du Pape* had reached thirteen editions in 1856, twenty-three in 1873.

Scepticism, nay Sansculottic Jacobinism' with their own, market-insulated, conservative mechanisms.

Cullen, though Anglophobe, was liberal in comparison with the Vatican; he won over the most formidable rebel from the English clerisy, Newman, and although the Catholic University in Dublin was a misfire, Newman's own brand of liberalism scorched Anglican muscular Christianity, in the shape of Charles Kingsley, in the 1860s: as painful a setback as Huxley roughing up Samuel Wilberforce in 1860. Cullen also echoed Carlyle on Empire, emigration, and 'the organization of labour'. The spirit of Abbot Sampson seemed present in the Jacobin management of the Christian Brothers and Jesuit colleges, which resembled a regiment, or a ship and its crew, with authority uncontested.[64] Such Foucaultian total institutions dominated the industrial society of the second, transport-orientated, phase of industrialization; in which collegiate forms of control organized workers' lives *outside* small houses, at school, in male workplaces, male pubs, and male sports; and in the Irish, remittance-sending case, organized their finances *outside* the prosperity of the nuclear family. In a civic order which was corporate rather than democratic, the English politico-religious establishment—itself the residue of older electoral hegemonies—would be weakened by secular reform *and* confronted by the new Catholic hierarchies which reinforced parish organizations with the Ancient Order of Hibernians or the St Vincent de Paul Society, Glasgow Celtic Football Club, or the Gaelic Athletic Association.[65]

The devotional revolution, with its stress on ceremonial, parochial organization and missionary self-sacrifice, furthered the capitalist virtues of centralization, promotion by merit, mission statements, education, building investment (overwhelmingly in 'English gothic' churches), and attention to the consumer qua parishioner. The dogma of the Immaculate Conception, promulgated in 1854, followed by the vision at Lourdes in 1858, enabled animistic or localized cults venerating pre-Christian deities (the norm on the Continent) to be standardized into the universal blue-shawled Madonna: mass-produced in statuette, print, and medal form, this was a useful copy of—and counterweight to—the projection of Victoria by the British state through coins and stamps. Coupled with this was the fire and strength of missionary effort, *particularly* in the Empire, where the new hierarchies were (unlike in Britain itself) of Irish origin.[66] Catholicism could outbid the Protestants on heroism and sacrifice, though sometimes making common cause. Joseph Lee writes that Cullen 'constantly objected to conventional official calumnies concerning the nature of poverty, censuring the managers of the Poor Law who "treat poverty as a crime to be dealt with more severely than murder"'.[67] The salience of the welfare mission may help explain something common to Britain and Ireland: the absence of radical anticlericalism. The Church aligned itself with two other post-Carlyleians: Mill, who stressed distribution as the keynote for the next phase of political economy, and T. H. Green, whose 'Liberal Legislation and Freedom of Contract' lecture of 1881 gave a philosophic rationale not only for the Irish Land Act but for the later Anglo-Catholic Lux Mundi

---

[64] Lee, *Modernisation*, 47.      [65] Ibid. 45.
[66] Gilley, 'Edward Irving', 241.      [67] Lee, *Modernisation*, 45.

movement.[68] The Gladstonian 'Union of Hearts' gained the sort of resilience that overcame the vicious but overdriven Unionist assault on Home Rule.[69]

In fact, the Home Rule division within Protestantism allowed a British Catholic 'heroism' to emerge, evident in Cardinal Manning's mediation in the London dock strike in 1889, Robert Louis Stevenson's *Father Damien* tract in 1890, and the obsequies for Newman and Manning in 1890 and 1892. That the monumental *Cambridge Modern History* was trusted to a Catholic Home Ruler in 1895, though Lord Acton was neither Irish nor orthodox, was as significant as Edward Elgar's inauguration of the English musical renaissance in 1899 with his setting of Newman's poem of 1865 *The Dream of Gerontius*—or for that matter Conan Doyle's personification in Sherlock Holmes (1891) of the detective as imperial patriot. Protestant prejudice became passé in England, ironically, just when clericalism provoked the 'revolt of the intellectuals' in France, during the Dreyfus affair. By 1906 anti-Dreyfusard Catholics like Belloc and Chesterton were taken as paracletes for 'the people of England, who have not spoken yet'. In 1914 a crusade could be mounted against Prussian (and unquestionably Protestant) *Kultur* on behalf of Catholic Belgium, and even in the sensitive region of Scotland Tom Devine writes that 'any doubts about the loyalty of the Irish in Scotland to the British State were conclusively removed'.[70]

## V   WHERE WERE THE HERO-SISTERS?

But if this reconciliation left Protestant Ulster to one side, with an identity created by fear of 'the other', the society of Catholic Ireland still had a quality remote from that of other UK provinces: the absence from its debates of the secular womenfolk of the majority religion. Lay Catholic Irishwomen were either subordinate or symbolic in such a way that they presented few parallels with an increasingly feminized mainland politics. Here, too, the Carlyleian shadow lay long. On the mainland women had been indirect beneficiaries of the 'heroic' in the theoretical or practical instances of George Eliot or Florence Nightingale. An early history of the suffrage movement like Ray Strachey's *The Cause* (1928) is typical in its personalization of political action. But Irish Catholic women were not just non-political but, until the 1960s, almost unknown to history.

---

[68] John Stuart Mill, *Principles of Political Economy* (London: Longmans, 1992), chap.7; Melvin Richter, *The Politics of Conscience: T. H. Green and his Age* (London: Weidenfeld and Nicolson, 1964), chap. 4.

[69] Harvie, *The Lights of Liberalism*, 235 ff.

[70] Tom Devine, *The Scottish Nation* (London: Allen Lane, 1999), 496. I have my doubts about this, not just in view of post-war sectarianism. The war memorials of the Scottish railway companies show proportionately fewer Irish names than the Irish share of the population would suggest, so there may have been continuing discrimination against the community in the working-class elite and, as Ian Wood argues, in the military. See his 'Protestantism and Scottish Military Tradition', in Graham Walker and Tom Gallagher, eds., *Sermons and Battle Hymns: Protestant Popular Culture in Modern Scotland* (Edinburgh: Edinburgh University Press, 1990).

Carlyle's advancement of symbol over system, much criticized by contemporaries, was particularly pronounced when he handled gender.[71] While the masterpiece of his own hero, Goethe's *Faust*, ends with the ringing line 'Das ew'ge weiblich zieht uns hinan' ('The eternal female leads us on')—and woman in *Faust* is flesh and blood, Eros as well as Agape—the Carlyleian woman is as abstract as her Catholic sister. The only female to appear in the whole of *Past and Present* is Irish *and* crucial: the widow who, denied alms in Edinburgh, succumbed to exhaustion and typhus, infecting and so killing another seventeen people: 'Nothing is left but that she prove her sisterhood by dying, and infecting you with typhus. Seventeen of you lying dead will not deny such proof that she *was* flesh of your flesh; and perhaps some of the living may lay it to heart'.[72] The Irish widow negates materialism, just as the Irish peasant of *The French Revolution* negates Burke. Yeats may have followed Burke in transmuting Marie Antoinette into the 'anti-modern symbol' of Cathleen ni Houlihan, but Carlyle's juxtaposition is both more brutal and more ambiguous.

Protesting against their designation as drudges, pampered but constrained passengers, or remittance collectors, Englishwomen took up social work or literary protest.[73] In *fin de siècle* Continental nationalism, feminism identified with social democracy. This was intensified in the British seaboard cities, where women took leading roles in voluntary and educational organizations. The educationalist Blanche Clough and the welfare campaigner Eleanor Rathbone were both from Liverpool, the Potter sisters were Lancashire, the Pankhursts' Women's Social and Political Union was born in Manchester. But in Ireland until the Gaelic revival Catholic women were either silenced, made into reifying images of the Madonna or Cathleen ni Houlihan, or completely overshadowed by rebellious Protestant sisters.[74]

What had disappeared was sex. Carlyle's last, unpublishable, *Latter-Day Pamphlet* was 'The Phallus and the Money-Bag', an attack on the moral decadence of utilitarianism and the sensuality of such as George Sand, whose title has a visual symbolism which would have intrigued Freud.[75] Carlyle had already painted a far different Marie Antoinette from Burke's—'within the royal tapestries, in bright boudoirs, baths, peignoirs, and the Grand and Little Toilette': exquisite, erotic, parasitic.[76] Her ineptness compromises the throne in the 'Diamond Necklace' affair; her image might, intriguingly, be that of Boucher's toothsome Miss O'Murphy.[77] Sublimating the latter—and Limerick's Lola Montez (the only woman who caused a revolution in 1848, in Munich, albeit a Protestant causing a conservative clericalist one)—ensured that the salience of Carlyleian-Catholic women would be slight. They appear seldom even

---

[71] For example, by W. R. Greg in *Literary and Social Judgements* (London: Trübner, 1877), i, 143–83.

[72] Carlyle, *Past and Present*, 144. This incident was taken from Dr W. P. Alison's *Observations of the Management of the Poor in Scotland* (Edinburgh: Blackwood, 1840).

[73] See Bonnie S. Anderson and Judith P. Zinsser, *A History of their Own*, 1988 (Harmondsworth: Penguin, 1990), ii, 167–96.

[74] As far as I can see, there isn't a single reference to an Irishwoman, of any religion or none, in the index of Anderson and Zinsser.

[75] See Fred Kaplan, *Thomas Carlyle* (Cambridge: Cambridge University Press, 1983), 322–3.

[76] Carlyle, *French Revolution*, i, 27.          [77] Ibid. 46.

in recent histories of Ireland, the Irish abroad, and the Catholic Church itself. In imaginative writing they are passive in Boucicault or Trollope; even Shaw failed to come up with a female lead in *John Bull's Other Island*, flawing perhaps his most serious play. Joyce's females in *Dubliners* are uniformly frustrated; Molly Bloom was as unhelpful a role model as Somerville and Ross's psychopathic Charlotte Mullen; while O'Casey's heroines, who *are* the power-and-feelings people of his plays, all end tragic.

The Cullenite clergy had decided that Catholic female destiny was vocation, home-making, and, a poor third, career: something reinforced by an institutional religion which (substituting gender for ethnie) oddly paralleled Irish subordination to Britain. Despite population decline, the number of nuns rose from 120 in 1800 to 1,500 in 1851 and 8,000 in 1901.[78] Katherine Tynan found in the early 1870s in Drogheda an archaic but cultivated existence; 'convents are really small, self-contained totalitarian states where life is lived according to a rigid schedule,' the writer Mary Colum remembered of the late 1890s.[79] Similar in some ways to the effective running of dissent by women on the mainland (a numerical comparison between the spinster daughters and sisters of the Scots clergy and the Irish nuns would be interesting), such *Past and Present*-like examples advertised celibacy to the wives, widows, and daughters who sustained their (ageing) husbands, sons and brothers: a difficult burden to shift.[80]

The feminist reaction, in the shape of Lady Gregory, Edith Somerville and Martin Ross, Alice Stopford Green, and on the far fringe Maude Gonne and the Gore-Booth girls, was firmly post-Protestant. Authoritarian male dominance produced several important female rebellions. One of the greatest Mazzinian novels, with a European reputation, particularly in the communist East, in which nationalism is seen as the road out of Catholic tyranny, was *The Gadfly* (1892) by Ethel Voynich, the daughter of the Cork mathematician George Boole. A similar stance was taken in the Trollopian novels of Mary Laffan Hartley, a convert to Protestantism.

In part this isolation was because Catholicism grafted class constraints on to its own authoritarianism. Irish nuns found themselves subject to the English class system and ended as lay sisters rather than choir nuns.[81] It was the 1960s, Edna O'Brien's era, before the others escaped, and thereafter tales emerged—of the Magdalene laundries, or the orphanages run by the Church—whose horrors almost outbid *Maria Monk*.[82] As Carlyle would say, think of that.

---

[78] By the 1950s the number stood at 19,000. See Caitriona Clear, *Nuns in Nineteenth Century Ireland* (Dublin: Gill, 1987) and Mary Peckham Magray, *The Transforming Power of the Nuns: Women, Religion and Cultural Change in Ireland, 1750–1900* (Oxford: Oxford University Press, 1998).

[79] *Life and the Dream*, 1947, quoted in Mary Luddy, ed., *Women in Ireland, 1800–1818: A Documentary History* (Cork: Cork University Press, 1995), 116.

[80] J. J. Lee, 'Women and the Church since the Famine', in Mary MacCurtain and Donncha ó Corrain, eds., *Women in Irish Society*, 1978 (Dublin: Arlen House and Women's Press, 1984).

[81] Susan O'Brien, 'Lay Sisters and Good Mothers: Working-Class Women in English Convents, 1840–1910', in Sheils and Wood, eds., *Churches*, 460.

[82] £700 million was offered in compensation to orphanage victims in 2003 (*Birmingham Post*, 15 Oct. 2003); and see Gemma Hussey, *Ireland Today: Anatomy of a Changing State*, 1993 (Harmondsworth: Penguin, 1995), chap. 18.

## VI   HIDDEN IRELAND OR PLAIN PEOPLE?

Following Immaculate Conception, a deeply conservative Vatican Council, convened in 1869, pronounced Papal Infallibility in 1870. Cullen died in 1878 and a year later the Council ended. Its last year saw—as well as the rise of the Land League and Parnell—Ireland's own vision at Knock. In this way the dogmas of the post-Thurles Church filled a political vacuum while, with population and agricultural prices declining, land as an issue per se was relatively speaking in retreat. The post-1879 agitation revived anti-landlordism of a very Carlyleian sort (Carlyle's venom was totally lacking, for instance, in an ex-Fenian like Charles Kickham); it also gave the priests a role bridging community and politics, while they in turn created quasi-religious fetishes for the nation.

Irish agriculture 'modernized' better than post-high-farming Britain, though less effectively than that of Denmark (which had also gone through a clerical-modernizing process under Bishop Nicholas Grundtvig, 1783–1872).[83] Yeats's 'dream of the noble and the beggar-man'—and the nationalism of ascendancy types from Yeats and Douglas Hyde to Maude Gonne and Constance Markiewicz—was an Irish variation on the power of the 'traditional intelligentsia' which in its British form puzzled Gramsci.[84] But it did little for manufacturing, depressed after the 1870s, and the Gaelic culture of Daniel Corkery's 'hidden Ireland'—religion, nationalism, and the land—proved illusory if emotionally satisfying: dependent on strong farmers, auctioneers, and the clergy as much as on British demand for agricultural products. In *John Bull's Other Island* the bullying Father Dempsey backs the Englishman Broadbent; operating his religious machine, he would have been quite at home in the France of Balzac or Stendhal.[85]

With 25 per cent of the national intelligentsia in orders by 1925 (compared with less than 10 per cent elsewhere in the archipelago) and 39 per cent by 1939, the Church laid its shadow across the country: a retrospect like Brian Friel's *Dancing at Lughnasa* (1988), set in that year, shows it as semi-imperial and stiflingly conservative. Contrast George Boyce on the Cullenite Church, 'the fixed point of nationalist identity in a changing world, and indeed the guardian of a complete, satisfying and noble faith', and Joe Lee on its later career: 'Rarely has the Catholic Church as an institution flourished more, by material criteria, as in the Free State. And rarely has it contributed so little, as an institution, to the finer qualities of the Christian spirit.'[86]

---

83  O'Grada, *Ireland*, 255.

84  Antonio Gramsci, 'The Intellectuals', in *Prison Notebooks*, trans. Quintin Hoare and Geoffrey Nowell-Smith (London: Lawrence and Wishart, 1971).

85  Daniel Corkery, *The Hidden Ireland: A Study of Gaelic Munster in the Eighteenth Century* (Dublin: Gill, 1925); and see Vivian Mercier, 'Literature in English', in J. R. Hill, ed., *A New History of Ireland*, vii: *Ireland 1921–84* (Oxford: Oxford University Press, 2003); O'Grada, *Ireland*, 255; Shaw, *John Bull's Other Island*, Act III.

86  Liam O'Dowd, 'Intellectuals and Irish Nationalism', in Graham Day and Gareth Rees, eds., *Regions, Nations and European Integration: Remaking the Celtic Periphery* (Cardiff: University of

Shaw and most 'modernizers' argued that Ireland could only escape this sort of stasis if it included Ulster, where a Scottish-enlightenment-inspired 'Drennanite' liberalism, like that of the 1790s, could be revived, just as Arthur Griffith saw a Belfast-built Irish merchant marine as a unifier along with his dual monarchy. Shaw assured the Protestants that they would soon run the whole show and, given Lord Pirrie's support for Home Rule and the 'reformed' unionist episode of 1906–10, this wasn't utterly forlorn.[87] But it was damaged by the extremism of the Tory Party in 1910–14 and destroyed by its co-option into the wartime coalition. Subsequently, partition meant that the twenty-six counties stayed a conservative component of the UK economy, with an agrarian economy and clerical control. A depressed Ulster economy no longer attracted, while Free State industrialization was unable to take off.[88] Only in 1958—two years after Suez, one year after the Treaty of Rome, and in the same year as a new and radical Pope, John XXIII—did Sean Lemass's commissioning of the Whittaker Report start to break the spell.[89]

If 'the Condition of Ireland' between 1860 and 1960 was framed by two concentric 'worlds'—the Irish Sea, encircled by the Atlantic—the Catholic blend of ultramontanism and nationalism fitted snugly into them. The Church was a focus for a people who got more complex and multifarious as they expanded perforce into new environments; nationalism was confronted by the symbol of the 'machine'. This was both Ireland's 'eternal nay' *and* an effective metaphor for the ganglions of the diaspora. In the larger world their own technical machine failed: the catastrophe of the 1840s meant that Irish industry never went from experiment to process, except in the Hong Kong-like Lagan Valley. But through the Church and its organizing of Irish human resources, there continued what Marx called the 'subjective' ordering of industry. 'Bitter wisdom' derived from the country's experience, vectored through the Church, would crucially contribute to the conscription crisis and the separation struggle of 1918–21. Ireland also helped others to succeed. The Irish political machine triumphed in America and contributed notably to the British Labour Party. The great success of the 1924 Labour government was John Wheatley as Minister of Health and his creation of state housing policy, while the reprints of *The Ragged Trousered Philanthropists* by 'Robert Tressell', which 'won the 1945 election for Labour', would provide an icon for activists often from an Irish background whose loyalty to Moscow paralleled the way the religious machine had buttressed the ultramontane papacy.[90] It

---

Wales Press, 1991), 127; George Boyce, 'Culture and Counter-Revolution', *Nationalism in Ireland* (London: Croom Helm, 1982), 118, and J. J. Lee, *Ireland, 1912–1985* (Cambridge: Cambridge University Press, 1989), p. 159; and see Terence Brown, *Ireland: A Social and Cultural History, 1922–79* (London: Fontana, 1981), chaps. 1 and 2.

[87] Patrick Colum, *Arthur Griffith* (Dublin: Browne and Nolan, 1959), 87 ff.; Shaw, *John Bull's Other Island*, 'Preface of 1929'.

[88] Lee, *Modernisation*, chap. 8.          [89] Brown, *Ireland*, 213–14.

[90] See Ian S. Wood, *John Wheatley* (Manchester: Manchester University Press, 1990); Sheridan Gilley, 'Catholics and Socialists in Scotland, 1900–1930', in Sheridan Gilley and Roger Swift, eds., *The Irish in Britain* (London: Pinter, 1989); and Alan Sillitoe's introduction to the Panther edition of Tressell's book (London: Panther, 1965), 7.

was a Carlyleian outcome: the 'mechanical age' transfixed the Irish, while the Catholic nation became an insistent but ever-changing *fata morgana*. Offering a means not just of catching up but of unifying these experiences, it hovered until the 1960s in one shape or another—enticingly, but always out of reach—before the Irish people.

# III
# IN TIME OF THE BREAKING
# OF NATIONS

# 7

# Muscular Celticism: Sport and Nationalism

From the moment when the drums beat *Johnnie Cope* at sunrise until it became too dark to see in the evening, the steady thump-thump of a boot on a ball could be heard somewhere in the barracks. It was tolerated because there was no alternative; even the parade-ground was not sacred from the small shuffling figures of the Glasgow men, their bonnets pulled down over their eyes, kicking, trapping, swerving and passing, and occasionally intoning, like ugly little high priests, their ritual cries of 'Way-ull' and 'Aw-haw-hey'. The simile is apt, for it was almost a religious exercise . . .

George MacDonald Fraser, 'Play up, play up, and get tore in!', 1970 [1]

Sing on: somewhere at some new moon,
We'll learn that sleeping is not death,
Hearing the whole earth change its tune,
Its flesh being wild, and it again
Crying aloud as the racecourse is,
And we find hearteners among men
That ride upon horses.

W. B. Yeats, 'At Galway Races', 1909[2]

## I  SPORT AND STATEHOOD

In 1888 the small borders town of Peebles opened the baronial-revival Chambers Institute, endowed by the great Provost of Edinburgh and publisher William Chambers and his brother Robert, pioneer of evolutionary thought in his *Vestiges of Creation* (1844). Its central feature was a half-scale reproduction in plaster of the Parthenon frieze: its charioteers, athletes, and wrestlers. Sport was integral to both doric worlds, observed John Buchan, who as a teenager had wolfed down the Institute's books: 'A sport [is] a contest with wild Nature in some one of her forms, a contest in which there is commonly some risk; a game, a contest under agreed rules with other human beings.' Writing in the 1920s, he noted that both had become very big business, nowhere more so than along the littoral: 'we may go to bed at Euston and wake on a western sea-loch; we may sit at the play one evening and be on a Scots moor after breakfast.'[3]

[1] In *The General Danced at Dawn* (Glasgow: Collins, 1970), 36.
[2] In *The Green Helmet and Other Poems* (London: Macmillan, 1912).
[3] John Buchan, ed., *Great Hours in Sport* (Edinburgh: Nelson, c.1925), pp. v, 277–88.

In *John Bull's Other Island* Bernard Shaw's entrepreneurs—Tom Broadbent and Larry Doyle—are in the leisure business. Their light railway and hotel might go bust—historically these things nearly always did—but Rosscullen's golf course will still be thriving. Another awkward Irishman, Sean O'Casey in *The Silver Tassie* (1928), doubly exiled his Dublin war-wounded from the new Free State, as casualties of 'England's war' and as association footballers. The shadows still lie long on 'These Islands', absurdly over-represented in sport because of international lethargy in shrinking the grandiose British representation which came from the early establishment of the national leagues: an ironic concession towards a 'Europe of the regions'.

In Germany and in France spectator-sport organization came late—most German football teams date from the 1900s—when a complex sport landscape had already developed in the urban UK. Fastidious market liberals as well as Marxists may regard sport-fixation's demotion as long deferred, inhibiting *real* priorities—economic development, technical training, literary culture, and sexual equality, a condemnation inherited in Scotland from Victorian divines who, according to Christopher Smout, 'were especially jealous of football, for it above all aroused exactly the heart-warming zeal and total devotion which they themselves had tried, so painfully and so totally unsuccessfully to arouse for God'.[4] As hostile was the influential 'bourgeois' social critique of the Swedish-American Thorstein Veblen:

The culture bestowed in football gives a product of exotic ferocity and cunning. It is a rehabilitation of the early barbarian temperament, together with a suppression of those details of temperament which, as seen from the standpoint of the social and economic exigencies, are the redeeming features of the savage character.[5]

A more plaintive 'if only' refrain remained. In 1910 the American psychologist William James, ally of such as gentle environmentalist souls as John Muir and Thomas Davidson, concerned at swelling international bellicosity, saw sport as potential contributor to a 'moral equivalent of war'. In the 1920s the Scots diplomat Robert Bruce-Lockhart remembered introducing football to a British-owned factory in St Petersburg, and its beneficial contribution to morale, and speculated whether 'fitba-daftness' might not have acted as an antidote to Bolshevism.[6]

In most histories of the labour movement written before the 1980s, sport rarely appears.[7] Yet within the national traditions the interminable discourse about it, football in particular, does not seem a case of substance-abuse, misplaced patriotism, or rampant false consciousness, football being *diplomatically* as important to Scotland as the Olympics were in 1992 to Barcelona and Catalunya, 'a country *in* Spain'.

---

[4] T. C. Smout, *A Century of the Scottish People* (Glasgow: Collins, 1986), 202.

[5] Thorstein Veblen, *The Theory of the Leisure Class*, 1899 (London: Allen and Unwin, 1925), 262.

[6] William James, 'The Moral Equivalent of War', 1910, in Leon Bramson and George W. Goethals, eds., *War: Studies from Psychology, Sociology, Anthropology* (New York and London: Basic Books, 1968).

[7] For instance, Ian Donnachie, Christopher Harvie, and Ian S. Wood, eds., *Forward! Labour Politics in Scotland 1888–1988* (Edinburgh: Polygon, 1989), and Stuart Macintyre's study of militant socialist Scots communities, *Little Moscows: Communism and Working-Class Militancy in Inter-War Britain* (London: Croom Helm, 1980), although sport resurfaces prominently in the text of the latter.

If the 1850s saw industrialization—the Glasgow of Lord Kelvin, John Elder, MacQuorn Rankine, and Co.—develop a culture, it also became acceptable to its workers. Along with co-ops and building societies, the first music halls, and crucially the Saturday half-holiday, sport began to encroach on a non-work time hitherto largely given over to drink.[8] The 'sport-and-nation' relation dates from 1860–80, both enhancing and frustrating political mobilization, but it had a distinct inflection when it hit the western seaboard. The public-school cult of games, with the equality it conferred on strength and character, rather than class, status, or brains, had some parallel to the 'national' ideal. It made its breakthrough when the Macmillan brothers (once radical crofters in the *Toper-na-Fuosich* mould) published *Tom Brown's Schooldays* by Clough's schoolmate Thomas Hughes (1857)—just after the navvies saved the Crimean soldiers from clueless aristos, and just before the Volunteer movement. Soccer was codified in 1863 by the new Football Association, its activists drawn from the public schools, but by the 1880s they were being pushed out by professional teams from industrial towns, and amateurs were turning to rugby. Both tendencies may have had American roots. Baseball grew rapidly during the Civil War. Played by bored troops behind the front lines, it began to go professional as early as 1871. American football (to which Veblen referred) was related to British soccer and rugby, and also stressed links to secondary and higher education, which may explain why it took until the 1890s to go professional.

Athletics was by then proudly patriotic. In Ireland the rise of the Gaelic Athletic Association (GAA) would after 1884 provide a role for such of nationalist youth (most of it) which was leery about the evening classes of the Gaelic League and could be persuaded to reject the seductions of such 'garrison games' as soccer and rugger. In 1919–21 the exploits of GAA men such as Michael Collins, whose physique kept him ahead of the Black and Tans, seemed to justify its discipline, and the revival of the Tailteann Games in 1924 became a founding ceremony of the Free State.[9] The Games didn't last long, but even a critical nationalist such as Joe Lee has written that the success of the GAA, being 'based on the co-option of intense local loyalties into a wider sense of national identity, reflected a capacity for organisation and a sense of communal coherence more developed than that in much of Mediterranean and eastern Europe.'[10]

In Wales rugby union *was* a conscious 'garrison game', promoted by Anglican clergy to keep miners out of the chapels as well as the pubs. The Nonconformist-nationalist establishment held it at a distance. For David Lloyd George in 1896 'The English were a nation of footballers, stock exchangers, public house and music-hall frequenters.'[11] This line scarcely lasted ten years. Wales's victory over New Zealand's otherwise triumphant All Blacks at Cardiff Arms Park on 16 December 1905 united

---

[8] See Iain Levitt and Christopher Smout, *The State of the Scottish Working-Class in 1843* (Edinburgh: Scottish Academic Press, 1979).

[9] W. F. Mandle, *The Gaelic Athletic Association and Irish Nationalist Politics, 1884–1924* (London: Christopher Helm, 1987), 218 ff.

[10] J. J. Lee, *Ireland, 1900–1985* (Cambridge: Cambridge University Press, 1989), 80.

[11] Anthony Mason, *Association Football and English Society* (Brighton: Harvester Press, 1980), p. ix; Gareth Williams, *1905 and All That* (Llandysul: Gomer Press, 1991), 16.

nationalists with the 'new' Welsh of the valleys—and kicked the last and greatest religious revival into touch. To Tom Jones, editing *Welsh Outlook* in 1914,

Rugby is . . . the game of the Welshman. The international records of the past twenty years show that the Principality can hold an equal if not superior hand in the game . . . The Association code in Wales is new and alien and comes in on the back of its popularity elsewhere: it is the game of the alien of the valleys whose immigration and de-nationalising tendency is one of the major problems of our country [and] the social context of the game [is] cosmopolitan . . .

Wales possesses in Rugby football . . . a game democratic and amateur—a unique thing to be cherished and . . . the concern of thinking men who value the complex influences making for higher levels of citizenship.[12]

In Scotland sport became part of national identity—but of a fractured one. Football obsessed most males, but did not disturb divisions of skill and of religion as well as the complex border between the middle and working classes, in a society of achieved rather than ascriptive status.[13] Political Liberals like Lord Kinnaird, W. H. Gladstone MP, and Quintin Hogg, who played for Scotland in the 1870s, gave the upper-class Association game a Liberal-reformist ethos, which it never altogether lost.[14] Cricket and rugby union, the achievement of the Anglicized middle class, gained working-class support, respectively among coalminers in the 1860s and textile workers in the Border burghs, Peebles included, in the 1870s.[15]

The national revivalists of the Scottish renaissance were as unhappy about sport's surrogate politics as the socialists of the ILP had been. Hugh MacDiarmid, both nationalist and ILPer, was, for a Langholm man, a dead loss to rugby, and contemplated Ibrox transformed into a vast lecture hall. His companion as a founder of the National Party of Scotland in 1928 Compton Mackenzie, who had also attended the Tailteann Games, made the autobiographical John Ogilvie in *The North Wind of Love* (1944) deeply critical: 'A nation which thinks that the news of the world in the six o'clock bulletin is a tiresome postponement of the football results is marching in blinkers along the road to ruin.'[16] He proposed the abolition of all professional sport, indeed of 'all idle games after childhood . . . [substituting] walking, forestry, shooting and sailing, according to the locality and the season'.[17]


## II  HOMO LUDENS

In 1938, in *Homo ludens*, the Dutch historian and philosopher Johan Huizinga disputed Veblen's thesis: sport, he argued, facilitated the equilibrium of the physical and the mental, the social and the individual. With their conventions and rules, games

---

[12] Dai Smith, *Wales! Wales?* (London: Allen and Unwin, 1984), 35.

[13] James Littlejohn, *Westrigg: The Sociology of a Chevioy Parish* (London: Routledge, 1963), 194.

[14] Jim Hossack, *Head Over Heels: A Celebration of British Football* (Edinburgh: Mainstream, 1989), 53–5.

[15] W. Hamish Fraser and Robert Morris, eds., *People and Society in Scotland*, ii: *1830–1914* (Edinburgh: John Donald, 1990), 252; Williams, *1905 and All That*, 22–3.

[16] Compton Mackenzie, *The North Wind of Love* (London: Rich and Cowan, 1945), 30.

[17] Ibid. 28.

could be a structure for socializing mass society; they could also be a means of promoting the coordination and communication of elites which controlled or sought to control it. The commercial rationalism of the nineteenth century, which Marx and Veblen exemplified, was a distortion, not the main line of development.[18]

Elements of Veblen's 'barbarian' model still applied in Scotland: the 'normal and characteristic occupations' of its elite were 'government, war, sports and devout observances'.[19] This would describe the Scottish itineraries of the British 'upper 10,000', after the Duke of Atholl had published *The Art of Deerstalking* in 1838 and Queen Victoria settled at Balmoral a decade later: the shooting of grouse and deer and the catching of salmon overtook sheep farming and fishing as highland employers. Sporting estates in 1900 took up about 60 per cent of the land area of Scotland (unsurprising, since only 25 per cent of the land was cultivable, and far less in the six 'crofting counties' of Argyll, Inverness, Ross and Cromarty, Sutherland, Orkney, and Zetland). David Thomson recollected his uncle Lord Finlay staffing his Nairnshire mansion with forty retainers in the less-than affluent 1920s, not counting the folk in the farms and lodges.[20] His class had tried to stabilize highland society after the post-1815 crisis and the Scott-inspired reinvention of the clans, producing not-totally-phoney highland gatherings, derived from clan contests and 'Wappenshaws'—at Braemar in 1817, St Fillans in 1819, and Lonach in 1823, and going into overdrive with royal patronage, tourism, and tartans after 1848. From one of the means of getting to the north, the private yacht, came the 'Cowal fortnight', which became the northern Cowes.

Yachting had a practical role for west-coast capitalists and engineers. It surged forward between 1851, when in a competition associated with the Great Exhibition the Americans unexpectedly won a race with the British, and 1870, when regular 'America's Cup' challenges started. The competitive element was also seen in the Australian grain and China tea races by three-masted clippers, British and American, reaching a climax in the duel between the *Ariel* and the *Taiping* in 1866, and the 'Blue Ribands' first awarded about the same time to the fastest Atlantic steamer. But the great clipper-bowed steam yachts with their white hulls and buff funnels were Schillerian *Spieltrieb* combined with luxury: the maritime equivalent of the private trains of America's 'Gilded Age' magnates, combining office and hotel, pleasure and communication. The Assheton-Smiths, who moved from Lancashire cotton to the Dinorwic slate quarries, were pioneer builders in the 1830s. Forty years later Lipton's *Erin* allowed him to flit between the Irish suppliers of his chain-stores and his city warehouses, while his successive *Shamrocks* kept on gallantly failing to win the America's Cup. Experiments in testing hull design and new steam engines, from Lord Kelvin to Sir Charles Parsons, were also encouraged; although ostentatious affluence probably won out. 'If you ask how much it costs to run a yacht, you shouldn't own one,' as an American millionaire put it. Alike for steam and sail, crew (around thirty for a

---

[18] Johan Huizinga, *Homo ludens* (Basel: Pantheon, 1938), 312–13. One indirect result of the Scottish revival of the 1990s has been Pat Kane's *The Play-Ethic* (London: Macmillan, 2004), which gives such arguments vivid contemporary relevance.

[19] Hossack, *Head Over Heels*, 53–5.

[20] David Thomson, *Nairn in Darkness and Light* (London: Hutchinson, 1987).

J-class or a steamer), moorings, repairs, and fuel came to about £ 35,000 a year in the money of the time, at least a million in our terms, though modestly paid government ministers could cut a subsidized dash in the Scottish Office's fishery cruisers or with the First Lord Winston Churchill and entourage on the Admiralty's *Enchantress*.[21] The modest 'messing about in boats' business, which Meredith's Nevil Beauchamp enjoyed in the 1870s, had in fact contributed to Churchill's somewhat alarming rise. The cruise of Erskine Childers's ten-ton sloop *Asgard* along the Frisian coast in 1902 gave rise to *The Riddle of the Sands* (1903) with its invasion-scare plot, and fanned the accelerating naval race. A decade later the same boat would land rifles at Howth for the Irish Volunteers, bringing, through inept army reaction, the first blood splashing on Dublin's streets.[22]

Another variant of *Spieltrieb* combined business, exercise, and pleasure after the 1860s: the milder ritual of golf. This became institutional in lives of elite and middle class alike, owing to the cheap gutta-percha golf ball of 1848, the settling of the rule-making Royal and Ancient Club in its clubhouse at St Andrews in 1853, and the first Open Championship in 1860. When H. H. Asquith visited in 1876, 'golf was then so little developed that he and his modest-living student companions were able to hire the services of the British open champion to carry their clubs'. In 1907, when he rented, as Prime Minister, an East Lothian house with its own nine-hole course, facilities ranged from over 300 local courses to the big railway-owned projects of Turnberry in Ayrshire and Cruden Bay in Buchan, to be followed by the gigantic Gleneagles.[23] Probably this reflected a rise in 'lower-upper-middle-class' incomes and, because of agricultural depression, a drop in the cost of land for golf courses, over 1,000 Britain-wide in 1910, played on by some 2,000 clubs, most densely on the Celtic fringe. Between 1902 and 1914 Britain was literally governed in summer from North Ber-wick.[24] Before Asquith took Archerfield, the donnish aristocrat Arthur Balfour, at nearby Whittinghame, was the first premier to use the socialization involved in golf and tennis as an instrument of political discussion, ritualizing an informality and approachability, in his case thoroughly deceptive.[25] 'Fear may ride behind the horse-man, he does not walk with the caddy' was one of Balfour's *mots*. Golf was unknown before 1870 in Wales or Ireland, but reached them via London and Liverpool, to which it had been carried by Scottish migrants in the 1860s. Lloyd George became equally enthusiastic, playing on the recent links at Criccieth and Harlech, as well at Walton-on-Thames, near his London villa.[26] By 1938 37 per cent of a sample

---

[21] Peter Heaton, *A History of Yachting in Pictures* (London: Tom Stacey, 1972), chap. 2.

[22] Andrew Boyle, *The Riddle of Erskine Childers* (London: Hutchinson, 1977). 'Messing about in boats' came from the small, furry, but certainly paranoid world of Kenneth Grahame's *The Wind in the Willows* of 1908.

[23] Roy Jenkins, *Asquith*, 1964 (London: Fontana, 1967), 26; Gleneagles was projected in 1910 but not opened until 1925. The crucial export of the game to America occurred in the 1870s.

[24] *Scottish Biographies* (Glasgow: Maclehose, 1938); 'lower-upper-middle-class' was a George Orwell coinage denoting the 'scholarship boy made good' level.

[25] Blanche Dugdale, *Arthur James Balfour* (London: Hutchinson, 1939), i, 146–7.

[26] Figures from Dr Jane George, who is currently researching the Scottish golf club as a social institution. And see Walter Stephen, *The Man who Took Golf to the World: The Life and Legacy of Willie Park, Junior* (Edinburgh: Luath, 2005).

of entries in *Scottish Biographies* golfed, against 17.5 per cent who fished, with the golf club replacing the urban 'howff' (bar) as the main place for middle-class male socialization. At arm's length, in independent clubs, it did wonders for the women's movement. The fellowship of the links could not, however, hold the opponents of the British elite at bay. Another recreational innovation, the bicycle, became, in the hands of the Clarion Cycling Clubs, an instrument of radical propaganda. Bicycle-borne Suffragettes caused unpleasant things to happen between tee and green.

For a more sympathetic Scottish nationalist, Eric Linklater (born and brought up a sea captain's son in the coal port of Barry and surely conscious of the Welsh *annus mirabilis* of 1905, when he would be six) the rugby–football distinction emphasized a line of division between working and middle class inimical to the creation of a national community. In his satire on nationalism *Magnus Merriman* (1933) he wrote flatteringly of a rugby international crowd in Edinburgh that 'To see them walking in clear spring weather is almost as exhilarating as the game itself, for their shoulders are straight, they are tall and lithe, they are square and strong, their eyes are bright, and their skin is toughened and tanned by the weather'.

By contrast, the supporters of the Edinburgh soccer teams Heart of Midlothian (Protestant) and Hibernian (Catholic) seemed another nation, predestined to frustrate the romanticism of Linklater's *homo ludens* Merriman:

To look at them it seemed obvious that work was a perversion, for it had not given them the upright bearing and the swinging stride that play had bestowed on the others, but rather it had kept their faces pale, and though it had toughened them it had not given them grace.[27]

Or, put in other ways by other people, work hadn't paid them much. Scottish sport simultaneously offered and withdrew the possibility of the full and balanced life, the *mens sana in corpore sano*. To adapt Marx, sport made the Scots 'of a nation' but not 'for a nation': conscious that they were 'agin' others, but also that they were internally divided by class and religion. The paradox was that Scotland, while failing to match the highly politicized pattern shown in Ireland, developed a tradition of interpreting sport's relations with society which was uniquely strong.

## III   GAMES AND THE SOCIOLOGISTS

Closer to Huizinga than to Veblen, the Scottish sociologists of the enlightenment had merged sport and political activity. Games were neither social control exercised as class hegemony, nor the random choices of consumers. Adam Smith, Bentham, and Marx might see sports as recreation or pleasure; emotional releases which could also be secured by card-playing or shove-ha'penny. For others they were socially constitutive rituals which were peculiarly infectious under print-capitalism. In the 1880s historians and anthropologists analysed sport organization. Local antiquarians set out to give rugby in the Scottish Borders or South Wales a historical pedigree, linking it

---

[27]  Eric Linklater, *Magnus Merriman* (Harmondsworth: Penguin, 1959), 128–9.

to 'hand-ba' or 'cnappan',[28] while the great James George Frazer in his *Golden Bough* (1890) argued that such rough field games, usually played in Lent, were connected with ritual purgation and scapegoating.[29] He was only following a tradition which had partly homogenized a games culture. In his *Essay on the History of Civil Society* (1767), Adam Ferguson regarded hostility between communities as a means of conferring an identity on them. Military virtues and sporting prowess existed in a continuum:

Every animal is made to delight in the exercise of his natural talent and forces. The lion and the tyger sport with the paw; the horse delights to commit his mane to the wind, and forgets his pasture to try his speed in the field; the bull even before his brow is armed, and the lamb while yet an emblem of innocence, have a disposition to strike with the forehead, and anticipate in play the conflicts they are doomed to sustain. Man too is disposed to opposition, and to employ the forces of his nature against an equal antagonist; he loves to bring his reason, his eloquence, his courage, even his bodily strength, to the proof. His sports are frequently an image of war; sweat and blood are frequently expended in play; and fractures or death are often made to terminate the pastimes of idleness and festivity.[30]

Sport was a necessary component of civic life. Casting back to the Greek games, and anticipating William James's 'The Moral Equivalent of War' (1911), Ferguson equated sports with the exercises of militarism: both disciplining and organizing youth and enacting a collective ceremony of community solidarity. Ferguson was born on the highland line, at Logierait, and had been as a Gaelic speaker a chaplain in the Black Watch (1745–54). In his ironic description of classical Greece the similarities to his own Highlands are clear:

They come abroad barefooted, and without any cover to the head, wrapt up in the coverlets under which you would imagine they had slept. They throw all off, and appear like so many native cannibals, when they go to violent sports and exercises, at which they highly value feats of dexterity and strength. Brawny limbs and muscular arms, the faculty of sleeping out all nights, of fasting long, and putting up with any kind of food, are thought genteel accomplishments. They have no settled government that I could learn; sometimes the mob, and sometimes the better sort, do what they please: they meet in great crowds in the open air, and seldom agree about any thing.[31]

More than a foretaste here of George MacDonald Fraser's post-1945 Scottish regimental football team!

Practical sport-sociology took two forms. Ferguson, demobbed, deployed his enthusiasm for Machiavellian civic virtu in the attempt to secure a militia for Scotland in 1760–1.[32] This awoke little resonance outwith the literati, and when a militia was

[28] Williams, *1905 and All That*, 80.

[29] J. G. Frazer, *The Golden Bough: A Study in Comparative Religion*, 1890 (London: Routledge Curzon, 2003), 184.

[30] Adam Ferguson, *An Essay on the History of Civil Society* (Edinburgh: Edinburgh University Press, 1966), 24.

[31] Ibid. 197.

[32] John Robertson, *The Scottish Enlightenment and the Militia Issue* (Edinburgh: John Donald, 1985), *passim*; Bruce Lenman, *Integration, Enlightenment and Industrialisation: Scotland 1746–1832* (London: Edward Arnold, 1981), 30–1.

set up in the 1790s the Scots rioted against it. But, after political reform, the Volunteer movement of the late 1850s[33] would influence the religious organizations which after 1870 developed the amateur football game, not to speak of a multitude of formal and casual local athletic bodies.[34]

The old philosopher was still alive and maybe even present when his son's friend Sir Walter Scott presided at Carterhaugh on 14 December 1815 over a famous football match between his Selkirk team and the Earl of Home's men, organized by James Hogg; not a step towards the League (over 150 took part!) but an occasion which helped revive the Common Ridings of the Border Burghs.[35] Given his popularity in translation, Ferguson may also have had a direct influence on the role played by gymnastics in national revivals in Europe: on Schiller's *Spieltrieb* (the compulsion of the game)[36] and on the German response to the Napoleonic invasion in 1806 through the liberal and nationalist *Turnvereine* of Friedrich Ludwig Jahn (1778–1852). First organized after 1811, their outdoor exercises were linked to an appreciation of folklore and history, developed on the left and the right, and replicated in other national movements, most notably the Czech 'Sokol' (Falcon) movement founded in the 1860s.

Another looming presence was Carlyle. On the face of it, someone prone to dismiss sport as extreme foolishness, Carlyle was deeply influenced in his thought by Ferguson in 'Signs of the Times' (1829) and 'Characteristics' (1831). His cult of effort in *Heroes and Hero-Worship* (1841) was to be transformed into 'muscular Christianity' by his Christian Socialist acolytes Tom Hughes and Charles Kingsley. 'From the cradle to the grave', wrote Hughes in *Tom Brown*, 'fighting, rightly understood, is the business, the real highest, honestest business of every son of man.'[37] Hughes combined radicalism and support for trade unionism with 'fighting, rightly understood' in the Volunteers and sports clubs, and Carlyle, in *The French Revolution* (1837), gifted a language to this, a style of descriptive writing able simultaneously to capture and analyse fast-moving events. Henry Boothe Luce claimed it as the origin of *Time*'s breathless style, and it provided the basic technique of that under-researched transatlantic performer, the sports journalist:

See Huissier Maillard, the shifty man! On his plank, swinging over the abyss of that stone Ditch; plank resting on parapet, balanced by weight of Patriots,—he hovers perilous: such a Dove towards such an Ark! Deftly, thou shifty usher: one man already fell; and lies smashed, far down there, against the masonry; Usher Maillard falls not: deftly, unerring he walks, with outspread palm. The Swiss holds a paper through his porthole; the shifty Usher snatches it, and returns. Terms of surrender: Pardon, immunity to all! Are they accepted? —'*Foi d' officier*, On the word of an officer,' answers half-pay Hulin,—or half-pay Elie, for men do not agree

[33] Hugh Cunningham, *The Volunteer Force: A Social and Political History, 1859–1908* (London: Croom Helm, 1975), 46–7.

[34] A. S. Neill, *Neill! Neill! Orange Peel!*, 1973 (London: Quartet Books, 1977), 63–4.

[35] John Gibson Lockhart, *Life of Sir Walter Scott*, 1837 (London: Dent, n.d.), 283–5.

[36] See Fania Oz-Salzberger, *Translating the Enlightenment: Scottish Civic Discourse in Eighteenth Century Germany* (Oxford: Clarendon Press, 1995), especially 304 ff.

[37] Edward Norman, *The Victorian Christian Socialists* (Cambridge: Cambridge University Press, 1987), 90.

on it, 'they are!' Sinks the drawbridge,—Usher Maillard bolting it when down; rushes-in the living deluge: the Bastille is fallen! *Victoire! La Bastille est prise!*[38]

Carlyle was, as Young Ireland's magus, as influential on T. F. Meagher's deployment of Celtic games against Anglo-Saxonry as he was on Macaulay's 'Horatius' in *Lays of Ancient Rome*, or Almond of Loretto's apotheosis of the rugger captain.[39]

The resonances of 'radical militarism' and Carlyleian hero worship give Scottish individual and team sports a much denser context than either the stereotypes of the urban *Untermensch* as gawping spectator or the cultivated paragons of physical fitness and social unity. The formative years of European sport as a mass movement, in the 1890s, coincided with the Wandervogel in Germany, the nationalistic Central Committee for the Promotion of National Youth Games of the Carlyle-like 'cultural pessimist' Julius Langbehn, with Pierre de Coubertin's propaganda in France for the revival of the Olympic Games, and an overall concern about 'degeneration' as a result of the move to a mass urban society.[40] Not to speak of such Scottish initiatives as Sir Hugh Munro of Lindertis making up in 1891 his celebrated list of 276 peaks above 3,000 feet—to this day the 'Munros'—and James Bryce MP presenting his Access to Mountains Bill in 1888, and a resolution on the same lines in 1892.[41] Although his project was felled by 'the polite but massive opposition of a vested interest and a national passion'—shooting and stalking—its land-reform principles echoed in the founding of the National Trust in 1896, with early properties in Cumbria and North Wales. Bryce had been a founder of the Alpine Club in 1861 and the spread of enthusiasm for climbing reached, with branch lines and horse-buses, Snowdonia and the Lakes in the 1870s. The building of a light railway to Snowdon was one of numerous projects of the elective Welshman Sir Edward Watkin, and his corrugated-iron mansion at Rhydd-Ddu would in 1894 host Gladstone, Lloyd George, and Tom Ellis. The nearby hotel at Pen-y-Pass became the centre of the rock-climbing movement which brought to the precipices of Eyryi such as George Mallory, Robert Graves, Richard Hughes, and I. A. Richards.

Coubertin of the Olympics came like Langbehn from an ultra-conservative, clericalist background, but was liberalized by English muscular Christians, Tom Hughes in particular. After a visit to England in 1883, he set up the Committee for Physical Exercises in Education in 1887, and the Olympic Games, set in motion by 1896 in Athens, promoted a version of Ferguson's medication for mass society: common games, competitively undertaken, as a formula for renewing coexistence and diffusing aggression. Coubertin's republican rival Paschal Grousset, Dreyfusard and

---

[38] Thomas Carlyle, *The French Revolution* (London: Chapman and Hall, 1895), 152–3. I owe the Boothe-Luce quote to the late Sir Alastair Dunnett, former editor of *The Scotsman*.

[39] Christopher Harvie, 'Carlyle and the Scottish Mission', in Priscilla Metscher, ed., *Regionalismus in Grossbritannien* (Hamburg: Gulliver and Argument Verlag, 1992), *passim*; Owen Dudley Edwards, 'Ireland', in *Celtic Nationalism* (London: Routledge and Kegan Paul, 1968), 122–4; Mandle, *Gaelic Athletic Association*, 16, 154; Williams, *1905 and All That*, 22.

[40] Eugen Weber, 'Pierre de Coubertin and the Introduction of Organised Sport', in *My France: Politics, Culture, Myth* (Cambridge, Mass.: Belknap, 1991), 207–12; Fritz Stern, *The Politics of Cultural Despair: A Study in the Rise of the Germanic Ideology* (New York: Knopf, 1961), 172.

[41] H. A. L. Fisher, *James Bryce* (London: Macmillan, 1927), i, 280–3.

cycling publicist, promoter of *barette* or *pelota* (the national game of the Basques), also developed links with British education, in particular the child-centred 'learning through play' of the 'progressive school' tradition in which Robert and Roland Muirhead, Whitmanites, Fabian socialists, and ardent Scottish nationalists were prominent. Margaret MacMillan, who had started as a preacher in the Bradford Labour Church, was similarly influential on the evolution of Board of Education policy under Sir Robert Morant.[42] This informally organized 'play' element led in 1902 to the setting-up, in advance of England, of the Royal Commission on Physical Training (Scotland). Evidence to it, particularly that of Dr W. L. Mackenzie, the Edinburgh school medical officer, stressed the importance of spontaneous games over drill. Somewhere here lurk J. M. Barrie's Lost Boys and John Buchan's Gorbals Diehards, as well as Patrick Geddes and A. S. Neill.[43] The non-coercive sports encouraged by Patrick Pearse at St Enda's School in Dublin were paralleled more ambiguously by the fieldcraft of Countess Markiewicz's Republican boy scouts, the Fianna.

## IV  TO THE TAILTEANN GAMES

But what of the GAA? It influenced Ifan ab Owen Williams (son of the Welsh educationalist Sir Owen M. Williams) to found the Urdd Genethlaedol Cymru (the Welsh League of Youth) in 1932, and some contemporary Scottish nationalists, Compton Mackenzie, William Power, and John L. Kinloch, tried to emulate it with the 'Clan Scotland' youth movement later that decade. So why did it not become a paradigm for the creation of a national sports movement, playing distinctive Scots or Celtic games? In the 1870s organized shinty made considerable strides; several early soccer sides, particularly those of the textile-and-dyestuff district of the Vale of Leven, were shinty teams as well.[44] Nationalists and land reformers—John Stuart Blackie, John Murdoch, Captain Chisholm of Strathglass—helped organize the game, and Scotland actually led Ireland in codifying its rules. Yet after some success between 1880 and 1900, shinty retreated to the eastern Highlands, and was further confined by the demographic damage inflicted by World War I.

The GAA had ostensibly been provoked by the organization, on a popular basis, of 'English' sports in Ireland. Its patron Archbishop Croke (who as Catholic Bishop of Auckland, 1870–5, coincided with the rise of New Zealand rugby, and drew appropriate conclusions) took a line similar to that of 'sport politicians' such as Henry Drummond and Stuart Blackie in Scotland:

If we continue travelling in the next score years in the same direction that we have been going in for some time past . . . effacing our national features as if we were ashamed of them, and

[42] W. David Smith, *Stretching their Bodies: The History of Physical Education* (Newton Abbot: David and Charles, 1974), 110–12.
[43] For Barrie's influence on Neill see Jonathan Croall, *Neill of Summerhill* (London: Routledge, 1983).
[44] Grant Jarvie, 'Sport, Gaelic Nationalism, and Scottish Politics, 1879–1920', unpublished paper, Warwick University, 1992, 228; Roger Hutchinson, *Camanachd! The Story of Shinty* (Edinburgh: Mainstream, 1989), 107.

putting on, with England's stuffs and broadcloths, her masher habits, and such effeminate follies as she may recommend, we had better at once, and publicly, abjure our
nationality.[45]

But there are paradoxes in the GAA story. Michael Cusack, its moving spirit, pillor-
ied by James Joyce as 'the Citizen', had himself made a fortune in cramming Irish
candidates for the British Civil Service.[46] Michael Davitt, who wrote to the founding meeting at Thurles pleading for 'athletic sports peculiar to the Celtic people' and
condemning 'the degenerate bearing of most of our young men at home', would be
a patron of Glasgow Celtic Football Club in 1888.[47] Even Michael Collins found
it desperately hard work compelling Irish exiles to play Gaelic games in London in
the 1900s. All but three teams dropped out when the ban on 'garrison games' was
enforced.[48]

But the real reason why the GAA succeeded while shinty never spread beyond
Inverness-shire, the Gaelic community in Glasgow, and the universities was political. As W. F. Mandle's research in government and police archives has shown, the
bulk of the organizational input into the GAA at its first peak in 1888–91 came from
the Irish Republican Brotherhood (IRB). Although it claimed over 600 branches by
1887 (Scotland had only twenty-six shinty clubs a decade later) the GAA as an effective 'sport police' was unimpressive: 'for its first few years athletics were virtually all
the GAA had to offer'.[49] Any impulse towards 'national sports' was subordinate to
the IRB's desire to keep its place in a national struggle largely taken over by Parnell
and Davitt's parliamentary and land campaigns. Not only was there no conspiracy
tradition in Scottish nationalism, but there was, even more significantly, no Irish conspiratorial tradition in Scotland either.[50]

Three IRB men were among the thirteen who attended the GAA's inaugural meeting. The politicos and clericals restricted themselves to sending letters. The games
of hurling and Gaelic football, which the IRB promoted in its ascendancy—until it
was engulfed by the Parnell split in 1890–1—seem to have been closer to bando (or
folk football) on one side or to rugby, until codified by R. T. Blake in 1895.[51] The
camans (hurling sticks) ritually shouldered at meetings in the 1880s, and at Parnell's
funeral, were at this stage more symbolic rifle substitutes than evidence of a distinctive sport culture. It was to be when GAA nationalism coincided with clerical control and formal 'no-politics' rules—between 1895 and the revival of the IRB within
the GAA around 1910—that Gaelic games developed as impressively as football in
England. They had, however, no element of professionalism, and a far higher degree

[45] T. F. O'Sullivan, *The Story of the Gaelic Athletic Association* (Dublin: Gaelic Athletic Association, 1916), 9–10.
[46] David Greene, 'Michael Cusack and the Rise of the GAA', in Conor Cruise O'Brien, ed., *The
Shaping of Modern Ireland* (London: Routledge, 1960), 76.
[47] Arthur Mitchell and Padraig O'Snodaigh, *Irish Political Documents, 1869–1916* (Dublin:
Irish Academic Press, 1989), 61–2.
[48] Tim Pat Coogan, *Michael Collins* (London: Hutchinson, 1990), 14–16.
[49] Mandle, *Gaelic Athletic Association*, 204.
[50] Bill Murray, *The Old Firm* (Edinburgh: John Donald, 1984), 66–75.
[51] Mandle, *Gaelic Athletic Association*, 105.

of county as opposed to urban organization. They were patently a godsend to the underused Midland and Great Western Railway system, far denser than the thin network in the Scottish Highlands, which provided their main challenge cup.[52] Further, the Ireland of the market towns was a relatively cohesive peasant-based society with a stable middle class of shopkeepers, auctioneers, publicans, teachers, and clergy. It could sponsor and control its own internal sporting system, as it already did with horse racing, for its own reasons. Gaelic sports could curb emigration, while young men who played 'garrison games' well would simply clear out.

The GAA was unique. There was no calibration, with it at one end, Scottish football in the middle, and English cricket and rugger on the right. It had, uniquely, a conspiratorial and physical force connection which consciously patronized athletics, but in fact it coincided with the rapid adoption in the Empire of 'English' games *and* anti-English sentiments which were expressed in success in them: rugby in South Africa, cricket in India, Australia, and the West Indies: the strategy deftly described by C. L. R. James in *Beyond a Boundary* of adopting the conquerors' games and then beating them hollow.[53] The GAA was as much a one-off as the 'real' English public-school elite's commitment to playing soccer rather than rugby.


## V  THE CIVIC MODE

James and Muirhead Bone reflected in 1901 that Glasgow working men arguing about football in the bars were talking a complex 'politics': they were as influential as any political party member, as the performance of their team reacted symbiotically with its supporters and their self-respect.[54] This elaborated some Victorian ideals and distorted others: revolutionary discipline for national liberation; ceremonies of community identity; socialization through collective enjoyment.

Scotland *had* been influenced by a pro-sport propaganda, like that of the *Turnvereine* and 'Sokol'. Robert Owen at New Lanark and in his *New View of Society* (1816) copied the—anything but effeminate—dancing of the Scottish regiments. The utility of games in school education was also advocated by the influential David Stow at the Glasgow Normal Seminary in 1836: 'The playground animates, invigorates, and permits the *steam* which may have accumulated to escape, not in furious mischief, but in innocent, joyous and varied amusements, under the superintendence of the master.'[55] Physical education in fact drew strongly on Swedish or Swiss theory and practice, institutionalized in Scotland when the wealth of Andrew Carnegie funded the Dunfermline College of Physical Education in his native town in 1905.[56]

---

[52] Ibid. 147–53.

[53] C. L. R. James, *Beyond a Boundary*, 1963 (London: Serpent's Tail, 1994).

[54] 'James Hamilton Muir', *Glasgow in 1901* (Glasgow: William Hodge, 1901), 188.

[55] Smith, *Stretching their Bodies*, 81. For the power of music and dance in a Highland regiment in the 1950s see James Kellaway's acclaimed novel *Tunes of Glory* (London: Putnam, 1956).

[56] I. C. MacLean, *History of the Dunfermline College of Physical Education* (Edinburgh: Blackwoods, 1972), chaps. 1–3.

In Europe the division in national physical training organizations tended to lie between advocates of military drill and advocates of sports.[57] The 'militarists' saw drill instilling discipline and obedience, the 'sportsmen' sought a more flexible, autonomous citizenry. The Volunteer movement combined both, but the attractiveness of drill alone seemed to decline in the 1880s, not just with the rise of commercialized sports, but with new technologies and tactics which diminished the importance of the highly drilled 'square' in favour of the 'skirmishing' attack, something which was to gain its expression in the popularity of Baden-Powell's *Scouting for Boys* (1908), much aided by Kipling. Adopted in part from experience of the *veldtkraft* of the Boer commandos, scouting quickly attained an anti-imperial form with Countess Markiewicz's Fianna of 1912.

Scotland played a particular role in the transition from the 'military' to the 'civic' mode. The Vale of Leven, the cradle of Scots soccer, had been an important centre of the Volunteers in the 1860s, part of the paternalism of the dyemaster families of Orr-Ewing and Wylie.[58] They were Tories, but a strong Liberal element went into the creation of the Scouts' precursor, the Boys' Brigade, founded in Glasgow in 1883 by (Sir) William A. Smith, a Free Church Sunday school teacher and officer in the First Lanarkshire Rifle Volunteers (who fielded one of the first Scottish football elevens).[59] In 1873 Glasgow Rangers had been founded as a club with Presbyterian connections: not perhaps the best of precedents for civic tolerance. But in the aftermath of the successful, and highly ecumenical, Moody and Sankey mission of that year Smith, concerned at the inability of Sunday schools to hold youngsters' attention, found that they responded to physical training—parading with wooden rifles—combined with sports. BB (Boys' Brigade) companies were set up, invariably linked to churches and missions, but rarely without athletic, swimming, and above all football clubs. If in 1910 the bulk of amateur teams in England were linked to churches, then the situation must have been even more apparent in Scotland.[60]

The rationale was spelt out by Professor Henry Drummond, Liberal politician, scientist, explorer, and charismatic Free Church leader:

The wise Officer, the humane and sensible Officer, in short makes as much use of play for higher purposes than parades, and sometimes more. The key to a boy's life in the present generation lies in athletics. Sport commands his whole leisure, and governs his thoughts and ambitions even in his working hours. And so striking has been this development in recent years that the time has come to decide whether athletics are to become a curse to the country or a blessing.[61]

[57] I. C. MacLean, 85.    [58] Macintyre, *Little Moscows*, 82–3.

[59] J. Cunnison and J. B. S. Gilfillan, eds., *The Third Statistical Account of Scotland: Glasgow* (Glasgow: Collins, 1958), 703–4; Percy F. Young, *A History of British Football* (London: Stanley Paul, 1968), 108.

[60] N. Fishwick, *English Football and Society, 1910–1950* (Manchester: Manchester University Press, 1989), 12. In fact, relations between the 'Old Firm' teams were pretty good until an influx of Ulster workers in the 1900s and the Scots reaction to the Troubles. See chap. 4.

[61] George Adam Smith, *The Life of Henry Drummond* (London: Hodder and Stoughton, 1899), 459.

Drummond had his doubts about commercialized sport, regarding BB football as 'the making moral of what, in the eyes of those who really know, is fast becoming a most immoral and degrading institution'. But he admitted that the most effective captains were those who coached their teams during the week and acted as referees on Saturday afternoons. By the 1950s the Glasgow Battalion of the BBs was running 'the largest football league in the world', fielding 200 teams every Saturday.[62]

This elaborate amateur spirit lay behind the SFA's withdrawal from 'British' football in 1887, after a pitch invasion at Preston North End on 30 October 1886 by genteel Queen's Park supporters. But an all-British league, paradoxically, was really only accessible to the better-off, a 200-mile rail return journey being necessary to reach the most northerly English ground. These were not the classes, increasingly being attracted as supporters, who would be the mainstay of the professional game.[63]

At this point of crisis in the 'amateur' game the Irish Catholic Nationalists became significant. The Catholic equivalent of the YMCA, the Catholic Young Men's Society, had helped Canon Hannan found Edinburgh Hibernian in 1873. Fifteen years later Glasgow Celtic was founded by another priest, Brother Walfrid of the Marist order. The motives were dual: a Catholic football culture would stop a migration to the BBs and enhance community prestige, in the classic C. L. R. James mode. Celtic was from the start the flagship of an entire community, many of whose members were unable to afford to be amateurs but took pride in Celtic as a top club and a well-run business, able by 1893 to build a stadium with a 30,000 capacity. This deliberate challenge, and the Rangers' response, gave Scottish football both a sectarian and a gladiatorial aspect which marked it indelibly.[64]

Davitt planted a shamrock sod at Parkhead in 1893, but the ethos behind Celtic was as far from the GAA as it was from Canon Hannan's teetotalism. Not just because six out of its seven directors in 1897 were publicans.[65] Celtic's backers were Home Rulers, but although some may well have been IRB members, they stuck with the old Nationalist Party, and did not, like the GAA after 1910, move to Sinn Fein. Team and enterprise having put the community on the Scottish map, in 1914 Celtic was patriotic.[66] Celtic's growth was less to do with nationalist solidarity than with showing that the Catholic community could create its own social overhead capital on a grand scale and claim equality of esteem in west central Scotland. By the 1920s this identity counted for more than 'anti-British' sentiment. Glasgow Catholics would be for a further half-century the pillars of Labour unionism.

The career of an archetypal footballer-as-publican, James Kelly, 'the fastest centre half-back that Scotland has produced', was surely emblematic. Kelly was a member of the 1888 Celtic team, and was subsequently capped sixteen times for Scotland; in 1911 he had become JP for Blantyre and a member of the school board, as well as

---

[62] Cunnison and Gilfillan, eds., *Third Statistical Account*, 626.
[63] Young, *History of British Football*, 122–3.   [64] Murray, *The Old Firm*, 35–55.
[65] Tom Gallagher, *Glasgow: The Uneasy Peace* (Manchester: Manchester University Press, 1987), 55, 61.
[66] Murray, *The Old Firm*, 126.

President of Celtic.[67] But, as he started his career by playing for Renton, he would have been a 'soccer and shinty' man, with the option of a GAA-type development open to him. Instead, the 'star' soccer of the 'Old Firm' supervened.

And yet . . . The problem with sociological explanations is the assumption that the actors in society are always content with the injunction 'be this' instead of 'do this'. And this is dodgy when applied to that gamut of activities which stretches from 'play' with its anarchic implications to 'organized sport' with its harsh motivators, whether nationalism, personal excellence, or money. And probably nowhere else was wayward individuality so well developed as in Scotland. Sport came to exercise a socially constitutive function, but this activity sits midway between a primitive, pre-social, and possibly destructive individuality, and that post-industrial identity that can create its own conscious balance of body and mind out of the security that civil society gives. At the first level we have the Cromarty tearaway Hugh Miller running wild, pulling knives on his schoolfellows, but also geologizing and collecting folklore. At the second we have the ingenuity of the Glasgow Catholic community in coming from far behind to capture a position at the top of the soccer scale. At the third? Perhaps another quote from a novel of the thirties sets the tone:

He was now past the half-way line, a little distance ahead of one of the Clausons, with no colleague near him, and with Charvil racing to intercept him. For one of Jaikie's inches there could be no hand-off, but he had learned in his extreme youth certain arts not commonly familiar to rugby players. He was a most cunning dodger . . .[68]

*Castle Gay*, John Buchan's inspired Peacockian comedy of ideas, is also structured like a huge game, in which the forces of a Scottish *Gemeinschaft* reconcile the ideologies—an inert conservatism, a socialism threatened by conspiracy—which threaten to tear it apart. Buchan announces this by having wee Jaikie Galt, slewing from one mode, and social class, to another, employ the arcane and unanticipated skills of the Gorbals Diehards to score the winning try.

## VI  'THE FINEST PLAY UNDER THE SUN'

In 1885 John Lavery's *The Tennis Party* was exhibited at the new Glasgow Art Club. An informal scene of sportive effort—'Love-thirty, love-forty, Oh what a joy!', etc.— framed by a tight structure of nets, shadows, and textures, it was a stunning success and was sold to the Neue Pinakothek in Munich: a coup which put the 'Glasgow Boys' on the map.[69] This name itself had an outdoors Irish, frontier, quality. It showed the way in which the 'Second City' drew to it talent from around the inland sea—Lavery being a Belfast Catholic from a poor working-class background. In 1916

---

[67] *Stothers's Glasgow, Lanarkshire and Renfrewshire Xmas and New-Year Annual, 1911–1912* (Glasgow: James Stothers, 1911), 226–7.

[68] John Buchan, *Castle Gay*, 1930 (London: Pan, 1967), 17–18.

[69] Duncan Macmillan, *Scottish Art, 1460–1990* (Edinburgh: Mainstream, 1990), 260–2.

he was a war artist, two years short of his knighthood, yet as an Irish nationalist he would paint at the Old Bailey 'Casement on trial, / Half-hidden by the bars'—to be echoed in Yeats's great life-reprise 'The Municipal Gallery Revisited' of 1938. His wife's portrait—

> Hazel Lavery living and dying, that tale
> As though some ballad-singer had sung it all.

—decorated for decades the banknotes of Free State and Republic.

Lavery emphasizes the modernity of art along the littoral. He was trained as a photographer, in the country where photography was first recognized as an art form, through D. O. Hill and Robert Adamson's calotypes of the worthies of the Disruption and the world-ranging reportage of John Thompson.[70] Scotland reflected the uneasy relationship in nineteenth-century Europe, running parallel to sport, between painting, democracy, and nationality. In a formal sense nationalism was weaker in 1880s Glasgow than earlier. The 'Boys' took their cue from the French realists, from Millet and Corot via the Barbizon school to Bastien-Lepage, yet beneath their west-coast pastorals was a democratic programme, and with it would come a more fundamental level of national consciousness. Earlier in the century nationalism had been more explicit: in Ireland (or rather 'painting for Ireland in London') James Barry, William Mulready, and Daniel Maclise used historical painting as a form of propaganda for Repeal in huge canvases such as *The Marriage of Strongbow and Eva/Aife* (1854).[71] If there was a parallel to sport it lay in their centring of interest in the human form, male and female, and the Greek precedents which lay behind this, influenced not least by the physiological studies of William Etty of York, who was to the human form what Stubbs had been to the horse.

This had mixed consequences in the regions. Did painters follow the grand style of Reynolds and Gainsborough (with inputs from Gericault and Ingres) or the more domestic programme of David Wilkie (1745–1841)? Scotland, under the baleful influence of Sir Walter Scott, produced monumental historical essays whose ambition was rarely matched by the talents of painters like David Scott. Wilkie, who followed Galt rather than Scott, was sympathetic to his Irish subjects and influenced their subsequent treatment.[72] In Wales he influenced an ironic artisan concentration on political caricature which coexisted with the pierhead painters' depiction of schooners or later steam-colliers bucketing through lead-blue seas.

It was evident by the mid century, however, that a 'British' critique had come into play, ironically through the 'Scot of Scots' John Ruskin, and his insistence on either the minute and accurate depiction of nature or the moral atmospherics of Turner.

---

[70] Richard Ovenden, *John Thompson: Photographer* (Edinburgh: National Library of Scotland, 1997).

[71] See Peter Harbinson, Homan Patterton, and Jeanne Sheehy, *Irish Art and Architecture* (London: Thames and Hudson, 1993), 187–234. Maclise's father was in fact Scots.

[72] Fintan Cullen, 'Romanticism', in W. J. MacCormack, ed., *The Blackwell Companion to Modern Irish Culture* (Oxford: Blackwell, 1999).

This appears to have produced a bifurcation in patronage: between the London patrons and dealers who went for big names who progressively reflected the Pre-Raphaelite impact, and localities which evolved their own subject-matter and artistic establishments. Some at least of this was due to another congeries of talent and influence, started by the Bristol-born Ruskinian Edward Godwin. In the 1860s Godwin simultaneously discovered Celtic and Japanese art, building Dromore Castle, Kerry, in 1863 and the White House in Chelsea in 1872 for Whistler. Godwin's private life was as tangled as Rossetti's. His mistress Ellen Terry gave birth to Edward Gordon Craig, the revolutionary stage designer, and his second wife, Beatrice, was the daughter of the Scots sculptor Birnie Philip, who went on, after Godwin's early death, to marry Whistler: the reason why most of the great radical's *oeuvre* ended up in Glasgow's Hunterian Museum.

This was the situation in which Scotland's west became *avant-garde*, almost literally in the powerful seascapes of William MacTaggart (1836–1910), which carried the values of Turner.[73] Scottish artistic independence was fortified by enlightened buyers and agents, taking full advantage of easy steamship access to France and more exotic situations: art became the often-complex treatment of a comfortable, largely rural bourgeois existence. The 'Boys' also nailed their Atlantic colours to the mast by campaigning in 1882 for Glasgow Corporation to purchase Whistler's 1872–3 *Arrangement in Grey and Black: Portrait of Thomas Carlyle* for its collection.[74]

Technique and ideology made some of them, like Charles Grant Murray, influential on a later generation of Welsh painters, not least because the developing Welsh art colleges, set up under the Science and Arts Act of 1857, were often staffed from Scotland, where art education had lain with the Trustees for Manufacturing and Fisherys since 1728, sustaining the remarkable development of painting and aesthetics at the time of the enlightenment. The Betws-y-coed school throve in the foothills of Snowdonia, reinforced by the remarkable talent of the Londoner Clarence Whaite and the Bavarian Hubert von Herkomer, who took the Welshness that he married into seriously and in the 1890s designed the costumes for the National Eisteddfod. For all these painters, and their Irish colleagues, Continental rather than London developments were central, particularly the clash between academic and 'secessionist' art. Although there was a continuing output of portraits, in Scotland historical and sentimental scenes ebbed, and the secessionist element became, unlike elsewhere, dominant.

This gave its cue to the other western countries. This whole movement and its outdoor ambience were reinforced after the 1870s by a flight westward by north European artists—to Brittany, Cornwall, Ireland, and Wales—in search of tranquillity, clear light, and unspoiled folk culture. A central figure was Stanhope Forbes, of a Scots-Irish engineering family, who settled at Newlyn in the 1890s. What was

---

73 Macmillan, *Scottish Art*, 245–52.

74 Whistler's ancestry was almost emblematic. His father, George Washington Whistler, was a railway engineer who died while building the Moscow–St Petersburg line. His mother was from a Scottish settler family.

significant, however, was the recoil of this activity on the national capitals, through portraitists, museum organizers, critics, and dealers, producing a fusion of the Continental avant-garde and native nationalism: as in the case of Glasgow's Alex Reid, the only man to sell a Van Gogh painting in the artist's lifetime. Dublin's Sir Hugh Lane, Lady Gregory's art dealer nephew faced the 'gombeen man' treatment of his donation to Dublin (largely from the Staats Forbes Collection). This provoked the wrath of James Larkin as well as W. B. Yeats.

In the 1890s this produced a remarkable forward movement into the European avant-garde. Scotland's own version of post-Impressionism, fronted by the activities of Patrick Geddes in Edinburgh and a host of architects, painters, and designers, ranged from John Duncan and Phoebe Traquair to Charles Rennie Mackintosh and Baillie Scott. A decade later the German theoretician Hermann Muthesius would see this playful ruralism as an alternative to the 'hotel life' of the great cities, with all its artificialities and tensions. In Ireland it produced crisis, when Lane offered his collection of European art to Dublin Corporation. It refused it in 1913—would Glasgow have done so? The result fused with the industrial unrest of the time into one of the powder trails which led to the Post Office in Eastern, 1916.

Outside the Geddes circle, Scots art tended away from the figurative. Duncan Macmillan has argued that in MacTaggart's huge beachscapes the figures dissolve into the paint—a reflection of the break-up of rural, Gaelic Scotland? Even a sharp social observer like Muirhead Bone created a Glasgow of tiny human figures crawling under huge ships, cranes, and guns, far different from the monumental historicism of his Welsh friend Christopher Williams, or the working-class realists whom Grant Murray and the Davies sisters were encouraging.

Comparisons with Continental schools don't really help, but athleticism does. The rhythmic elements of post-Impressionism, Augustus John or William Orpen's gypsies, the bacchantes of J. D. Ferguson, Stanley Cursiter's adoption of futurist methods of registering motion, seem to yearn for the fusion of play and intellect which the Olympic ideal—and indeed Olympia itself, the re-emerging confederal sport-city excavated by the Germans after the 1870s in the Greek Peloponnese—represented. Ferguson would be the model for the anarchic artist-hero Gulley Jimson of Joyce Cary's *The Horse's Mouth* (1940), and two other idiosyncratic interpreters of the littoral, John Arden and Alasdair Gray, started like Cary in Scottish art school.

In a painting of W. B. Yeats's brother Jack—friend of Masefield, *Punch* cartoonist—a girl lays a flower on Bachelor's Walk, where in 1913 panicked Scots soldiers shot at crowds accompanying the rifles that Erskine Childers had smuggled into Howth. With his taste for the melodrama, the boxing ring, the racecourse, Jack remained in touch with those his brother spurned, yet at the same time yearned for:

> An affable Irregular
> A heavily-built Falstaffian man
> Comes cracking jokes of civil war
> As though to die by gunshot were
> The finest play under the sun.

I count those feathered balls of soot
The moor-hen guides upon the stream,
To silence the envy in my thought;
And turn towards my chamber, caught
In the cold snows of a dream.[75]

[75] W. B. Yeats, 'Meditations in Time of Civil War', 1923, in *Collected Poems* (London, Macmillan, 1934).

# 8

# John Bull's Other Irishman: Bernard Shaw, Capitalism, and the Celts

Ireland has changed. The patriotism of the Irish is the same, but the expression of it is different. The boy who used to want to die for Ireland now goes into a rage because the dispensary doctor in County Clare has been elected by a fraud. Ireland is no longer a sweetheart but a house to be set in order.

W. B. Yeats, address in Detroit, 19 February 1913[1]

## I  THE VIEW FROM BAKER STREET

The Court Theatre, London, 1 November 1904: Act I of *John Bull's Other Island*. We have been here before. A consulting room in central London, shared by two bachelors, and a shifty-looking character about to enter. Could this be 221B Baker Street? Bernard Shaw playing Holmes-and-Watson? Indeed, and not for the last time: Professor Higgins and Colonel Pickering would come in 1914.

Matt Haffigan, Irish and voluble, entrances Watson; Holmes enters and destroys him:

No Irishman ever talks like that in Ireland, or ever did, or ever will. But when a thoroughly worthless Irishman comes to England, and finds the whole place full of romantic duffers like you, who will let him loaf and drink and sponge and brag as long as he flatters your sense of moral superiority by playing the fool and degrading himself and his country, he soon learns the antics that take you in.[2]

Our heroes then go off on their venture to modernize Ireland, Watson packing a revolver.

The outcome, however, is Watson (or Tom Broadbent) triumphant, the Irish knocked over like ninepins by his tourist schemes, Holmes (his partner Larry Doyle) reduced to sullen acquiescence, Rosscullen's local madman-visionary patronized into speechlessness. *John Bull's Other Island* is a sort of omnibus introduction both to the dilemma of *fin de siècle* West Britain and to the synoptic seer-politician-playwright it produced. It combines knowing contemporary parody, the cosmic, savage humour

[1] Quoted in Roy Foster, *W. B. Yeats: A Life*, i: *The Apprentice Mage* (Oxford: Oxford University Press, 1997), 513.

[2] George Bernard Shaw, *John Bull's Other Island* (London: Constable, 1907), 14.

of Carlyle in *Latter-Day Pamphlets*, and that sense of personal maiming which Conor Cruise O'Brien regards as the mark of the Irish writer. 1904 seemingly saw Irish affairs at their most soluble, with even the Tories, in the person of Chief Secretary George Wyndham, playing with Home Rule, but 'there are five separate tragedies in the thing besides the Broadbent comedy', Shaw wrote to his director, Harley Granville-Barker, in October. When it reached Dublin, on 25 September 1916, these were already unfolding, and the mocker of nationalist pieties had become the passionate defender of the Easter rebels.[3]

'Irish' Shaw appears as a tragic hero, rather than the gabby know-all of his later years, something picked up by perceptive critics. Michael Holroyd's biography, usually richer in incident than in analysis, still nails *John Bull* as 'sombre and self-revealing'; for Keith May it is 'a model play of ideas', while Arnold Kettle sees in it Shaw's subtle knack of playing off ideological and personal confrontations. *John Bull* went beyond comedy—even of the ambiguous Chekhovian sort—to become an omen of incipient, if scarcely perceived, crisis. It made Shaw's reputation, though it was not outside Ireland very successful, seldom performed because too long—even a cut version plays for nearly two-and-a-half hours—and with too slight a female lead, however apposite in symbolizing the plight of Irish Catholic women. Yet, regarded as 'one of the three great plays of the Irish repertoire in the first half of the twentieth century', it contained some of Shaw's best writing, and in the apocalyptic Father Keegan perhaps the greatest of those shape-changing figures whom he repeatedly and calculatingly played against his own dogmatism.[4]

In his preface to the 1912 revival Shaw wrote that changes since 1904 meant that *John Bull*, 'which had up to that moment been a topical play, immediately became an historical one'.[5] Few of his other plays had such direct influence. Though *Man and Superman, Caesar and Cleopatra*, and *The Devil's Disciple* had won acclaim in New York in the late 1890s, which Shaw used to prise open the London theatre, it was only with *John Bull* that Shaw became *the* political oracle, *the* GBS. The Conservative premier Arthur Balfour—'Bloody Balfour' in Irish political mythology—loved it and went no fewer than five times, taking the men who turned out to be his successors, Campbell-Bannerman and Asquith, along with him. Edward VII laughed so much that he fell through one of the Court Theatre's chairs. In far different circumstances, Sean O'Casey saw it in Dublin in the autumn of 1916 and said it made him into an Irish playwright. Though its direct influence on him was most observable in the inferior *Purple Dust*, his style of tragicomedy—the tension between Nora Clitheroe and her husband in *The Plough and the Stars*, the 'flight into eloquence' of his paralysed poets in *The Shadow of a Gunman*—was surely derived from the 'man of action'/'man of feeling' dichotomy of Broadbent and Doyle.[6]

---

[3] Shaw to Granville-Barker, 3 Oct. 1904, in *Bernard Shaw's Letters to Granville-Barker*, ed. C. B. Purdom (London: Phoenix House, 1956), 39.

[4] Christopher Fitzsimons, *The Irish Theatre* (London: Thames and Hudson, 1983), 126.

[5] Shaw, preface to the 1912 reprint of the play. Although *John Bull* did not reach Ireland until after the Easter Rising, it was in the Abbey's annual repertory until 1928.

[6] George Bernard Shaw, *Collected Plays* (London: Constable, 1955), 410.

The play came at a critical juncture. The seasons run by Harley Granville-Barker and Louis Vedrenne at the Court, 1904–7, were a crucial episode in the London theatre—the greatest thing since Shakespeare at the Globe, some said—but reflected a profounder change on the littoral. 'In the theatre, the mob becomes a nation', Yeats had grandly intoned; it could also become a city or a region, or go international: all were outcomes of the repertory movement which, starting in Ireland in 1898, spread to Manchester (1908) and Glasgow (1909), and rarely lacked an input from across the pond.

Dismissive of Shakespeare, Shaw would probably have compared his tour de force of eleven premieres to Wagner's *Ring des Nibelungen*, premiered at Bayreuth between 1863 and 1870, against the competing leitmotif of Bismarck's wars of conquest. Shaw's overture, *Man and Superman*, written in 1901–3, had been an exfoliatingly Atlanticist farrago of travel, sex, speculation, and politics, so complex as to be almost unperformable. *John Bull*'s contemporary, un-legendary Ireland was more manageable chamber music. Yet it failed to impress its original patrons, Yeats and the Celtophiles of the Irish Literary Theatre. This despite the fact that Shaw's common sense about Home Rule would by 1914 concur with Yeats's own middle-aged realism and the civic irony Joyce showed in *Dubliners*. Its fate would be one of periodical revivals, nearly always successful, and then decades on the shelf. Its autobiographical, ideological, and nationalist discourse: Irish *and* British, rather than Atlanticist, its powerful poetry and allusion (Shaw wrote that 'a man can no more be original . . . than a tree can grow out of air'), had a relevance which would be destroyed, or at least indefinitely deferred, by the violent end of Anglo-Irish politics after 1916.[7] *John Bull*'s neglect also reflects the lacunae in Shaw scholarship. No one has researched the huge, and virtually unparalleled, cuts that he made in the text, how and when he drafted and revised his prefaces, or what sources he used. Although Shaw is almost automatically associated with Ibsen and Wagner, this intensely didactic play, which still keeps safely away from the political pamphlet, restates a type of social criticism which we could call 'peripheral British', the tradition of Edgeworth's *Castle Rackrent*, Carlyle's *Chartism*, much of Thackeray and Trollope, and Ruskin's *Unto this Last,* only to see it overwhelmed.

## II  THE INTELLIGENT FABIAN'S GUIDE TO WEST BRITAIN

*John Bull* was wise to its audience, as were the plays that followed. Its writer was a politician; one of its producers, Vedrenne, had been a Cardiff businessman and consul. Shaw surveyed Londoners in his first plays, but he regarded their economy as eccentric. As a post-Marxian, a founder Fabian in 1885, he had as his real subject and market the industrial areas, ports, and coalfields, and what Antonio Gramsci would call the 'organic intelligentsia'—managers, skilled workers, local politicians,

---

[7] Michael Holroyd, *Bernard Shaw*, i: *The Search for Love* (London: Chatto and Windus, 1988), 99.

and administrators.[8] Their municipal and joint-stock operations were (as far as manufacturing industry was concerned) starting to take over from the family firms while landed authority based on farming—the unquestioned background of mid Victorian novelists from the Brontës to Meredith—was at an end: killed by the post-1873 slump and buried by the Ashbourne Land Act. Nick L'Estrange, the Ross-cullen squireen, has been sold up before *John Bull*'s action starts: big house and demesne figure nowhere. This is Cherry Orchard country after the Ranevskys have cleared off.[9]

In its place, Shaw recognized, was an industrial scene far different from that once dominated by dissenting millowners. An evolutionary new order of great concerns, susceptible (so Fabians thought) to state direction, was expanding from the transport utilities: railways, docks, electric tramway and power companies.[10] These were substantially regional: most of the 120-odd separate railway companies, such as the Hull and Barnsley and the Taff Vale, hauled coal from mine to port. Fabian confidence reflected the control of railway charges by government; their own influence marked electricity generating after the 1880s, in which private power companies were constrained by a preference in legislation for municipal enterprise.[11] In place of agriculture, primary production meant energy, and energy (given the infancy of oil and hydroelectricity) meant coal. Giant companies—D. A. Thomas's Cambrian Combine or Sir Adam Nimmo's Fife Coal Company—underpinned enterprise and urbanism. An output of 81 million tons in 1860 rose in 1905 to 240 million tons.[12]

Fabians suspected that such concerns implied a retreat from manufacturing to primary production, 'trustification', and an orientation towards a rapidly industrializing Europe which demanded power: north European cities needed above all to be heated and clothed. Along the littoral huge outward flows of coal, ships, machines, and cotton piece goods balanced inward traffics of iron and copper ore, guano, bauxite, frozen meat, grain, and what the Germans called *Kolonialwaren* (tea, coffee, tinned foods, etc.: the basis of Sir Thomas Lipton's fortune). Britain and coal occupied for two decades the role, reliable and uniform—'financial and commercial services were similar throughout the world before 1930'[13]—that American oil dynasties like the Rockefellers were only beginning to aim at, and which Saudia Arabia would fill in the 1960s and 1970s. Only after 1908 was oil from Persia

---

[8] Antonio Gramsci, 'The Intellectuals', in *Prison Notebooks*, trans. Quintin Hoare and Geoffrey Nowell-Smith (London: Lawrence and Wishart, 1971).

[9] Chekhov died as Shaw was writing *John Bull*, on 15 July 1904. His plays were given their British premieres by Alfred Wareing's Glasgow Repertory Company. *The Seagull* was welcomed on 3 Nov. 1909 by the critic of the *Evening Times* (the young James Bridie?) as 'a drama of realism which ought to be seen by anyone who is a serious student of the stage'. Quoted in Victor Emeljanow, ed., *Anton Chekhov: The Critical Heritage* (London: Routledge, 1981), 86–7.

[10] See Graham Wallas, *The Great Society: A Psychological Analysis* (London: Macmillan, 1914).

[11] Martin Chick, Nationalisation, Privatisation and Regulation', in Maurice W. Kirby and Mary B. Rose, eds., *Business Enterprise in Modern Britain* (London: Routledge, 1994), 319–20, and see E. Eldon Barry, *Nationalisation in British Politics: The Political Background* (London: Jonathan Cape, 1965).

[12] B. R. Mitchell, ed., *European Historical Statistics* (London: Macmillan, 1975), 185–8.

[13] D. C. M. Platt, *Business Imperialism, 1840–1930* (Oxford: Clarendon Press, 1977), 1.

and America being considered for European navies, and the Continent had scarcely 100,000 automobiles, but the scramble for energy and raw material had already gone global. Shaw's *jetés* in *Man and Superman* from London to the Spanish Sierra Nevada or the Algerian Atlas Mountains were scarcely exotic to those reared on Conrad, Kipling, Thomas Cook, or the Stock Exchange.[14]

Shaw disbelieved in the ability of pure market economics to correct a capitalism grown rampant rather than cultivated—not a view confined to the Left. 'New' Liberals such as J. A. Hobson, Norman Angell, and Noel Brailsford around the *Manchester Guardian* blamed low working-class wages and cramped housing for inflating capital export and inhibiting consumer-goods manufacturing and the domestic market that ought to accompany it.[15] Such critics, while radical, were still internationalist and pacific, but into this investment vacuum had surged four less reassuring factors: first, the mounting demand for armaments, after von Tirpitz's *Flottenpolitik* met the Dreadnought revolution in battleship construction of 1905–6; second, an attempt by the owners to rationalize production by the introduction of American technology and scientific management; third, a bourgeois political economy not of Samuel Smiles-like effort but of conspicuous consumption—regional elites realizing their gains in the south, with their earlier solidarity breaking up. Finally there was an evolving 'military socialism', of the sort advertised by German paternalist entrepreneurs, Theodore Roosevelt, and the 'national efficiency' school, with whom the Fabians—and Shaw: see *Major Barbara*—would also be identified, not to speak of David Lloyd George, since 1906 the expansionist of the Board of Trade, enthralled at 'twisting industrialists around my little finger'.[16]

Shaw had already got the ideologues of 'social Darwinian' capitalism in his sights. Roebuck Ramsden in *Man and Superman* was a caricature of Herbert Spencer, the prophet of an absolute marketism, who rose to his zenith as the Muse of the Millionaires in the 1890s, and was the near-constant companion of Richard Potter, father of Beatrice Webb.[17] Potter's fairly typical wealth was derived from textiles, coal, steel, railways, engineering, and shipbuilding: activities which in the Production Census of 1906 amounted to around 50 per cent of GDP, but which now faced what David Landes has called 'short wind and second breath'. *Man and Superman*'s four-way conflict between Ramsden (market liberal), John Tanner (revolutionary socialist), Malone (Irish-American millionaire), and 'Enry Straker (cockney engineer) reflects the culture of an Atlantic capitalism, only just resolving its contradictions beneath the deceptive solidity of joint-stock, professionally managed concerns.[18]

[14] For an estimate of car numbers in 1913 see Mitchell, *European Historical Statistics*, 350–2, though half of these were in Britain, an eight-fold increase on 1905.

[15] See Jules Townshend, *J. A. Hobson* (Manchester: Manchester University Press, 1990), 47–75, and P. F. Clarke, *Lancashire and the New Liberalism* (Cambridge: Cambridge University Press, 1971).

[16] See G. R. Searle, *The Quest for National Efficiency: A Study in British Politics and Political Thought, 1899–1914* (Oxford: Blackwell, 1971), chaps. 3–5.

[17] Beatrice Webb, *My Apprenticeship*, 1926 (Cambridge: Cambridge University Press, 1979), 22–42.

[18] David Landes, *The Unbound Prometheus* (Cambridge: Cambridge University Press, 1969), chap. 5.

The routes of the wealthy could be out, into an affluent private life, into philanthropy—and into specialist industry. The classic animator was Andrew Carnegie, back in Britain after 1895, when he settled at Skibo Castle, near Dornoch, and started to give money away (not least to a needy Liberal Party). See, too, the coal-owners D. A. Thomas and David Davies and his sisters in South Wales, the Booth-Potters of Liverpool, the Lithgows on the Clyde, who were married into the coal-owning Nimmos. They were constrained by a dependence on exports, whose fluctuations often inflamed labour relations, while secularized versions of the Nonconformist conscience drove them towards the Carnegie type of philanthropy.[19]

The coal-owners, with their cash in shipping, local railway lines, and Scotland, north-east England, and South Wales, coexisted uneasily with other, younger entrepreneurs who profited from transport, energy, and technical advance: electrics, soap, confectionery, photography, chemicals, mass-produced foodstuffs, mass-circulation papers. Their market had hitherto been middle-class patrons who were prepared to pay for innovation (cars seem, even then, to have been different: appealing more to the landed gentry or would-be landed gentry) or the new 'white-collar' classes. They wanted to broaden it through markets and products hitherto developed by European or American firms: a matter of imagination and psychology not distant from social reform or the theatre. 'James Bridie', Dr Osborne Henry Mavor (1889–1951), perhaps Shaw's closest disciple as a satirist, was from a Glasgow family of electrical engineers. His uncle, the economist Professor James Mavor, had been Shaw's colleague in the Fabian Society. For Bridie, a working doctor until his fifties, a practical profession was essential; to be called 'a man of letters' was to be insulted.[20]

Observing and envying inter-war Britain, the Austrian J. A. Schumpeter noted how the old Whig nobility persisted: families of traditionally 'progressive' views felt relatively isolated after the constitutional crisis of 1910, yet were still prepared to use their local power and often their scientific or academic prestige.[21] Haldanes, Grosvenors, Aberdeens, Pentlands, Devonshires, and Russells had to cope with the philistinism of the bourgeoisie, but many had already strengthened their position by marrying into *haut bourgeois* academic or manufacturing families to produce that hybrid which Noel Annan christened 'the English intellectual aristocracy'. Old industrial wealth was constrained by its preoccupation with exports, and its desire to depress wages in this cause; the agrarian Whigs had already, in the 'high farming' era, rationalized their labour force.[22] The result, in terms of fashion and style, was an interestingly indeterminate conflation of gentry and bohemian. If Keir Hardie scandalized

[19] Beatrice Webb, *My Apprenticeship* (Harmondsworth: Penguin, 1935), started a vogue for family-based prosography unique in Europe, although Kate Chorley, *Manchester Made Them* (London: Faber & Faber, 1950), another convert from individualist Liberalism to socialism, is subtler. The biographical information on the next two pages is derived from a wide range of sources; for the sake of conciseness, nearly all these can be accessed in the *Oxford DNB* (2005).

[20] James Bridie, *One Way of Living* (London: Constable, 1939), 113.

[21] J. A. Schumpeter, *Capitalism, Socialism and Democracy* (London: Allen and Unwin, 1942), 290–1.

[22] Noel Annan, 'The Intellectual Aristocracy', in J. H. Plumb, ed., *Studies in Social History* (London: Longman, 1955).

the Commons in 1893 by turning up in a tweed suit, ulster, and cap, this get-up was little different from that of a duke on his estate, or an artist sketching a Cornish harbour—or indeed Lloyd George as the caped crusader of Gwynedd, 'looking like someone the Romans were after'.

Generated and employed by all these groups was what Friedrich Engels had in the 1850s called the *avocati*, the idea-brokers and journalists whom they bankrolled. Their own motivations were a mixture of idealism, ambition, and survival: what we would now call networking. John Buchan (1875–1940) was a Tory-imperialist version, always canny enough to keep open his links to 'the other side'; Thomas Jones was his Labour-Nonconformist opposite number (and later on, in gloomier days, collaborator in the Pilgrim Trust). The two were united by education at Glasgow University, penetrated by the Balliol reformism of Edward Caird, and regaining the sort of role it had exercised under Francis Hutcheson and Adam Smith in the 'Scottish enlightenment'. The name itself was coined in the 1890s by another Ulsterman, the economist Professor W. R. Scott; Glasgow's leading philosopher in the 1900s was the Welsh Liberal Henry Jones.[23]

Education and the arts also provided a very effective method of mobilizing middle-class women. The arc was remote from the decorative, subservient role their sisters were expected to fulfil at Court, the cathedral close, or north Oxford—and perhaps also from the aggressive suffragette campaign which was its reflex. The anti-suffrage campaign of Sir James Knowles in *The Nineteenth Century* in 1889 had mainly been supported from the south-east. The western coast was much more woman-friendly. One Scottish engineer's wife, Marion Reid, had revived literary feminism with *A Plea for Woman* in 1843, and another, Margaret Elder, widow of the Clydeside pioneer of high-pressure steam, not only continued to run his shipyard, but poured funds into the education of women in the west of Scotland. Of other educational pioneers Blanche Clough was in origin Liverpool Welsh, and her influence extended into the organization of the first state secondary schools erected under the Welsh Intermediate Education Act of 1887. Liverpool capital also produced the likes of Eleanor Rathbone and Beatrice Webb, and there was an energetic Manchester organization around Lydia Becker, the Pankhursts, and Ellen Wilkinson. By the 1900s, it was even extending to Ireland, where southern Protestant women had always been as active as their Catholic sisters were downtrodden. Both the Gore-Booth girls of Lissadell, near Sligo, went Left, but while Constance became an Irish nationalist her sister Eva went to organize women's trade unionism in Lancashire: 'A Helen of social welfare dream, | Climb on a wagonette to scream' commented Yeats, sourly.[24] But he and the Abbey Theatre were bankrolled by the Quaker Annie Horniman, who went on to fund after 1908 the 'Lancashire Renaissance' at Manchester's Gaiety Theatre, just

---

[23] See E. L. Ellis, *TJ: A Life of Dr Thomas Jones* (Cardiff: University of Wales Press, 1992), 54–131.

[24] Sean O'Faolain, *Constance Markiewicz*, 1934 (London: Cresset, 1987), 22–5. Linked to this seems to have been at least a tolerance of single-sex unions: the ladies of Llangollen, Somerville, and Ross, Eva Gore-Booth and Esther Roper, Eleanor Rathbone and Elizabeth Macadam; given ideological form by the Whitmanite Edward Carpenter in his 'intermediate sex' pamphlets of 1894–5.

as the Cheshire-born Harriet Weaver, editor of *The Egoist*, would after 1913 subsidize James Joyce.

A regional Britain had to be integrated and sustained in an otherwise artificial nationalism: arc had to be bound to core. This was the role of the press lords, themselves almost to a man from the west, like many of their journalists. Robert Donald and Hugh Dalziel of the *Daily News* were Scots, like James Riddell of the *Chronicle*; the Harmsworth brothers of the *Daily Mail* were Dublin Protestants; the Berry brothers, who ran the *Telegraph*, were from Methyr Tydfil. Beaverbrook of the *Daily Express* had like Bonar Law, his protégé, drifted in from the Canadian Maritimes, a region which, with the improvement of St Lawrence Seaway, was now past its economic prime. J. L. Garvin of *The Times* wasn't simply an Irishman, but a Catholic who had started life as a Home Ruler.[25] Literary flair and opportunism counted more than wealth or business prestige, something lost on Balliol-bred Asquith but not on his Welsh Chancellor.

E. M. Forster in *Howards End* (1910) distinguished between the City-based Wilcoxes in their world 'of telegrams and anger' and the intellectual Schlegels; he was echoed by Michael Frayn fifty years later and his 'carnivores and herbivores'.[26] But how helpful is the distinction? Bloomsbury was always uncomfortably conscious of the proximity of Wells's 'Bladesover': the official metropolitan life of court, parliament, law, and the City: bland and well-spoken but nervous and vengeful. On the littoral industrial politics could obviate telegrams by experimentation, consultation— and distance. Schemes of 'scientific management' were competitors with the welfarism that produced Sir William Lever's Port Sunlight or the conciliatory industrial politics of Brunner Mond at their Cheshire chemical works. There was similar 'enlightenment' in Scotland: the Liberal shipbuilders Dennys of Dunbarton, the Birkmyres of the Greenock Ropework Company, successors of Robert Owen at New Lanark, who subsidized Keir Hardie. A Renfrewshire tannery sustained the progressive educationalist Robert Muirhead and his brother the Scottish nationalist Roland, both Fabians and Young Scots. The brothers Principal John Caird and Edward Caird, Master of Balliol, were sons of a Greenock shipbuilder. The Allans of the shipping line were the 'socialist millionaires', treasurers of the Glasgow ILP. With liner-route consolidation in the 1900s this cosmopolitanism reached as far as the efforts of Jewish shipping magnates such as Sir Ernest Cassel and the Hamburg–Amerika line's Alfred Ballin to promote Anglo-German cooperation on the main Atlantic routes, and pacific policies in general, in which they were joined by the likes of Lord Pirrie, boss of Harland and Wolff, Lord Haldane, and the Glasgow coal shipper Sir Daniel Macaulay Stevenson, of the famous engineering-art critic-literary family.[27]

---

[25] Piers Brendon, *The Life and Death of the Press Barons* (London: Secker & Warburg, 1982), 108–25.

[26] E. M. Forster, *Howards End*, chap. 4; Michael Frayn, 'Festival', in Michael Sissons and Philip French, *The Age of Austerity* (Harmondsworth: Penguin, 1964), 331.

[27] See the description of the Manchester electrical magnate Sir William Mather in Chorley, *Manchester Made Them*, chap. 5, and the contrast between his benevolence and a more apprehensive younger generation.

Cosmopolitanism was necessary to an order which required joint-stock company organization, patent acquisition, and foreign trade representation or branch-plant manufacture. Its owners holidayed elsewhere on the littoral or on the Continent—the 1900s were boom years for Italian resorts—but tended to settle off the fashionable track, calculating on health and cost: they wanted money for investment, not show, and the express train, motor car (which gets its first onstage role in *John Bull*; an aircraft is similarly premiered in *Misalliance* (1911)), motor yacht, and telephone facilitated such dispersal. Sir Denis Forman, later the boss of Granada TV, recollected how, before World War I, his father, a Liverpool merchant, could leave that city at 4.15 and dine at his mansion near Moffat before eight.[28]

So they peopled resorts on the Clyde estuary, in Ulster, or in west Wales. The last became an outlier to industrial Lancashire, replicating to some extent the life of the Lakes in the Victorian period (Wordsworth, Coleridge, Arnold, Ruskin) but further from the anglophone mainstream, with linkages which missed out on Oxbridge and London, and replaced hunting and shooting with climbing, hillwalking, sailing—and golf. The fringes of Lloyd George's Criccieth—to take just one habitat—found the Great Central Railway Chairman Sir Edward Watkin at Rhydd Dhu under Snowdon, not far from Mrs Gaskell's kin the Hollands, Lancashire cotton masters turned Welsh slate and railway owners. Twenty miles south, at Harlech, Thomas Davison of Eastman Kodak, patron of Glasgow's Sir J. J. Burnet, had another Glaswegian architect George Walton (brother of the 'Glasgow Boy' E. A. Walton) build his mansion, later followed by a golfing hotel. Just to the north was the summer home of Alfred Percival Graves, author and Gaelic revivalist, married to a daughter of the great Leopold von Ranke. T. E. Lawrence had been born to a Scots-Irish family at nearby Tremadog. Clough Williams-Ellis, descended from the Williamses of Parys Mountain, also holidayed locally, and would later settle at Portmeirion. When in 1910 David Davies rebuilt Owain Glyndwr's Parliament House at Machynlleth, he commissioned murals from his friend the Scottish artist Murray Urquhart, of the cosmopolitan Scots-Catholic family. This was a society—experimental, artistic, quasi-nationalist, radical—quite different from that of the outer suburbs of London and the Surrey hills, miniatures of Bladesover peopled by MPs, civil servants, editors, and financiers, where the once-cosmopolitan Kipling communed with his rediscovered rural England.[29]

A notable example of the hybridity of this elite was D. A. Thomas, Lord Rhondda, boss of the Cambrian Combine. Thomas represented economic rationality, not unlike Gerald Crich in D. H. Lawrence's *Women in Love* (1921); he was also related by marriage with the tinplate magnates, the Vivians, to Douglas Haig. Yet he used some of his funds to bankroll Keir Hardie as his fellow MP for Merthyr Tydfil, his wife was a prominent feminist, and his daughter Margaret Haig Thomas, a central

---

[28] Denis Forman, *Son of Adam* (London: Deutsch, 1990), 37; two classic narratives of this itinerary were R. B. Cunninghame Graham's short story 'Beattock for Moffat' (1900) and Richard Hannay's flight from London in John Buchan's *The Thirty-Nine Steps*, 1915 (Oxford: Oxford University Press, 1993).

[29] As well as the *Oxford DNB*, see Richard Perceval Graves, *Richard Hughes* (London: Deutsch, 1994) and Peter Lord, *The Visual Culture of Wales*, ii: *Imaging the Nation* (Cardiff: University of Wales Press, 2000), 336.

figure on the Cambrian board, founded the feminist weekly *Time and Tide* in 1920. In 1917 Lloyd George would make him head of the Local Government Board. Tom Jones, Lloyd George's confidant, stuck with his ILP past and would never trust a coalowner, but Rhondda proved outstanding, and went to win further laurels as Food Controller: the original of Arnold Bennett's *Lord Raingo*, the symbol of the 'men of push and go'.[30]

## III   THE ROAD TO ROSSCULLEN

On to this huge and complex panorama, enter village politics in the west of Ireland. Although its sense of local identity is strong—Yeats wrote that it was 'the first of Shaw's plays that had a geography'—*John Bull* dealt with a country that its author had quit with relief over a quarter of a century earlier.[31] Shaw's own Irish experience is certainly present: work as a land agent, long holidays at Killiney, south of Dublin, a youthful love affair. More than anything, perhaps, the character of Larry Doyle personifies Shaw's escape from the tensions and traumas of his family life, and their Irish converse—'the torturing, heartscalding, never satisfying, dreaming, dreaming, dreaming, dreaming!'—into the self-discipline of the autodidact social engineer.

Another influence must have been his reawakening of interest in Ireland through marriage to a wealthy Irish heiress, Charlotte Payne-Townsend, in 1897. The Payne-Townsend estate was at Rosscarbery, County Cork, whose similarities to the fictional Rosscullen—size, landscape, distance from a railhead—seem considerable. In November 1896 he wrote to her, much in the style of Doyle, that 'all Ireland's failures have been due to her incapacity for believing in success or happiness—for talking like Lefanu whilst Irishmen are going out into all lands and putting them on as a shepherd putteth on his garment'.[32] Three years later came the foundation of the Irish Literary Theatre by Yeats, George Moore, Edward Martyn, and Lady Gregory. An alternative to the folklorism of the Gaelic League, this was urban-based, and the Catholics Martyn and Moore wanted to make it Ibsenite and realist. Shaw belonged, at first glance, to their side. He was already minded to write an Irish play. In 1900 Yeats reported to Lady Gregory:

I saw Shaw today. He talks of a play on the contrast between Irish and English character which sounds amusing. He came to the 'Three Kings' on Saturday. I replied to a speech of his and pleased the Fellowship very much by proving that Shaw's point of view belonged to a bygone generation—to the scientific epoch—and was now 'reactionary'. He has never been called reactionary before. He was not in very good form however.[33]

Yeats was perceptive in identifying the limitations of Shaw's rationalism, but wrong to dismiss his adaptability. In the 1890s Shaw had discovered, or created,

---

[30]  See Chapter 9.

[31]  Hesketh Pearson, *Bernard Shaw*, 1942 (London: Allen and Unwin, 1987), 246.

[32]  Shaw to Charlotte Payne-Townshend, 4 Nov. 1896, in *Bernard Shaw: Collected Letters, 1874–1897*, ed. Dan H. Laurence (London: Max Reinhardt, 1965), 691.

[33]  W. B. Yeats to Lady Gregory, 12 Mar. 1900, in W. B. Yeats, *Letters*, ed. Alan Wade (London: Hart Davis, 1954), 335.

a social-democratic Ibsen and a social-democratic Wagner, much to the benefit of an English stage hitherto confined to the Savoy operas, the melodramas of Boucicault, the simplicities and prejudices of Pinero, and the 'well-made play' which cast its shadow even over Wilde. But he was also alert to the qualities in his masters which could not be fitted into a political conspectus: the white horses of the Rosmers, the powerful sexuality (never one of Shaw's strong points) of *Tristan und Isolde*.

And that remarkable familiarity with unvisited post-Parnellite Ireland? Shrewd, Kailyardish observers such as George A. Birmingham were in fact creatures of the later Edwardian period. Shaw had anticipated them. One clue might be a reference which appears in the preface to *Major Barbara* to the unusual source—by Shaw's standards—of Charles Lever, the high-Tory projector of appealing stage Irishmen. Shaw took after the later, more nationalistic Lever of *Lord Kilgobbin* (1872), where the Irish paralysis drives all the novel's more active characters away. Joe Atlee, modernizer and nationalist, comes rather close to that of Larry Doyle. Broadbent might be Conan Doyle's Dr Watson; Stanley Weintraub has suggested young Winston Churchill; but he might also be Lever's friend Anthony Trollope, another big, booming and apparently insensitive Englishman, who said he loved the Irish and gave them their postal system—though he certainly stopped short of Home Rule.[34]

Ibsen is of course present, and that setting of small Norwegian seaports which he made municipal and universal. Shaw realized the limitations of Ibsen qua social democrat, the fact that the Norwegian prophet was more interested in moral dilemmas and their impact on his characters and their autonomy than in social solutions. Peer Gynt's encounter with the Boyg—his quest for the heart of the onion—was also present. Broadbent could be an extended version of the caricature figures whom Peer encounters on his travels. If Rosscullen is the Gudbrandsdal, and Nora the faithful Solveig, then Doyle and Keegan are a sort of composite Gynt: the first the practical opportunist, the second the visionary and fantasist. Shaw, in fact, burrows deeply in *John Bull* into early and late Ibsen, both of which are remarkably sensitive to the over-stressed and irrational: Pastor Brand and Master Builder Solness itch to get at their ice-cathedrals or spires. To go back to early Ibsen is also to go back to the fairy-tale epics on which he drew, such as Wilhelm Hauff's 'The Cold Heart' (1827), in which a young Black Forest woodcutter sells his soul to 'the Dutchman', a timber rafter, and is rewarded with wealth screwed from the misery of those around him. How much was this more disturbing element apparent in *John Bull's Other Island*, a play seemingly convinced of the invincibility of capitalist rationalism?[35]

In an 1888 address to the British Association, Shaw propagated Fabian gradualism, but ended with a plea for the socialist idealists who were not prepared to wait for evolution to take its course, but wanted to smash the entire system. His own version

---

[34] See Christopher Harvie, *The Centre of Things: Political Fiction in Britain from Disraeli to the Present* (London: Unwin Hyman, 1991), 102 ff.; Shaw, preface to *Major Barbara* (London: Constable, 1907), 150, and see Owen Dudley Edwards, 'Trollope the Irish Writer', *Nineteenth Century Fiction*, 38 (1983–4), 3.

[35] Wilhelm Hauff, *Das kalte Herz* dates from 1824; my guess derives from general similarities of the plots, but it was widely available throughout Europe and was translated into English as *Heart of Stone* in 1844.

of the 'thin crust' was never wholly overlaid.[36] The challenge could come from the Right as well as the Left. The pacific atmosphere surrounding *John Bull*'s premiere was misleading. In 1904 the Unionists under Arthur Balfour, who had first made his reputation as Irish Chief Secretary in 1887–92, had been in power for nearly two decades, but were in severe trouble through a split over economic policy between free traders and protectionists. The Balfourian process of 'killing home rule with kindness' had ended by corrupting its Unionist authors. Under the secretaryship of George Wyndham, an English literary landowner who was a patron of Morris and Company and Philip Webb, the socialist architect, the Ashbourne Land Act was passed in 1903, virtually establishing peasant proprietorship. In 1904 the Irish Permanent Secretary, Sir Antony MacDonell, convinced himself that he had persuaded Wyndham to agree to discussions on a measure of political devolution, but this initiative was frustrated by a furious Unionist reaction, and Wyndham resigned in March 1905.[37]

This would certainly have registered on Shaw, had *John Bull's Other Island* been written a year later: evidence that Unionist resistance to Home Rule (even when attained through consensus among British parties and between them and moderate Irish nationalists) could be inflamed into mania. Throughout the summer of 1904, as Shaw worked on his script, provisionally entitled *Rule Britannia*, in a series of uncomfortable Scottish hotels, he had political goals in mind. 'It would be very bad business to produce *Rule Britannia* before parliament meets again,' he wrote to Granville-Barker, 'You will sell a lot of stalls to the political people, and the Irish MPs will fill the pit'.[38]

Shaw underestimated the risk of a Unionist reaction, although a section in his preface, on the Denshawi incident in Egypt, in which natives were hanged for a minor assault on British occupying forces, showed that he knew the potential for dumb authoritarianism latent within even that element of the British elite who dined with the Sidney Webbs. Otherwise, he was remarkably foresighted. His characters embody the future of politics in the Free State and the Republic. Barney Doran, Rosscullen's entrepreneur, would be a serviceable Fianna Fáil TD, the shrewd, forceful Father Dempsey a bishop by the 1920s. Larry Doyles, with degrees in business studies and information technology, were still leaving Rosscullen in droves up to the 1980s. But Keegan would have stalked through the Post Office . . .

There are two main problems with a formidably intelligent play: one intellectual and the other ostensibly dramatic. The first is Shaw's shaky understanding of what makes social groups cohere, a facility which was, by contrast, always to hand in Ibsen. Shaw certainly drew on some aspects of the Scottish enlightenment, William Robertson and Adam Smith mediated through Carlyle and Marx, but his peculiar social situation, in lower-class-ascendancy Dublin, was one where the claims of

---

[36] Bernard Shaw, 'The Transition to Social Democracy', address to the British Association, Bath, Sept. 1888, in R. L. Smyth, ed., *Essays in the Economics of Socialism and Capitalism* (London: Duckworth, 1964), 38–64.

[37] See the present writer's *The Centre of Things*, 138–53; Roy Foster, *Modern Ireland* (London: Allen Lane, 1988), 434–5.

[38] Shaw to Granville-Barker, 20 Aug. 1904, in *Shaw's Letters to Granville-Barker*, 25.

society were limited.[39] Shavian religion tended to be either comic-commonplace or utopian-mystical. Broadbent's final confrontation with Keegan is, in these terms, a brilliant juxtaposition:

> BROADBENT (reflectively) Once, when I was a small kid, I dreamt I was in heaven. (They both stare at him). It was some sort of pale blue satin place, with all the pious old ladies in our congregation sitting as if they were at a service; and there was some awful person in the study at the other side of the hall. I didn't enjoy it, you know. What is it like in your dreams?
>
> KEEGAN In my dreams it is a country in which the State is the Church and the Church the people: three in one and one in three. It is a commonwealth in which work is play and play is life: three in one and one in three. It is a temple in which the priest is the worshipper and the worshipper the worshipped: three in one and one in three. It is a godhead in which all life is human and all humanity divine: three in one and one in three. It is, in short, the dream of a madman.[40]

The Broadbent bit of the dialogue comes directly from Shaw's experience of 'plantation nonconformity'. The Keegan bit is pretty certainly Ruskin, a presence in young Shaw's Killiney, with his tragic and fruitless love for Rose La Touche of Greystones. What both lack—although it's more present in *John Bull's Other Island* than in almost any other play of Shaw—is a sense of the 'moulding' qualities of the political community.

The second problem was the weakness of *John Bull*'s women. Shaw's 'matter of Britain' play *Heartbreak House* (1913–16) has three important female roles; *John Bull* has only Nora. Shaw wanted Barker to cast a strong actress in the part, but what could Ellen Terry, say, have made of this?

A slight, weak woman in a pretty muslin print gown (her best) . . . For Tom Broadbent, therefore, an attractive woman, whom he would call ethereal. To Larry Doyle, an everyday woman fit only for the eighteenth century, an invalid without the excuse of disease, an incarnation of everything in Ireland that drove him out of it.[41]

Nora had to be for didactic reasons the antipode of Kathleen ni Houlihan, but she therefore came all too close to the real wraiths of Irish Catholic womanhood: a near-nonentity, tragic only in the last moments, when she has been totally, hopelessly, trapped by Broadbent. Shaw suggests vaguely that she might be improved by life in London, and maybe, *Pygmalion*-like, some such transformation might have worked. More likely she would have been driven to an early grave by obstreperous Broadbent kids.

Why was this? Ireland wasn't lacking in forceful female characters—Maria Edgeworth, Lola Montez, 'Speranza' Wilde (mother of Oscar), Lady Gregory herself. One thinks of Charlotte Mullen in Somerville and Ross's *The Real Charlotte* (1894), a figure located in a Rosscullen-like environment but whose obsession with and

---

[39] Michael Holroyd, *Bernard Shaw*, ii: *The Pursuit of Power* (London: Chatto and Windus, 1989), 85.

[40] Shaw, *John Bull's Other Island*, 116.

[41] Ibid. 33; and see Shaw to Granville-Barker, 18 Sept. 1904, in *Shaw's Letters to Granville-Barker*, 30.

entrapment by a declining landed family ends psychopathic. Perhaps Shaw flinched from portraying relationships which came too close to his own family, for that matter to his own marriage. Or perhaps the sheer invisibility of Irish Catholic women meant that, for all the country's theatrical genius, it was impossible to portray them. Although Joyce's Molly Ivens in 'The Dead', written in 1906, credibly represents the new nationalist generation, his stab at Ibsenite drama in *Exiles* (1914) was unperformable.

*Heartbreak House*, started pre-war and finished post-war, benefited from Shaw providing much greater initiatives for his female characters, but the result is indulgent writing for actresses whom Shaw flirted with in that bloodless way of his, while Captain Shotover, meant to be England's Father Keegan, punctuates the action with his apocalyptic rantings, rather than forcing it along like the madman of Rosscullen. Shotover is elemental with the sea as symbol of England, but somehow stranded by the tidal wave of war in Bladesover country. Shaw seems—in the circumstances, understandably—to fumble the reality of the 'English character', before the *deus ex machina* of a Zeppelin raid ends the play.

## IV   EARTHQUAKE

A year after *John Bull*, Shaw's *Major Barbara* achieved an even greater success, its theme apparently far from any Irish pastorale: the clash of religious idealism and the military-industrial complex. This ominously volcanic comedy, juggling rearmament and destruction, was launched on 28 November, only a month after the monstrous HMS *Dreadnought* was laid down, which could sink any ship in the world. The creation of an equally volcanic playwright, the eponymous heroine finds herself checkmated by the unflappable cynicism of her father, funding William Booth's crusade out of his gun-and-warship profits. In her despair Barbara relates how, when she was a child, an earthquake at Cannes had shattered her security: '. . . how little the first shock mattered compared to the dread and horror of waiting for the second? That is how I feel in this place today. I stood on the rock I thought eternal; and without a word of warning it reeled and crumbled under me'.[42]

Carlyle's 'thin crust' again; but in Shaw's hands it now became part of a complex dialectic between rational reform and darker human dispositions. Shaw's creation was dragging the playwright after him. He wrote to the actor Louis Calvert, down to play Undershaft, 'The part of the millionaire cannon-founder is becoming more and more formidable. Broadbent and Keegan rolled into one, with Mephistopheles thrown in . . . Undershaft is diabolically subtle, gentle, self-possessed, powerful, stupendous . . .'.[43] In 1901 at the *Manchester Guardian* J. A. Hobson had related imperial expansion to domestic social inequality and under-consumption, which caused the drive for profit to balloon into international speculation. In 1903 Erskine

---

[42]  *Major Barbara*, Act III.
[43]  Holroyd, *Bernard Shaw*, i, 100 ff.

Childers had raised the spectre of German invasion in *The Riddle of the Sands*. Only days before *John Bull* opened, the Russian Baltic fleet, lumbering towards the Far East and the war with Japan, opened fire on Hull steam drifters off the Dogger Bank, believing them to be enemy torpedo boats. This was to be the prelude to a vertiginous series of crises, partly socio-industrial, partly diplomatic, which undermined the bipartisanship of the politicians in the Court Theatre stalls. In December 1904 the same Russian warships would be annihilated at Tsushima by a Japanese fleet (largely built on the Tyne). Japan had been an ally of the UK since January 1902; in April 1904 an entente was concluded with France, drawing the country yet closer to the European alliances. This remote war detonated revolution in Russia, beginning on 22 January 1905 and lasting all year.[44]

The crisis foregrounded the port-centred bourgeoisie, crucial to both British *and* German politics, both because the struggle for markets and raw material was basic to Atlantic capitalism and also because of a looming domestic confrontation in both countries: the struggle for the levers of constitutional power.[45] The monarchic German constitution was threatened by the rise of the Social Democrats (SPD) in the one-man-one-vote Reichstag, and by the authoritarian leanings of the military. This was inhibited—though less and less convincingly—by the blocking power of Prussia in the upper house or Bundesrat through the three-class franchise of the Prussian Diet, which frustrated any possible proletarian majority. In Britain the post-1905 crisis was somewhat similar. Joseph Chamberlain's crusade for Tariff Reform, a somewhat analogous strategy to that of the German National Liberals, wrecked the Tory Party before he was felled by a stroke. The Conservatives now turned to the Lords, where the constitution had allowed the now-archaic landed class to maintain its control through a Whig–Tory alliance. The upper house was now a Court and London oligarchy, electoral and local government reform having eroded its regional dominance.[46]

The Lords felled Gladstone over Irish Home Rule in 1893. They upheld conservative legal judgments against the trade unions, impelling the 1903 MacDonald–Gladstone pact, by which the Liberals stage-managed Labour's entry into the Commons in 1906. The political structure remained skewed against working-class political rights, with only half the adult male population qualified to vote and ill-distributed constituencies. If religious bias in Liverpool and west central Scotland is added, the result was highly undemocratic. But it kept a rural Liberalism in existence and also enhanced a devolutionary politics, not just in proposals for 'Home Rule all round' but in elective county government (1888 in England, 1894 in Scotland, and 1896 in Ireland) and after 1908 in the effective government of Ireland by the

---

[44] At Tsushima nearly 4,400 Russian sailors died, compared with 170 Japanese, so defeat could mean annihilation. Armoured ships, once holed, sank like stones, further increasing the apprehensions of the admirals. See <www.wikipedia article: battle of tsushima>.

[45] Volker Berghahn, *Germany and the Approach of War* (London: Macmillan, 1973), 9–15.

[46] This was reinforced by the limited number of Scots representative peers elected per parliament (16), and Irish representative peers elected for life (28), along with 71 Irish peers with English titles. These were too few to form regional groupings, although the Irish Viceroy and the Scottish Secretary had usually been peers.

National Party under John Redmond, cooperating closely with the Liberal Chief Secretary Augustine Birrell, Liverpool-born but of Scottish descent.[47] Would a restruc-
turing of British polity be necessary in a genuine democracy? Was county government
a permanent or merely experimental tier? Was Ireland exceptional in loathing British
rule, or could Home Rule propel a general regionalization of British politics?

In Germany the National Liberals, mediating between an aristocracy increasingly
militarized as agriculture declined, had hoped to collar the urban bourgeoisie as its
allies, through the Tirpitz programme for a big fleet (1899), enthusiastically backed
by Wilhelm II. It was a gamble, and by 1911 it was sinking, since the few port
cities—Bremen, Lübeck, Hamburg—were a weak base. In Britain, however, naval
arsenals and the steel industry had traditionally looked to the Tories. Here the whole
potential of the west coast clicked menacingly together. In October 1905, only eight
years after Parson's' tiny *Turbinia* had stirred up the Diamond Jubilee Review, the
*Dreadnought* was laid down at Devonport dockyard; a year later she took to sea.
Mounting twelve 11-inch guns (previous battleships had four) and turbine-powered
at 21 knots, she instantly made the UK's 100 other battleships obsolete, at a blow
putting the country on all fours with her competitors.

In December 1905 Conservative rule, which had lasted a generation, ended. The
January 1906 election was a Liberal landslide. Balfour equated it with the Russian Revolution, the anti-clerical triumph in France, the gains of the German SPD.
Nevertheless, the 'Cawdor Programme' of his First Lord, a great Scots and Welsh
landowner, would be carried on by the Liberals, partly because of the catastrophic
international depression which caused a fall in shipping orders between 1907 and
1909. This had by 1914 resulted in a fleet of twenty-nine Dreadnoughts (plus
thirteen building), the most recent mounting 15-inch guns, which left the ships
of 1906 obsolescent. Germany had, under the Tirpitz plan, eighteen (with nine
building).[48]

Britain's army of 160,000 men and a small reserve, with minimal artillery and
machine-gun cover, was a tenth of Germany's wartime strength. If it were to invade,
Bismarck quipped, 'I would send a policeman and have it arrested.' The invasion pan-
ics of the sensationalist press before the war were essentially about home defence, not
a full-scale European war, and in 1913, when 'military conversations' with France
were under way, no one anticipated what trench-based 'attrition' would be like, any
more than the provincial, progressive bourgeoisie reckoned just how unstable its
social and political foundations were. Yet there was a growing fear of Armageddon.
Erskine Childers's *Riddle of the Sands* came from a public servant whose sympathies
lay on the Whiggish left. His great-uncle Hugh had been Gladstone's Chancellor; Erskine ancestors had patronized Burns, been romantic Scottish nationalists
and later *Edinburgh Review* Whigs. The maternal Bartons, Wicklow landowners,

---

[47] See León Ó Broin, *The Chief Secretary: Augustine Birrell in Ireland* (London: Chatto and
Windus, 1969), Clarke, *Lancashire and the New Liberalism*, Chap 9, 'Men of Light and Learning',
is particularly illuminating about this milieu.
[48] For the naval component of marine construction, see the table in A. W. Kirkaldy, *British
Shipping: Its History, Organisation and Importance* (London: Kegan Paul, 1914).

were radicals and Parnellites. Erskine's wife was American. Childers admired the Germans, and *The Riddle* is a grand yachting novel, but as salient as the sandbanks of the Wattenmeer is the Hobsonian notion that European capitalist dysfunction could force its masters into military expansion.[49]

## V    PASSIONATE DREAMING

Rosscullen might seem remote from all this, though Shaw's feel for a west Ireland, visited only in youth, is unerring. *John Bull* has the texture of a great Jack Yeats painting—tumbling together people, weather, land, legend—in Doyle's passionate declaration of love and hate:

Here, if the life is dull, you can be dull too, and no great harm done. (Going off into a passionate dream.) But your wits cant thicken in that soft moist air, on those white springy roads, in those misty rushes and brown bogs, on those hillsides of granite rocks and magenta heather. Youve no such colors in the sky, no such lure in the distances, no such sadness in the evenings.[50]

Yet Rosscullen stood on a technological frontier. In 1901 another young engineer, half-Irish, Guglielmo Marconi, whose mother was from nearby Limerick, transmitted successfully across the Atlantic from the headland of Poldhu in Cornwall. In 1912 his radio telegraphy system was chosen for an Empire-wide network, with a government participation in Britain which would bring the reputation of Lloyd George into peril. By 1914 its masts would loom over the Rosscullen-like village of Clifden in County Galway. Five years later Alcock and Brown's Vimy bomber nosedived into the nearby Derrygimlagh bog, sixteen and a half hours out from Newfoundland, beginning a process which in fifty years would sink the Atlantic ferry.

Doyle was the Childers sort: wanting to bring Rosscullen within three hours of Colchester, and New York within twenty-four hours of London (Childers's *Riddle of the Sands* predicted that Colchester (more or less) would be where the Germans would invade). And what are he and Broadbent actually doing? Promoting a premature 'heritage industry', speculating in real estate in a low-wage economy. This could be a post-industrial play about an overweight, overstuffed society dissipating its wealth, en route to the England—owned by the multinational Breakages Limited, making chocolate creams for the American market—in *The Apple Cart* over thirty years later. So, if Broadbent and Doyle are a political metaphor of the Anglo-Irish union: then, for good or ill, Broadbent, in Michael Holroyd's words, 'brings to Ireland a terrible corruption of Shaw's belief in improvement; but he brings it cheerfully, expansively', annexes the Irish drive to material success which thrust itself from the ruins of the land struggle and Parnell's martyrdom.

There is a parallel here to another, darker work of the same year, Joseph Conrad's *Nostromo*, and the matter-of-fact Americans with their National Central Railroad

---

[49]  See Jim Ring, *Erskine Childers* (London: John Murray, 1996).
[50]  *John Bull's Other Island*, 18.

who arrive in South American Costaguana and tear through its romantic corruption and stasis. Shaw may have had foreknowledge of Conrad's novel. 'Don Roberto' Cunninghame-Graham, the mordant Scottish writer and radical—elements of whom turned up in Conrad's *fainéant* mine-owner Charles Gould—had been a friend since the mid 1880s, whom he, too, had used in *Captain Brassbound's Conversion* (1900).[51]

Doyle rejects cheerful expansiveness, but submits. He is cold, super-rational, lyrical: better at being an Englishman than Broadbent, but barred from success by thought and conscience: Hamlet rather than Fortinbras. But what might happen if Doyle takes on the determination of Broadbent, or if the Irish destroy Broadbent's self-confidence? There are elements of the first in Eamon de Valera, in his pilgrimage to nationalism, and of the second in the numskull reaction of the British military and politicians to the Rising in Dublin in 1916.

Peter Keegan is the centre of the play, and perhaps the most lyrical of all Shaw's characters, with speeches in the final act which swing between Shakespeare in their power and beauty and Beckettian nihilism, heightened by the sublime banalities of Broadbent.

> KEEGAN . . . It is a place where the hardest toil is a welcome refuge from the horror and tedium of pleasure, and where charity and good works are done only for hire to ransom the souls of the spoiler and the sybarite. Now, sir, there is only one place of horror and torment known to my religion; and that place is hell. Therefore it is plain to me that this earth of ours must be hell, as the Indian revealed to me—perhaps he was sent to reveal it to me—to expiate crimes committed by us in a former existence.
>
> AUNT JUDY (*awestruck*) Heaven save us, what a thing to say!
>
> CORNELIUS (*sighing*) Its a queer world: thats certain.
>
> BROADBENT. Your idea is a very clever one, Mr Keegan: really most brilliant: *I* should never have thought of it. But it seems to me—if I should say so—that you are overlooking the fact that, of the evils you describe, some are absolutely necessary for the preservation of society, and others are encouraged only when the Tories are in office.[52]

There are elements of Yeats's 'System' hovering around, but Keegan is autobiographical: Shaw as somewhat premature Prospero—not yet 50 when he wrote *John Bull*—but far from being in charge of events on his island. At the Court Theatre in these astonishing seasons he could invoke but not command. Keegan sees the creatures of Milan, or of the island itself, taking over, while his medieval learning, his sea of faith, has flooded back to overwhelm his reason. He is more than Irish: 'Father Peter' suggests the rock of the medieval papacy; the attempt to recover wholeness which had marked the Victorian sages—Newman, Carlyle, and Ruskin above all—on whom Shaw and his generation had fed, as well as Ibsen and Wagner: 'My wandering fit is on me . . . *He goes for his hat and stick*' might be Wotan exiling

---

[51] See Christopher Harvie, 'Industry, Identity and Chaos: Cunninghame Grahame and Patrick Geddes': Millennium Address to the National Museum of Scotland, 9 Dec. 1999, in *Scottish Affairs*, 32 (summer 2000).

[52] Shaw, *John Bull's Other Island*, 89–90.

himself from the flawed paradise of Valhalla. Keegan's final dismissal *and* co-option by Broadbent—'What a regular old Church-and-State Tory he is! Hes a character: he'll be an attraction here. Really almost equal to Ruskin and Carlyle'—shows the way the social critics' apocalyptic denunciations of industrialism and greed were apparently effortlessly digested by bourgeois liberalism.[53]

The result is what, writing about the same time, James Joyce would call paralysis, and 1904 was the year he followed Doyle's example and left Dublin. By 1910 he was in Trieste, sea port of the Austrian Empire, the friend of an Italian-German-Jewish entrepreneur-novelist who had made his fortune in marine paint. Ettore Schmitz, nom de plume Italo Svevo, supplied much of the character of Leopold Bloom in *Ulysses* (1922). Joyce had bought the Fabian vision: the would-be positive figures of *Dubliners* try to think of themselves as part of a European Left. In 1911 he returned, with the project of giving Ireland progress's *dernier cri*: the cinema. The Volta in Mary Street, Dublin, was Ireland's first picture house, and (being managed from Italy) perhaps the first transnational media concern. It didn't prosper, and the Joyce brothers sold out a year later at a loss.[54]

But Shaw would surely have approved. The tragedy is that he, with his bitter, intelligent nous about modernization, did not become 'the Old Man Eloquent to the new governing generation', but the embattled, aristocratic Yeats. Vatic incantations, as well as cold-blooded endorsements of murderous dictators, might have been avoided.

## VI 'ORDER THE GUNS AND KILL!'

Dictatorship was never very far away. Shaw's vertiginous vision is even more explicit in the 'Britishness' of *Major Barbara*, which he wrote in 1905—its premiere was in November—during another period of violent European upheaval. Barbara's religion, the fundamentalist evangelicalism of the Salvation Army, is cynically countered by the collectivist Fabianism of her father and (later) of her lover Adolphus Cusins. It may also reflect turmoil in Shaw's own political 'family', with H. G. Wells's idealistic descent on the Fabian Society. Where in *John Bull* Peter Keegan ends in a way triumphant—the Dublin GPO and de Valera's rural utopia latent in his great final rant—the arms king Andrew Undershaft is a quite different proposition. He represents a type of industrialist rare before the 1890s, but multiplying thereafter. Gustav Krupp and Sir William Armstrong of Newcastle provide prototypes, and the Andrew Carnegie who bankrolled Patrick Geddes's town-planning schemes out of the profits of United Steel. His warfare-welfare state forecast accurately the way in which society would evolve during the war.

The imagery of *Major Barbara* is emphatically English; a Broadbent-made society, with Lady Britomart, Undershaft's alienated wife, as one of those well-built Britannias from the *Punch* cartoons. It has absorbed the Victorian sages in

[53] This argument is specifically documented in J. L. Wisenthal, *Shaw's Sense of History* (Oxford: Clarendon Press, 1988), esp. 150–7.

[54] Richard Ellmann, *James Joyce* (New York: Oxford University Press, 1959), 310–22.

homeopathic doses, and it uses their lessons defensively. Not least it saw 1904–5, the Russo-Japanese War, the Dreadnought, and the Anglo-French entente as the writing on the wall for 'Little Englandism'. Despite the Liberal victory of 1906, there was a stressing of class conflict *and* an appeal to patriotism identified with Lloyd George and Winston Churchill. Against the playful, argumentative world of Rosscullen, Undershaft symbolized the ease with which armaments made politics move to the metropolis, taking the intellectuals with it, even under a party pledged to decentralize. Internationally, events were ominously accelerating. British academics who habitually stirred up European minorities during their vacations—A. V. Dicey and the Jews, John Westlake and the Finns, James Bryce and the Armenians, R. W. Seton-Watson and the Slavs—were finding that the multinational empires crumbled too swiftly. Cusins, a fictionalized Gilbert Murray, sees off his best student, pledged to fight for Balkan freedoms. He gives him a revolver, not in Broadbent's daft apprehension about Ireland, but in deadly earnest. Is it surprising that he will become the next Undershaft? Late in life, Shaw confessed he did not like at all where the last act was taking him.[55]

A more downright line came from Rudyard Kipling, sulking at the Liberal victory and writing ingenious but shop-talk-ridden parables of mechanistic, elite-driven, transatlantic utopias, with an undertow of determined class warfare, like 'As Easy as ABC' (1907), in which the Aerial Board of Control crosses the Atlantic by some sort of aircraft to suppress race conflict in Chicago.[56] Kipling's international civil servants are a dull BBC-governorish bunch, but the rioters' anthem 'McDonough's Song' seems to betray its author's intemperance:

> Whatsoever, for any cause,
> Seeketh to take or give
> Power above or beyond the Laws,
> Suffer it not to live!
> Holy State or Holy King—
> Or Holy People's Will—
> Have no truck with the senseless thing.
> Order the guns and kill!

Also in 1907, a year after another earthquake devastated San Francisco, John Griffith 'Jack' London published *The Iron Heel*. It was soon out in a cheap edition from Newnes and being serialized in the newly founded Glasgow socialist weekly *Forward*: a remarkable success for something close to unadulterated Marxism. *The Iron Heel* is not an ingratiating book. Set (implausibly) thousands of years in the future, it details how a socialist revolution in 1913 led by Ernest Everhard is ruthlessly suppressed by

---

[55] Pearson, *Bernard Shaw*, 1961 (London: Foursquare, 1964), 252. The revolver business really happened. Murray gave the gun to Noel Brailsford, the radical journalist and historian.

[56] See Christopher Harvie, 'The Sons of Martha: Technology, Transport and Rudyard Kipling', *Victorian Studies*, 20/3 (spring 1977), 269–82. The poem is in *A Choice of Kipling's Verse*, ed. T. S. Eliot (London: Faber, 1941), 268.

the eponymous Iron Heel, a corporatist alliance of business, government, and labour 'traitors' which captures Everhard and secretly executes him in its aftermath. If 'As Easy as ABC' is remote from the zest and sympathy of *Kim*, London's *Iron Heel* is wooden compared with his nature stories and his unsparing memoir of his alcoholism in *John Barleycorn* (1913). While America slides towards civil war, Everhard pops up every couple of chapters reeling off theory from *Capital*, which either converts people—like the 'author' of the account, his wife—or makes them want to murder him. London seems to sketch in greater detail the appallingly destructive civil wars which William Morris predicted in *News from Nowhere* (1891) would end class society in the West.

The intriguing thing is the rapidity with which this vision of conflict in America spread. This was fanned not only by the upheavals of 1905–6, but by the explosion of trade union militancy in Britain and Ireland, triggered by the slump of 1907–10. In 1910 another Irishman, 'Robert Tressell', wrote *The Ragged Trousered Philanthropists*. Robert Noonan, then a Hastings house painter, was in fact a member of the Anglo-Irish Croker family, folklorists and Tories, as much of the ascendancy as the Childers or Bartons. The charismatic revolutionary was being reborn, a late industrial version of General Ludd, Captain Swing, or Captain Moonlight, and such figures appeared in fact as well as in fiction.[57]

G. K. Chesterton's Adam Wayne in *The Napoleon of Notting Hill* (1906) recaptures romance and imagination through a bloodbath—and inspired the young Michael Collins as much as Undershaft's 'When you shoot, you pull down governments' had done.[58] There was a wave of high-risk-taking secular evangelists: Victor Grayson, 'Labour's lost leader', Jim Larkin, the fiery, theatrical, dockers' leader in Belfast and Dublin, John MacLean MA, the revolutionary teacher of the Clyde. An intellectual input came from the anarchist ideas wolfed down by the socialist movement, from Georges Sorel's philosophy of action, and from the rise of ultra-democratic and workers' control movements.[59] It was as if the 'blood and fire' of Chartist and Young Ireland radicalism of the 1840s, later transmuted into the vitalist religion of Moody and Sankey, Catholic revivalism, and the Salvation Army, had resumed the political crusade.

Patrick Geddes, whose historical-sociological masques made him part of the dramatic movement, was in Dublin in 1913 as the guest of the Viceroy, Lord Aberdeen. He was heartened by such stirrings, particularly by the literary and cooperative movements and the intellect and humanity of Jim Larkin, who had plunged the city into the dockers and tramwaymen's strike, yet also supported the Lane Art Gallery. Dublin he saw as the new geotechnic city, with its food-processing industries,

[57] Harvie, *The Centre of Things*, 136–7.
[58] This connection was made in the novel *The End of the Hunt* by Thomas Flanagan (New York: Warner Books, 1995), but given Flanagan's status as an authority on Irish literature, and the fact that his novel does everything an historical novel ought to do, I accept it.
[59] Logie Barrow and Ian Bullock, *Democratic Ideas and the British Labour Movement* (Cambridge: Cambrdige University Press, 1996), 246–304.

its bicycle factories, its slums to be recovered by conservative surgery, and its grand classical streets and squares to be reanimated, not least by its looming capital status. With his Boston colleague John Nolen, he and Lord Aberdeen persuaded the council to run a competition for a Dublin plan. The award went in 1916 to the young Liverpool Scot Patrick Abercrombie, but the outbreak of war on 4 August 1914 delayed the adjudication. When the plan became reality, in 1922, Ireland was no longer part of the United Kingdom.[60]

[60] Helen Meller, *Patrick Geddes: Social Evolutionist and City Planner* (London: Routledge, 1990).

# 9

# Men who Pushed and Went: West-Coast Capitalism, War, and Nationalism

The manufacturing resources at the disposal of the Allies are enormously greater than those which Germany or Austria can command . . . and the seas being free to them [they] can more easily obtain material. I do not believe that Great Britain has even yet done anything like what she can do in the matter of increasing her war equipment . . . All the engineering works of the country ought to be turned to the production of war material. The population ought to be prepared to suffer all sorts of deprivation and hardships whilst this process is going on.

David Lloyd George to the Cabinet, 22 February 1915[1]

'The lungs are engorged—congested with blood. At least, one of them is, in your case. The air has to make room for the blood, and so the lung is put partially out of action. This means that the part that isn't out of action has to work harder. That's why you're breathing quicker. And it's the heart that has to bear the strain. That's about all there is to it.'

Arnold Bennett, *Lord Raingo*, 1926[2]

## I  FRONTISM AND REMEMBRANCE

In September 1914, a month into war, the Norwegian tramp *Themis* sailed with 7,000 tons of iron ore from Nova Scotia to Rotterdam. There, the ore was transferred to Rhine barges and towed upriver to the blast furnaces of Duisberg and Essen, and cheques in settlement were mailed from the Rotterdam offices of RheinStahl and Krupp to Jacks and Company of Glasgow, the family iron-broking firm of Andrew Bonar Law, Leader of His Majesty's Opposition. Telegrams were intercepted by British intelligence, and six months later Jacks was prosecuted for trading with the enemy. The case was brought to trial in the Scottish High Court, and two directors were jailed, though Law's brother John, the firm's chairman, got off. Bonar Law, interviewed the following autumn as Colonial Secretary in the new Coalition—his Unionists had entered it only on condition that Lord Chancellor Haldane was ejected for

---

[1] Cab. 42/1/39, quoted in R. J. Q. Adams, *Arms and the Wizard* (London: Cassell, 1978), 21.
[2] (Leipzig: Tauchnitz, 1927), 285.

'pro-Germanism'—said that in the circumstances, he would have done the same as his brother.[3] Coming from a politician noted for inflammatory rhetoric, this seems extraordinary, yet it also emphasizes the leap involved in the transition to war, and the civil self-confidence that would respond to such a challenge. The legal team under John Clyde KC who defended the Jacks directors would shortly enforce 'dilution' on the Clyde engineering industry.

Jacks and Company *was* Germanophile; its founder, Dr William Jacks, a Scots Liberal MP who wrote about German culture and politics, had been honoured by Emperor William II, and had endowed the Chair in German at Glasgow University. Law, a Carlyle enthusiast, shared this culture—in this he differed from his friend Rudyard Kipling, who was vociferously pro-French—and his Unionist colleague in the Lloyd George War Cabinet after December 1916, and its effective coordinator, was Alfred Viscount Milner, the former imperial proconsul, educated in the gymnasia of the university towns of Göttingen and Tübingen. Both politicians would, with the 'Welsh home ruler and radical'—*Dod*'s description—David Lloyd George (once Milner's fiercest critic, during the Boer War), front Britain's resistance to 'the Hun'. Of Lloyd George's five-man Cabinet, Law was from New Brunswick, Arthur Henderson a Scots-born engineering trade unionist. Only the Marquess Curzon was an Englishman, English-born.[4]

Milner, raised a Balliol Liberal, became in 1886 a Unionist of the first hour, when Gladstone adopted Irish Home Rule. Law led the Ulster resistance which brought Ireland in July 1914 to the brink of civil war. They, and the businessmen whom they summoned into government, secured victory over a well-coordinated military-conservative regime, but they also helped destroy the political and economic balance which had sustained West Britain. Their contribution both promoted the climacteric of British power—never was the world map redder, or merchantman tonnage greater, than after 1918—and its rapid destruction.

On 23 October the *Clan Grant*, a day short of its destination of Madras, was intercepted by the German light cruiser *Emden*. Kapitän Karl von Müller, punctilious in observing the rules of engagement, allowed the passengers and crew, properly provisioned, to take to the boats, and then sent the liner to the bottom. With it went Patrick Geddes's 'Cities and Town Planning' exhibition, the apogee of the civic gospel which had matured along the Atlantic littoral, which he was sending to his friend Lord Pentland, Governor of Madras. Geddes apparently recovered; his Indian and Palestinian town planning ventures were still to come. But by 1916 his son Alastair was dead in France and his wife dying. Resilience was difficult for a

---

[3] Christopher Harvie, 'Scandal and the True-Blue Clyde', in *Travelling Scot* (Colintraive: Argyll, 1999), 100–8. This was based on the Bonar Law papers in the House of Lords library.

[4] An impression increased by Sir William Orpen's painting of Versailles, 1919, *The Signing of Peace in the Hall of Mirrors*. Twenty-six statesmen fill the central three bays. Twelve represent the Empire. Aside from the Indian, Canadian, and South African, four are Scots (Law, Balfour, Barnes, and Riddell), two Welsh (Lloyd George, Hughes). Only Hankey and Montagu could plausibly be claimed as English, though the first was Australian-born and the second Jewish. Orpen was an Irish nationalist, whose complex outlook was featured in an exhibition at the Imperial War Museum in 2005.

man in his sixties. Lewis Mumford, his American disciple, found him infuriatingly disorganized in the 1920s, quixotically trying to recreate a Scots college at Montpellier in France, although only months before he died, in 1932, Ramsay MacDonald gave him a knighthood. In the wake of 'war socialism' an altogether different sort of planning, dominated by airports, motorways, giant 'harmonica cities'—fascist, communist, New Deal, Modern Movement—was taking over.[5]

Against this an apparently untroubled English patriotism thrived. Stanley Baldwin would succeed Bonar Law as Tory premier in 1923, his 'steady as we go' the keynote of the inter-war establishment: a reaction to war's disruptions and to what he called, shudderingly, the 'dynamic force' of Lloyd George. Baldwin was a South Wales steelmaster, and Kipling's cousin on the MacDonald side, but presented himself as a Worcestershire yeoman. His famous monody 'On England'—'the sound of the scythe against the whetstone, the sight of a plough team coming over the brow of the hill'—could have been drafted by Buchan, who like Richard Hannay had gone as native in the Cotswolds as Kipling had in Sussex. Refugees from the collapsing democracies and 'hotel civilizations' of Europe—J. A. Schumpeter, Karl Popper, Nikolaus Pevsner, Geoffrey Elton—marvelled at the combination of intelligence and diplomacy, tradition and manoeuvre that this sort of thing represented. Yet the scars and doubts didn't heal.

A formal temple of memory existed in the war grave culture over which Kipling presided. The Western Front, and the fates settled there, became Gethsemane, a biblical metaphor for the isolation, betrayal, and martyrdom borne by the men of the trenches. This could be both a conservative and radical impulse. Kipling's terse epitaphs—

> *Common Form*
> If any question why we died
> Tell them, because our fathers lied.
>
> *Batteries out of Ammunition*
> If any mourn us in the workshop, say
> We died because the shift kept holiday.

—pointed the finger at organized labour, aliens, intellectuals. Yet his greatest contribution to war literature, *The Irish Guards in the Great War* (1923), was, for his biographer Charles Carrington, a belated act of contrition for his violent unionism in 1914, made to an Ireland now lost: another instance of the way Kipling's skill could transcend his prejudices. But it could not make the broken vessel appear whole, or explain 'Cousin Stan' as anything but 'lost to socialism'.[6]

A cognate alienation from the metropolis was 'frozen' in the literature and particularly the poetry of the war's victims. This would climax a decade after its close,

---

[5] Philip Boardman, *The Worlds of Patrick Geddes* (London: Routledge, 1978), 253; and Helen Meller, *Patrick Geddes: Social Evolutionist and City Planner* (London: Routledge, 1990), chap. 7.

[6] *A Choice of Kipling's Verse*, ed. T. S. Eliot (London: Faber, 1941), 164; and see Charles Carrington, *Rudyard Kipling*, 1955 (Harmondsworth: Penguin, 1970), 508–13, and 'War Graves', in *Encyclopaedia Britannica*, 12th edn.

when the work of such as Robert Graves, Siegfried Sassoon, R. H. Mottram, and R. C. Sheriff re-presented that of casualties like Wilfred Owen and Isaac Rosenberg. This pattern has been repeated in a torrent of recent interpretations: Pat Barker's *Regeneration* (1996) or Sebastian Faulks's *Birdsong* (1997), reinforced by the histories of Lynne MacDonald, Richard Holmes and Martin Middlebrook and the prolific Niall Ferguson's *The Pity of War* (1996).

This 'Western Front industry', with its postmodern imprint, has tended to overshadow the social interpretation of the war's effects on British society, which seemed two decades ago to have much more salience. The work of Arthur Marwick and Jay Winter in *The Deluge* (1965) or *The Great War and the British People* (1983), with its thesis of war-induced, state-driven home-front reform, placed the war in the context of the evolution of the mixed economy and the welfare state. After 1991 this seemed to become a dead end. Was this because the West had been war-free for nearly sixty years, disengaging social reform from military necessity? Or because its bloodless victory of 1989–91 cut down—through civilian 'progress': communications technology and classical economics—the great revolutionary product of the war, Soviet Communism?

As the state shrank, research retreated from the big themes—modernism, collectivism, and the formal literary canon—and became both imaginatively pluralistic, concentrating on the war's implications for women, say, or for the psychology of memory, or for local identity, and predictably market-driven. In the identity politics of analysing 'Britishness', the discourse still seemed to pass inexorably through the blood and mud of the trenches.[7] Hew Strachan's massive *The First World War*, truly global in its reach, may provide a new if darker synthesis, reflecting the tormented aftermath of 1989–91,[8] but Marwick–Winter's British home-front lay in the shadow of earlier collective, pacifist-inclined interpretations. A disaster had to be recovered from, made worthwhile. In 1939–45 this was the achievement of Britain's 'People's War', meaning the 'myth of the Blitz' rather than the front line. The global brutality of that conflict, with a death toll over three times greater than that of 1914–18, didn't obscure this; but tended instead to reinforce the 'never again' spirit: war as sacrifice. Benjamin Britten's *War Requiem*, with its use of Wilfred Owen's poems, inaugurated the new cathedral at Coventry in 1961. The bomb victims of Coventry and its German twin, Dresden, were commemorated by a soldier's poems about soldiers, an irony that no one remarked on.[9]

If Britishness was trench-trapped, Irishness lay on the road from the General Post Office. Mapped by the Catholic Church, republican ideologues, and historians, this

---

[7] Angela Gaffney's statistics on research on memory and memorials show that most of this came after 1980; see *Aftermath: Remembering the Great War in Wales* (Cardiff: University of Wales Press, 1998), 182–8.

[8] Hew Strachan, *The First World War*, i: *To Arms* (Oxford: Oxford University Press, 2001). Though only a third of the great work is so far in print, Strachan's briefer *The First World War: A New Illustrated History* (London: Simon & Schuster, 2003) and *The Oxford Illustrated History of the First World War*, which he edited (Oxford: Oxford University Press, 1998), have provided the necessary narrative for this chapter.

[9] For a perceptive survey of Owen's literary reputation see Merryn Williams, *Wilfred Owen* (Bridgend: Seren Books, 1993), chap. 2.

ran far distant from the now-pallid spectre of West Britain. Only in the 1990s, with the imminence of some sort of settlement in the north, did a prosperous Republic come to terms with its citizens' role in 1914–18: a process accelerated by Joseph Lee's cool comparison between independent Ireland and its European coevals.

The change in the discourse, from a confident Britishness to something much more fractured, also tends to underline the ethnic uncertainty of nearly *all* the 'British' war writers: less representative of the mass of soldiers than of a less-than-United Kingdom intelligentsia. Siegfried Sassoon and Isaac Rosenberg were Jewish, Robert von Ranke Graves Irish-German, John Buchan and Ian Hay Scots, Frederic Manning Australian, John MacCrae Canadian. Ellis Evans 'Hedd Wyn' had far greater wartime signific-ance than Owen (born only twenty-five miles distant from him). Though his lan-guage was spoken by only a tiny percentage of Britons, one of them was the Prime Minister, who used the text of the poet's 'black chair' at the August 1917 Birken-head Eisteddfod—he had been killed at Passchendaele—to stage a remarkable rhet-orical rally.[10]

Sexual deviance gave a particular edge to Sassoon's and Owen's rhetoric—not to speak of the Irishness, illegitimacy, and masochism of the war's one romantic hero, T. E. Lawrence. In approaching it, even as original a work as Paul Fussell's *The Great War in Modern Memory* (1975) becomes, seemingly, only an overture. Pacifistic accounts since 1964 which leave out Lawrence Binyon's 'For the Fallen', John MacRae's 'In Flanders Fields', and the poppies of the British Legion become distorted. But so too are those which pass by the Easter Rising commemoration in Dublin in 1966, marked by an apparently moribund IRA blowing up the Nelson Column outside the GPO. In the same year Welsh Nationalism made its break-through, when Gwynfor Evans won Carmarthen, hitherto the seat of Megan Lloyd George. The frontist ethos—the BBC's *Great War* series in 1964, Churchill's funeral a year later—coincided with the start of the break-up of Britain.

'I want to sketch some of the ways in which Europeans imagined the postwar world as composed of survivors perched on a mountain of corpses. How to relate to the fact of mass death, how to transcend its brutal separations and cruelties, were uni-versal dilemmas,' Jay Winter has written.[11] But war competed with other narratives and other disruptions, and when the templates of technology, civics, and national-ism are placed over it, a much more contested Britishness emerges. Drives towards integration and disintegration compete, economic mobilization both converting pro-vincial societies into a British society *and* setting up strains which would undermine it. In 1926 Arnold Bennett, writing *Lord Raingo*, his verdict as an insider on wartime politics, and looking for a useful metaphor, found it in the pneumonia which afflicted his hero the industrialist-turned-minister Sam Raingo, a composite of Lords Beaver-brook and Rhondda. His illness scarcely has to be elaborated to explain the fate of the provincial bourgeoisie, Lloyd George's 'men of push and go'. He probably meant

---

[10] Peter Lord, *The Visual Culture of Wales*, ii: *Imaging the Nation* (Cardiff: University of Wales Press, 2000), 354–7.

[11] Jay Winter, *Sites of Memory, Sites of Mourning* (Cambridge: Cambridge University Press, 1995), 17.

the phrase as irony, contrasting inarticulate generals and their 'big pushes', which failed to go more than a few blood-soaked miles, with the bourgeois entrepreneurs who armoured them and also recast society. They became the hyphen between 'munitions' and 'reconstruction', and in 1918 the precipitators of earthquake-like political change. But did they know where to stop? When did they become, in Bonar Law's words, 'hard-faced men who have done well out of the war', the profiteers and ornaments of—was it Cardiff or Liverpool?—which some wit dubbed 'the city of dreadful knights'? How much were they to blame for the lasting constitutional crisis of the period: the exit of southern Ireland, and the end of West Britain?[12]

What were the consequences of war for a hitherto decentralized industrial and political structure? What effect did wartime politics and policies have on existing trends? And how far can we, both through these factors and through their reflection in the 'ideal types'—formal political writing, political fiction, the first great monuments of modernism—understand the reasons for the countervailing mobilization of nationalist ideas and organizations in provincial Britain?

## II  EXPECTATIONS AND ACTUALITIES: AUGUST 1914–FEBRUARY 1916

There is a narrative of technology and logistics and another, by no means separate, of ideology and morale. The first might initially seem remote from the pacific world of the littoral, but it was the latter's adaptation to become a war machine that was crucial: what Marx had in 1864 called 'the objective ordering of industry', applied to the business of killing men and wrecking economies. At the same time there was, particularly in Britain, a 'subjective' element—convincing citizens that the sacrifices were necessary—and this inevitably caused an increasing divergence between industrial and non-industrial Britain, and between the quite different, though so far complementary, economies of the western industrial basins and that of southern Ireland. The people who would run the machine would probably—even if only as opponents—recognize the Marxian thesis. Think of Milner or Balfour, or anyone who had seen Shaw's plays and read his prefaces. But there was also the incalculable business of stimulating emotions, and then trying to control them; particularly difficult after the machine had been set in motion.[13]

The soldiers who took to arms in 1914 were overwhelmingly peasants and conscripts—except in Britain, where they were proletarians and volunteers. What did they, and behind them the politicians and civilian populace, believe they were letting themselves in for? Expectations about mobilization and war's effect on business and industry would be more sensitive than elsewhere. 'Plucky little Belgium' was transformed remarkably from the brutal tyrant of the Congo only six years earlier,

---

[12] The phrase 'hard-faced men' was first recorded by C. F. G. Masterman in *Britain after War* (London: Hodder, 1920).

[13] Karl Marx, 'The Working Day', in *Capital*, i, 1864, trans. Eden and Cedar Paul (London: Dent, 1951, 230–311).

its Catholicism a definite bonus for propagandists with Ireland in their sights, but this couldn't play indefinitely. Niall Ferguson believes the Asquith Cabinet could have held aloof, but this seems to overdo counterfactuality, and to underestimate the lure of national unity—particularly when set against labour disputes, party hatred, and Ireland. More persuasively, Hew Strachan has seen a mixture of short- and long-war appraisals on all sides: the first hoped for, the second insured against. Yet few commentators have troubled to distinguish between the 'war psychosis-recruitment' phase, when most of Lord Kitchener's New Army expected to be in Berlin by Christmas (quite implausibly, given the time taken to train), and the preparations for a long conflict.[14]

Sir Douglas Haig is credited with foreseeing the latter as Commander of the First Army Corps. He transmitted this view to Kitchener, the new War Minister, and Kitchener took it to the Cabinet, convinced apparently both that the war would last at least three years and that his New Army would not be in Europe until the last of these. But did Haig himself believe this? He was an *arme blanche* man, a believer in a war of movement rather than 'industrialized' attrition. Did he expect Germany's Schlieffen plan to fail, leaving her fighting a two-front war, and thus vulnerable to additional British forces?[15] In this context a balance between the *longue durée* and decisive intervention was foreseeable, but did this mean Britain as the hegemonic Ally, or pursuing the limited sort of naval and finance role she had done in 1793–1815?

By early September it was clear that the Germans had misplayed Schlieffen. Because Russia had mobilized earlier than expected, in late August Moltke had to transfer six army corps eastward. This enabled the French to hold firm on the Marne. When the Russians were worsted at Tannenberg on 26–31 August, German forces could again concentrate on the west, but the trench war was now sclerotically present: 'It is *stalemate*; we cannot turn them out of their trenches and they cannot turn us out'[16] wrote the Chancellor of the Exchequer, David Lloyd George, to his wife after his first visit to the front, on 20 October. Only a month earlier he had addressed his Queen's Hall speech to the London Welsh, its motif a democratic crusade by 'the little five-foot-five nations' against Prussianism; a 'progressive' motivation as remote from the aristocratic diplomats who had been dragged into hostilities as it was from the 'Pro-Boer' of 1900.[17]

How did Lloyd George learn the lessons he taught the Cabinet in February 1915? Arguably, this was a civilian revelation, drawing on alarmed businessmen as well as Shaw's inchoate radicals, through the sort of public intellectuals Charles Masterman had assembled at his propaganda HQ, Wellington House.[18] The popular patriotic literature generated for the war, for example the *Daily Mail Illustrated History*,

---

[14] Niall Ferguson, *The Pity of War* (London: Allen Lane, 1998).

[15] The Schlieffen plan, formulated in 1897, envisaged a devastating German assault on France, knocking her out before Russia could mobilize. See Strachan, *To Arms*, chap. 1.

[16] Quoted in John Grigg, *Lloyd George: From Peace to War, 1912–1916* (London: Harper Collins, 1985), 181.

[17] Kenneth O. Morgan, *Keir Hardie: Radical and Socialist* (London: Weidenfeld and Nicolson, 1975), 56.

[18] Ibid. 161–73; David Wright, 'The Great War, Government Propaganda, and English "Men of Letters", 1914–1916', *Literature and History*, 7 (spring 1978). The Germans remained fixated

wasn't wholly devoted to tub-thumping patriotism and stories of gallant allies and German atrocities. The response of 'prestige' authors, like the future-minded H. G. Wells, anticipates his distinctly ambiguous war novel *Mr Britling Sees it Through* (May 1916), which would run through several registers of pacifism, liberal outrage, and anti-Germanism only to return, chastened, to 'pacifism-plus' in the shape of 'the people's war against war', which was broadly the Lloyd George line. Once there, few options were ruled out.[19]

Questions remained while the pattern of war was unclear and the New Army was under training. On land, how long would preparation take, and what hardware was needed? Was the Russian steamroller real or (as in 1904) illusory? Reverting to the orthodoxy of 1906–12, could the Grand Fleet win on its own? Early British naval successes against isolated German commerce-raiders, including the *Emden*, sunk off the Cocos-Keeling islands on 9 November—quickly evaporated. A single U-boat sank three cruisers off Holland on 22 September; the Admiralty had to keep quiet until 1918 about the mining of the Super-Dreadnought *Audacious* off Ulster on the 27th. Admiral Cradock's antique armoured cruiser squadron was sunk by von Spee's modern cruisers at Coronel on 1 November, Spee in turn being annihilated by British battlecruisers off the Falklands on 8 December. Some 2,500 British and German sailors drowned in minutes as their heavily armoured ships went down, showing the risks of naval battle. The Falklands ended most commerce-raiding by surface ships, and seemed to prove that bigger was better, but British gunnery was shown up as ominously poor.[20]

These new menaces were embodied in Tirpitz's unrestricted U-boat campaign from 1 February 1915. This was the brainchild of the hitherto pacific Alfred Ballin, now *Kriegsmarineamt* under-secretary: disorganization and insurance costs wrecked the nerve of much of the British merchant marine. Matters were ultimately remedied by the creation of the Ministry of Shipping in December 1916, but west-coast shipping had already lost out to rail for munitions traffic, suffering a setback from which it never recovered.[21] Air reconnaissance and radio forced the Admiralty to defer the clash of capital ships which were now seen as vulnerable: kings, not queens on the chessboard. Churchill famously said that Admiral Jellicoe could lose the war in fifteen minutes. He could not win it, even given fifteen months. What was worse, he could still lose it in months without a single one of his Dreadnoughts putting to sea, until the Americans gave him breathing space by forcing Tirpitz to call off in August 1915.[22]

Naval failings haunted alternative strategies intended to draw on Britain's world connections. First Sea Lord Fisher's notion of an attack on the Baltic was squashed by the vulnerability of the capital ships, and the fact that the sea was anyway frozen

by the success of British propaganda, if the accessions to stock in the modern languages library of Tübingen University, particularly those of 1933–45, are anything to go by.

[19] H. G. Wells, 'Will the War Change England?', *The Daily Mail History of the War: Illustrated* (20 Feb. 1915); this was edited by the Scots-born journalist Sir J. A. 'Sandy' Hamerton, from the milieu of Robertson Nicoll and Arthur Mee.

[20] Strachan, *To Arms*, 478–9; Arthur Marder, *From the Dreadnought to Scapa Flow*, ii: *The War Years: To the Eve of Jutland, 1914–1916* (Oxford: Oxford University Press, 1965), 119–29.

[21] 'Shipping', in *Encyclopaedia Britannica*, 12th edn, xxxii, 451–64.

[22] Eberhard Rössler, *The U-Boat* (London: Arms and Armour, 1981), 16–29; and see B. J. C. McKerchar, 'Economic Warfare', in Strachan, *Oxford Illustrated History*, 126–8.

for four months. But the Cabinet's 'Easterners' Winston Churchill and Lloyd George eyed their underused fleet and the continuing Balkan crisis as relations with Turkey worsened. No longer was Turkey the Disraelian keystone of British Near Eastern policy, instead the Young Turks feared the Russian advance on the region. Britain's neo-Gladstonian backing of the Balkan Christians in 1912–13 didn't help, nor the impounding in 1914 of two Turkish Dreadnoughts in British yards. Turkey became further tied to the Central Powers by the arrival at Constantinople on 11 August of the new German battlecruiser *Goeben*, which could single-handedly have wiped out the Turkish fleet and so became a gift impossible to refuse—perhaps the only strategic victory a Dreadnought won. Turkey declared war on 29 October, slamming the door on 95 per cent of Russian trade and the huge grain traffic from the Black Sea to Britain.[23]

Lloyd George had thought to counter this with an activist anti-Austrian policy, but the furthest he and Churchill got was when in January 1915 Britain and France attacked the Dardanelles, intending to gain a warm-water link to Russia. The expected Italian alliance (she declared war on 24 May) ought, they thought, to open a mobile, navy-driven southern front. A bombardment by surplus pre-Dreadnoughts (with the new *Queen Elizabeth* to see off the *Goeben*) was supposed to destroy the Turkish forts and force the Bosphorus. Instead Turkish mines sank three of the old battleships. The admirals took fright and, realizing the proximity of the *Goeben*, transformed the attack into a landing. Risky anyway (combined operations were always notoriously accident-prone), this hit fierce Turkish resistance under Liman von Sanders and the young Kemal Pasha and cost 130,000 casualties, which the Irish, Australians, and New Zealanders neither forgot nor forgave. Bulgaria's accession to the Central Powers in October was the last straw, and the Allies evacuated in November. Other eastern campaigns—at Salonika (occupied in October 1915) and in Mesopotamia in the winter of 1915–16—fared no better.

Berlin sought to reverse Schlieffen by conciliating Russia. The Russian steamroller recovered from the setback of 1914 and until 1916 inflicted considerable damage on the Austrians. Germany meanwhile mastered trench warfare in the west, digging in instead of taking the offensive, and allowing French and British assaults to break bloodily on bunker, machine-gun nest, and barbed wire. In 1915 the Germans' hardened front left the French exposed on two sides of the Verdun salient. The Germans determined to use this advantage to waste them after February 1916, dragging Britain into a war of attrition. The consequent commitment of Britain's New Army to a 'great push' was planned for mid 1916.

By then, the economics of adaptation facing Whitehall had become starkly explicit. As John Terraine once put it, in extenuation of the brasshats' performance:

> When Lloyd George says that 'our Generals had the most important lessons of their art to
> learn' he states no less than the truth; they had indeed. What that generation of naval
> and military leaders, no longer young, brought up in Victorian society and accustomed
> to a leisurely process of technical and social change, had to face was this:

[23] Strachan, *The First World War*, i, 644–80.

the first war of aviation, with all the implications of that;

the first real under-sea war, entirely altering the nature of naval power;

the first war of the internal combustion engine, therefore also the first war of mechanics, a new breed of men in uniforms;

the first chemical war, using (among other things) poison gas and napalm (flame-throwers, petroleum-based);

the first war of modern mass production, mass logistics and mass administration (by 1916 British G.H.Q. in France was administering a population bigger than any single unit of control in England, except Greater London); and much else besides.[24]

The specifically industrial nature of this challenge was emphasized by the entry 'Munitions of War' in the huge resource of the *Encyclopaedia Britannica*. Its twelfth edition, produced in 1923 under the editorship of Hugh Chisholm, Glasgow Tory and *Times* leader writer, was (besides being the last wholly British edition) a 3,000-page treatment of the conflict, succinctly summed up:

When the British army of six divisions took the field in 1914 it possessed about 900 field guns, less than 200 field howitzers, about 60 heavier weapons of 6-in. and upwards, and perhaps about 200 obsolescent types, such as the 4.7 in. and the 85-pdr. howitzer, a reserve of ammunition of less than a million rounds weighing some 20,000 tons, and less than 2,000 machine-guns. By the end of 1918, the army had received 10,000 field guns, 6,000 heavier guns and howitzers; 217 million rounds of artillery ammunition weighing 5.25 million tons and nearly 225,000 machine-guns.[25]

Even the traditional infantryman's supplies doubled in the course of the war.[26] After it the influential critic Captain Basil Liddell Hart would make a distinction between the traditional attributes of generalship and the management of the modern army: 'Compared with the manifold personal initiative of a Marlborough or a Napoleon before and during battle, the decisions of an army commander in 1914–18 were necessarily few and broad—his role was more akin to that of managing director of a huge department store.'[27] Strategic and logistical remits combined to harness the industrial west coast. Whether the generals could direct this materiel was another matter.

The fulcrum of military reform in 1906–11 had been the partnership between R. B. Haldane and Sir Douglas Haig. Campbell-Bannerman had sent Haldane to the War Ministry as punishment for Liberal-imperial intrigue. Haldane, from the Scots landowning-religious elite (his brother was J. S. Haldane, the Oxford scientist and father of J. B. S. Haldane and Naomi Mitchison), had already created the civic universities, his 'British Charlottenburg'; Haig was of the Scotch whisky distillers,

---

[24] John Terraine, *The Smoke and the Fire: Myths and Anti-Myths of War, 1861–1945* (London: Leo Cooper, 1992), 172–3.

[25] *Encyclopaedia Britannica*, 12th edn, xxxi, 1013.

[26] Martin van Creveld, *Supplying War: Logistics from Wallenstein to Patton* (London: Cambridge University Press, 1977), 141.

[27] Basil Liddell Hart, *The First World War*, 1934 (London: Pan, 1970), 32.

with a middle-class, academic Clifton-and-Brasenose education. His knowledge of French and German, and of the German military, helped him design the Imperial General Staff. His wife, Dorothy Vivian, was of the Cornish-Welsh tinplate-making family, well connected at court, with the coal-owner J. A. Thomas related by marriage. Jellicoe, in command of the vastly expanded navy, had a similar marriage connection with the Cayzers, the Scottish shipowning dynasty. The two men were a foretaste of a different sort of military-political elite from the accustomed one: provincial, administrative, connected to industrial and finance capital. Their challenge was to hold the line while coping with the disruption Kitchener had wreaked on labour supply.[28]

This was met by the animating genius of Lloyd George and after May 1915 his establishment of a central Ministry of Munitions, which drew on the collectivist expertise of the French, through his friend the socialist War Minister Albert Thomas. To this was added the chemical and engineering capabilities of Fletcher Moulton, a Cambridge radical of the 1870s, and the engineering expertise of Ernest Moir of Pearson Longman, who had started his career with the Forth Bridge, and William Weir of Cathcart, along with the organizational skill of Dr Christopher Addison, Hubert Llewellyn Smith of Toynbee Hall and the Board of Trade, and D. A. Thomas of the Cambrian Combine. This combination of centralization, elite recruitment, and pragmatic, profit-driven devolution meant that Lloyd George made remarkably few mistakes, but he was aided by economic circumstances.[29] More ambiguously, he would change the parameters of high and low politics in ways which destroyed the balance of civic, ethnic, and parliamentary politics on which littoral and core had traditionally depended.

## III  'THE WORKSHOPS ARE OUR BATTLEFIELD'

In August 1914, along the west coast, the exporting economy seemed to run into a brick wall, endangering the jobs of miners, steelworkers, and shipbuilders. Recruitment in such areas was predictably enthusiastic, and beneath the heroic propaganda it was propelled, as Jay Winter has reminded us, by local loyalties: Kitchener posters and Belgian atrocities mattered less than workmates joining up. The Belgium story, however, had political and Irish significance. Belgium was overwhelmingly Catholic; when German *Kultur* burned the Catholic University of Louvain, it echoed Bismarck's *Kulturkampf* against the ultramontane church in the 1870s. Scots, Welsh, and Ulster volunteers were propelled to the front by clever tracts like *The First Hundred Thousand* and *Private Spud Tamson VC* (both 1915), the solidarity of the

---

[28] The American sociologist Morris Janowitz, surveying military elites in the 1940s, thought they ought to be somewhat archaic, to stop Napoleonic threats of *coups d'état*, etc. See *Sociology and the Military Establishment* (New York: Russell Sage Foundation, 1959).

[29] Adams, *Arms and the Wizard*, chap. 4, 'The Men of Push and Go', 38–55.

Ulster Covenanters, and Lloyd George's claim on the Welsh chapels.[30] The Scots contributed about 40 per cent more than their proportion of the UK population; the Welsh contradicted their pacifist reputation and showed bloodthirsty.

Southern Ireland was less enthusiastic, but so was rural England. The war brought prosperity to farm work (a reserved occupation), recruitment levelled off, and politics—with British-minded youth in the forces and British intelligence agents off chasing German spies—continued on somewhat more nationalist lines.[31] Yet the 'western' literati were distracted from criticism: propaganda was high-level and literate, whether under Masterman, an early example of a sociologist in government, the egregious and learned John Buchan, or the Protestant Dubliner Alfred Harmsworth, whose *Daily Mail* had from the 1890s embodied populist imperialism at its zenith. Viscount Bryce's 'Committee on Belgian Atrocities'—led by an Ulster-Scot Home Ruler, critic of British imperialism, and popular ex-ambassador to Washington—showed that in exposing German 'barbarism' intellectuals packed rather more of a punch than blockaded Dreadnoughts.[32]

Initially and perhaps unexpectedly, 'business as usual' continued. War wasn't followed by state control; rather the opposite. In Europe there was conscription, true, and Whitehall's control of the railways, under an act of 1871, took effect. Otherwise, regimes, desperate to get supplies, bid against one another in an international market free of conferences or cartels.[33] Entrepreneurs found they had to replace trade to enemy-controlled regions, but could capture overseas markets served by the enemy. Even a year after the outbreak of war, they were still assessing profit and loss in such terms. The west-coast ports benefited; the Atlantic trade avoided the Thames for safety reasons, and because southern harbours from Plymouth to Yarmouth were filling up with transit traffic to the front.[34]

Nor was there much centralization. Politicians handed over control to the military—Asquith didn't convene his Cabinet with a war agenda for months. Once fighting actually started, it devolved right down to the private or at least his section leader, battle being so noisy and close communication so non-existent (the walkie-talkie wasn't there until World War II) that any sophisticated response was impossible. Britain had plenty of war experience through colonial conflicts, but how useful would this prove?

Mid 1915 would demonstrate the result. British forces attacked in May, at Ypres, Lens, and La Bassée. Artillery proved inadequate, and the Germans retaliated with

[30] See David Goldie, 'Laddies who Fought and Won: Scottish Popular Culture and World War I', paper given at Strathclyde University, 12 Dec. 2000.

[31] Keith Jeffery, *Ireland and the Great War* (Cambridge: Cambridge University Press, 2000), 1–26.

[32] *Encylopaedia Britannica*, 12th edn, xxxi, 1146–8.

[33] See Chris Wrigley, ed., *World War I and the International Economy* (Cheltenham: Edward Elgar, 2000); and Kathleen Burk, *Britain, America and Sinews of War, 1914–1918* (London: Allen and Unwin, 1985).

[34] See Christopher Harvie, *No Gods and Precious Few Heroes: Scotland since 1914*, 1981 (Edinburgh: Edinburgh University Press, 1999), chap. 1, which draws extensively on the twenty-two printed but unpublished volumes of *The History of the Ministry of Munitions* (London: Stationery Office, 1922–3). Rex Pope, ed., *Atlas of British Social and Economic History* (London: Routledge, 1989) is useful here, particularly chap. 3, although handicapped by the lack of Irish material.

poison gas. Breakthroughs on narrow fronts could not be sustained. This led to the highlighting of munitions production. Tirpitz's unrestricted U-boat war quickly provoked a crisis, though maritime losses—actual and expected—benefited shipping entrepreneurs. Grain, for instance, usually came as return cargoes for coal, from Argentina or the Black Sea. With war and Turkish hostility, charges for Argentinian grain went from a 'listless' 12*s*. 6*d*. per ton to 50*s*. by January 1915, and by mid 1916 to 183*s*. 6*d*. Even after Chancellor Reginald McKenna's excess profits tax, this 'meant higher profits than, in pre-war years, could ever have been thought possible'.[35] The price of cargo steamers rocketed, enabling the Glasgow merchant William Burrell to offload his entire fleet of twenty-eight ships and put his cash into the fine arts. Similar inflation was also seen in coal, agriculture and textiles, notably jute for sacks. It took until well into 1915 for these to be curbed by being brought under government control.[36]

In November 1914 the first steps to organize ordnance, high-explosive shells, and machine-gun production on the scale necessary were taken, in the Crayford 'shells and fuses agreement'. This gradually took effect, but only in May 1915 did the munitions theme become politics. Fomented by a bitterly critical report in *The Times* of 14 May, a Liberal-Conservative coalition was forced through on the 21st.[37] Behind it was the realization that a breakthrough would need huge quantities of high-explosive shell to penetrate German dugouts, and supplying it would mean partially reversing volunteering, and remodelling industry and government. Kitchener had in March appointed an 'armaments output committee' under George Macaulay Booth, merchant and shipowner, of the Booths of Liverpool, son of the pioneer sociologist Charles and a cousin of Beatrice Webb. Booth turned out the original 'man of push and go' and set up a munitions regime, restraining skilled workers from volunteering, coordinating management and resources, even before Lloyd George's appointment as Minister of Munitions in May. Soon the momentum had increased, implying conscription and collectivized production.[38]

Lloyd George not only dynamized production but rewrote the history of the war. While the Pals' battalions trained for the 'big push', he and his assistant Dr Christopher Addison geared up management and recalled soldiers and female and immigrant labour to produce armaments on a scale the Germans had never anticipated. Britain became *the* arsenal of the Allies (in World War II, by contrast, its armaments production was scarcely a third of that of the USA or the USSR).[39] The demand after early 1915 was also a highly specific one: for heavy artillery, particularly high-elevation howitzers (a cross between a field gun and a mortar) and their shells. Such guns wore their barrels out rapidly, which had been rare in earlier, short wars; their

[35] *Encylopaedia Britannica*, 12th edn, xxxii, 452.

[36] E. M. H. Lloyd, *Experiments in State Control*, Carnegie Endowment (Oxford: Clarendon Press, 1924).

[37] Arthur Marwick, *The Deluge: British Society and World War I*, 1965 (Harmondsworth: Penguin, 1967), 59.

[38] Duncan Crow, *A Man of Push and Go: The Life of George Macaulay Booth* (London: Rupert Hart-Davis, 1965), and Strachan, *To Arms*, 993–1113.

[39] Richard Overy in *Der Spiegel* (June 2001).

shells were steel, packed with high explosive, not shrapnel—intended to break open reinforced concrete. This demand soon exceeded the capacity of the traditional armaments firms—Vickers, Coventry, Armstrong-Whitworth—which the War Office's Director of Purchasing, Sir Stanley von Donop, favoured. His guess as to likely cost had been a *total* of £1.6 million. In December 1915, von Donop went. On 29 September 1918 a single day's barrage against the Hindenburg line cost £3.9 million.[40]

Lloyd George took over from Booth the reorganization of civilian engineering and machine-tools concerns, a move which brought huge pressure on technology, particularly the demand for lathes (for boring out cast-steel barrels and shells) and explosives, and on labour. Industrial relations had been fraught, pre-war, as employers had tried to replace skilled male labour with new technology and 'scientific management' of the semi-skilled. So the largest of the new munitions districts, Clydeside, became at this stage a battleground more important than Flanders. Lloyd George replaced joint munitions committees with the autocratic rule of William Weir, the 38-year-old boss of Weir Pumps, who shared his sense of urgency, and provoked a crisis which ran from August 1915 to April 1916. Although there were radical socialist overtones—American far-leftism had made inroads since 1906, and many in the local ILP favoured the ethical pacifism of Keir Hardie, Ramsay MacDonald, and the influential weekly *Forward*—this was essentially a confrontation between Weir, and behind him the London-based Munitions Directorate under William Beveridge, and the engineers' elite: skilled men who often became officers once afloat, overwhelmingly Protestant and often Unionist in their politics. The Tory ex-Scottish Secretary, Lord Balfour of Burleigh, mediating in 1915, found kirk elders jailed in Barlinnie and furious about it, as they had sons at the front. 'Dilution' was achieved by early 1916, but the quid pro quo for this was statutory rent control, a robust assault on inflation which penalized 'dispensable' capitalists, the urban rentiers who had been in happier times the sponsors of civic reform.[41] By this time, too, fifteen National Projectile and Shell factories had been built in the main industrial districts, and a giant explosives plant commissioned at Gretna, where three of the Anglo-Scottish railways and the Newcastle–Carlisle line converged, at which 30,000 workers prepared gun cotton for the shell cases. Once the Clyde had conceded, the other districts fell into line, and the great push could be supplied.[42]

Munitions was a matter of administration and high politics. This was unusual. Economic and social policy had hitherto been remote from 'statesmanship', devolved to the mundane level of bureaucrats and local authorities. It now provided the locomotive of social and eventually political change, driven by Lloyd George. A figure alien from the traditional political establishment—Welsh home ruler, dissenter, class warrior—he had come to the political centre in 1906 with his own social reform

[40] Adams, *Arms and the Wizard*, 2.
[41] See Harvie, 'Scandal and the True-Blue Clyde' and Iain S. McLean, *The Legend of Red Clydeside* (Edinburgh: John Donald, 1983).
[42] Adams, *Arms and the Wizard*, 66–70; the Gretna project created one of the biggest contracting firms, Laings of Carlisle. See Ray Coad, *Sir John Laing* (London: Hodder, 1979), 66.

agenda. Now he was commissioned to squeeze production out of a hitherto decentralized industrial and political structure. Its celebration was partial and obscure: the twenty-two volumes of the *History of the Ministry of Munitions* (1922–3), printed but never published, Maurice Elvey's film epic *The Life Story of David Lloyd George*, shot in 1918 but never released, memoirs and novels and poems by those in his entourage (or against it) and not least the premier's own justification, his *War Memoirs* of 1932–4. These in their turn bore the mark of a frustrated political revolution.[43]

Munitions was only one of three main war production areas. The first was concerned with replacing, in manufacturing and services, the men who were now under arms, some two million by mid 1915, and also with backing them up. There could of course be some shuffling around of production, as normal peacetime demands fell and labour was 'diluted'. The second—the most crucial mandate for the new ministry—was high-explosive shell in unprecedented quantities. Finally, enemy action had to be made good: not just the destruction of resources, notably by U-boats, but the replacement of German technology in chemicals, precision equipment and electrics, explosives, and fertilizers. In optics the British were so desperate in 1914 that they were willing to buy German Zeiss binoculars through Swiss intermediaries, but the Glasgow firm of Barr and Stroud rapidly devised mass-produced products. In magnetos, where another German firm, Bosch, had a pre-war monopoly, similar adaptations were carried through, to supply the military vehicles whose numbers rose from 20,000 in 1914 to 200,000 in 1918.[44]

More significant than high explosive ought to have been the British blockade of Germany. But the world's greatest naval power was almost instantly immobilized by U-boats and mines, which ruled out any 'close blockade' of German seaports. A 'distant blockade' meant intercepting German ships in foreign ports, and stopping trade by neutral vessels (which handled about a third of Germany's supplies) via neutral Holland. Tirpitz's ruthless answer was discredited when U 20 torpedoed the great Cunarder *Lusitania* off Kinsale on 7 May, though many of the doomed merchantmen were sunk by U-boats cruising on the surface, and mostly close to the British coast. American protests gained protection for neutrals from 1 September. Yet, even during the ensuing lull, Walter Runciman, President of the Board of Trade *and* prominent shipowner, believed that Britain would be brought to its knees by the summer of 1917.[45]

The 'fleet in being' had already moved north and west: the old bases of Chatham, Portsmouth, and Devonport—too close to the U-boats—were forsaken for Rosyth, Invergordon, and Scapa Flow. But when it met the High Seas Fleet off Jutland on 31 May 1916, only a month ahead of the Somme offensive, the Grand Fleet's superiority

[43] Elvey had been a pioneer of the 'new drama' of Chekhov in Britain. His film, if uneven, had some spectacular scenes which anticipate Eisenstein. See Simon Berry and David Horrocks, eds., *David Lloyd George: The Movie Mystery* (Cardiff: University of Wales Press, 1998). The portrait of Lloyd George as 'Chester Nimmo', in Joyce Cary's *Not Honour More* (London: Michael Joseph, 1955), captures the frustrated radicalism of a fading 'dynamic force'.

[44] Michael Moss and Iain Russell, *Range and Vision: The First 100 years of Barr & Stroud* (Edinburgh: Mainstream, 1988).

[45] A. J. P. Taylor, *English History* (Oxford: Clarendon Press, 1965), 99.

in numbers, tonnage, and firepower was betrayed by inaccurate gunnery and inadequate armour plate, and three modern capital ships and 6,000 men went down. Afterwards the German fleet left harbour only once, but remained menacing in its intactness, while its submarine arm—never more than seventy strong at any time—took a further deadly toll when unrestricted U-boat warfare resumed on 31 January 1917.

This provoked the Americans to declare war on 6 April, but such were the losses inflicted—40 per cent of the British merchant fleet was sunk in the course of the war—that Lloyd George (Prime Minister since 6 December 1916) demanded, and eventually got, a change in policy to convoy protection.[46] His new Shipping Ministry, a Scots-dominated operation under Joseph Maclay, John Anderson, and Eric Geddes, ultimately prevailed over Jellicoe by the end of April.[47] Submarine warfare had, however, further implications for the cohesion of the western littoral, not only shifting freight to northern ports and to rail (for U-boats were particularly deadly in 'the antechamber of Britain') but reorientating naval construction to escort craft, aircraft carriers, and aircraft, and anti-submarine and anti-mine vessels. The result—on top of replacement merchantmen—was huge orders to the shipyards, notably those of Belfast, which kept demand running at nearly its pre-war level, itself a record.[48]

The immensity of munitions demand was one thing. The use of technology and ingenuity to circumvent it was another. Convoying was the brainchild of a young naval officer, Commander Reginald Henderson; perhaps the most successful weapon of the trench war was the Stokes mortar, a drainpipe-like rocket launcher which did the work of most heavy guns for a fraction of the cost.[49] The tank (in action from September 1916) drew on a scratch team from the navy under the patronage of Churchill. The ever-ingenious Erskine Childers followed up the propaganda success of *The Riddle of the Sands* by experimenting with torpedo-launching planes and motor boats, just as another Anglo-Irish freelance, T. E. Lawrence, stirred up the Bedouin. The duel of Shavian genius with military boneheadedness—and the shadow of Thomas Carlyle's 'Captains of Industry'—hovered around Lloyd George's Downing Street. Its negative consequences were immense: could the horrors of the Western Front in 1916 and 1917 have taken place *without* the success of the munitions drive? But so too were its other ostensibly positive, implications.


IV  FROM RECONSTRUCTION TO VICTORY

Lloyd George was never behindhand with a parable, and his account of the ministry's dealings with Dr Chaim Weizmann of Manchester University strikingly fused military necessity with reform. Explosive works were short of acetone, a key fixative for

[46] A. J. P. Taylor, *English History* (Oxford: Clarendon Press, 1965), 167.

[47] John Grigg, *Lloyd George: War Leader 1916–1918* (London: Allen Lane, 2002), 50–3.

[48] For the Belfast record see Jonathan Bardon, *A History of Ulster* (Belfast: Blackstaff Press, 1992), 456–7.

[49] John Grigg, *Lloyd George: From Peace to War, 1912–1916* (London: HarperCollins, 1997), 276–7; Grigg, *War Leader*, 50–1; Patrick Wright, *Tank* (London: Faber, 2000), chap. 2.

stabilizing shell propellant. Herbert Samuel introduced the minister to the Zionist scientist, who had devised a process which could mass-produce the stuff from maize. His quid pro quo for this came in the shape of the Balfour Declaration of 2 November 1917, in which Britain came out in favour of a national home for the Jews.[50]

The reality was less straightforward, but typical of the imagination of Lloyd George's agenda, something reflected in his *War Memoirs*, in which industrial dynamism alternated with radical political initiatives. If Churchill's *The World Crisis, 1911–1918* (1923–9) was in style military-political, Lloyd George's version was almost a British manifesto for Franklin Roosevelt's directly contemporary New Deal. They portray our hero in his struggles against the generals, his own military miscalculations—the Dardanelles, the Nivelle offensives of 1917—being played down. Events are elided to give more of an impression of dynamism than there was. Yet they show him responding to the doubts of the likes of H. G. Wells about whether the country could hold together, in part simply by co-opting those thinkers of a 'national efficiency', New Liberal, or Fabian cast who could live with a centralizing, collective state. There was a Committee on Reconstruction from early 1916, and in June 1917, following Lloyd George's Whitehall takeover, it became a full-blown ministry under his Munitions aide Christopher Addison.[51]

In functional terms the reconstruction drive—something quite unprecedented in Britain—was Lloyd George's means of securing sufficient public commitment to the allied cause to justify the conscription he had always seen as essential. Some reconstruction would have come about anyway—new housing was necessary for the new factories; factory crèches, catering, and welfare provision stemmed from an increasingly female labour force; licensing hours restriction followed from the need to keep workers sober in highly dangerous munitions plants.[52] Even educational reform was near-automatic, as recruitment interrupted the supply of teachers to the classrooms and made forward planning necessary. The art of Lloyd George was to use the demands of conscription and war production to mould these into a continuous programme, at least of promises. Even an opponent of the war like the Labour leader Ramsay MacDonald noted the boost such measures had given to social reform. 'Reconstruction' in fact underlined how far the political-economic landscape had changed: the German word *Umwälzung*, or 'enforced revolution', seemed apt. This amounted to a reversal of Herbert Spencer's theory of the evolution from military to industrial society. Command took over from contract; programmes and policies from party debate and market forces. The cost of this was that awkward, time-wasting issues which didn't fit the delivery mechanism of war production—like Ireland—were shelved, or made over to the second-rate, who wouldn't cause trouble.

[50] Lloyd George, *War Memoirs* (London: Odhams, 1932–4), 348.

[51] Jane and Kenneth Morgan, *Portrait of a Progressive: The Political Career of Christopher, Viscount Addison* (Oxford: Clarendon Press, 1980). This is vividly presented in Elvey's film, with Lloyd George and Addison interviewing trade unionists and managers in their cramped office, the action segueing into vast panoramas of munitions workers and shells.

[52] My great-uncle Ebenezer Harvie, an engineer at Gretna, recollected workers lying under tank waggons to soak up drips of industrial alcohol, and going mad. The measure against this was the Carlisle State Liquor Scheme, which lasted until the 1970s.

For example, two social policy breakthroughs came directly from 'resolving' the Red Clyde crisis. Rent control provided a precedent, though it wasn't in itself enough. Asquith's Scottish Secretary Henry Tennant reactivated the Royal Commission on Scottish Housing, which had been set up at the behest of miners' leaders in 1913, and suspended on the outbreak of war. When it reported in 1917, it condemned the 'idle' capitalism of the Glasgow rentiers, while approving the arms drive of the engineering bosses, and placed before them and the unions the prospect of a major social housing programme—up to 250,000 houses—as a pay-off. By co-opting liberal philanthropists and left-wingers into reconstruction, from Tom Jones and R. H. Tawney to G. D. H. Cole and H. G. Wells, 'reconstruction' both gave the government's cause an eloquence that it had hitherto lacked and immobilized many of its potential critics.[53] In 1917, Lloyd George's Scottish Secretary Robert Munro, doubtless with Ireland at the back of his mind, set out to bring the voluntary and impoverished Catholic schools within the Scottish state sector, with total autonomy, before the 1918 election. His Catholic supporters were prepared to get Rome to coerce the Archbishops of Edinburgh and Glasgow when they refused to cooperate. Although there was some Sinn Fein activity, Scotland's Catholics would stay loyal to the party of Redmond and Dillon.[54]

This didn't just apply to the Left. H. A. L. Fisher moved from Sheffield and the fringes of Bloomsbury to become Education Minister and pilot through the Education Act of 1918, an attempt to bring education abreast of that of the Central Powers.[55] In agriculture the 1917 Corn Production Act was necessary to get land turned over to the plough, since arable faming was nutritionally far more productive than pastoral farming. The task of setting up County Agricultural Production Executives went to a Tory Oxford don, R. E. Prothero, later Viscount Ernle. Housing was featured in another inquiry under Lord Salisbury, as was the Tory-collectivist enterprise of a Transport Ministry, carried in 1919 by Sir Eric Geddes, another graduate from Munitions. An Edinburgh engineer who had knocked about in the Americas and India, Geddes was an innovatory general manager of the North-Eastern Railway, who became during the war first a general (when managing railway communications with the front line) and also an admiral (when controller of the navy).[56]

1916 had been dominated in a 'linear' way by the build-up of men and supplies for the Western Front, but in 1917 the outlook was obscure and Lloyd George was on the qui vive. The markers of old Europe vanished as in February Tsarist Russia collapsed, Austria tried to exit, and the USA intervened. Attempts to sustain the Russian republic were disastrous. The French Protestant general Nivelle, whose spring offensives Lloyd George backed, failed. French armies mutinied and thereafter remained on the defensive. In April America entered the war, but it would take months for her troops to arrive in adequate numbers, while the German General Staff's inspired decision to ship Lenin

---

[53] Keith Middlemass, *Politics in Industrial Society: The Experience of the British System since 1911* (London: André Deutsch, 1979), 68–93.

[54] Richard Finlay, *Modern Scotland* (London: Profile, 2004), 95–9.

[55] Grigg, *War Leader*, 569 ff.

[56] For Geddes's pre-war career see Keith Grieves, *Sir Eric Geddes* (Manchester: Manchester University Press, 1989), 1–11.

from Zurich to Russia by special train was by the autumn paying off. Lloyd George had to give in to the generals and their demand for a Flanders offensive to keep Kerensky in play. The result was the catastrophe of Third Ypres (Passchendaele), and in October the Russian army was voting with its feet. The Germans could now concentrate on a single Western Front, and to this were added the toxins of revolution filtering out from Bolshevik Petrograd. The only glimmers of hope were the introduction of convoys, docking the Dreadnoughts, as it turned out, for good (though it took until 1942 for the message to reach the admirals), the 'globalizing' of the British war effort, under the Imperial War Cabinet, sitting from March 1917, and in June a coup in Greece which brought Lloyd George's pro-Allied protégé, Eleftherios Venizelos, to power and promised that the army mouldering in Salonica could at last strike northwards.

In Scotland working-class truculence had now been co-opted to supply tanks and aircraft and hundreds of freighters and escorts: the Unionist *Glasgow Herald* wrote in December 1917:

The arrangements regarding the recognition of shop stewards are also significant as a sign of the times. They may portend syndicalism or they may not, but they certainly mean that the actual workers will be in closer touch with the machinery of their unions, and also with their employers, and familiarity is more likely to breed friendship than enmity.[57]

The Clyde was quiet. Trouble came in 1917 from Sheffield and South Wales. Arnold Bennett, ensconced in propaganda thanks to his and Lloyd George's friend Max Aitken, Lord Beaverbrook, observed the new ganglions which connected the metropolitan headquarters with the industrial provinces. In his mildly risqué *The Pretty Lady* (1918)—London's war seen from the boudoir of a well-doing French courtesan—the Clyde's capacity to shock and convert eventually energizes her dégagé lover G J, whose former fiancée, a welfare volunteer in the factories, is seared by seeing one of 'her' girls scalped and killed by unguarded machinery. Addison, recruited from a medical school, proved a safe and sympathetic pair of hands to tackle such traumas: a prototype, perhaps, of the fictional doctors who, in A. J. Cronin, Francis Brett Young, or James Bridie, figured so much in the inter-war years. He went on to Housing in the peacetime government, taking his Munitions associate the Scots building contractor James Carmichael with him.[58] Haldane, out of office but never far from the corridors of power, contributed his 'Machinery of Government' report in 1918, which acted as a blueprint for many subsequent reform ventures. His own transfer to the Labour Party (Addison followed) would be another verdict on the waning of Asquithian Liberalism.

The 'eternal nay' of this situation was precisely the sort of politician who had inhabited Victorian 'high politics': most notably, in Lloyd George's view, the urbane, indolent Asquith. Addison had it in for the Tory President of the Local Government Board, Hayes Fisher. Both were lawyers when law, insofar as Lloyd George needed it, meant the unorthodox and unnerving figures of Carson and Birkenhead. What emerged in

---

[57] *Glasgow Herald Industry and Trade Supplement* (31 Dec. 1917).
[58] Kenneth O. Morgan, *Consensus and Disunity. The Lloyd George Coalition Government, 1918–1922* (Oxford: Clarendon Press, 1979), 89.

1917 was certainly effective, but also dangerously narrow. Bennett observed in *Lord Raingo* (1926) that despite the demand for coordination self-obsessed departments fought each other more bitterly than the Germans. Whitehall was Kenneth Morgan's 'mighty machine of centralised power', but as Sam Raingo found out, centralization didn't mean coordination. It soon aggravated the policy fractures that would rapidly dissolve a substantial part of the British state: the Irish union. The interpretative debate between Marwick and Winter and Ross McKibbin has also shown how the Reform and Redistribution Act of February 1918, though passing through Westminster the previous six months, was underestimated as a disrupter of the political situation. Eight million new voters were enfranchised, three-quarters of them women. There would be one MP per 70,000 in Britain, and one per 43,000 in Ireland.[59]

This sort of shift was neither unprecedented nor unpredictable: the 1884 Reform Act had had a similar effect on Whiggism in rural Scotland, Ireland, and Wales, triggering the rise of the Parnellite nationalists and in Scotland the Crofters' Party. The Liberals reached a modus vivendi with both, but also lost in the longer term to a renascent west coast Unionism, particularly in Scotland. Their problem in 1918–24 was more fundamental, responding to a tripartite crisis experienced along the littoral: the division within the Liberal Party, the disjunction between the Liberal-commercial businessmen of the west coast and the 'professionals' of the south-east, and a new electorate and new constituencies which the divided party couldn't manage. The last was more proletarian, with a new agenda: trade-union-based Labour and its wartime victories of rent control, full employment, regulation of hours worked, and (in Scotland) confessional education.[60]

More securely liberal in ideology was the formulation of war aims, concentrated by the Fourteen Points of President Woodrow Wilson on 8 January 1918, just as Ludendorff concentrated his forces on the Amiens front. The central ideas of a League of Nations plus national liberation (aimed at multinational Austria) had been advanced by a group under Viscount Bryce after 1915, whose language—the stress on 'open covenants'—reflected its Scots Presbyterian origins.[61] In the ruins of socialist internationalism, this made progress. Ludendorff's armies lost momentum and then started to retreat across northern France in the summer of 1918. By the end of September the *Kaiserreich* was crumbling, and on 3 October a reform ministry under Prince Max of Baden started to sue for peace. Germany's admirals tried a last throw, but on being mobilized on 3 November, the High Seas Fleet mutinied. When the armistice took effect on 11 November, Wilhelm II had already abdicated and left for Holland. In the *Kriegsmarineamt*, Alfred Ballin shot himself.

The 'coupon' election of 15 December 1918, in which the government endorsed those who supported it in the Maurice debate, split the Liberals irrevocably and

[59] *Annual Register* (1918), 52.

[60] Ross MacKibbin, *The Evolution of the Labour Party, 1910–1924* (Oxford: Clarendon Press, 1974), 70–1.

[61] See Edmund Ions, *James Bryce and American Democracy* (London: Macmillan, 1968), chap. 22, and Thomas Kleinknecht, *Imperiale und internationale Ordnung: Eine Untersuchung zum anglo-amerikanischen Gelehrtenliberalismus am Beispiel von James Bryce, 1838–1922* (Göttingen: Vandenhoeck und Rupprecht, 1985).

confirmed Lloyd George's leadership of a right-wing coalition. But although the coalition Liberals were momentarily successful in the west, they had lost the largely Asquithian activist base of the party, even if this were only local solicitors. This situation might have been repaired, either by a reunited Liberal Party or by flexible coalition Liberals. However, the Liberals were immobilized by two further factors: the preoccupation of the coalition with the post-war international settlement, involving a huge dissipation of government effort; and the economic slump which hit the UK in late 1920 and forced the dispersal of the assets of the Liberal business elite. Liberalism was increasingly vulnerable to Labour, with a new agenda tailored to urban discontents, or to business-led Conservatism, with its 'anti-socialist' agenda. The progressivism of the coalition's programme couldn't be discounted, but in most respects this favoured the new power brokers. Within six years the once-great Liberal party had plummetted. Its decline was even more marked along the western littoral. In Scotland its seats fell from 58 to 27 in 1922 and to 8 in 1924; in Wales from 26 to 10 in 1924 alone.

The consequence was something more than the eclipse of a Liberal-philanthropic elite, whose indirect links to high politics in London gave way to a localized confrontation of businessmen and socialists: one in which the priorities of civics were suspended for a decade. In war, politics had become managerial. The 'men of push and go' entered a milieu in which executive action was crucial, in supplying the front, keeping the military under control, and offering reconstruction to the home front. Parliament stopped being any sort of forum, and what T. S. Eliot would call a 'disassociation of sensibility'—or in political terms the absence of 'joined-up thinking'—set in. This suggests a type of trauma, wherein the collective mind of government, and the usual public and habitual checks on it, simply ceases to function.[62] That this 'shaking to bits' as John Buchan, in psychoanalytical mood, put it in 1924, was a situation more apparent to imaginative writers on the fringes of government than the leading actors themselves may be significant.[63] In Ireland it would prove disastrous.


## V  THE UNIVERSITY OF FRONGOCH

In 1924 W. B. Yeats, a Free State senator since 1922 (appointed, intriguingly, to conciliate *both* the Protestant Ascendancy and the pro-Treaty Irish Republican Brotherhood, or IRB), published his long and complex 'Meditations in Time of Civil War'. The terrific events of a European decade were concentrated into eight sections, yet

---

[62] I can suggest an example of this tunnel vision from my own experience. When I wrote *Fool's Gold: The Story of North Sea Oil* (London: Hamilton, 1994), I consulted the three standard biographies of Harold Wilson, premier when the British government legislated to control the oil industry in 1975. In none of them (by Austin Morgan, Ben Pimlott, and Philip Ziegler) was there a single mention of the oil, although it was crucial to the balance of payments issue. I taxed Ben Pimlott with this and he admitted that as a highly technical matter, it tended to drop out of sight of Cabinet ministers, and hence of historians.

[63] John Buchan, *The Three Hostages*, 1924, in *The Adventures of Richard Hannay* (London: Hodder and Stoughton, 1930), 857–62.

the imaginative heart was two simple, ballad-like poems, 'The Road at my Door' and 'The Stare's Nest by my Window', in which the matter became the clash of Republican Irregulars and Free Staters in the Galway countryside, atrocities inflicted by Irishmen on Irishmen:

> A barricade of stone or of wood;
> Some fourteen days of civil war;
> Last night they trundled down the road
> That dead young soldier in his blood:
> Come build in the empty house of the stare.
>
> We are closed in, and the key is turned
> On our uncertainty; somewhere
> A man is killed, or a house burned,
> Yet no clear fact to be discerned.
> Come build in the empty house of the stare.[64]

A global problem was framed in an ideal type taken from Irish history. A quite different form of conflict had flared up from that expected in Ireland in early 1914, when capital was ranged against labour, William Martin Murphy against Jim Larkin. Yeats's predicament also reflected how far and fast Ireland had drifted from the 'war socialism' of Whitehall. If the British munitions drive had been the triumph of the 'objective' ordering of industry, which Marx in the 'Working Day' section of *Capital* (1867) would have recognized if not approved, Ireland had become a disaster of the 'subjective' ordering of industry. The Anglo-Irish War of 1919–21, in which the total of dead didn't reach that of an average day on the front, where casualties in battle were rarely numbered in tens, in which the capture of half a dozen rifles or a machine gun was a triumph, ended with the dishonourable defeat of the world's greatest military power. Establishing why means investigating imperial dysfunction as much as nationalist energy.[65]

This isn't the place to advance yet another account of an episode both exhaustively researched *and* deftly packaged in poetic quotes, usually from Yeats: 'terrible beauty', 'All changed, changed utterly', and so on. Yet lacunae remain, which can be filled only with reference to the politics of the littoral. What happened to 'Home Rule is Rome Rule', so prominent in F. S. L. Lyons's account of 1912–14, so obscure when he turns to 1917–21?[66] Why did Lloyd George's handling of the Catholic Irish, so shrewd and successful in Scotland, crumble in Ireland itself after 1917?

---

[64] W. B. Yeats, 'Meditations in Time of Civil War', in *The Tower*, 1928, in *Collected Poems* (London: Macmillan, 1934), 225–32; see also Roy Foster, *W. B. Yeats: A Life*, ii: *The Arch-Poet, 1915–1939* (Oxford: Oxford University Press, 2003).

[65] This contention may be seen by contrasting the treatment of the Irish rebellion in F. S. L. Lyons, *Ireland Since the Famine*, 1971 (London: Fontana, 1973), which runs to 155 pages for the years 1912–22, and Joseph Lee's allowance of 55 pages for the same period in *Ireland, 1912–1985*. This isn't to criticize Lyons, but to emphasize how much the underlying priorities had changed over that quarter-century.

[66] Contrast Lyons, *Ireland Since the Famine*, chaps. II.9 and III.5.

In 1914, despite the sabre-rattling of Carson, Birkenhead, and Bonar Law, the undercurrent *in Westminster* had still been one of underlying agreement in terms of a semi-federal, two-Ireland approach, with the exclusion of Ulster. This had continuity with the traditional minimal-cost administration, whereby Ireland was run by retired military officers and Irish civil servants at arm's-length collaboration with the Catholic Church and the National Party, a society stabilized by English Tories through the Ashbourne Land Act of 1905. The conservative, property-owning peasantry which Ashbourne endowed was placed to do well out of the war, and duly raised its real wealth by 154 per cent.[67] This seemed to have overcome the pre-war tensions partly generated by a 'British' crisis brought on by trying to rationalize labour in the heavy industries of West Britain, mirrored in the labour-intensive port culture of Dublin, whose Catholic bourgeoisie supported Murphy, an imperial railway and tramway magnate who had once been a Nationalist MP, against the infant Irish trade union movement under Jim Larkin. This caused sleepless nights for Bryce's successor the Chief Secretary, the amiable *littérateur* Augustine Birrell, whose option to remain in London, while his Permanent Secretary at Dublin Castle, Sir Matthew Nathan, governed the place in consultation with John Redmond and his party, seemed to have paid off.[68] Belfast, with Unionism in unchallenged power at municipal level, yet with northern industry represented by a (truly) liberal unionist, Lord Pirrie, the boss of Harland and Wolff, was allowed to go its own way.[69]

The problems came when the economic matrix changed. U-boats made Irish agriculture unprecedentedly prosperous and enlistment increasingly difficult (30 per 10,000 in the Irish west by 1916, much lower than Norfolk's 80 per 10,000). Ireland also did well through new opportunities for emigrant labour. Small wonder that in rural Leitrim the young Patrick Kavanagh found his family rubbing their hands at the prospect. Why shouldn't war be popular? A crusade for little, Catholic Belgium, in alliance with Ireland's old ally, Catholic (and republican) France.[70] Longtime Irish sympathizers in England such as G. K. Chesterton and Hilaire Belloc held their usually energetic fire; Tom Kettle and Erskine Childers changed from running guns for the Irish Volunteers to, respectively, soldiering and flying. Catholic loyalty to the cause seemed in calculated contrast with the mutinous (and even pro-German) north. A war cabinet like Lloyd George's might have prioritized this. Asquith did not. Although he had depended on Irish Nationalist support since 1910, he knew little about the country (his visit after the Easter Rising was only his second, and his first to Belfast) and was more worried about curbing the Conservatives at Westminster than about integrating Ireland into high politics.[71]

---

[67] Jeffery, *Ireland and the Great War*, 18.

[68] León ÓBroin, *The Chief Secretary: Augustine Birrell in Ireland* (London: Chatto and Windus, 1969), 210.

[69] Herbert Jefferson, *Viscount Pirrie of Belfast* (Belfast: Mullan, 1946), 141 ff. This, in my experience perhaps the worst biography ever written—largely given over to speeches made by mayors presenting caskets to Pirrie—sunk its important subject faster than the *Titanic*.

[70] Patrick Kavanagh, *The Green Fool*, 1938 (Harmondsworth: Penguin, 1976), chap. 7, 'The War', 57–66.

[71] Roy Jenkins, *Asquith*, 1964 (London: Fontana, 1967), 311, 447–8.

Less predictable was an educated Irish public opinion long disposed to be critical of the British government. Ireland might breed Harmsworths, but it still had its own nationalist press, locally based, with a strong circulation among emigrants to the USA, where ethnic politics were well developed, and a large German community, usually on the Left, was active. Such opinion was critical, particularly when Ulster Unionist leaders entered the coalition in May 1915. It was further inflamed by firebrands such as Larkin, working for the Germans. Radical Irish nationalism was more Catholic and more Gaelic; yet it could be at its most fanatical when positioned on the imperial–Anglo-Irish divide: the daughters of the greatest Unionist landlord, the Earl of Midleton, became Sinn Feiners, as did the Gore-Booth sisters and Madame Despard, the sister of Sir John French, the British Commander-in-Chief and later Viceroy. Sir Roger Casement, the leading colonial reformer, offered his services to the Germans. Even Southern Unionists, fearing partition, which would reduce Protestants to less than 10 per cent, tended to argue for a united Ireland where they would be 25 per cent.

Within a context of fitful and unexpected affluence, the breakdown of traditional authority, and the imposition of a war-induced British nationalism, Irish reactions were unpredictable. Generally integrated into the Empire—through the diaspora and the Catholic Church—more than into the United Kingdom, yet increasingly subject to the political tensions of the mainland, the Irish nationalist intelligentsia looked rather ingenuously to allies in the United States and France. This did not rule out co-option, which Whitehall had managed quite efficiently in the cases of its former Boer opponents, Botha and Smuts, so why wasn't this replicated? What changed the events which motivated Ireland, deeply unpopular when they occurred, into revolutionary milestones?

In 1914 the Ulster Volunteers were incorporated into the New Army, the Irish Volunteers were not. Why? This is usually put down to protestant prejudice among the officer class, lately demonstrated at the Curragh, but it was fairly logical. Export-orientated Ulster faced war-induced unemployment, the twenty-six southern counties required manpower in agriculture. Moreover the Irish Volunteers were only nominally an armed force: the 900 rifles of Howth were, in comparison with the 36,000 of Larne, minor stuff. If the Ulstermen could be harmlessly incorporated as the Ulster Division then Liberal politicians, hitherto careful to let John Redmond have his way, regarded this as well and good.

Ireland was pro-war. Lord Midleton told the Lords that in eastern Ireland 127 men per 10,000 had enlisted in August–November 1914: low compared to Scotland at 237, but better than the largely agricultural west of England at 88. Besides this the numbers involved in the 'extreme' element of the Irish Volunteers scarcely reached 5,000, of whom fewer than 1,000 would take up arms. The socialist Citizen Army of James Connolly never numbered more than 250, and in 1915 lost the anti-insurrectionary Sean O'Casey. Plans for an insurrection went ahead, after an IRB-convened meeting on 3 September 1914. Ireland had to strike while Europe was at war, went the argument: delay might leave republicans looking as forlorn as the Fenians of the 1860s. Pearse and Connolly (respectively disillusioned with Irish-American populism and the strike weapon) determined on a formal uprising, with German assistance, rather than guerrilla war. How much was this Pearse's near *Blut und Boden* belief in sacrifice stoked up—as embarrassingly as Rupert Brooke's—by the war? 'The last sixteen months have been the most glorious in the history of Europe. Heroism has come back to the earth . . . the old heart of the earth needed to be warmed by the red wine of the battlefields.'[72] Or, through Connolly and his Dublin workers, had the sort of non-national revolutionism that Jack London had talked of in 1907 surged up, which lurked in the psyche of Jim Larkin, in the lyrics of Jim Connell's 'Red Flag', and in Robert Tressell's *Ragged Trousered Philanthropists*, posthumously published in 1914? The 'Irish War of Liberation' was seen as romantic nationalism, yet it would be a bundle of competing discourses, some archaic, some ultra-modern. The great art of Yeats or O'Casey—'Meditations' and 'The Plough and the Stars'—was produced with the ink scarcely dry on the treaty, yet the exploits of the rebels in 1919–21 were simultaneously celebrated in street ballads and compared to cowboy movies.

Fortunes were mixed for the Allied cause in the Catholic south. Belgium and the *Lusitania* sinking—frightfulness brought home to west Cork—aided Britain, the Irish casualties at Suvla Bay, Gallipoli, in May 1915, did not. Among the potential rebels, the IRB's conspiratorialism, stiffened by the return of the old Fenian Tom Clarke, inhibited full mobilization. British containment failed. Room 40 in the Admiralty was technically effective—German moves were identified by the code crackers, and the guns of the *Aud* and Sir Roger Casement intercepted—but politically, Dublin Castle (which had switched surveillance to the German spy peril) showed complacency, then panic and ineptitude, when on Easter Monday 1916, in circumstances close to the Fenian farce of the 1860s, 700 insurrectionists seized strongpoints in central Dublin, proclaiming another republic to add to Europe's existing three: France, Switzerland, and San Marino.

General Sir John Maxwell (like Birrell, of a Liverpool-Scots Protestant family) was demoted from Egypt to handle the insurrection. Pearse surrendered on 30 April; his forces were hissed by the Dublin crowds, though Irish opinion seems to have been baffled if not divided. But his subsequent court martial and execution, with the other fifteen ringleaders, thought by the dim and complacent 'Conky' Maxwell a minatory but measured solution, exploded in the government's face. It *was* moderate, in comparison with the bloodbath of the Paris Commune and some imperial police actions, but it netted Pearse's bill exactly, particularly when accompanied by the arbitrary internment of 3,400 suspects, mostly jailed at a disused Welsh distillery near Bala, which they used to plot a further insurrection under the gifted leadership of Michael Collins, and so nicknamed it 'the University of Frongoch'.[73] Connolly was the last to die, on 12 May. Shortly, the sixteen dead faces would be on every Irish pub wall, and a barrage of cables from Ambassador Spring-Rice in Washington, registering American

---

[72] Quoted in Jeffery, *Ireland and the Great War*, 24.

[73] Bala was the spiritual centre of Welsh Nonconformist nationalism, later deeply influenced by the Easter Rising, and also only thirty miles from Lloyd George's home base at Criccieth, but there might have been contacts. Tim Healy, the old foe of Parnell, through a visitor to Frongoch (11 Aug. 1916) and closely in touch with both Northcliffe and Beaverbrook. See Tim Healy, *Letters and Leaders of my Day* (London: Butterworth, 1928), chap. 42, and Lyn Ebenezer, *Frongoch* (Talybont: Y Lolfa, 2005).

revulsion and German glee, was already arriving. Asquith chose that day to change policy. He crossed to Ireland, and met representative figures, including some rebels. When he returned to London, it was to announce 'the breakdown of the existing machinery of Irish government'. On 25 May Lloyd George was deputed to open negotiations.[74]

Might these restorative concessions have worked? They were sidelined, not least by Asquith's appointment of Sir Henry Duke, an obscure West Country Tory, as Birrell's successor. Lloyd George's energetic attempts (from the Munitions Ministry: he never visited Ireland) to neutralize Irish discontent ended ambiguous. He nearly got Home Rule operational in 1916, only to be defeated by Asquith's sloth in arranging legislation and by Lord Lansdowne, the last of the Whigs, who whittled away Dublin's powers—and Irish representation at Westminster—to a point which no Nationalist MP could tolerate. This was the same Lansdowne who on 27 November 1917 would demand a compromise peace. His motives were similar in both cases. He could see that the war was shaking the old social order to bits, and hoped to reach a conservative European compromise before this happened.[75]

Under Lloyd George the Convention of Irishmen was suggested at the Imperial War Cabinet, convened in April, and propelled forward by Jan Christiaan Smuts in May 1917. This had also an Atlantic context: it was a response to Redmond, who had already quit Westminster, with an eye on the imperial leaders and on Woodrow Wilson, who had just entered the war in April. Lloyd George hoped that Irish-American pressure might be harnessed, at least to keep Ireland at peace through the crucial year of 1917.[76] It met from July 1917 to May 1918, during which time Sinn Fein's by-election impact slackened, while the National Party's support held up, perhaps giving Lloyd George the false confidence that conscription could be bought with Home Rule.[77] With Ludendorff flinging his armies on to the Western Front, hoping to break through before the Americans arrived, reinforcements of any sort were needed, not least to inspire the French, now depressed and immobile. Conscription had been necessary in industrial Britain, given the competing demands of the military and of war production, but prospering Irish agriculture demanded labour, otherwise migrating to unskilled or semi-skilled jobs in the British industrial regions. So the threat of it pressed on 'strong farmers' who felt within grasp of Home Rule, yet inhibited by the power of Ulster Unionists in Whitehall and—in the feline shape of the Chief of the Imperial General Staff, Sir Henry Wilson—the War Office.

The irony was that, throughout the war and in particular in 1917–18, Ireland was where 'business as usual' prevailed. Its economy did what was required of it—supply the rest of Britain with food and with unskilled manpower—without the drastic collective intervention that mainland society required and, through the expansion

---

[74] *Encylopaedia Britannica*, 12th edn, xxxi, 564; Keith Robbins, *Sir Edward Grey* (London: Cassell, 1971), 341. Spring-Rice's sister was a nationalist, involved with Childers in the Howth gunrunning.

[75] Grigg, *From Peace to War*, 342–55.

[76] Max Beloff, *Wars and Welfare* (London: Edward Arnold, 1984), 84.

[77] Michael Laffan, *The Resurrection of Ireland* (Cambridge: Cambridge University Press, 2000), chap. 3.

of the Ministry of Munitions, got. Because Ireland hadn't a munitions-organization problem (there was little activity outside the Lagan Valley and Kynoch's Arklow explosive works) it was devolved to its farmers, its own conservative Catholic establishment, and dugout generals like Maxwell.[78] Arguably this set-up made a critical contribution to the narrow margin of survival against the U-boats and the westward switch of German troops, in 1917–18. But this conservatism meant that its traditional politics, dominated by the resentful nationalism of frustrated priests and teachers, continued, gaining momentum with the South Longford by-election of May 1917, and the death on 1 August after force-feeding of the IRB's Thomas Ashe.[79]

The Convention reported on 13 April 1918, only five days before the Conscription Bill was finally passed. It proposed an Irish parliament of 200 members, 40 per cent of whom would be Unionists, with forty-three MPs sent to Westminster.[80] Again the Ulstermen stood in Lloyd George's way, and American involvement—Woodrow Wilson's Ulster-Protestant background had been underestimated—also frustrated compromise. Sinn Fein, which hadn't taken part, felt justified. Childers, seconded from the Naval Air Service to the Convention Secretariat, felt so too.

In the event, radical action came from the Catholic Church. On 18 April 1918 Cardinal Logue received anti-conscriptionists, including Sinn Fein's Eamon de Valera. Opinions among the Irish bishops had hitherto been divided. They had deplored the Rising, but were split between a Redmondite majority and Sinn Fein sympathizers. In August 1917 Pope Benedict XV had advanced a peace initiative. His motives, ironically, were similar to those of Lord Lansdowne: dynastic Europe was under immediate threat, a compact was necessary before the radicals took over. It was welcomed in Vienna, but nowhere else, even though the content differed little from President Wilson's Fourteen Points (of January 1918), but Whitehall dismissed it unread, without seemingly considering what the impact would be on a Catholic society facing conscription. It wasn't the nationalism of the Irish Church that paid off for Sinn Fein, but its ultramontanism: its *detachment* from government. 'My country is not Ireland or England but the whole mighty realm of my Church', as Shaw's Peter Keegan had put it. If this meant that the participation of a priest at a militant's funeral was read as nationalist solidarity, this was the cost to the British of spurning the Holy Father.

German involvement had long since stopped: Ludendorff had his spring offensive on his mind. Whitehall, fighting this off, deferred any sort of Home Rule concession and fabricated a 'German plot' out of the arrest of a single agent in May 1918. Opponents of conscription were again interned, which simply made matters worse. Lloyd George's preoccupation with the war's last decisive phase allowed an understandable sequence of blunders—sweeping arrests, fitful negotiations and amnesties—to take place: not just in Ireland. By the end of the year there were serious breakdowns in public order along the littoral (often taking the form of race riots), and throughout the Empire, in Quebec and Australia and most seriously in India, Britain's claim to rule was being questioned in the streets.

---

[78] Jeffery, *Ireland and the Great War*, 30–2.
[79] Charles Townshend, *Political Violence in Ireland* (Oxford: Clarendon Press, 1983), 317 ff.
[80] *Annual Register* (1917), 76.

An undistracted government *might* have managed a solution. In January 1917 the Speaker's Conference had unanimously recommended replacement of first-past-the-post by proportional representation. Lloyd George dismissed it in March as 'a device for defeating democracy', yet if adopted before the 1918 election it might have kept enough moderate Irish National Party MPs in being to cramp the style of Sinn Fein's militants.[81] Instead, electoral upheaval supervened. The circumstances, had Lloyd George noticed them, were similar to those which had first brought him into parliament in 1887. The Scots electorate rose by 183 per cent, the Welsh by 50 per cent, the Irish by 176 per cent. In the first two countries war-weariness, Liberal division, and trade union organization led to a swift growth in Labour organization, though a breakthrough in seats (in Scotland from 7 to 29 out of 72; in Wales from 10 to 18 out of 36) didn't come until November 1922. In Ireland the National Party's ineffectuality after the failure of the Convention meant that the drift of its supporters into Sinn Fein registered itself electorally in the election of December 1918.[82] A republicanism swelled which had in 1914 enthused only a small minority. Two Redmondites survived.

Lloyd George, however, had to deal with the Peace Conference in Paris, begun on 19 January 1919, to restrain French *revanchisme* and handle an America becoming steadily more irresolute, particularly after the congressional elections of autumn 1918 returned a Republican majority. The inauguration of Dáil Eireann three days later passed near-unnoticed—Ireland had retreated even further into British 'low politics'—and continued to do so until the middle of the year. Yet the Dáil's preoccupations were ambitious: the goal of the republic had displaced Home Rule, and it had Paris, not Westminster, in mind. Not far behind was the USA, to which Eamon de Valera had been dispatched in June 1918, staying for eighteen financially profitable if diplomatically frustrating months.

For Lloyd George the federal Government of Ireland Bill was still the terminus. In January 1919 he replaced the mild and ineffectual Edward Shortt as Chief Secretary with the 38-year-old Ian MacPherson. MacPherson was a Gaelic speaker, a land reformer and Young Scot, but when in June systematic republican hostilities started against members of the Royal Irish Constabulary and civil servants, aimed at breaking down the authority of Dublin Castle, he proved a hard-liner, and proscribed Sinn Fein and the Dáil. Over the next two years the IRA would kill around 300 in an imaginative but brutal campaign, provoking retaliation and atrocity from British forces who more and more seemed to resemble the Germans in Belgium. MacPherson got the bill to its second reading on 31 March 1920, but resigned within a week. His successor Sir Hamar Greenwood, a Welsh-Canadian temperance enthusiast, was rhetorically backed by a rattled, indecisive premier. With unrest growing in Egypt, India, and Quebec—and transmitted to Downing Street by the Imperial War Cabinet—Ireland had become far more than a domestic difficulty: 'De Valera has practically challenged the British Empire. Unless he is put down, the Empire will look silly',

---

[81]  Grigg, *War Leader*, 105–6.

[82]  Leon Ó Broin, *Just like Yesterday* (Dublin: Gill and Macmillan, 1986), 21. Much of Sinn Fein's impact was down to National Party capitulation, sometimes through coercion, sometimes through organizational decrepitude.

wrote Lloyd George to Churchill in 1919. Distracted by the economic crisis and the industrial challenge of the 'Triple Alliance', he allowed Greenwood to supplement the army and Royal Irish Constabulary by 10,000 auxiliaries and Black and Tans in the summer, recruits varying from the inexperienced to the psychopathic. When Greenwood proclaimed martial law on 9 August, the premier seemed to become the creature of the Unionists: condemned not just by journalist allies like C. P. Scott on the *Manchester Guardian* but by Northcliffe. Only in April 1921, faced with the possibility of trade union action on Ireland, did Lloyd George put out feelers to the Irish, but when a policy change came, it was in June, via Smuts and the Glasgow academic A. D. Lindsay acting as go-betweens. A truce in July led to convoluted negotiations, dominated by the lethally abstract question of the oath of allegiance, until a treaty came on 6 December.[83]

John Anderson, an Edinburgh civil servant, was Lloyd George's instrument, backed up by Alfred Cope, George Booth's aide in Ministry of Munitions days. Anderson found the man drafting the Treaty was Booth's kinsman, Crompton Llewellyn Davies, now committed wholly to the Sinn Fein side. Lindsay's negotiating partner was Erskine Childers, who had gone from *The Riddle of the Sands* via gunrunning in 1914 for the Irish Volunteers, to the Fleet Air Arm and pioneer work on motor torpedo boats. Reverting to Irish nationalism, he became Minister for Publicity of the Sinn Fein government, turning the skills of Whitehall against it. Childers was secretary to the Irish delegation at the peace talks. He would in 1923 be shot by Free Staters as an irreconcilable republican—hearing of this, Frank O'Connor, a young Irregular on the run in County Cork, found himself speaking Whitman's threnody on the dead Lincoln.[84] The death toll of the Civil War in 1922–3 may have reached 3,000.

In retirement, Birrell was astonished at the surrender:

'Government' capitulates and signs a treaty with 'Sinn Féin' and declares Ireland (minus an undefined Ulster) to be a Free State, with full control over both Customs and Excise, with her own police and her own army . . . In pursuit of this Treaty, and without waiting for parliamentary approval, Dublin Castle is 'surrendered' to rebels, and our soldiers evacuate the land.[85]

The cultural damage was longer-lasting. British forces burned Sir Horace Plunkett's dairies; republicans fired the Ascendancy's mansions in revenge, and proceeded to burn even more belonging to those like Plunkett himself, who supported the Free State. What the young Yeats had feared in the 1890s came to pass:

> How should the world be happier if this house
> Which passion and precision had made one,
> Time out of mind, become too ruinous
> To breed the lidless eye that loves the sun?[86]

---

[83] Morgan, *Consensus and Disunity*, 125 ff., and see Jim Ring, *Erskine Childers* (London: John Murray, 1996), chap. 16.

[84] Frank O'Connor, *An Only Child* (1961), in Frank O'Connor, *An Only Child and My Father's Son: an Autobiography* (London: Penguin, 2005), 165–66.

[85] Ó Broin, *The Chief Secretary*, 210.

[86] Yeats, 'Upon a House Shaken by the Land Agitation', in *The Green Helmet*, 1900, in *Collected Poems*, 106.

Conflagration on a Carlyleian scale left, besides police barracks and town centres, great houses roofless from sea to sea—destruction far beyond what German battle-ships and Zeppelins had inflicted on England. Ireland, Kenneth Morgan concluded, 'was the blackest chapter of the government's policy in any theatre, a monument to ignorance, racial and religious prejudice, and ineptitude'.[87] Restitution also had its price. On 26–8 July 1922 British field guns, on loan to Free State troops, were used to bombard republicans in Dublin's Four Courts. Gandon's great dome was left an empty shell, and the Irish archives a heap of ashes.

[87] Morgan, *Consensus and Disunity*, 132.

# IV
# AFTERMATH

# 10

# 'Night's Candles are Burnt Out'

Alles geben Götter, die unendlichen,
Ihren Lieblingen ganz,
Alle Freuden, die unendlichen,
Alle Schmerzen, die unendlichen, ganz.

Goethe

The Gods give without stint
To those they love,
All joy, illimitably,
All grief, illimitably.

My translation. This was the epigraph to Hamish
Henderson's Elegies, 1948.

A bottle swings on a string. The matt-grey iron ship,
Which ought to have been the future, sidles by
And with due auspices descends the slip
Into an ocean where no auspices apply.

Louis MacNeice, 'Alcohol', 1942[1]

## I  DYNAMIC FORCES

In 1928 the Electricity Supply Board of the Irish Free State allowed the painter
Sean Keating to document the opening of the Shannon Power Scheme. The river
had been diverted fifteen miles upstream from Limerick, and its waters carried along
a ten-mile head-race to one of Europe's largest hydroelectric power stations. Pylons
took 152 megawatt hours throughout the new country.[2] This was a young man's
ploy: the engineer Thomas McLaughlin was only 27, and his political boss as Minister of Commerce Patrick McGilligan 34, when the scheme was decided on in 1923,
as the civil war ended. Keating's 'Night's Candles are Burnt Out' was as ambiguous as
his master William Orpen's Versailles paintings had been six years earlier. The dam,
under construction, looms up in the background, but the central figure is a coarse,

---

[1] In *Collected Poems* (London: Faber, 1966), 208. The ship was the *Titanic*, which steamed past
Carrickfergus Rectory in 1912 when the poet was 5.
[2] *Annual Register* (1925), 139. In 2004 consumption was 23 gigawatt hours.

grasping-looking businessman—Barney Doran of Shaw's *John Bull*, two decades on? To the right a fatigued war veteran is begging from him, to the left, two drunks contemplate a rag-clad skeleton, hanging from a branch. Further to the right a young couple and their child strain forward with enthusiasm, while behind and below them a priest reads, shyly and shiftily, in a breviary. It is at best a painting of severely qualified hope.

'Ardnacrusha', as the Irish knew it, cost £5.2 million and—though scarcely on the scale of Stalin's hydro projects and Roosevelt's Tennessee Valley Authority—pioneered the sort of public works which Lloyd George would demand in his Liberal *Yellow Book* campaign of 1929, and which Tom Johnston got in his North of Scotland Hydro-Electric Board of 1943. It served notice on coal and palaeotechnology.[3] Mulvaney and Dargan would have appreciated it, even if its technology was German, from the firm of Siemens-Schuckert, a forebear of which had built Ireland's first electric railway at the Giant's Causeway in 1883. Perhaps in such boardrooms the thought wasn't entirely absent that Swift's great curse—'Burn everything English except their coal!'—might help Germany in another conflict. It was supposed to show off the progressiveness of the Cosgrave administration, but was opposed by business and the banks, and by the cities whose own generating plants were taken over by the Electricity Supply Board. Within three years Cosgrave had fallen, and the incoming, and much more aggressively nationalist, Fianna Fáil government of de Valera wasn't disposed to dwell on this achievement. Keating's painting ended up in the Oldham Art Gallery.

More poignant, though less noticed than the burned-out mansion, the power station as the symbol of progress frustrated by patriotic romance and the gun would lour over that most Shavian of Free State tragi-comedies, Denis Johnston's *The Moon in the Yellow River* (1931).

> Li-Po has drowned
> He tried to capture
> The moon in the Yellow River.

Johnston's haiku—from a collection of Ezra Pound's—could stand for other tragedies provoked not just by hubris but by the economic tsunami of 1920–1. Political and economic crisis produced Schumpeter's 'creative chaos' in reverse. New factories stood empty, and industrial regions suffered poverty and vast population outflows for the rest of the decade. Lloyd George perished politically in October 1922, through domestic instability plus the attack of an enemy whom Liberals had contemned from Gladstone's day, but who had already worsted him and through this acquired a nationalist modernizer.

The Treaty of Sèvres (1920) had promised the Greeks territories in Thrace and west Turkey. Their troops invaded, but were defeated by the same Kemal Pasha who

---

[3] The scheme is remarkably little documented, failing to turn up in Lee's otherwise comprehensive text: but see Annette Becker, John Olley, and Wilfried Wang, eds., *Architektur im 20 Jahrhundert: Irland* (Munich: Prestel, 1997), 82–5, 104–5. Patrick Geddes was a major influence on the Tennessee Valley Authority's planning theory. See Walter Stephen, ed., *Think Global, Act Local: The Life and Legacy of Patrick Geddes* (Edinburgh: Luath, 2004), 42–3.

had driven the British from Gallipoli. They were pushed back on Smyrna (Izmir), where, in August, tens of thousands of soldiers and civilians—the Christian merchants who had kept the Ottoman Empire going, as seamen, agents, and warehousemen for half a millennium—were treated to the same fate as the Armenians after 1914 and slaughtered. In October Lloyd George reaped the consequences of his affinity with the Greek liberal Venizelos ('Karolides' in Buchan's *Thirty-Nine Steps*, and another provincial: he came from Crete). After a British force had checked the Turks at Canakkale (Chanak), Lloyd George proposed a peace process for the eastern Mediterranean and a convention was signed on 11 October, but his Tory allies had had enough of his 'dynamic force' and were preoccupied by the British slump. On 19 October they met in the Carlton Club, and persuaded their leaders (Bonar Law was ill, and hit by the collapse of Jacks and Company, but approved) to end the Coalition. This symbolically refounded the Tory Party: its backbenchers are still represented by the 1922 Committee.[4]

Law became premier. He did not last long, as cancer gripped him and he resigned on 19 May 1923. Most of the west coast's coalition men—the likes of Lord Weir, Sir Eric and Sir Auckland Geddes, and Lord McLay—left politics. Beset by the woes of his unravelling industrial empire, Lord Pirrie died off Panama in 1924. The patrimony of Scotland and the littoral had changed: half of the Clyde-owned shipping lines and banks and all of the railways passed under southern control; the rest, an interlinked complex of mines, steelworks, shipyards, and shipping lines, took the slump on the chin, an episode which would end symbolically with the jailing for fraud of Lord Kylsant, Pirrie's successor, in July 1931.[5]

'And saw the merry Grecian coaster come . . .' This eclipse contrasted, again, with upheavals in the eastern Mediterranean. Finding themselves on the Aegean rocks, the Greeks fought their expulsion from Turkey by going on the qui vive in commerce. Merchants in tobacco and grain, forced out of the Asia Minor, survived by purchasing wartime freighters, now going cheap—the sort of ship William Burrell had swapped for his Cézannes. This and from the 1930s flags of convenience would in due course allow the likes of Stavros Niarchos and Aristotle Onassis to tap the West's new addiction: to oil. The first Greek tanker had an emblematic history. The *Petroil* had been built as the *Pennoil* at Greenock in 1903. Sold on as the *Gargoyle* and *Oswego*, she became in 1923 the *Queen Maeve* as one of the first Free State merchant ships, before being sold to Piraeus owners in 1931. Onassis bought her in 1938. In the same year Eric Ambler was among Levantine exiles in Nice, writing *The Mask of Dimitrios* (1939), altogether more hard-bitten than Buchan's 'shockers' in capturing the ruthless dealing involved in this recovery, the murky milieu of Balkan arms-and-finance players like Sir Basil Zaharoff, hired by arms suppliers trying to unload

---

[4] A. J. P. Taylor, *English History* (Oxford: Clarendon Press, 1965), 251–2. Harvie, 'The Jacks Case', in *Travelling Scot* (Colintraive: Argyll, 1999), 100–8. Law left about £50,000; Lloyd George three times that.

[5] 'Owen Cosby Philipps, Baron Kylsant' (1863–1937), in *DNB*. See Keith Middlemas, *Politics in Industrial Society: The Experience of the British System since 1911* (London: Deutsch, 1979), chaps. 6 and 7; Christopher Harvie, *No Gods and Precious Few Heroes: Scotland since 1914*, 1981 (4th edn, Edinburgh: Edinburgh University Press, 1999) chap. 2.

munitions which were dragging them down. Shortly after *Petroil* was scrapped in 1950, another Lloyd George pledge—the Balfour Declaration—had come home to roost. The abortive Anglo-French assault on Egypt in October 1956 would enable Greek shipowners to take advantage of the Suez closure and radically increase the size of tankers and their own vast fortunes. Onassis would share his yacht with the ancient Churchill (thoughtfully rounding the Dardanelles in darkness) and his bed with Maria Callas and Jacqueline Kennedy. His new world—of the VLCC or 'Very Large Crude Carrier' and containerization—would write off the British merchant-man and the British shipyard.[6]

The experience of 1860–1930 ended prophetic of ultimate decline, for the demo-cracy as well as the hero. 'Their school a crowd, his master solitude', as W. B. Yeats wrote in his *éloge* of Parnell. Could the new mass age yield 'bitter wisdom that enriched his blood'? 'Parnell's Funeral' is loaded with Frazerian as well as Swiftian symbolism. Might a juxtaposition of the sort—of cultural past and incalculable present—work in assessing Ireland? Was something cognate shared by Scotland or Wales, or by the complexities of the British state? The argument of this epilogue, which analyses the various ways the episode was recollected, reimagined and re-enacted, is that it was, but that this must be placed in the context of an economy dwindling from world hegemon to gallant obsolescence.[7]

## II  INTO THE DOLDRUMS

Hard-bitten, ruthless . . . The terms that orthodox parliamentarians would use of the Balkans could be applied nearer home. If the new leaders of 1923, the Conservat-ives' Stanley Baldwin and Labour's Ramsay MacDonald, had one point of principle, it was not to do with technology but with keeping Lloyd George as far from the levers of power as was humanly possible. By 1926 he was reduced to leading a family fac-tion within the Liberals; even more vividly, his power dwindled in Wales along with that of the Nonconformity he had so briskly exploited. In 1925, only three years after *Dod's Parliamentary Companion* had removed 'Welsh home ruler and radical' from his entry, nationalists, many of them anti-war, but including such former sol-diers as Saunders Lewis, formed Plaid Genedlaethol Cymru, the National Party of Wales, on his doorstep, in a tearoom at Pwllheli during the National Eisteddfod. It would take forty years for the Blaid to win a seat, as the politics of *y fro Gymraeg*

6 See Christopher Harvie, *Fool's Gold: The Story of North Sea Oil* (London: Hamilton, 1994), chap. 2, and http://visseraa.topcities.com/UK/id326.htm. 'Irish-American tankers'.

7 W. B. Yeats, 'Parnell's Funeral', in *A Full Moon in March*, in *Collected Poems* (London: Macmillan, 1934), 319–20 and see Roy Foster, *W. B. Yeats: A Life*, ii: *The Arch-Poet*, 1915–39 (Oxford: Oxford University Press, 2003), 481–2. For the 'deep structure' of regional culture see Robert D. Putnam et al., *Making Democracy Work: Civic Traditions in Modern Italy* (Prin-ceton: Princeton University Press, 1993). The result of a twenty-year study of the new Italian regions (1971), this found continuity between medieval civic republicanism and industrial-age competence.

(the Welsh-Language community) were sharply divided, but only a year for American South Wales to meet its own Golgotha.[8]

The initial response to peace had been dominated by reconstruction, and loosening the financial constraints on this. Britain came off the gold standard on 31 March 1919. £380 million was raised for investment in 1920 alone, to the alarm of conservative City financiers like Herbert Wagg, who wrote that 'The war profiteers and in particular the shipowners of Cardiff, "that city of dreadful knights", were busy unloading their fleets and factories on a credulous public through mushroom issuing houses, long since sunk without trace. Values were monstrously inflated, but every offering was oversubscribed.'[9]

Cash surged into cotton and coal: the last grand mills and modern collieries, while in the 'green revolution' many great estates—often with heirs killed in the war, like Nanteos and Gogerddan—were broken up and sold to tenant farmers. Then inflation set in, pre-war labour disputes revived, and by late 1920 boom turned into what *The Economist* called 'one of the worst years of depression since the industrial revolution'.[10]

Worse was to come. Slump reached the coalfields late because of the European unsettlement which Lloyd George had tried to calm and the compromise he had cut with the British miners. Fortuitously the French occupation of the Ruhr in 1922–3, and the German resistance to it, choked output, which kept up the demand for Welsh steam-coal. When Ramsay MacDonald, as Labour's first (and only) premier-cum-foreign secretary, brokered a settlement in 1924, German coal exports could resume, and with a saturated market came confrontation. Once back in power, Baldwin bought a year's grace in 1925, but in May 1926 the coal-owners locked their men out. The Trades Union Congress (TUC) called out the dockers, railwaymen, and printworkers in sympathy, and the General Strike began. It lasted only nine days, until the TUC surrendered. It shifted politics away from direct action, and also compelled creative writers as well as politicians to take stock. Probably with Dublin 1913–16 in mind, Baldwin had been ostensibly tactful (and infiltrated the unions without scruple), so the outcome was rather more of a moral victory for 'Britishness' than for the coal-owners. The strike was where the radical cultures of Britain and Ireland finally diverged. Class politics, factored through parliament, imposed themselves for half a century.[11]

---

[8] Kenneth O. Morgan, *Wales in British Politics, 1868–1922*, 1963 (Cardiff: University of Wales Press, 1980), 302–3, and see Alan Butt Philip, *The Welsh Question: Nationalism in Welsh Politics, 1945–1970* (Cardiff: University of Wales Press, 1975); in 1918 Lewis was working under, and was influenced by, Compton MacKenzie, later a founder of the National Party of Scotland, and head of British intelligence at Athens. A future and even more incandescent nationalist, Christopher Grieve, 'Hugh MacDiarmid', was then at Salonika, but had no connection with them.

[9] A. J. Youngson, *The British Economy, 1920–57* (London: Allen and Unwin, 1960), 26 ff. 'In the Doldrums' was a phrase coined by A. C. Pigou in his *Aspects of British Economic History, 1918–1925* (London: Macmillan, 1947).

[10] *Economist Commercial History and Review of 1921* (London: Economist Publications, 1922), 290. And see John Davies, 'The End of the Great Estates and the Rise of Freehold Farming in Wales', *Welsh History Review*, 7 (1974–5).

[11] Treatments of the General Strike, in the 1980s popular among German students, seemed to decline as those on the Western Front, and on nationalism, rose after 1989. Margaret Morris, *The*

In Scotland Hugh MacDiarmid and Lewis Grassic Gibbon made the strike central to their epic projects the poem-cycle *A Drunk Man Looks at the Thistle* (1926) and the novel trilogy 'A Scots Quair' (1932–4). It cast a long shadow over the work of the first generation of Welsh writers in English: Lewis Jones, Gwyn Thomas, Idris Davies, Richard Hughes. In the case of all of them the tensions between nationality and class struggle were unmistakable: intellectually stimulating but politically weakening. This also applied to the most socialist of the Irish writers, Sean O'Casey, a deserter from the blood-sacrifice of the Citizen Army. His Dublin trilogy—in historical sequence *The Plough and the Stars* on the Easter Rising (first performed 1926), *The Shadow of a Gunman* on the war with the British (1923), and *Juno and the Paycock* on the Irish civil war (1924)—didn't only become a central text of radical drama between the wars, but was immediately copied in the lockout by the Scottish miner Joe Corrie, whose *In Time of Strife* (1926), touring to raise funds for the Fife pitmen, got as far as a radically expressionist staging in Leipzig. O'Casey's breach with nationalism was total by the time he wrote *The Silver Tassie* in 1928, a symbolic-realist verdict on World War I. Its surreal central act, set around a huge gun, with his Dublin footballer-soldiers as proto-Beckett clowns, resembled in spirit Orpen's or Keating's paintings. But this was a past Ireland didn't want to be reminded of.

There was also realignment at the centre. In his *roman à clef* about contemporary politics *The New Machiavelli* (1911), H. G. Wells had forecast an Undershaft-like alliance between the most dynamic elements in the Liberal party and the Conservatives. By 1917 this was a fact, regretted by 'establishment' novelists like Stephen McKenna: 'For thirty years I have lived among what the world has agreed loosely to call "the Governing Classes",' wrote the nephew of Asquith's Chancellor, in *Sonia* (1917), 'The title may already be obsolescent; sentence of proscription may, as I write, have been passed on those who bear it.'[12] Reginald McKenna, sitting for Newport, Monmouthshire, was the son of an O'Connellite Catholic, who converted after settling in London as a civil servant, a type of career that the war would destroy, just as the overthrow of Asquith wrecked the Liberal Party. The sort of focused elite that he and the McKennas belonged to, already failing fast, could not survive electoral expansion, the collapse of Liberal organization, and cheaper technologized entertainment. Nonconformity and caucus politics dwindled before the mass media of radio (1923), the talkies (1928), and cheap books, nearly all of which were firmly centred in south-east England: two archetypal cockneys, Charlie Chaplin and Alfred Hitchcock, became idols of the new art.[13] European or American intellectuals, used to large-scale wars and steeped in Marx or Veblen, had at least a foothold on a situation where

*General Strike* (Harmondsworth: Penguin, 1976), has a useful section on regional responses. John Buchan's verdict, in *A Prince of the Captivity* (London: Hodder and Stoughton, 1932), was subtle: the substitution of welfare for self-government was, on balance, a loss for democracy.

[12] Stephen McKenna, *Sonia* (London: Methuen, 1917), 2. Fictional summings-up of World War I are covered in Christopher Harvie, *The Centre of Things: Political Fiction from Disraeli to the Present* (London: Unwin Hyman, 1991), chap. 5.

[13] John Stevenson, *British Society, 1914–1945* (London: Allen Lane, 1984), 398–9. The Glasgow origins of another silver screener aren't widely known, though Stan Laurel provoked Oliver Hardy's 'Another fine mess you've got us into!', maybe the pithiest summing-up of the inter-war world.

the Russian Revolution ended any notion of a return to the pre-war world, while maintaining a continuity with carbon-fired progressivism. Patrick Geddes, who most resembled them, was in virtual (though productive) exile after 1918, in Palestine, India, and from 1924 his Scots College in Montpellier. In England the transition was more awkward.

*Mass* modernism consisted largely of the technology-transmitted values of American business and entertainment. *Literary* modernism was the traditional elite trying to comprehend mass society, not empirically but through metaphors which would restore a pre-democratic, pre-industrial unity of feeling: really a counter-enlightenment sanctioned by the recovery of 'consciousness'. Where Victorian progressives like Meredith, Shaw, Wells, and Geddes had anticipated a growth of mental capability, modernists saw habit and ritual circumscribing realism, and revived romance and the epic: this became explicit in the three literary monuments of 1922–3: the Homeric-Vergilian structure of Joyce's *Ulysses*, the Wagnerian leit-motifs of Eliot's *The Waste Land*, and the national history of Yeats's 'Meditations in Time of Civil War'.[14] Literary resistance was regional, but shifted to the provinces of the English language—to Ireland, Scotland, the American Midwest and South. The country, not the city, was dominant; the stress was on pre-print-capitalist modes, on the intimate and introspective. The irony was that both conservative and radical stresses would be found in the 'radical' John Maynard Keynes, whose apprehensions of volcanic menace were almost word-for-word those of Carlyle.[15]

## III 'A GENERAL UNSETTLEMENT'

Dominic Medina, *schreck* of perhaps the greatest of John Buchan's 'shockers', *The Three Hostages* (1924), and prototype of countless super-villains in Ian Fleming and elsewhere, was Irish. Parallels with de Valera ought not to be discounted. But Buchan's psychoanalyst, Dr Greenslade, arguing that war-induced breakdown made extremes of behaviour inevitable, was grist to the mill of the best-seller author.[16] Trauma had been around for fifty years as a concept, first developed to analyse the non-physical damage inflicted by railway crashes. What was new was the publicity it got from 'oh what a literary war', as Paul Fussell called 1914–18, as its writers sifted the rubble. There was a directly political background. Having shattered the Liberal Party in 1916, Lloyd George was forced to court the great beasts of the press, of whom Piers Brendon has commented that their most striking characteristic was 'an individuality so pronounced that it constantly teetered into eccentricity', and in that package came their literary satellites, the hard-working culture politicos, the Bennetts

---

[14] Malcolm Bradbury, *The Social Context of Modern English Literature* (Oxford: Blackwell, 1971), 65 ff.

[15] See J. M. Keynes, 'My Early Beliefs', in *Collected Writings* (London: Macmillan, 1972), Vol. X, 447.

[16] See P. N. Furbank, 'The Twentieth-Century Best-Seller', in Boris Ford, ed., *The Penguin Guide to English Literature*, vii (Harmondsworth: Penguin, 1961).

and Buchans.[17] Conversely, in fictionalized retrospects, from Virginia Woolf's *Mrs Dalloway* and Grassic Gibbon's *Sunset Song* to Pat Barker's *Regeneration*, the war's human impact was symbolically portrayed by shell shock: the destruction of Septimus Warren-Smith, the recovery of Siegfried Sassoon, the suicidal desertion of Ewen Tavendale.

The first two novels stressed the peril of the individual when a more social breakdown could be diagnosed. Barker, perhaps, got closer to the heart of the matter. *Regeneration* is set in the sanatorium of Craiglockhart in Edinburgh, where Sassoon's tormented dreams were analysed by the Cambridge psychiatrist W. H. R. Rivers. As important, however, was Rivers's colleague A. J. Brock, who not only worked with Wilfred Owen but encouraged him as a writer. Brock was from an Edinburgh therapeutic tradition whose literary links ran back to James Hogg's friendship with Dr Andrew Duncan, arguably the first clinical psychiatrist, in the 1820s. A disciple of Patrick Geddes, he had as his modus operandi—'ergotherapy'—to get shell-shocked officers to recover their links with civil society.[18] Sent to Geddes's headquarters at Edinburgh's Outlook Tower, Owen made an enthusiastic response:

It stands to disarm The Exclusive, by which I mean in Science the over-specialist locking himself in a groove, in letters the Pedant, in Religion the Fanatic, in Ethics the Egotist and in Society the Snob. They are all its enemies, more even than Ignorance, indifference and Ugliness . . .

The Tower is suggestive of the great Method of Philosophical Thinking which is Correlation or Coordination.[19]

It was thanks to Brock that Owen's poetry broadened from protest to a universal meditation on social alienation. Acknowledged as the most profound statements about the war—*The Pity of War*, the title of Niall Ferguson's best-seller, comes from Owen's draft preface—his poems recognized trauma as a part of social pathology, and its treatment as a conscious process of recuperative therapy. As such psychiatry, or 'psychotherapy' (for such is the entry in the twelfth edition of the *Encyclopaedia Britannica*), became a hyphen between the war and the modern movement.

Psychiatry had already been part of the establishment mobilization against the Central Powers. John Buchan (serving the far from cerebral talents of Northcliffe and Beaverbrook) found himself reading the standard texts of Freud and Jung, and finding behind them the patterns and archetypes of *The Golden Bough*. It also became an acceptable method of treating the disruptions of war, appealing to the factory manager as much as to the medical man or the poet. Production lines were now 'manned' by women, so old prohibitions had to be discarded, and new ones invented to keep women in their place—and after the war to reconcile them to domesticity. The

[17] Piers Brendon, 'Northoleon', in *The Life and Death of the Press Barons* (London: Secker and Warburg, 1982).

[18] A. J. Brock, 'The Re-Education of the Adult: The Neurasthenic in War and Peace', *Sociological Review*, 10 (1918); and see Karin Straub, 'Psychological Disturbance in the Scottish Novel of the Nineteenth and Twentieth Centuries', PhD thesis, Stuttgart University, 2005.

[19] Owen, quoted in Dominic Hibberd, *Wilfred Owen: The Last Year, 1917–1918* (London: Constable, 1992), 22, 36.

industrial traumas of dilution and the 'scientific management' of Taylor and Bedaux (which proved far from the panacea which the likes of William Weir had expected) demanded elaborate hierarchies to handle a more complex labour force. Industrial psychology directly stemmed from the arms drive, and led to modern personnel management, evolved at Glasgow and Dundee under Dr Charles Oakley and Dr James Bowie.[20]

Buchan's post-war causerie *The Island of Sheep* (1919), set in the same myth-laden milieu as Eliot's *The Waste Land* (1922) attempts to heal the 'centre of paralysis' salient in pre-war works like *Dubliners* or *John Bull's Other Island*.[21] Psychology had a distinctive geographical dispersal. The Hogarth Press's translating of the basic Freudian texts came late, with James Strachey in the mid 1920s, but it was above all significant in the urban, industrial north-west area. Ernest Jones, the friend and biographer of Sigmund Freud, was Welsh, and Ronald Fairbairn, an early and productive Freudian, Scots. The first British Jungian analyst was Maurice Nicoll, son of Lloyd George's ally, the literary entrepreneur Sir William Robertson Nicoll, one of whose first subjects was Edwin Muir. Psychiatry could relativize the sexual liberation of the war (Marie Stopes's paean *Modern Love* came out in 1919) and cope with the assaults of a popular press whose controllers likewise emanated from the same regions.[22]

More generally, the emergency called for a reappraisal of traditional prejudice as well as a critique of the rough-and-ready socialization provided by trade unions, churches, or pubs. Just before the war Sophie Bryant, a Dublin psychologist who was to become a prominent London headmistress, wrote *The Genius of the Gael* (1913), holding that the Celtic peoples argued by extension, while the English argued by exclusion, something given plausibility by the regular confrontations between Lloyd George's entourage and laconic brasshats. Arguably it underlies the articulate reinterpretation of society to be found in the West in the 1920s, whether the restoration of the civic epic in *Ulysses*, MacDiarmid's *Drunk Man*, or the Welsh-language revival associated with Saunders Lewis and Plaid Cymru.[23]

More debatable in all of this was the prospect for urban life, embraced so confidently by Geddes. Edwin Muir along with Saunders Lewis made a hero of James Connolly, a socialist who seemed ultimately to surrender to rural ethnic nationalism.

[20]  Buchan's psychological interests are covered by Catherine Carswell in *John Buchan, by his Wife and Friends* (London: Hodder and Stoughton, 1947). He and C. J. Jung were born in Calvinist manses in the same year, 1875. For the political background to 'industrial psychology' and personnel management see Bernard Waites, *A Class Society at War, 1914–18* (Leamington: Berg, 1987), 271–9, and also Arthur McIvor, 'Were Clydeside Employers More Autocratic?', in William Kenefick and Arthur McIvor, eds., *Roots of Red Clydeside, 1910–14* (Edinburgh: John Donald, 1996), 41–65.

[21]  Buchan's book is not the same as his Richard Hannay thriller of 1934, but was co-written with his wife Susan as 'Cadmus and Harmonia' (old and wise serpents): it makes a strong case for the liberal Buchan. See also Torsten Hitz, 'Shell Shock and the Literature of World War I', MA thesis, Tübingen University, 1997.

[22]  For the early history of psychoanalysis see Jock Sutherland, *Fairbairn's Journey into the Interior* (London: Free Association, 1989); his psychoanalytical portrait of John Buchan, in the *John Buchan Journal*, although from a Freudian rather than a Jungian position, is also fascinating.

[23]  Luke Gibbons, 'This Sympathetic Bond: Ossian, Celticism and Colonialism', in Terence Brown, ed., *Celticism* (Amsterdam: Rodopi, 1996), 274–91.

Was this a way of combating a general sense of cultural displacement, a tension between a civic ideal which had been paternalist and small-scale—from Adam Ferguson to Thomas Chalmers and the Kailyard—and the huge market- or war-driven structures which actually prevailed?[24] This casting-back—what the Welsh called *hiraeth*—afflicted other immigrant groups, according to the Welsh-Jewish Dannie Abse, and provided another motif for pioneer psychoanalysts as well as journalists, architects, and town planners. Was it not also the internalization of sexual problems by a middle class enjoined to sublimate sexuality to the task of preserving social control—through Emmanuel Todd's 'authoritarian families' and a political pattern of family life which stressed sexual puritanism? William Buchan suspects that the large and talented Buchan clan was 'somewhat undersexed', with few of its members marrying; A. S. Neill commented on the lack of pleasure in sex in his parents' generation, as did Margaret Stansgate, even although her parents were noted freethinkers. R. D. Laing believed that his parents copulated only on the occasion of his conception. A survey of Ulster attitudes to sexual mores in the 1930s found abstention from intercourse widespread in both religious communities, which seemed to increase *with* secularization and urbanization and the decline of infant mortality.[25] At its best literary revival encouraged reflection and subtlety, what Max Weber called *Verstehen*, but it sacrificed the blunt confidence and energy, the 'Tom Broadbent' element, of the pre-war years.


## IV  INQUESTS

Lloyd George fell in a European aftershock, in the racket caused by other Dynamic Forces: Italian fascism, German inflation, and the Kapp putsch, the Ruhr occupation. British ideas of social evolution retreated to a moralistic version of the old two-party system. Novelists were sharp in sensing this, even before George Dangerfield's evocation of 1909–14, *The Strange Death of Liberal England* (1934), claimed with Meredith that fiction was 'the purest form of history'. Max Beloff attributed prophetic qualities to McKenna's *Sonia*, with seventeen editions between March and December 1917: humdrum sub-Disraelian stuff but, like Edward Marsh's memoir *Rupert Brooke* (1915) and Ernest Raymond's *Tell England!* (1922) an upper-class tragedy set against a new and mechanistic commercial leadership.[26] It foregrounded a preoccupation with 'Englishness' that would continue.

[24] See Helga Woggon, *Integrativer Sozialismus und nationale Befreiung: Politik und Wirkungsgeschichte James Connollys in Irland* (Göttingen: Vandenhoeck und Rupprecht, 1990), 11–44.

[25] Jonathan Croall, *Neill of Summerhill* (London: Routledge, 1983); William Buchan, *John Buchan: A Memoir* (London: Buchan and Enright, 1982), chap. 1; Adrian Laing, *R. D. Laing: A Biography* (London: Peter Owen, 1994); Margaret Stansgate, *My Ticket of Leave* (London: Hutchison, 1992); B. M. Browne and D. S. Johnson, 'Social Change in Inter-War Northern Ireland: Fertility Control and Infant Mortality', in Rosalind Mitchison and Peter Roebuck, eds., *Economy and Society in Scotland and Ireland, 1500–1939* (Edinburgh: John Donald, 1988).

[26] Harvie, *The Centre of Things*, 154–5, and see Max Beloff, *Wars and Warfare* (London: Edward Arnold, 1984), 37–8; Raymond's book was High Church and homoerotic, but Anthony Asquith's film of 1931 was as powerful an anti-war manifesto as Lewis Milestone's *All Quiet on the Western Front*, 1938.

In 1926, two Edwardian heavyweights joined in. Ford Madox Ford published the third volume of *Parade's End*, a meditation on 'the public events of a decade', and Arnold Bennett *Lord Raingo*. Ford's grandfather had been Ford Madox Brown, the painter of *Work* (1857), and as an 'English Tory' he carried on the nationalist element in Christian Socialism.[27] His hero Christopher Tietjens, a Bolingbroke-like 'country' man, distrustful of Whitehall, refuses as a senior civil servant to falsify military statistics, in an echo of the Maurice case. He is replaced by an ambitious, pliable Scot Vincent MacMaster and goes to the front, expecting to be killed. His neurotic Sheela-Na-Gig of a Catholic wife Sylvia intrigues against him; her confessor, Father Consett, is shot for his part in the 1916 Rising. Though he was writing after *Ulysses*, with a narration equally marked by stream of consciousness, Ford was conservative in a deeper sense than Disraeli. General Maurice was the grandson of the 'Christian Socialist' F. D. Maurice, portrayed alongside Carlyle in *Work* as prophets of an English nationalism.[28] Consett was the honest enemy, MacMaster the deracinated, opportunistic provincial, bending politics to selfish ends: Lloyd George—or John Buchan?—writ small.

Bennett wrote *Lord Raingo* out of his stint at the Ministry of Information in 1918 with Beaverbrook, who aided him with details. Old friends from the Coalition clustered round. Churchill praised; Birkenhead, always after ready cash, denounced. *Raingo* sold nearly 20,000 copies in its first fortnight, and effectively became the opening shot in the battle over wartime strategy which was fully joined when Lloyd George started to publish his *War Memoirs* in 1930.[29] In the novel he is Andrew Clyth, a Scots-Irish Catholic, who summons his fellow townsman the ailing Sam Raingo to the Ministry of Records and the House of Lords. Raingo's new career brings disaster on his wife, who crashes her car and is killed, and his mistress, shattered by the death of a former lover at the front, who commits suicide. He is trapped in Whitehall, where ministries fight each other more than the Germans. In the Lords he performs badly but saves face by breaking the news of a German mutiny at Brussels—the first sign of total collapse. His efforts overtax him and he contracts pneumonia. He recovers, but the strain is too much for his heart and, on the last night of the war, he dies.

Sam Raingo is the Liberal Britain which shifted from provincial industry to finance and the City: a 'solid' provincial who took on the war effort, partly out of patriotism, partly out of pride. But 'push and go' also means the blood in the lungs, the death and waste of the front. Clyth is carrying a bill to extend conscription to the middle-aged and to Ireland. Raingo has to organize visits to London by the American editors on whom Britain now depends. His death symbolizes the costs of victory. Yet out of this comes change. Raingo is surrounded by female bureaucrats, drivers, and typists, at their top the Prime Minister's secretary Miss Packer (a composite of the

[27] For this part of Ford's career see Arthur A. Mizener, *The Saddest Story* (London: John Lane, 1971), 365–81.

[28] For the Maurice incident see Taylor, *English History*, 146–7, 172–3.

[29] Birkenhead in *Daily Mail* (Nov. 1926), quoted in James Hepburn, ed., *Arnold Bennett: The Critical Heritage* (London: Routledge, 1981), 475–83.

Cabinet Secretary Maurice Hankey and Lloyd George's secretary and mistress Frances Stevenson). Not only are women realizing themselves in such new occupations; they *are* Geddes's 'geotechnics' symbolically overtaking the male engineer elite of a literally exploding palaeotechnology.

Ford's Tietjens sought a similarly holistic image in Bemerton, the parish of the Jacobean poet George Herbert, where 'a man might stand up on a hill'. This reflected a search for the undivided sensibility of Shakespeare's time, or the Pre-Raphaelite virtues in William Dyce's great painting of the slight cleric dwarfed by massive-boled oaks, Salisbury spire in the distance. Ford saw the old elite felled by the intrigues of Whitehall arrivistes, where Bennett saw the opposite, the honest businessman trapped and throttled in the web. Was this unduly gloomy? Bennett ended pessimistic. In 1926, although he called himself a socialist, he condemned the General Strike, which he saw as a revolutionary act directed at a collapsing economy.[30]

These novels emphasize the paradox of the 'War to end War'. Woodrow Wilson's world order was rooted in seventeenth-century notions of contractual, divided sovereignty: a League of Nations grounded in a covenant. Yet Britain's own attempt at this—Irish Home Rule—had failed dishonourably. The intellectual reaction to this rootlessness was a retreat to another seventeenth century, reflected in *Parade's End*. T. S. Eliot's essay 'The Metaphysical Poets' in 1921, drawing on the scholarship of the Shetlander Herbert Grierson, rehabilitated Herbert and his contemporaries, setting their 'unity of thought and feeling' against a greedy, vain, unstable age. A year later came *The Waste Land*. Eliot took after Bergson, Sorel, Freud, and Jung: emphasizing the role of the habitual and ritual in keeping civilized life from falling apart. He was echoed by more orthodox Conservatives, such as Buchan and Walter Elliot MP, who regarded post-Newtonian physics as unable to provide certainties on which to construct the natural, let alone the social sciences.[31] A restatement of the Kiplingite 'Law' through the hierarchy of Christian Socialism and paternalism, this pragmatism would later be applauded by refugees like J. A. Schumpeter and Karl Popper, and fitted snugly into the Tory reaction to the Lloyd George coalition and its explicit technocracy. Its atmosphere, in Lord Blake's words, 'hard, glittering, sophisticated . . . heartless and insincere', provoked the same sort of revulsion in another literary-minded romantic, Stanley Baldwin.[32]

## V   AFTER IRELAND

Victory disguised for only months the fragility of the British state. Bernard Shaw pirated Ruskin and flaunted him in *Heartbreak House* (1919): 'Rome fell, Venice fell, Hindhead's time will come!' The Irish crisis was taken by radicals in Scotland and

---

[30] *The Journals of Arnold Bennett*, 1933, ed. Frank Swinnerton (Harmondsworth: Penguin, 1954), entries of 4–13 May 1926, 402–3.

[31] See Walter Elliot, *Toryism and the Twentieth Century* (London: Philip Allen, 1928), 95.

[32] Robert Blake, 'The Right', in John Raymond, ed., *The Baldwin Age* (London: Eyre and Spottiswoode, 1960), 35.

Wales, as well as India and Egypt, as the first stage of collapse, with Lloyd George looking less of a world statesman than one of Rome's latter-day 'barbarian Emperors', like Magnus Maximus (also a Caernarfon man: Macsen Wledig to the Welsh) who briefly and bloodily took over in 388. It was Asquith, 'the last of the Romans', who patronized Lytton Strachey's post-Freudian *Eminent Victorians* (1917).[33] Both appeared only the temporary kings—J. G. Frazer's coinage seemed apt—of a provisional, not-quite-civic state. Strachey's lover J. M. Keynes called Lloyd George 'a man rooted in nothing', which, if condescending and snobbish, still captured a new class kept in power on military sufferance, sapped by the democratization of 1918, its cultural resources made unstable with the crumbling of Nonconformity; its coal-and-steam technology threatened by oil, chemicals, electricity, and the consumer goods demanded by its workers; its investment power taken over by Wall Street.[34]

All of this was complicated by the absence of the Irish. In 1910 the Redmondites had really been part of the Liberal coalition at Westminster; now Gladstone's 1886 scheme for an independent, non-federal Irish parliament was a fact, with greater powers but not the protectionism Liberals had then feared. Free State fiscal conservatism appeared as conciliatory as the ex-guerrilla W. T. Cosgrave, President of the Council of Ministers, at Commonwealth Conferences in London, singing from the same worthy sheet as that other ex-guerrilla Jan Christiaan Smuts.[35] But the treaty and the withdrawal of the Irish Party shifted British politics to the Right and to forces recruited from Bulpitt's 'low politics'. Irish emigrants, since 1921 largely barred from the USA, faced a hostile establishment in Britain.[36]

Liberals and Tories had wheeled and dealed with the National Party and the Catholic hierarchies; Balfour's 1900 'Khaki' election victory owed more to bribing Catholics than beating Boers. The 1918 Education (Scotland) Act was this sort of politics, playing into extra time. But Labour's recruitment of the Irish after 1921 drove many surviving Liberals into local government alliances with the Tories, and under Baldwin politics moved, if not towards explicit repression, then towards an accentuated Englishness or Scottishness which implied this. The English Catholic hierarchy was patriotic and conservative—if Cardinal Manning took the London dockers' side in

[33] Shaw was adapting Ruskin in *The Stones of Venice*, 1848, on the maritime empires of Tyre, Venice, and England: 'Since first the dominion of men was asserted over the ocean, three thrones, of mark beyond all others, have been set upon its sands: the thrones of Tyre, Venice, and England. Of the First of these great powers only the memory remains; of the Second, the ruin; the Third, which inherits their greatness, if it forget their example, may be led through prouder eminence to less pitied destruction' (*The Works of John Ruskin*, ed. E. T. Cook and Alexander Wedderburn (London: George Allen and Longmans Green, 1903–12), xix, 17).

[34] J. M. Keynes, 'Mr Lloyd George', in *The Economic Consequences of the Peace* (London: Macmillan, 1919), 123.

[35] W. T. Cosgrave, 'Address of the President of the Council of Ministers, Irish Free State', in *Contemporary English Rhetoric: Speeches at the 1925 Conference of Imperial Prime Ministers* (Berlin: Humblot, 1926). The former Taoiseach Dr Garrett Fitzgerald remembered de Valera at the end of his career, feeling himself emotionally closer to Smuts, and indeed to the Queen Mother, than to the 'New Commonwealth'; conversation with the writer, Dec. 1973.

[36] The Immigration Act of 1 July 1921 'restricted immigration to 3% of the persons of that nationality resident in the United States in 1910'. This gave a figure for the whole UK of 77,200. 'Immigration', *Encyclopaedia Britannica*, 12th edn.

1889, Cardinal Bourne went beyond King, premier, and Canterbury in condemning the General Strike in 1926—but attacks on Catholicism mounted. In Scotland the Established Kirk, traditionally Conservative, captured the drive to Church reunion, under a powerful clerical Tory, the Revd John White. His Church and Nation Committee combined Milnerite social reform with deep hostility to Catholic immigrants; and the United Free Church dissented little. Once united, in 1929, the Kirk's prescription against the slump of 1929–32 was a further dose of the same.[37]

Baldwin's Scottish Secretary in 1924–9 created modern administrative devolution. Sir John Gilmour was also an Orangeman. His bureaucratic centralization, replacing semi-representative central boards with British civil service departments in 1926 and ending elected local education authorities and parish councils in 1929, could be seen as a pre-emptive strike on areas where Catholics might take democratic power. It was opposed by Scots Labour MPs but forced through, while Tory litigants racked John Wheatley, the ablest and most left-wing of the Red Clydesiders, and a Catholic, to an early grave.[38] Almost exclusively Protestant, Tory MPs remained the majority in Scotland until the 1950s, overwhelmingly so between 1931 and 1945; while the bureaucracy of St Andrews House was a Protestant redoubt. Although in 1913 the Catholic Sir Antony MacDonnell, formerly Under-Secretary at Dublin Castle, had recommended an integrated Scottish Office, it took half a century for a Catholic, James McGuinness, to reach permanent secretary rank. In the 1850s the Orange Order had been suppressed by the Whigs; now anti-Catholicism extended from Hugh MacDiarmid on the Left (despite all his enthusiasm for Yeats and Connolly) to such as George Malcolm Thomson or Andrew Dewar Gibb on the Right. John Buchan's Gorbals Diehard-turned-journalist Jaikie Sim in *Castle Gay* (1931) wants a reborn Scotland without the Irish, though there was nothing on the Scottish Left as venomous as J. B. Priestley's assault in *English Journey* (1934) on the Liverpool Irish as a savage, squalid nuisance. Anti-Catholic nationalism was troubling to Roland Muirhead, the ex-Young Scot and dour utopian who bankrolled the Scottish National Party (1934), but he couldn't wish it away.[39]

There were counter-currents. The high-profile nationalism of Compton Mackenzie and the Dominican monk and seafarer Peter Anson was Catholic and corporatist. Buchan at the end of his career went ecumenical as Governor-General of Canada: his autobiographical Sir Edward Leithen, in *Sick Heart River* (1941), dies in the care of a French-Canadian priest, in a Eucharist of Canadian ethnic and religious diversity. Within the Kirk after 1938 the coming man was the emotionally Catholic, socialist, and pacifist George MacLeod, whose Iona Community combined social work in Glasgow slums with rebuilding Columba's abbey. The far right, Catholic as well as

[37] See Tom Gallagher, *Glasgow: The Uneasy Peace* (Manchester: Manchester University Press, 1987), chap. 4.

[38] William S. Marshall, *The Billy Boys: Orangeism in Scotland* (Edinburgh: Mercat, 1996), 127–31. The order had been banned from public life in Ireland by Under-Secretary Thomas Drummond in the 1830s.

[39] See George Pottinger, *The Secretaries of State for Scotland* (Edinburgh: Scottish Academic Press, 1979), 29–37; interview, James McGuinness and the writer, Oct. 1986; J. B. Priestley, *English Journey* (London: Heinemann, 1934), 235–6.

Protestant, tripped over itself. In the early 1930s anti-Catholic parties were polling high in Glasgow and Edinburgh, producing a uniquely Scottish rightist movement; but they regarded fascism as a Catholic conspiracy—despite a largely Scots 'general staff' Mosley roused no one in the north—and were alienated from Catholic nobility like the Maxwell-Scotts, who propagandized for Mussolini and Francoist Spain. Their propaganda, however, divided Labour supporters in the west in the late 1930s, and liberal Tories such as Walter Elliot were quite content to profit by it.[40]

The inter-war years did little for such Protestant Irish socialists as John Hewitt, a desponding Geddesian regionalist confronting such ethnic dystopias as de Valera's ruralism and Craigavon's eighteen-year stewardship of 'a Protestant State for a Protestant People'.[41] At the same time, the Atlantic arc lost out on new Fordist industry: the early Ford plants at Cork and Trafford Park were almost all that the western seaboard saw of car making between the 1920s and the 1960s. The rise of Cowley, Longbridge, Luton, and Dagenham in the English heartland, luring redundant Welsh colliers or low-paid agricultural workers willing to take on jobs assembling components from the smallware factories of Birmingham and the Black Country, would wipe out the Scottish car industry by 1930. The period 1939–45—'The Emergency' in Ireland—would not help. World War II brought a boost to the Ulster economy, whose living standards increased from being roughly level with those of the Free State to 75 per cent higher than those of the new Republic in 1949.[42] This boosted the British connection, against a rural and inturned south. Eire had been a model of sorts for an independent Scotland: no longer. Its example kept many Scots leery of Scottish independence until the late 1960s.

## VI   AMERICAN DREAMS

In 1922 a young Scottish radical headed across the Atlantic to study newspapers and society in Chicago. Once there, John Grierson decided that print was finished and went south-west to Hollywood, where he blagged his way into the company of D. W. Griffith, Charlie Chaplin, and John Feeney, who called himself John Ford. He came back with the message that film was a truly popular culture—far more people in Europe recognized Chaplin than Haig or Ludendorff—and was sustained in this even by the apparently antithetical politics of the Soviet Union. Under Lenin's New Economic Policy, Communism was to mean 'electrification and power to the

[40] See Christopher Harvie, introduction to John Buchan, *The Leithen Stories* (Edinburgh: Canongate, 2002); Ronald Ferguson, *George MacLeod* (London: Collins, 1990); Neil Stewart, 'The Far Right in Scotland in the 1930s', PhD thesis, Edinburgh University, 1993.

[41] See Edna Longley, 'Progressive Bookmen', in *The Living Stream* (Newcastle: Bloodaxe, 1994), 110–29; Norman Vance, 'Pictures, Singing and the Temple', in Eve Patten, ed., *Returning to Ourselves* (Belfast: Lagan Press, 1995); Patrick Buckland, *James Craig, Lord Craigavon* (Dublin: Gill and Macmillan, 1980), 115 ff.

[42] David Johnson, *The Interwar Economy in Ireland* (Dundalk: Economic and Social History Society of Ireland, 1985), 43; and see Johnson and Liam Kennedy, 'The Two Economies in Ireland in the Twentieth Century', in J. R. Hill, ed., *A New History of Ireland*, vii: *Ireland 1921–1984* (Oxford: Oxford University Press, 2003).

Soviets', but in fact it continued the Atlantic worship of scientific management and new technology. So the ideologically more acceptable innovations of Eisenstein and Vertov could be taken on board. In 1926, helping Stephen Tallents to set up Baldwin's Empire Marketing Board—a weak substitute for the Empire free trade that the Prime Minister wanted—Grierson showed the Soviet greats to Rudyard Kipling, who was enthralled; Britain should not lose out on such 'pageants of Empire'.[43]

A further Scots-Atlantic blowback was the rise and dissemination of Douglas Economics, or social credit, which stemmed from a somewhat imaginative rationalization of the economics of one war production factory by Clifford Douglas, an engineer of Scots origins. Noting that the payments for material and wages were always lower than the price gained by the goods, Douglas attributed this to the appropriation of credit by the financial industry. Taken up by A. R. Orage and the *New Age*, this spread rapidly through nationalist ranks and, following tours by Douglas, influenced politics in Alberta and British Columbia and New Zealand; its role was also significant in the ideology of the Scottish national movement—MacDiarmid and Edwin Muir were both devotees, and Tom Johnston was more pro than contra—probably reflecting Scots and Scots settler resentment at the relative success of Scottish banking while the rest of the economy pitched into recession. Bafflement at translating Douglas's ideas into policy led to what W. B. Yeats called the politics of the 'revolutionary simpleton'. It led Ezra Pound to the far Right, though a whiff of it continued in the policies of the Scottish National Party.[44]

Symbolically, Douglasism and Grierson's career—he crossed to Canada in 1938 to head the National Film Board—showed the littoral hit by a centrifuge. The geography of success was shifting east and west from the arc, and from north to south within Britain. Although in World War II the north and the Clyde would be as crucial as in World War I—making good huge merchant shipping losses and acting as the air and sea marshalling yard connecting America with Russia and the second front—the psychological and media centre of the war was London. The 'Myth of the Blitz' and Priestley's *Postscripts* were its propaganda: the lineal successor to the pipe-and-beer patriotism of Chesterton and Belloc, albeit with a north-western flair. The metropolitan triumph was further projected by Ed Murrow's broadcasts, newsreels of St Paul's riding out the flames, the films and essays of Humphrey Jennings and George Orwell, the cheery cockneys from the shelters—with a Celtic theme park of MacNeice, Dylan Thomas, Colquhoun, and MacBryde quartered usefully on Fitzrovia.[45]

Irish neutrality, and revulsion from it in anti-Nazi circles—MacNeice's furious poem 'Neutrality' for instance—was only a partial explanation. The answer may

---

[43] H. Forsyth Hardy, *John Grierson: A Film Biography* (London: Faber, 1979), 49.

[44] C. B. MacPherson, *Democracy in Alberta* (Toronto: University of Toronto Press, 1953); Hugh MacDiarmid, 'The Creator', in Lewis Grassic Gibbon and Hugh MacDiarmid, eds., *Scottish Scene: or, The Intelligent Man's Guide to Albyn* (London: Routledge, 1934).

[45] See Angus Calder, *The Myth of the Blitz* (London: Cape, 1990), and Richard Weight, *Patriots: National Identity in Britain, 1940–2000* (London: Macmillan, 2002), chap. 1; the tenor of this milieu was unforgettably captured by the Scots-sounding J. MacLaren-Ross in *Memoirs of the 1940s*, 1966 (Harmondsworth: Penguin, 1984); more profound is his empathy with the displaced historian Alun Lewis, whose poems and short stories equate Wales with a pre- and post-imperial world.

lie, ironically enough, in an inversion of Atlantic-consciousness. When America formally entered World War I in 1917, encouraged by old hands like James Bryce, its intelligentsia was set up to appropriate Anglo-Britain, by framing it in American experience. This produced an ethos closer to that of the European nation states than earlier projections of a diffused, schismatic United Kingdom. Such modern accounts as Samuel Hynes's *The Soldier's Tale* (1995) or Paul Fussell's *The Great War in Modern Memory* (1975) are still marked by the impact on English Studies—and indeed on Irish Studies—of America's own total war of 1861–5, as bloody and almost as literary as 1914–18.[46]

The weakness of the littoral after 1920 meant that the American initiative, and identification, was with *England*, something made specific later on in the Tory patriotism of T. S. Eliot's *Four Quartets* and *Notes towards the Definition of Culture* (1948). Eliot was on the right of the scene, but this also applied to left-wing social democracy. Aneurin Bevan and his wife Jennie Lee, deeply influenced by the radical Uruguayan sociologist José Rodo, quartered themselves with the Canadian Ulster Scot Beaverbrook and the ex-Irish nationalist Brendan Bracken.[47] Bevan was far from the caricature Welsh-revivalist-preacher-and-primitive-Marxist—Dai Smith's 1993 study shows him endlessly eclectic—but after 1931 he was embedded in London. West Britain's America in the 1900s had been socialist, absorbing both the revolutionism of the Wobblies and the progressive Democracy of Bob La Follette and Eugene Debs. After 1918 in the propaganda of Grierson, and in the continuity that David Caute has seen between the 'westward look' of the enlightenment and the technocratic ingenuousness of the fellow travellers, it paralleled the other new world of the Soviet Union. A similar collectivism influenced perhaps the last gasp of the Atlantic impulse, the drive from the 1940s to the 1960s for high-rise housing, on the back of rearmament, something foreshadowed in a Glasgow delegation which visited the New Deal New York of Fiorella La Guardia for the World's Fair in 1939, a parallel to Glasgow's own ambitious Empire Exhibition in 1938.[48]

Huge 'conurbations' (a Geddes coinage) presented a negative image, also transmitted. Transport and power companies had to be made subject to 'virtue' or they would corrupt. Another Marlowe, Raymond Chandler's, was en route to his own Heart of Darkness, down the mean streets of a dystopic, unmelting pot, where defensive neighbourhoods had replaced communities.[49] Richard Hughes's dangerously carefree children, first in *A High Wind in Jamaica* (1930) and then in *The Wooden Shepherdess* (1961), are one aspect of this, all too close to the wandered souls of Chandler's Los Angeles. Dystopias continued to fascinate, explaining much of the affinity between the American Marxist Howard Fast and Gwyn Thomas, when the optimism had

[46] Samuel Hynes, *The Soldier's Tale* (London: Pimlico, 1998) and Paul Fussell, *The Great War in Modern Memory* (New York: Oxford University Press, 1975).

[47] Jose Rodo, *Ariel: Liberalism and Jacobinism*, 1900, trans. William F. Rice (Chicago: University of Chicago Press, 1929).

[48] David Caute, *The Fellow-Travellers: A Postscript to the Enlightenment* (London: Weidenfeld and Nicolson, 1973).

[49] Dai Smith, 'Pagans and Public Eyes', in *Aneurin Bevan and the Culture of South Wales* (Cardiff: University of Wales Press, 1993), 298–317.

departed. A sense of community could also, however, mutate into the 'fortress Wales' element of Richard Llewellyn's xenophobic *How Green was my Valley* (1939), which projected Saunders Lewis's anti-industrial ideology internationally, via the conservative Irishness of John Ford, who filmed it. This defensiveness wasn't far from the social ethos of Atlantic Protestantism which still marks contemporary Northern Ireland, its sequences of bungalows, shopping malls, and churches strung out beyond the periphery of decayed, violence-scarred inner-city areas.[50]

But westward look! America could still be radical. In 1938 the great black actor, singer, and communist Paul Robeson starred in Pen Tennyson's *Proud Valley*, set in the South Wales coalfield; in 1942 Woodrow Wilson Guthrie (was a name ever more Presbyterian?) came off a troopship in the Clyde and discovered Burns. After World War II, when MacCarthy assaulted New Deal radicalism, Guthrie's successors Pete and Peggy Seeger and Alan Lomax came back, feeding into the nationalist and radical movements, and into the Irish Folk Song Commission. Communists like Hamish Henderson and Norman Buchan rediscovered, and re-created, a popular voice of Scottish folk culture, which also mediated between the Protestant and Catholic traditions, and between (in the cases of Henderson in Scotland and Gwyn Thomas in Wales) other European cultures: the Italy of Gramsci, the America of the hobos, the crime novel, and the *film noir*, the Andalusia of Lorca, homosexual, friend of the gypsies, martyr to the fascists, allured and repelled by the mass society of New York.[51] Things might have been more radical had economic depression persisted, but after 1935 rearmament, war, and the bombing of enemy industries brought an orthodox heavy industrial upswing, which the Americans supplemented with light manufacturing and service concerns to maintain a European manufacturing presence and absorb women workers. Industry supplying America was replaced by industry owned by America.

Progressivism had been white—aggressively so in such expat Welsh products as Jack London and D. W. Griffith—but this changed with economic eclipse and World War II. Just as Robeson became an honorary Welsh miner, singing to the Eisteddfod over the radio when banned from travelling, Martin Luther King and the civil rights movement were taken, rather vaguely, as models for the early stages of anti-Unionist protest in Northern Ireland. Seamus Heaney, in *The Listener* in 1968, took a line which was still civic rather than national:

The civil rights marchers who were banned from entering the walls and business centre of the city . . . represented after all the grievances of the Catholic majority; unemployment, lack of housing, discrimination of jobs and gerrymandering in electoral affairs. They were asking to be accepted as citizens of Derry also; they wanted at least the rights, too long the prerogative of the minority, to demonstrate and express themselves in public.[52]

[50] See John Harris, ' "A Hallelujah of a book": *How Green was my Valley* as Best-Seller', *Welsh Writing in English*, 3 (1997).

[51] Hamish Henderson, 'Lorca and Cante Jondo', in *Alias McAlias: Writings on Songs, Folk and Literature* (Edinburgh: Polygon, 1992), 313–18.

[52] Seamus Heaney in *The Listener* (24 Oct. 1968), quoted in Bob Purdie, *Politics in the Streets: The Origins of the Civil Rights Movement in Northern Ireland* (Belfast: Blackstaff, 1990), 246.

The small but articulate Communist Party regarded such street politics as inappropriate, and likely to provoke sectarian confrontation. Perceptive, for the outcome of civil rights campaigns on both sides of the Atlantic turned out bleakly ironic by the 1990s. Black mayors, like their Ulster Catholic counterparts, were landed with undercapitalized, run-down inner cities from which the more affluent had fled.[53]

America would in the 1970s deliver the *coup de grâce* to west-coast heavy industry. The demand for oil from the North Sea after the Middle Eastern crisis of 1973 led to a frenzy of off- and onshore activity which sucked investment away from conventional shipbuilding and engineering. It was followed by the huge Anglo-American Trident missile programme in the Gareloch and Loch Long, two-thirds complete when its *raison d'être*, the cold war, vanished in 1990.[54] The boom in 'hotel ships', once the Clyde's speciality, had to be met elsewhere. The commissioning of the giant *Queen Mary II* at Lorient in 2003 coincided with the bulldozing of the last remains of John Brown's Clydebank yard, birthplace of the first *Queen Mary*, to clear the ground for a supermarket.

A photograph of the mid 1950s shows two angular, elegant old men on an Italianate terrace, one dressed in tweeds and breeches, the other under a black wide-awake hat. Both Clough Williams-Ellis and Frank Lloyd Wright were Welsh by adoption, called themselves radicals, and were disciples of Patrick Geddes, yet there could have been few architectural statements as different as Portmeirion and Taliesin West. Williams-Ellis's hotel-village near Porthmadog, started in 1923, was a Prospero's Island, a refuge for the flotsam from wrecked mansions and forgotten cottages, created by the man who wrote the first history of the tank and would edit the first conservationist manifesto, *Britain and the Beast*, in 1938; Lloyd Wright's desert home in Arizona was a Whitmanite affirmation of American defiance of topography and climate, something only a car-borne and airborne civilization was capable of.[55] Peggy Guggenheim's cash would build Wright's last monument, off Central Park, container for a collection dominated by another extraordinary product of an Atlantic city, Barcelona's Pablo Picasso, but not before it had bankrolled—through her Australian leftist husband Douglas Garman—the novels of the Rhondda communist Lewis Jones.[56] Portmeirion would be outdone by the newspaper tycoon William Randolph Hearst's St Donat's Castle, whose form and contents were pillaged from hundreds of sites as a gift to his Welsh mistress Marion Davies. This monumental kleptocracy would be realized unforgettably by Orson Welles—briefly but notably at Dublin's Gate Theatre in 1929—in the Xanadu of *Citizen Kane*.[57]

---

[53] Ian Budge and Cornelius O'Leary, *Belfast: Approach to Crisis. A Study of Belfast Politics, 1613–1970* (London: Macmillan, 1973).

[54] See Harvie, *Fool's Gold*, chap. 5; and Brian Jamison, 'Scotland and the Trident Programme', PhD thesis, Glasgow University, 2004.

[55] Clough Williams-Ellis, *Portmeirion* (published by the author, 1955); and the programme of the Vitra Design Museum's Frank Lloyd Wright exhibition, Glasgow Art Gallery, 1999.

[56] Anton Gill, *Peggy Guggenheim: The Life of an Art Addict* (London: Harper Collins, 2002).

[57] Simon Callow, *Orson Welles* (London: Cape, 1995), chap. 3.

## VII  NATIONALISM REDUX

In 1918 the soap king Lord Leverhulme bought the Outer Hebrides and announced an energetic Tom Broadbent-like plan of industrialization and modernization, based on fisheries and Harris tweed. Lewis, a bleak, low-lying peat-raft floating on granite, and mountainous Harris would be linked up by electric railway, with factories and processing plants and their Port Sunlight-like workers' housing. Motorships would deliver their output to the Clyde and Merseyside, and to chains of MacFisheries retail shops on every high street. The last scheme worked, but it was the only part that did. The crofters wanted their land and invaded it; the Scottish Secretary fretted about rural bolshevism and interfered; grants to build railways and roads were cut by the Geddes axe; Lever's shareholders rose in revolt, and the scheme was dead even before Lever himself expired in 1925, its cadaver commemorated with morose jollity by MacNeice in 1938:

> The glass is falling hour by hour,
> The glass will fall forever.
> But if you break the bloody glass
> You won't hold up the weather.[58]

Planning ought theoretically to have been reinforced by politics, since the franchise extension of 1918 raised the issue of containing Labour through social engineering. Prompted (but not controlled) by figures like Geddes, town and country planning became a major element of bipartisan collectivism. All the Atlantic cities had development projects from an early date: the Glasgow City Improvement Trust of 1867, the Lever Town Planning School under Charles Reilly in Liverpool (1903), the Dublin Development Plan (1922), the Cathays Park project at Cardiff.[59] Planning's numerous failures, the grim slum-clearance schemes of the 1930s like Blackhill in Glasgow and Craigmillar in Edinburgh, and the high-rise panacea of the 1960s (though there were successes such as Glasgow's overspill schemes and the new towns), have to be set against two things: the sheer size of the problem, and the endemic industrial lethargy of the inter-war years.

Just when their sins were finding them out, the old elites withdrew in good order. Some, like William Weir, tried to apply industrial techniques to the housing problem, but failed owing to the suspicions and obstruction of the unions. Housing essentially made a return to the philosophy of 'improvement' inherited from Scots Georgian lairds. Besides Leverhulme's Port Sunlight there was Edgar Chappell in the Welsh Housing and Town Planning Association, and David Davies at Llandinam. Their efforts became legislation in the 1940s through politicians like Hugh Dalton from

---

[58] Louis MacNeice, *I Crossed the Minch* (London: Longmans, 1938); and see Nigel Nicolson, *Lord of the Isles: Lord Leverhulme in the Hebrides* (London: Weidenfeld and Nicolson, 1960).

[59] For Geddes's influence on Wales see David Michael, 'Before Alwyn: Early Social Thought, Action and Research in Wales', in Glyn Williams, ed., *Crisis of Economy and Ideology: Essays on Welsh Society, 1840–1980* (Bangor: British Sociological Association, 1983), 20–3.

Neath and Lewis Silkin from Cardiff, old enough to remember unplanned, polluted industrial sprawl in the South Wales of their childhood.[60]

'The city-state has lasted for over five centuries,' Fernand Braudel wrote in 1948, 'the nation state for scarcely 150 years.' But the challenge of the latter to civics was further impressed on the Scots or Welsh intelligentsias by increasing agitation throughout the British Empire by nationalists drawing on the Irish experience. Versailles could be seen as, in an odd way, Lloyd George's revenge for his rebuff in 1896 at the hands of 'cosmopolitan South Wales': since throughout Europe ethno-linguistic unity, not civic or economic community, would dominate the new settlement. Cardiff, as much as Vienna and Budapest, would be left, politically as well as economically, on the beach. The paradigm of social reconstruction in the 1920s, even among liberals, was the Scandinavian or central European nation state: Sweden, Finland, and Czechoslovakia, the Weimar Republic. The angle of the arc had changed.[61]

National literary movements flourished, claiming for Scotland and Wales the 'Versailles'-type identity granted to the Irish Free State. The conurbations might have housed and influenced such renaissances, but they were hit by the slump: *Ulysses* was the end of one evolution, not the beginning. More influential on the Free State was Daniel Corkery's *The Hidden Ireland* (1925), comforting to a largely clerical intelligentsia seeking a peasant past, untainted by Anglo-Irishness, where the city-region had no place. Even Scotland, a 'liberal' state, saw a sort of ethnic nationalism take over, small-town in origin and wary of multi-ethnic, print-capitalist urban culture. A third of the population might live in just four cities, but the 'renaissance writers' were rural. Of the group which came together in the mid 1920s in Montrose, a port, market, and small factory town of 12,000 people, Christopher Grieve was from Langholm, Tom MacDonald (Fionn mac Colla) from Montrose, Edwin Muir from Orkney, and Francis George Scott from Fraserburgh: professionals, proceeding through higher education—the Church, education, medicine, perhaps journalism—to a middle-class mobility considerably greater than that of Edwardian Scots businessmen, who were born, worked, and (even when rich) retired and died close to their works.[62] Indifference to urban issues also marked the organizations generated at the pit of the depression, the Scottish National Development Council, the National Trust for Scotland, the Scottish Youth Hostels Association (all 1930–6), whose non-political 'national awareness' was seen as a means of repairing the damage industrialization had inflicted. The Saltire Society's aims: 'not a mere revival of the arts of the past, but a renewal of the life which made them, such as the Scots themselves experienced in the eighteenth century' had an ethos which seems to come

---

[60] See preface to Edgar Chappell, *History of the Port of Cardiff,* 1939 (London: Merton Priory Press, 1994).

[61] Alice Headlam-Morley, *The New Democratic Constitutions of Europe* (London: Oxford University Press, 1928), 67 ff., and see Christopher Harvie, *The Rise of Regional Europe* (London: Routledge, 1993), 46–8.

[62] Sample taken from Cairns Craig, ed., *The History of Scottish Literature,* iv: *The Twentieth Century* (Aberdeen: Aberdeen University Press, 1987), and compared with businessmen alive in 1900 taken from *The Dictionary of Scottish Business Biography, 1860–1960* (Aberdeen: Aberdeen University Press, 1986).

straight out of the enlightenment. But they also implied a retreat *from* the Geddesian 'neotechnic city'.[63]

This was reinforced by political change. Middle-class angst expressed itself physically in a withdrawal to the countryside and England—'the future of Glasgow is buried in the cemeteries of Bournemouth'—and Conservative-Liberal solidarity against Labour. Unionist MPs, especially after the landslide right-wing victory of 1931, came from the courts in Edinburgh, the services, or London. Lady Elliot, widow of Walter Elliot, and Sir George Harvie-Watt, both of whose forebears had made their money from west central Scotland, said in the 1980s that they 'had never been near the place in years'.[64] An urban identity remained, but 'civics' tended to mean towns of the Montrose sort, and urban development as something 'planned', community-ordained, and harmonious, carried over from the Scottish enlightenment—the building of Eaglesham, Helensburgh, Edinburgh New Town, Fochabers, etc.—and with the stress on community of enlightenment philosophers such as Francis Hutcheson and Adam Ferguson.[65]

In Wales the reform of the franchise in 1918 ought to have transferred power from the privileged rural areas to the 'cosmopolitan south', yet the divergence between an articulate nationalism and urban problems became even greater. The growth of Labour in the 1922 contest from 9 to 18 seats out of 34, and in 1929 to 25, was chiefly made up of miners' MPs, while the cities, with their large number of business votes, became redoubts of Toryism. The miners had little interest in anything outside industrial politics, and the endemic problems of their industry confined their action to this losing battle. The ideology of Plaid Cymru was explicitly anti-urban, demanding the de-industrialization of South Wales—something which bound the Catholic Saunders Lewis to activists mainly drawn from rural Nonconformity. One positive and emphatically Atlantic factor was the Pilgrim Trust, formed in 1930 by the American multimillionaire Edward Harkness, of Dumfries descent, which had two Glasgow graduates as its *animateurs*: Thomas Jones and John Buchan. Relief of the plight of South Wales was one of its priorities, which both resulted in the huge inquiry headed by Hilary Marquand (of a prominent Cardiff shipowning family) and also involved Susan Buchan, who wrote movingly about the South Wales mining valleys in *The Scent of Water* in 1936. Wales certainly produced one major example of cultural criticism in 1937, Williams-Ellis's symposium *Britain and the Beast*, but this essentially rehearsed the National Trust agenda, and had as little to say about city or coalfield as the coming literary man, Dylan Thomas, whose diction was creepily prophetic of Richard Llywellyn's racial song-speech in *How Green was my Valley* (1939). Psychoanalysis, so liberating to the Scottish renaissance in enabling sex to be talked about, also affected Wales thanks to the work of Ernest Jones, Freud's friend and biographer and a member of Plaid Cymru. Yet this too chipped away at the civic image, suggesting a polity both more irrational and more ruralist than that of Geddes.

[63] Robert Hurd, *Building Scotland* (Edinburgh: Saltire Society, 1936).
[64] Interview with Lady Elliot, Apr. 1981; with Sir George Harvie-Watt, July 1983.
[65] See George Elder Davie, *The Scottish Enlightenment* (London: Historical Association, 1971).

In Ulster civics scarcely surfaced at all, crushed by a rigid puritanism among both communities. John Hewitt's own utopian socialism, with its naive faith in a benign Soviet revolution, took its cue from this situation, as did the constructive work that other Ulster people—MacNeice, Joyce Cary, Robert Lynd—were capable of, once well away from the place. In Belfast the depression was compounded by the new Protestant state, legitimated by the illiberalism of the conservative Catholic middle class which dominated Free State politics. The malign synergy of these two forces interdicted any sort of civic identity: froze the liberal intelligentsia out, between an indolent Unionist establishment and Catholic ghetto politicians of the Joe Devlin type. MacNeice castigated his fellow Irishmen every time he visited. More mysteriously, one of Ulster's potentially most distinctive voices, C. S. Lewis, became Anglicanism's most eloquent apologist since the young Newman.

## VIII THE BIG SHIP GOES DOWN

Before 1914 the Atlantic cities, juxtaposing traditional and modern, gave European culture a new and fundamental dialogue, stretching from the mysticism of Yeats and AE, the repertory theatre of Lady Gregory and Annie Horniman, the humanist architecture of Rennie Mackintosh to Geddes's sociology and the quarrying of the anthropological past in Frazer's *Golden Bough*. Much of the cash for this came from money made in coal or publishing or photographs, from the Davies family or George Davison of Harlech. The rediscovery of consciousness involved in *fin de siècle* sociology assisted this. War and slump were too much for the economic mainspring, yet they enabled the survivors to fend for themselves in all quarters, their vision being Joyce Cary's kinetic one of the pilgrim rather than the English rural certainties of Baldwin or Kipling. The fricative Whitmanite Kipling of the 1890s, or *Kim*, gave way to a private, paranoid, golf-club Toryism, transferred to Ulster in his vengeful and panicky 'Ulster 1914'.

Defensiveness, however, increased in the 'exhilarating prosperity followed by desolating slump', as Sir Glanmor Williams characterized the last decades of 'Atlantic Wales'.[66] In 1934, its twentieth year, Lord Davies closed down *Welsh Outlook*, concluding that if the 1920s had been bad, the 1930s would probably be worse. Nationalism was no panacea, probably the reverse, with Nazi regression paralleled by the conservatism of Saunders Lewis. Glasgow was similarly burdened through its ambiguous relationship with Belfast. However sophisticated the city—and (aided by rearmament) it did itself proud in the Empire Exhibition of 1938—Rangers and Celtic were there to subvert any idea of a unified Scottish people. If progressives fled from Belfast to England, they fled from Glasgow to the countryside: the artists settled in the southwest, while the literary men exited to Rose Street Edinburgh or the Highlands. Neil M. Gunn's only 'urban' novel, *The Serpent* (1943), exemplifies this. Geddes, the theorist of the neotechnic city, and his colleague during World War I Charles Rennie

---

[66] Glanmor Williams, 'A Prospect of Paradise: Wales and the United States, 1776–1914', in *Religion and Nationalism in Wales* (Cardiff: University of Wales Press, 1979).

Mackintosh, could not stay in the place and live. Another, unvolcanic, image took over: that of James Clerk Maxwell's Second Law of Thermodynamics: of the natural tendency of dynamics towards entropy, cooling-down, death.

The middle classes turned tail, but what happened to the working class? In few societies had the market, the technological processes of capitalism, and the idea of labour autonomy, and hence resistance, been so widely disseminated as on both Atlantic coasts, causing in the 1906–10 depression a distinct shift from liberal self-improvement to such hyper-materialist gospels as De Leonite socialism. The civic counter-movement—Geddes's Dublin mission in 1913—was interdicted by the outbreak of war; Labour was reinforced by the sudden democratization of 1918, but maimed by the crash after 1920. So the conclusions that younger readers (brought up during the depression) drew on encountering Muir, or Grassic Gibbon, were more political than cultural. The system was faulted; the geotechnic city unreachable.

Hence that simultaneous commitment to utopia, in the shape of the Soviet Union, and to the pre-modern Scottish countryside of literary renaissance and folk-song movement. Neither could provide a secure resting place and, as could be expected in a period of emigration, the 'positive' outcomes of the inter-war years were achieved abroad. Of the generation launched on their careers by the pre-1914 boom in the north, Cary went to the Balkans, Nigeria, and Oxford; Tyrone Guthrie, after trying to animate the Scottish National Players, went to London's West End with James Bridie, then to Edinburgh, then to Stratford, Ontario. Grierson's course took him from Clydeside to London and Canada. Muir went to Germany and Czechoslovakia and back to Newbattle Abbey College, A. S. Neill to Germany and Suffolk. John Buchan, particularly in his Canadian career, showed a remarkable cultural dualism: *Sick Heart River* (1941), his last work, is a plea not just for coexistence but for miscegenation, and its strong figures are French-Canadian priests and Inuit-Scots trappers. What's visible here could—seen from one angle—be what Patrick Geddes called synergy, summed up by the ILP's James Maxton MP (who popped up discreetly in Dublin, as well as more loudly in Westminster) with the phrase 'If you can't ride two horses at the same time, you've no place in the bloody circus.'[67] The problem was that, applied globally, this subtracted talent from maimed communities which desperately needed to innovate. The people could see on the cinema screen (in every village of over 2,500, often in a former church or chapel) the impact in America of electricity, cars, concrete, radio, civil aviation, encouraging migration from a polis once seductive but now tragically lacking in imaginative leadership.

London resumed its once-traditional Celtic capital status: publishing, journalism, the BBC, and less reputably the various interconnected Fitzrovian worlds of Griff's bookshop and Keidrich Rhys at the bar of the Wheatsheaf, along with 'the two Roberts', Colquhoun and MacBryde. Grassic Gibbon in Welwyn Garden City, and countless exiles from de Valera's Ireland, headed up by O'Casey, either went to ground in the English countryside or suburbia or created—MacNeice was only too accurate—'a factitious popular front in booze'. Such activities were notable for

---

[67] The Irish Maxton figures nowhere in Gordon Brown, *Maxton* (Edinburgh: Mainstream, 1986). I owe this information to his nephew, Prof. W. J. MacCormack, 'Hugh Maxton'.

*not* happening among the Atlantic cities themselves, apart from the Manchester of Sidney Bernstein, Howard Spring, L. S. Lowry, Ewan MacColl, Lewis Namier, and A. J. P. Taylor. The last succinctly accounted for its survival: 'You could easily convert a cotton mill into another sort of factory. You couldn't do that with a mine or a shipyard.' Even Birmingham, booming in the late 1920s, with a cultural and political scene which included Walter Allen, Auden, MacNeice, and Oswald Mosley, then regarded as Labour's next leader, contributed more than Liverpool or Cardiff.[68]

The Atlantic city's dependence on skilled men and exports failed to empower women and lower-status groups, while the bias to the old Liberal or *gwerin* establishment, grotesque in South Wales, had been destroyed by Lloyd George and franchise reform. The controllers of capital moved out. Where the old order had failed to organize unskilled or semi-skilled workers, the theoretical socialism of the new crumbled when confronted with endemic unemployment. Left politics rose, only to be cut down by the slump and the 1931 crisis. The Right stayed on, indolent and agrarian, in Scotland and Northern Ireland, while urban centres remained unchanged in the 1930s, even when their councils were Labour-run. A war-induced partnership grew up between prosperous and after 1934 radical London and the surviving heavy industries of the littoral reprieved by rearmament, the war, and the favourable market created by the destruction of German and Japanese plants. Supplemented by Board of Trade-promoted light industries and service concerns which absorbed women workers, often owned by American firms, the Atlantic economy was merely running in reverse. Ulster's per capita output increased, with the Beveridge reforms reinforcing the British connection, against the rural south. This would start to change only with the industrialization prescribed to Séan Lemass by the Whitaker Report of 1957. Five years before, John Hewitt, sick of party fights and patronage in Ulster—quit for Coventry, the British Motown—fertilized by a huge Scots as well as Irish immigration. Which Richard Hughes, no less, intended to make the scene of the final volume of his 'Human Condition' trilogy.

In the future, too, lay a more positive and ecumenical Scottish and Welsh nationalist agenda: based on incorporating the culture of the 'Welsh Wales' of non-Welsh-speakers and the Irish-Scots Catholics, vivid in William MacIlvanney's symbolically impressive *Docherty* (1975). Scottish nationalism, once strongly ethnic and Protestant, now rejoiced in furthering MacIlvanney's 'mongrel nation' and assessed incomers opportunistically—the latter often reciprocating, and becoming as nationalist as the native. This underlined the 'devolution of English literature' which Robert Crawford detected as a recurrent concern. Philip Hobsbaum would help generate literary revivals in Belfast and then in Glasgow: Heaney, Simmonds, and MacLaverty in one city, Gray, Kelman, and Torrington in the next.[69]

'The matt-grey iron ship, which ought to have been the future . . .' The 1929–33 slump saw the *Queen Mary* rusting on the Clydebank stocks. It would be completed

---

[68] A. J. P. Taylor, conversation with the writer, Aug. 1978.
[69] Robert Crawford, *Devolving English Literature* (Oxford: Clarendon Press, 1992), 285–6; Robert Crawford and Thom Nairn, eds., *The Arts of Alasdair Gray* (Edinburgh: Edinburgh University Press, 1991), 6.

only because of the threat of war. A later generation would take as the great symbol of the Atlantic economy the *Titanic* of 1912, emblematic of risks now seen as inherent in great ships and great cities. It carried down with it W. T. Stead—journalist muse of Gladstone and General Booth—as well as the luckless emigrants in the steerage. In 1915 in the *Lusitania* there perished Sir Hugh Lane, whom Yeats had seen as playing the Duke of Urbino to a re-civilized Dublin. From Dorset, the ironic Hardy saw the catastrophic drowning of Vulcan by Neptune as a punishment for hubris:

> In a solitude of the sea
> Deep from human vanity,
> And the Pride of Life that planned her, stilly couches she.

> Steel chambers, late the pyres
> Of her salamandrine fires,
> Cold currents thrid, and turn to rhythmic tidal lyres.

> Dim moon-eyed fishes near
> Gaze at the gilded gear
> And query: 'What does this vaingloriousness down here?'[70]

The sinking of the *Titanic* was filmed as an indictment of British imperialism by the Nazis in 1943. They never released the print, as it seemed too apposite to their own situation. In 1999 James Cameron's epic, involving a near-full-size replica, computer magic, and a corny plot, wasn't just a hit but enhanced (rather strangely, given the story) a boom in cruise travel. The German poet and cultural theorist Hans-Magnus Enzensberger in his long poem of 1968–77, written in both German and English, made the liner into a contemporary Apocalypse:

> Soaked to the skin I peer through the drizzle, and I perceive
> my fellow-beings clutching wet trunks, leaning against the wind.
> Dimly I see their livid faces, blurred by the slanting rain.
> I don't think it is Second Sight. It must be the weather.
> They are right on the brink. I warn them. I cry, for instance, Watch Out!
> There's the brink! You are treading slippery ground, ladies and gentlemen!
> But they just give me a feeble smile, and gallantly they retort: Same to you!
> I ask myself, is it just a matter of a few dozen passengers,
> or do I watch the whole human race over there, haphazardly
> hanging on to some run-down cruise-liner, fit for the scrapyard
> and headed for self-destruction? I cannot be sure. I am dripping wet
> and I listen. It is hard to say who the seafarers over there
> may be, each of them clutching a suitcase,
> a leek-green talisman, a dinosaur, or a laurel wreath.[71]

Enzensberger's theme was—like that of Yeats in 'Meditations in Time of Civil War'—contemporary, the collapse of European civilization, the *Titanic* being an

---

[70] Thomas Hardy, 'The Convergence of the Twain: Lines of the Loss of the Titanic', in *Poems of Thomas Hardy*, ed. T. R. M. Creighton (London: Macmillan, 1974).
[71] Hans-Magnus Enzensberger, *The Sinking of the Titanic*, Eng. version, 1981 (London: Paladin, 1989), canto 33, p. 73.

augur of August 1914. He saw this replaced by a permanent civil war between the propertied and the excluded, something all too visible in the nexus of fanaticism and criminality which is the world of the alienated paramilitary. This would make its own mark on New York, only yards from where the liner was heading, on 11 September 2001.[72]

Or was this too well-booked a metaphor? The Ship of Fools had been around almost as long as Charon the Ferryman: while the crisis looming over the millennium was new and terrifying. Thomas Hardy, hearing of war in 1914, expected that 'This will go onward the same,/Though dynasties pass.' He did not expect that the polar icecap would melt, or that as a by-blow of such global warming the warm currents keeping the littoral temperate might cease.[73]

## IX EPISODES: EPIPHANIES: IMPERIUM

In the autumn of 1986 I made a film for BBC Scotland called *Grasping the Thistle* about what autonomy might do for Scottish politics. One section was shot off the Scott Lithgow yard at Port Glasgow, where Henry Bell's *Comet* (1812), the revolutionary *Agamemnon* (1865), and Lipton's *Erin* (1897) had been built. The 30,000-ton *Ocean Alliance* was under construction, the world's most sophisticated drill-ship, commissioned by the state-run British National Oil Corporation for the deep fields west of the Shetlands. It was far behind schedule, 120 per cent over its estimate of £88 million, and the yard, sold in 1984 by Thatcher to the conglomerate company Trafalgar House, was going bust. The ship is still in service, and indeed on its findings much of our energy future might depend, but the yard was briskly demolished in 1999 and replaced by three call centres.[74]

Next door, in June 2005 the last locally owned Clyde shipyard, Fergusons, was fighting for a contract to build a fishery cruiser. Its bid was undercut by a subsidized Polish company, yet if the cruiser were to be classified as a warship—if it had a gun, however nominal—the Polish yard would be ruled out. The job was important, because Inverclyde (Gourock, Greenock, Port Glasgow) stood on the edge of ruin. It had never recovered from the closure of Scott Lithgow, and its big IBM factory had just been sold to the Chinese. The call centres had sopped up some unemployed but their future was uncertain, threatened by 'Macaulay's children' in India, who were better qualified and motivated, and cost less. Drug and crime problems

---

[72] Hans-Magnus Enzensberger, *Ansichten auf den Burgerkrieg* (Frankfurt: Surkamp, 1993), 123; Steve Bruce, *The Red Hand: Protestant Paramilitaries in Northern Ireland* (Oxford: Oxford University Press, 1992).

[73] Five writers were asked to write short stories for a symposium, published in Gerry Hassan, Eddie Gibb, and Lydia Howland, eds., *Scotland 2020: Hopeful Stories for a Northern Nation* (London: Demos, 2005), 56–88. Bad weather dominated three accounts: one (Pennie Taylor) thought Scotland would be more humid; two (Ken McLeod, Julie Bertagna) thought it would be freezing.

[74] Harvie, *Fool's Gold*, 309–10.

were pervasive, and the council had been given an ultimatum by the Scottish Executive in Edinburgh: sort yourselves out, before we send commissioners in.[75]

At the same moment, thousands were protesting against the developed world's leaders outside the Caledonian Railway's great golfing hotel at Gleneagles, while two Scottish-founded banks, the Hong Kong and Shanghai and the Royal Bank, had risen to be the world's largest on the back of the surge in Chinese manufacturing. Such were the grandeurs and miseries of the Atlantic world. Scotland was in some sort of post-industrial equilibrium, though the Inverclyde burgh example showed the wounds the experience had left, and the way an abstruse legal formula, not economic inevitability, might salve them. The world's wealthy were desperately insecure. As to the Chinese future, while it matched up to what Charles Pearson had expected in 1893, it was ominous in its neglect of civil rights and environmentally catastrophic *whether it succeeded or failed*. Was anyone drawing the connections? If not, why not? In 1941 the American scholar J. U. Nef published a study of the early British coal industry which argued that its impact had long preceded the Industrial Revolution of the late eighteenth century. He also observed that it had become increasingly difficult to organize such a debate, as specialization had become so extreme that hardly any common ground existed. This was particularly the case when two different methodologies were involved; because what was necessary to make imaginative connections required a Shakespearian boldness that came less and less to hand.[76]

Applied to the littoral, this suggested that while regional specializations (shipping, engineering, etc.) were efficient, and *did* integrate, they bore substantial systemic risks. It was possible to acquire a pragmatic but sophisticated overview: hence the importance in *A Floating Commonwealth* of book-driven urban philosophers like Carlyle, Shaw, and Joyce, not to speak of those who ran with their ideas on the other side of the pond. In terms of debates on development strategy or the synergies of economic integration, historical sequences could be identified and matched with geographic situations: for instance the 'cluster' theory, which could account for localized technological breakthroughs to do with steam at sea on the Clyde in the 1850s and narrow-to-medium-gauge railways in North Wales in the 1860s. Applied to more recent historical analyses this would downgrade the identity politics of Colley—religious dogmatism shrinks cooperation, it doesn't expand it—and Landes's tendency to jump from place to place in search of innovation without much regard to the social fabric. Did the community, be it town, river valley, or culture-nation, along with its supra-national partnership regions or, in Braudelian terms, 'world' matter more than the ethnic nation?

The political element of this is, as Landes correctly insists, the speed of technical innovation; given some strong drive, the rest of society will adapt itself. But it must also accumulate over time the sort of social overhead capital—the hard- and software of culture—which will remember, rationalize, and forecast this. Perhaps the

---

[75] See Christopher Harvie, 'Grasping the Thistle', in Kenneth Cargill, ed., *Scotland 2000* (Glasgow: BBC, 1987). Fergusons didn't get the contract, but limp on.

[76] Charles H. Pearson, *National Life and Character* (London: Macmillan, 1893), 355–7 (see Chapter 3); John Ulric Nef, *The Rise of the British Coal Industry*, 2 vols. (London: Routledge, 1932).

sheer persistence of west-coast names among the furniture of economic rationality—Lloyds, Dow Jones, Watt, Bell, Forbes, Ford, Unilever, Marconi—strengthens
this, thought it might also ease the rise of the snake-oil merchant trading under some
similar appellation: Murdoch, Maxwell, McDonald, etc.

There are parallel worlds of politics, business, culture. These have a 'high politics' of strategy, often (though variably) steered—by entrepreneurs, treaties, statesmen, civil servants—and below that a 'low politics' one of social adaptation, the
work of subordinate legislatures, middle management, artisans, and civil society. The
two are only indirectly linked by political doctrine, but plentifully linked by convention, 'imperium' (not empire but the accepted supra-regional political sphere)
both devolving day-to-day operations and coordinating the same in joint organizations, marketized and public services, running everything from time- and tide-tables
to business agencies, shipping conferences, and cooperative literary, dramatic, and
musical institutions. But a sense of 'world' is required for a strategy to be successful. These episodes and epiphanies have, I hope, shown how, in one critical epoch,
it worked.[77]

The risk is always twofold: that high politics corrupts and that the smaller gov-
ernmental worlds of 'low' politics become too self-preoccupied and don't interact.
Another threat besets the technology which ought to communicate if it becomes
encrusted and archaic; or that when unprecedented and unusual demands are made
on it—for example by war—these leave distortions. Here the control has to be recon-
figured, but meanwhile the integrative conventions may rapidly decline, and along
with them the ability of the system to sort itself out. Taking for granted relationships
which may have grown quite different will worsen matters.

John Buchan tellingly illustrated the impact of this in his *Thirty-Nine Steps*. The
high command has to explain how a spy, taken for the First Sea Lord, can walk into
a strategic conference and exit with all its details in his head. A French general remin-
isces: while fishing in Africa he had tethered his pony so that he could see it out of
the corner of his eye. A half-hour later he turned and found himself confronted with
a lion which had attacked and eaten the pony. His attention elsewhere, he hadn't
noticed the changes in the dun-coloured fleck on the fringe of his vision. This is as
much theory as Buchan allows himself—and the theorist is (of course?) French—but
it might explain a lot about the story we have been following.[78]

We come back to Patrick Geddes, a dishevelled thinker but an enduring voice
because of a practical interest in the business of living, working, and enjoyment.
There was along his littoral an exfoliating, contractual patriotism (folk), a known,
accessible geography (place), and economic and technical cooperation (work) which
he projected in his summer schools, exhibitions, and masques. Through pragmatic
interaction, different forms of socialization had reached similar goals and developed

---

[77] Thomas Kleinknecht, *Imperiale und internationale Ordnung: Eine Untersuchung zum anglo-
amerikanischen Gelehrtenliberalismus am Beispiel von James Bryce, 1838–1922* (Göttingen: Vand-
enhoek und Rupprecht, 1985), shows how this pluralism worked in the 'federal' studies of the
Ulster-Scot jurist.
[78] John Buchan, *The Thirty-Nine Steps*, 1915 (Oxford: Oxford University Press, 1993), 91–2.

their own conventions. In 1914–18 these relationships responded to, and saw off, the challenge of the Wilhelmine Empire's military-defined and deformed notions of folk and place. The habit of cooperation went first into overdrive, and then with victory disintegrated. The systems of the littoral became, with the nationalism of Versailles, separate, almost autistic, and cooperation dwindled away.[79]

## X 'THE O'ON OLYMPIAN'

In 1953, when I came in, the old material order was still hissing and clanging away on the banks of the Clyde. Later that year, like many other Scots children, I was taken to Sir Robert Lorimer's Scottish National War Memorial. This was built in 1928 in Edinburgh Castle by the son of the great international lawyer, the first to draft a constitution for Europe; at its centre there erupted the glistening volcanic black of the Castle Rock. The memorial did not just commemorate dead soldiers, but those mobilized to supply war and tend its casualties: miners, railwaymen, shipbuilders, women munitions workers, and nurses.[80] This was a cenotaph for a society, once formulaic for development along the seaboard, now crippled through the entropy of its failing industry which, even when revived, was controlled from abroad, by investment trusts devised by Victorian Scots capitalists, to further profit, not welfare. In contrast with the complex dialogues of Enrico Miralles's Holyrood Parliament—a remarkably kinetic, ship-like building which seemed to surge into the capital—it seemed the memento mori of Scotland's world moment. Writing this book largely *from* a changing Scotland may help account for its long gestation, but devolution has provided a model for the action—not as metaphor but as fact.

Was the reborn Scots Parliament a step towards Geddes's 'geotechnic' polis? Or an eccentricity in postmodern Britain? Was Sir Walter Scott's metaphor of the Union—'a deep and smooth river' as the symbol of historical progress—flowing into a postmodernist Never-Never Land? One winner, the egregious Niall Ferguson, thought so, alternately mocking the country's attempts at autonomy and intoning about American 'mission'. But did Ferguson himself not represent the quasi-nationalistic exclusions of commercially driven 'trophy history', which inhibited it from becoming a scientific instrument?

The task before the parliament stemmed from a breakdown in a pioneer industrial society; stuck in 1919, as Geddes would have put it, at the palaeotechnic

---

[79] See Patrick Geddes to his son Alastair Geddes, June 1915, in Paddy Kitchen, *A Most Unsettling Person: An Introduction to the Ideas and Life of Patrick Geddes* (London: Gollancz, 1975), 123, and compare this to the pragmatics-inspired analyses of industrial systems undertaken by Walter Shewhart in the United States at the same time. For this I am indebted to Noel Spare of Offenburg Technical University, and his paper 'Managing the Knowledge-Based Economy', Schiltach, 2005.

[80] See Christopher Hussey, *The Work of Sir Robert Lorimer, KBE* (London: Country Life, 1931), 123; see Christopher Harvie, 'Lorimer Invents Europe', in *Travelling Scot* (Colintraive: Argyll, 1999). The usually judicious, if conservative, architectural critic Gavin Stamp, praising Lorimer, regards the Miralles building as a failure; my own reaction runs in quite the other direction, believing that it makes highly imaginative, and continuously interesting, use of its site, materials, and textures.

stage. There would be no easy remedy, capitalist, nationalist, or socialist, but various diagnoses. Tom Johnston in his *History of the Working Classes in Scotland* of 1922 questioned national or religious discourse, stressing instead exploitation and division: coal-owners against collier-serfs, cotton magnates against spinners, engineering employers against shop stewards. Working-class solidarity dominated MacDiarmid's 'Ballad of the General Strike', the central section of his national epic *A Drunk Man Looks at the Thistle* (1926), but it also failed:

> A rose loupt oot and grew, until
> It was ten times the size
> O' ony rose the thistle afore
> Had heistit to the skies.
>
> And still it grew until it seemed
> The haill braid earth had turned
> A reid reid rose that in the lift
> Like a ball of fire burned.
>
> Syne the rose shrivelled suddenly
> As a balloon is burst;
> The thistle was a ghaistly stick,
> As gin it had been curst.
>
> A coward growth in that lorn stock
> That wrought the sorry trick?
> —The thistle like a rocket soared
> And cam' doon like the stick.[81]

MacDiarmid, Carlyle's successor, swayed between promethean social engineering and patriotism, yet was skewed by a sequence of victims from Wallace to John MacLean. With another atheist, Grassic Gibbon, he turned the Left's frustration into something Burns had ignored—a religious epiphany. The singing of Psalm 124—'When cruel men against us furiously, rose up in wrath to make of us their prey'—modulated into the crucifixion imagery of 'The Ballad of the General Strike' or the plea of the Good Thief, 'Lord, Remember me, when thou enterest thy kingdom', of *Cloud Howe*.[82]

The route out after 1926, for the MPs, for Gibbon, and (less successfully) for Mac-Diarmid, involved a personal high road to London, shared with another inconvenient man of the Celtic left, Sean O'Casey, when he broke with Yeats, and Irish piety, over the Abbey Theatre's rejection of *The Silver Tassie* in 1928. The Burnsian note is somehow appropriate. Their battle was shrill, bloody, and fought down south.

Yet Scotland somehow remained central, with a discourse which fused national, technological, and class consciousness, and maintained a European reach: Burns's 'social union', MacDiarmid's 'Wunds wi' warlds to swing'. The continuing reputation of Geddes was one element of this, casting back to Whitman's universalism, but

---

[81] Hugh MacDiarmid, *A Drunk Man Looks at the Thistle* (Edinburgh: Scottish Academic Press, 1987), 92.
[82] Lewis Grassic Gibbon, *Cloud Howe,* 1933 in *A Scots Quair* (London: Jarrolds, 1946), 154–7.

contemporary in its ecology. The imaginative, demotic element was typified by the
poet, critic, and folklorist Hamish Henderson, the first poem of whose *Elegies on the
Dead in Cyrenaica* (1944) ended with the lines:

> There were our own, there were the others.
> Therefore, minding the great word of Glencoe's
> son, that we should not disfigure ourselves
> with villainy of hatred; and seeing that all
> have gone down like curs into anonymous silence,
> I will bear witness for I knew the others.
> Seeing that littoral and interior are alike indifferent
> and the birds are drawn again to our welcoming north,
> why should I not sing *them*, the dead, the innocent?[83]

This is the argument of Owen's 'Strange Meeting', of the civic identity he hadn't
time to realize. 'Remember always whom you are writing for: the people of Glasgow, of Halifax, of Dublin,' adjured Henderson's friend E. P. Thompson. His
work as 'people's rembrancer', recorder and teacher, bears comparison with that of
Thompson, with Gwyn A. Williams in Wales and Field Day in Ireland. He took an
often-invoked martyr, John MacLean, and reworked his memory into a vigorous and
alert internationalism:

> Broken families in lands we've herriet,
> Will curse Scotland the Brave nae mair, nae mair;
> Black and white, ane til ither mairriet,
> Mak the vile barracks o' their maisters bare.
>
> . . .
>
> When MacLean meets wi' freens in Springburn
> A' the roses an' geans 'll turn tae bloom,
> An' the black boy frae 'yont Nyanga
> Dings the fell gallows o' the burghers doon.[84]

For Henderson, victimhood was overcome in World War II, by the soldiers of the
Eighth Army in North Africa and Italy, the 'D-Day Dodgers', purging imperial misdeeds in 'the last classical war', fighting alongside Italian partisans. This central singer
was a communist with a culture which bridged Whitman and Marx—poet, socialist, bisexual, cosmopolitan, and nationalist. 'Freedom Come all Ye' (1960) in a sense
completes the circle that Burns began in 1793, through its socialism, feminism, and
colour-blindness, set out to legitimize a post-imperial Scotland as a civic nationality,
with the pedigree of European learning—Croce's influence on Gramsci—and the
city republics behind it, reaching back to Macaulay's republican Rome. This meant
restoring to the old flyting with Marxism a scale of values—assessing the ambiguities

---

[83] Hamish Henderson, *Elegies for the Dead in Cyrenaica*, 1948 (Edinburgh: EUSPB, 1976),
17–18, 68–9.
[84] Hamish Henderson, *Collected Poems and Songs*, ed. Raymond Ross (Edinburgh: Curly Snake
Press, 2000), 143.

of progress or economic development or ecology—which put the nation in dialogue with other centres of identity.[85]

Henderson's agenda underlay the Scottish renaissance of the 1980s: the circumstances in which *A Floating Commonwealth* was conceived. This schema involved the attempt to redeem the country from industrial and social dependence, the reconciliation of different cultural communities, the overcoming of male aggression, the recovery of the geotechnic: a new but also old narrative for national history shown after the debacle of 1979 by Alasdair Gray's *Lanark* (1981).

This 'Life in Four Books' had an impact as great as *The Scots Quair*, and bears comparison with *Ulysses*. It plays itself out, not above the thin crust but *in* the post-industrial, entropic hell of a Scotland split into dying industrial Unthank and the Institute, an authoritarian, irresponsible 'civilization' which perpetuates the politeness of the enlightenment, observes the struggles on the surface through a camera obscura (like that which topped Geddes's Outlook Tower), and eats the reprocessed flesh of the victims. The recovery from this Swiftian vision—'man is a pie which bakes and eats itself'—is the subject of Book the Third, which the author regards as a 'Difplag' (diffused plagiarism) of *Faust*, with contributions from Carlyle, his disciple Charles Kingsley, and Geddes.[86] Post-enlightenment Scotland confronts industrial and ecological destruction. Individualism dies with the artist Duncan Thaw, who, like John Davidson, walks into the sea to drown. Reborn as the 'social being' Lanark, he struggles to save Unthank from the Institute's plan to drown it. At the final epiphany, when the floods rush towards the city, Lanark's girlfriend Rima (the water goddess), whom he has rescued from inclusion in the food-chain, re-enacts Goethe's Galatea:

'Tell me what's happening, please,' said Rima. She lay curled on the ground with her hands over her eyes. Everybody lay on the ground except Alexander, who knelt beside the radio transmitter earnestly turning knobs.

'The ground is level again,' said Lanark, getting up, 'and the fire is spreading.'

'Is it horrible?'

'It's wonderful. It's universal. You should look.'

Behind the burning buildings was a great band of ruddy light with clouds rising into it from collapsed and collapsing roofs. There were no other lights. 'First the fire, then the flood!' cried Lanark exultingly, 'Well, I have had an interesting life.'[87]

The city of Unthank is saved by a Geddesian triad of 'Makers, Movers and Menders', the eternal female triumphs, and the landscape of Scotland whole appears to the dying Lanark, clear and meticulous as in MacDiarmid's praise poems:

A blast of cold wind freshened the air. The rushing grew to surges and gurglings and up the low road between Necropolis and cathedral sped a white foam followed by ripples and

---

[85] Henderson, *Alias MacAlias*, 247–325.

[86] Gray, like Carlyle in *Sartor* always helpful with references, regards *Lanark* as a reworking or diffused plagiarism (difplag) of Kingsley's 'scientific' morality *The Water Babies* of 1863. Alasdair Gray, *Lanark*, 1981 (London: Granada, 1985), 419–20. See Christopher Harvie, 'Alasdair Gray and the Condition of Scotland Question' and Cairns Craig, 'Going Down to Hell is Easy', in Crawford and Nairn, eds., *The Arts of Alasdair Gray*.

[87] Gray, *Lanark*, 557.

plunging waves with gulls swooping and crying over them. He laughed aloud, following the flood with his mind's eye back to the river it flowed from, a full river widening to the ocean. His cheek was touched by something moving in the wind, a black twig with pointed little pink and grey-green buds. The colours of things seemed to be brightening although the fiery light over the roofs had paled to silver streaked with delicate rose. A long silver line marked the horizon. Dim rooftops against it grew solid in the increasing light. The broken buildings were fewer than he had thought. Beyond them a long faint bank of cloud became clear hills, not walling the city in but receding, edge behind pearl-grey edge of farmland and woodland gently rising to a faraway ridge of moor. The darkness overheard shifted and broke in the wind becoming clouds with blue air between. He looked sideways and saw the sun coming up golden behind a laurel bush, light blinking, space dancing among the shifting leaves. Drunk with spaciousness he turned every way, gazing with wide-open mouth and eyes as light created colours, clouds, distances and solid, graspable things close at hand. Among all this light the flaming buildings seemed small blazes which would soon burn out. With only mild disappointment he saw the flood ebbing back down the slope of the road.[88]

'More light!' cried Goethe on his deathbed. We are talking serious Difplags.

[88] Gray, *Lanark*, 557–8.

# Chronology

| | Economy and Technology | Culture | Politics |
|---|---|---|---|
| 1851 | Great Exhibition: Crystal Palace, London; gold discovered in Australia | Ruskin, *The Stones of Venice*; Newman's Catholic University, Dublin | Louis Napoleon's coup, Paris; reaction elsewhere in Europe |
| 1852 | First airship flight | Harriet Beecher Stowe, *Uncle Tom's Cabin* | Liberation Society founded to demand Church disestablishment |
| 1853 | Dublin Exhibition; Cayley's man-carrying glider; cholera epidemic | Wagner's *Ring des Nibelungen* begun | Gladstone's financial reforms; Forbes–MacKenzie act curbs drinking in Scotland |
| 1854 | | Henry Thoreau, *Walden* | Crimean War begins (March); Civil Service Commission; *The Times*, reporting from Crimea, fells government |
| 1855 | Irish 'Godless' Universities Act; newspaper stamp duty abolished | Longfellow, *Hiawatha*; Whitman, *Leaves of Grass* | Constitutional government in Australia; Jewish Disabilities Act |
| 1856 | Bessemer convertor starts mass production of steel; aniline dyestuffs; local police forces | Hugh Miller dies; Emerson, *English Traits*; Victoria Cross instituted | Crimean War ends; US 'Black Ships' visit Japan; Second Opium War in China |
| 1857 | First screw collier *William Bowes*; first Atlantic cable laid; divorce and women's property reform | H. T. Buckle, *History of Civilisation* | Indian Mutiny; Reform under Alexander II in Russia; Second Opium War in China |

|  | | | |
|---|---|---|---|
| 1858 | Universities (Scotland) Act; MacQuorn Rankine, *The Steam Engine*; SS *Propontis* with compound engine | Bernadette's vision at Lourdes; Owens College, Manchester | Indian Mutiny; Conservative government; Fenian Society founded in USA |
| 1859 | SS *Great Eastern* built; deaths of I. K. Brunel and Robert Stephenson; work starts on Suez Canal; electric light pioneered in New York; Loch Katrine water supply scheme, Glasgow | Darwin and Wallace on natural selection; Mill, *On Liberty*; Samuel Smiles, *Self-Help*; Iolo Morgannwyg's forgeries denounced at Welsh Eisteddfod | Foundation of Liberal Party; war in Italy between Piedmont and France and Austria; Volunteer movement in UK |
| 1860 | Atlantic telegraph broken; Cobden–Chevalier free trade treaty | J. S. Mill, *Representative Government* | Garibaldi's 'Thousand': most of Italy unified under Piedmont |
| 1861 | First British street tramway, Birkenhead | John Ruskin, *Unto this Last* | First British ironclad ship *Warrior*; outbreak of American Civil War (April) |
| 1862 | Limited Liability Act; Samuel Smiles, *Lives of the Engineers*; cotton blockade starts | | Founding of Red Cross; sinking of Confederate commerce-raider CSS *Alabama*; CSS *Merrimac* versus USS *Monitor*, first modern naval battle |
| 1863 | Festiniog Railway, first steam-worked narrow-gauge line; Co-operative Wholesale Society; Football Association rules drawn up | J. S. Mill, *Utilitarianism* | Polish rising against Russia; Reform League founded; Prussian–Danish war |
| 1864 | International Workers Association founded, London | | Palmerston dies |

| | | | |
|---|---|---|---|
| 1865 | SS *Agamemnon* built; first long-distance freighter; Clerk Maxwell on *Electricity and Magnetism* | Walter Bagehot, *The English Constitution*; J. S. Mill, *Sir William Hamilton's Philosophy*; Carlyle's Rectorial Address, Edinburgh | End of American Civil War |
| 1866 | Economic slump; cholera epidemic; Atlantic cable relaid; Sheffield outrages prompt Royal Commission on trade unions | Thomas Carlyle, *Shooting Niagara* | Hyde Park riots over Reform Bill; Fenianism; Austro-Prussian War; first moves for women's suffrage |
| 1867 | Death of William Dargan; Paris Exhibition; Nobel invents dynamite; Karl Marx, *Capital*, vol. i | Matthew Arnold, *On Celtic Literature*; *Essays on Reform*; Ibsen, *Peer Gynt*; George Eliot, *Felix Holt*; 'God save Ireland' composed | Disraeli's Second Reform Act; Canadian Confederation; Austro-Hungarian *Ausgleich*; German SPD founded; Meiji dynasty begins modernization, Japan |
| 1868 | Founding of Trades Union Congress | Charles Dilke, *Greater Britain* | Gladstone's Liberal victory; Henry Richard heads radical Wales |
| 1869 | Suez Canal opened (November); *Cutty Sark* clipper built; Charity Organisation Society and Co-operative Union founded; telegraphs bought by state | Matthew Arnold, *Culture and Anarchy* | Vatican Council convened; Manchester Martyrs; Irish Church disestablished |
| 1870 | Forster Education Act; Naturalisation Act, among most Liberal in Europe | Papal Infallibility; Benjamin Disraeli, *Lothair*; death of Dickens, June | Franco-Prussian War; Bryce and Dicey in America |

| | | | |
|---|---|---|---|
| 1871 | German Empire proclaimed at Versailles; Paris Commune; last religious and university tests abolished; Irish Home Rule Party founded | Aberystwyth College founded; Stanley finds Dr Livingstone in Africa; George Chesney, *The Battle of Dorking* | First railway in Japan; Mont Cenis tunnel links France and Italy; Street Tramways Act; Rugby Union rules; trade unions legalized (to 1875) |
| 1872 | Bismarck's *Kulturkampf* begins; *Alabama* judgment awards £3.5 million against UK | Ruskin, *Ethics of the Dust*; Charles Lever, *Lord Kilgobbin*; George Eliot, *Middlemarch* | Midland Railway modernization creates new facilities for mass transit; Glasgow Rangers |
| 1873 | | Moody and Sankey's crusade; John Stuart Mill dies | International economic crisis results in enduring agricultural depression |
| 1874 | Disraeli takes power; Alexander MacDonald, first trade union MP | Anthony Trollope, *The Way We Live Now* | International Postal Union; first refrigerated ship |
| 1875 | Public Health and Friendly Societies Acts | Mark Twain, *Tom Sawyer*; George Meredith, *Beauchamp's Career* | Disraeli buys Suez Canal shares |
| 1876 | Disraeli makes Victoria Empress of India; Gladstone denounces Bulgarian atrocities | Reform of Oxford and Cambridge; Anthony Trollope, *The Prime Minister*; William Alexander, *My Uncle the Bailie* | Gilchrist–Thomas steelmaking process; Bell patents telephone in USA; Plimsoll line adopted for marine safety |
| 1877 | UK annexes Transvaal | Ibsen, *Pillars of Society* | |
| 1878 | Congress of Berlin | William Booth founds Salvation Army; death of Cardinal Cullen | Collapse of City of Glasgow Bank; CID set up in Metropolitan Police |
| 1879 | Gladstone's Midlothian Campaign | Henry George, *Progress and Poverty*; the Virgin of Knock, Ireland | Tay Bridge disaster; Land League founded in Ireland |

| | Politics and society | Literature and culture | Science and social developments |
|---|---|---|---|
| 1880 | Liberal victory under Gladstone; Anglo-Boer War | Bradlaugh case, Westminster; Disraeli, *Endymion* | Social-Democratic Federation founded by H. M. Hyndman |
| 1881 | Irish Land and Coercion Act; Tsar Alexander II assassinated | Meredith, *Celt and Saxon*; T. H. Green, 'Liberal Legislation and Freedom of Contract'; Arnold Toynbee, *The Industrial Revolution* | First electric train; Canadian Pacific Railway founded; Panama Canal scheme fails |
| 1882 | Britain invades Egypt; Phoenix Park assassinations, Dublin | Anthony Trollope, *The Land Leaguers*; Gilbert and Sullivan, *Iolanthe* | Death of Karl Marx; Singer's sewing machine factory, Clydebank |
| 1883 | Ilbert Bill controversy, India | Robert Louis Stevenson, *Treasure Island*; Andrew Mearns, *The Bitter Cry of Outcast London*; Bernard Shaw, *The Unsocial Socialist* | First skyscraper, Chicago; Gaelic Athletic Association |
| 1884 | Reform and Redistribution Act; Imperial Federation League founded | *Oxford English Dictionary* begins publication | Fabian Society founded; Royal Commission on Housing (to 1886) |
| 1885 | Death of Gordon at Khartoum; Chamberlain's radical programme; Scottish Secretary; Conference of Berlin; Indian Congress founded | | Gold found in Transvaal; Second Tay Bridge; Daimler's automobile; highland 'land war' in Scotland; Special Branch set up |
| 1886 | First Irish Home Rule Bill; Gladstone loses to Salisbury's Conservatives | Gissing, *Demos*; James, *The Princess Casamassima*; Dicey, *Law of Constitution*; bicentenary of Burns's poems; Hardy, *Mayor of Casterbridge*; *The British Weekly* | American Federation of Labour founded; repeal of Contagious Diseases Acts, UK; Scottish Football Association |

|  | | | |
|---|---|---|---|
| 1887 | | Mark Rutherford, *The Revolution in Tanner's Lane* | Bloody Sunday in London (November); coercion in Ireland under Balfour; Welsh anti-tithe agitation; UK annexes Burma |
| 1888 | 'New unionism' organizes unskilled; first Glasgow International Exhibition; Glasgow Celtic | Mrs Humphry Ward, *Robert Elsmere*; Bryce, *The American Commonwealth* | County Councils Act; Scottish Labour Party founded; Railway Rates Act; Goschen Formula determines public spending in Scotland |
| 1889 | London dock strike; first London tube line; women's anti-suffrage petition; first government grant to universities | R. L. Stevenson, *The Master of Ballantrae* | Fabian Essays in Socialism; Welsh Intermediate Education Act; Second International Founded (to 1914) |
| 1890 | Forth Bridge completed; Scottish rail strike; McKinley Tariff, USA | Edward Bellamy, *Looking Backward*; J. G. Frazer, *The Golden Bough* | 1890–1902: A. T. Mahan, *Influence of Sea Power*; Lloyd George elected |
| 1891 | Papal encyclical on labour; Trans-Siberian Railway started; Charles Booth investigates London poverty | Anglo-US Copyright Treaty; Hardy, *Tess of the D'Urbervilles*; William Morris, *News from Nowhere*; *The Bookman* | Death of Parnell |
| 1892 | J.P. Holland's submarine | Conan Doyle, 'The Bruce-Partington Plans'; death of Tennyson | Last Gladstone government; Independent Labour Party founded |

| | | | |
|---|---|---|---|
| 1893 | Engineers' strike; Robert Blatchford, *Merrie England*; Charles Pearson, *National Life and Character* | Gaelic League founded, Ireland; Bryce Commission on secondary education; National University of Wales | Failure of Second Irish Home Rule Bill; Lord Rosebery PM |
| 1894 | Trans-Andean railway; Jewish emigration from Russia because of pogroms | *Scottish Students' Song Book*; Somerville and Ross, *The Real Charlotte* | Franco-Russian Alliance; Conservatives in office; Navy League founded |
| 1895 | Röntgen: X-rays; Lumiere: cinecamera; Marconi: wireless; UK Light Railway Act; West Highland Railway (to 1897) | Trial of Oscar Wilde; first best-seller list, USA | Imperial Federation League dissolved; Free Church Council funded |
| 1896 | Uranium radiation; Glasgow Underground; National Union of Woman Suffrage Societies | Harmsworth's Theodor Herzl, *Der Judenstaat* | Jameson Raid; Venezuela crisis |
| 1897 | Parsons's *Turbinia* | Dreyfus case begins; Kipling, 'Recessional' | First Zionist Congress; Queen Victoria's Diamond Jubilee |
| 1898 | Curie: Radium; Glasgow muncipalizes trams | | Marquis Curzon Viceroy of India (to 1905) |
| 1899 | | *Daily Mail*; Thomas Mann, *Buddenbrooks* | Outbreak of Boer War |
| 1900 | Planck's Quantum Theory; Carnegie sells steel holdings for £100 m; Taff Vale case | British Academy founded | Labour Representation Committee founded; Queen Victoria dies (22 January) |

|  | | | |
|---|---|---|---|
| 1901 | Telegraphy of pictures; transatlantic wireless messages | George Douglas Brown, *The House with the Green Shutters* | Conservatives win Khaki Election; death of Queen Victoria; end of Boer War |
| 1902 | J. A. Hobson, *Imperialism* | | Balfour Education Act; end of Boer War |
| 1903 | North British Locomotive Company; Wright Brothers' first flight; Rutherford at Manchester: radioactivity; Women's Social and Political Union founded; secret MacDonald–Gladstone pact ensures Labour seats in 1906 | Erskine Childers, *Riddle of the Sands*; Joseph Conrad, *Typhoon*; *Daily Express*; Jack London, *The People of the Abyss* | Chamberlain splits Conservatives over tariff reform; Committee of Imperial Defence |
| 1904 | Ashbourne Land Act, Ireland; Panama Canal begun; Imperial General Staff | Bernard Shaw, *John Bull's Other Island* | Anglo-French Entente; Russo-Japanese War; Battle of Tsu-Shima |
| 1905 | *Dreadnought* laid down; restrictive Aliens Act passed; Automobile Association founded | Conrad, *Nostromo*; Bernard Shaw, *Major Barbara*; Galsworthy, *The Silver Box* | Sinn Fein founded, Dublin; revolution in Russia; Norway separates from Sweden |
| 1906 | Slump on west coast (to 1908); *Forward* founded in Glasgow | Chesterton, *The Napoleon of Notting Hill*; Kipling, *Puck of Pook's Hill* | UK Liberals win in landslide; Haldane reforms army (to 1912) |
| 1907 | Transmitting photographs; first UK Census of Production; Trades Disputes Act | National Library of Wales founded; Jack London, *The Iron Heel* | Anglo-Russian Entente over Persia; Arthur Balfour coins 'Celtic Fringe'; James Bryce as Ambassador to Washington (to 1913) |

| | | | |
|---|---|---|---|
| 1908 | Graham Wallas, *Human Nature in Politics* | Buchan, *A Lodge in the Wilderness*; Conrad, *The Secret Agent* | Belgium takes over Congo from King; Young Turks take over in Constantinople |
| 1909 | Bleriot flies Channel; first employment exchanges; Miners' Union affiliates to Labour | H. G. Wells, *Tono-Bungay* | Lloyd George's People's Budget; Trade Boards Act against sweated labour |
| 1910 | Syndicalist strikes in France; Guild Socialism in Britain | Post-Impressionist Exhibition, London (December) 'Human Nature changed!' | UK general elections: Liberals win both |
| 1911 | Extensive rail and dock strikes in UK; Glasgow historical exhibition | H. G. Wells, *New Machiavelli*; Fletcher and Kipling, *History of England* | Parliament Act becomes law; National Insurance Act; Agadir incident |
| 1912 | RMS *Titanic*; *The Miners' Next Step* in South Wales; collapse of Argyll Car Company; first military use of aeroplanes in Balkans | James Joyce leaves Dublin; Vaughan Williams, *A Sea Symphony* | Balkan War (October) Christians beat Turks; women's suffrage crisis in UK; GPO takes over telephone system |
| 1913 | Record UK coal and steel production; Dublin dock and tramway strike; trade union support for Labour legalized | John Buchan, *The Power-House*; W. B. Yeats, *Autobiographies*; Compton Mackenzie, *Sinister Street* | Balkan War (June): Bulgaria versus other Christians; Ulster crisis (to August 1914) |
| 1914 | Empire-wide radio telegraphy network set up; Royal Naval Air Service (RNAS) and Royal Flying Corps (RAFC) founded | James Joyce, *Dubliners*; Rupert Brooke, 'The Soldier'; Vaughan Williams, *A London Symphony*; J. MacDougall Hay, *Gillespie* | War declared (4 August); Irish Home Rule and Welsh disestablishment carried, but 'put on ice'; Jacks case |

| 1915 | First use of gas in warfare; Patrick Geddes, *Cities in Evolution* | John Buchan, *The Thirty-Nine Steps*; Caradoc Evans, *My People*; Charlie Chaplin, *The Tramp*; D. W. Griffith, *Birth of a Nation* | Dardanelles campaign (March–November); Italy declares war on Austria (May); Conservatives and Labour enter Coalition government; Salonica occupied (October) |
|------|---|---|---|
| 1916 | Summer time introduced; first use of tank in Battle of Somme (June–November); Battle of Jutland (31 May); conscription introduced on UK mainland | H. G. Wells, *Mr Britling Sees it Through* | Irish Rising, Easter; Italy declares war on Germany (August); T. E. Lawrence in desert; formation of Lloyd George Coalition (December) |
| 1917 | Unrestricted U-boat warfare prompts convoy system (February); Bonar Law imposes government control on Bank of England; report of Royal Commisson on Scottish Housing; Lord Leverhulme buys Lewis | Siegfried Sassoon's poems published; Wilfred Owen at Geddes's Outlook Tower; Stephen McKenna, *Sonia* | Russian revolutions (February and November); Bolsheviks out of war (early 1918); papal plea for peace; USA enters war (6 April); 'Convention of Irishmen'; Balfour Declaration on Zionism (November). |
| 1918 | Influenza epidemic kills 30 million; R34 airship crosses Atlantic east–west; Fisher Education Act; RAF founded under first Air Minister William Weir; first Transport Minister Eric Geddes; trade union membership doubles from 4 million in 1914 | Scottish Catholic schools get government funding; Maurice Elvey, *Dombey and Son*; *The Life of Lloyd George* | Reform Act gives suffrage to women over 30; Ludendorff's last offensive (March); Armistice (11 November); UK election (December) won by Lloyd George; Montagu–Chelmsford report backs Indian self-government; Labour Party constitution |

|  | | | |
|---|---|---|---|
| 1919 | Paris Peace Conference ends (28 July); Amritsar massacre (June); Soloheadbeg attack, Ireland | Elgar, Cello Concerto; Robert Wiene, *The Cabinet of Dr Caligari* | Alcock and Brown fly Atlantic west–east; J. M. Keynes, *Economic Consequences of the Peace* |
| 1920 | League of Nations set up; guerilla war and repression in Ireland; Communist Party of Great Britain founded | Chaplin, *The Kid* | Post-war boom collapses in autumn; most Scottish banks and shipping lines amalgamate with English concerns |
| 1921 | Anglo-Irish truce; Franco-German crisis over Ruhr coalfield; Sankey Commission recommends coal nationalization | | Failure of Triple Alliance (miners, dockers, railwaymen); 'Geddes Axe' hits public expenditure; National Unemployed Workers' Movement founded |
| 1922 | Smyrna massacre (August); Chanak crisis (November); Lloyd George falls; Conservatives take power under Bonar Law; Irish Civil War | T. S. Eliot, *The Waste Land*; James Joyce, *Ulysses* | Dublin Development Plan |
| 1923 | Stanley Baldwin, PM, calls election over protection | W. B. Yeats, 'Meditations in Time of Civil War'; Fritz Lang, *The Nibelungs* | 'Grouping' of British Railways; BBC founded |
| 1924 | First Labour government under MacDonald | Buchan, *The Three Hostages* | Wheatley Act starts council housing |
| 1925 | Conservative government under Baldwin; founding of Plaid Cymru | Sean O'Casey, completion of Dublin trilogy; Sergei Eisenstein, *Battleship Potemkin* | Return to Gold Standard |

| | | |
|---|---|---|
| 1926 | | General Strike and miners' lockout |
| 1927 | Arnold Bennett, *Lord Raingo*; Hugh MacDiarmid, *A Drunk Man*; Abel Gance, *Napoleon*; Fritz Lang, *Metropolis* | Conservative Industrial Relations Act |
| 1928 | Lindberg flies Atlantic | Votes for women at 21; founding of National Party of Scotland |
| 1929 | Buster Keaton, *The General*; Al Jolson, *The Jazz Singer*, the first talkie | Labour government under Ramsay MacDonald |
| 1930 | Ardnacrusha power station | |
| 1931 | Sergei Eisenstein, *October*; O'Casey, *The Silver Tassie* | Conservative-dominated National Government under Ramsay MacDonald wins landslide victory |
| 1932 | John Ford, *The Informer*; John Grierson, *Drifters* | Ottawa Conference; ILP disaffiliates from Labour; de Valera's Fianna Fáil forms Irish government |
| | Wall Street Crash (October); Church of Scotland and Free Kirk amalgamate | |
| | Western economies in free fall | |
| | UK government comes off Gold Standard (November) | |
| | Introduction of limited protection; Scottish National Development Council funded | |
| | G. M. Young, *The Portrait of an Age*; MacDiarmid, *To Circumjack Cencrastus* | |

# Index

Note that compound surnames, such as Morris-Jones and Cunninghame Graham, are filed under their first element. Alternative names are given in (parentheses).

Index written by Gerard M-F Hill, 2008.